BODIES UNDER SIEGE

Self-mutilation and Body Modification
in Culture and Psychiatry

Second Edition

Armando R. Favazza, M.D.

Professor, Department of Psychiatry and Neurology
University of Missouri–Columbia School of Medicine

THE JOHNS HOPKINS UNIVERSITY PRESS
Baltimore and London

First edition, *Bodies under Siege: Self-mutilation in Culture
and Psychiatry*, 1987
Johns Hopkins Paperbacks edition, 1992
Second edition, *Bodies under Siege: Self-mutilation and
Body Modification in Culture and Psychiatry*, 1996
Printed in the United States of America on acid-free paper
05 04 03 02 01 00 99 98 97 96   5 4 3 2 1

The Johns Hopkins University Press
2715 North Charles Street
Baltimore, Maryland 21218-4319
The Johns Hopkins University Press Ltd., London

Library of Congress Cataloging-in-Publication Data will be found
at the end of this book.
A catalog record for this book is available from the British Library.

ISBN 0-8018-5299-4
ISBN 0-8018-5300-1 (pbk.)

This book is dedicated to the patient who wrote
the following to me:

Thank you for the opportunity to express my feelings and for the attention you are paying to my problem.

I believe there is a larger truth at work in the riddle of self-harm which is important for society as a whole to penetrate.

May you find the answers which you seek.

CONTENTS

vii

PREFACE
TO THE SECOND EDITION

▬ ▬ ▬ ▬ ▬ ▬ ▬ ▬

The awakened and knowing say: body am I entirely, and nothing else; and soul is only a word for something about the body.

Nietzsche, *Thus Spoke Zarathustra*

Bodies under Siege is my magnum opus—my singular contribution to patients and to my profession. The first decade of my professional career was devoted to developing the field of cultural psychiatry, a discipline that interfaces cultural anthropology and clinical psychiatry, and labors in this area achieved some measure of success. In 1978 my article "The Foundations of Cultural Psychiatry," featured on the cover of the *American Journal of Psychiatry*, helped to legitimize the topic among academicians, who generally had thought of it as exotic and not terribly relevant. Several years later, I cofounded the Society for the Study of Psychiatry and Culture.

Because of my cultural psychiatric expertise, I received a call in 1980 from a colleague at my university's counseling center who requested a consultation on a depressed patient. The patient was from the Sudan, the wife of an exchange student. After a lengthy interview, I determined that her depression was the indirect result of a childhood incident. At the age of nine, the patient, along with all of her friends, underwent a pharaonic circumcision. Her clitoris was snipped off, her labia scraped, and her vagina sewn [*infibulation*] shut except for a small opening to allow the exit of urine and menstrual fluids. The procedure effectively created a chastity belt of her own flesh. She eventually married and remembered a painful honeymoon. Sexual intercourse was not a particularly pleasurable event, but then again she did not have any great expectations. Only after she came to Missouri and listened over coffee to the American wives of students discuss their orgasms did she become curious. She read books about sexuality and watched soap operas on television. Thus, she came to learn that she would never experience an event so highly prized throughout the world. Her potential to have an orgasm had been surgically removed. Feeling cheated, she became demoralized and finally developed a clinical depression. Contact with this patient led me to my first awareness of mutilation.

Several months later, my interest in mutilation grew because of a teaching conference at my medical school. A resident psychiatrist was presenting for discussion the case of a young woman who chronically slashed her body with razor blades. I was asked to provide comments from a cultural psychiatric perspective. I went to my file cabinet, but the folder on self-mutilation was thin and not very helpful. I then turned to the two extensive annotated bibliographies I had published on themes in cultural psychiatry from 1925 to 1980. Over five thousand books and articles were cited, but I had not included self-mutilation in the index of either book. I spent several days in the anthropology section of my university library and called several colleagues in the anthropology department. Although I found many references to practices such as skin scarification and foot binding, in which individuals voluntarily participated in the mutilation of their bodies, I could not find any books that examined self-mutilation as a cross-cultural phenomenon. In fact, I found only two review articles: one dealt with finger amputation, the other with testicle crushing. Both were written in German and had been published half a century ago. The standard anthropological sources did not even include mutilation as a topic.

Next, I retrieved my fairly complete set of notes of all the conferences I had attended during the four years of my psychiatric training. I found that self-mutilation had not been presented at a teaching conference during my training, although I clearly remembered that the case of a chronic self-cutter was discussed at morning rounds. The patient had told of a dream in which a crow flew out of her head. Later, as the professor was commenting on the possible symbolism of this dream, an aide ran into the room and told us that the patient had just swallowed some glass and had cut her arms. The professor, noting that the patient had not improved during her six-month inpatient stay, threw up his hands and said, "We'd better transfer her to the state hospital."

In searching for material to present at the teaching conference, I came across an intriguing book about a contemporary Moroccan group of mystical Islamic healers. These healers work themselves into a ritual frenzy and slash open their heads. Bits of bread and sugar cubes are dipped in the healer's blood and given to the sick to eat (a fuller discussion of this appears in chapter 4). In this context, self-mutilation is a positive act performed to promote recovery from illness. This notion seemed far-fetched at first, but then I recalled the venerable therapeutic practice of bloodletting in Western culture as well as Karl Menninger's contention that some acts of self-mutilation serve to avert suicide. If ritual self-mutilation serves a therapeutic purpose for some cultural groups, then does it serve a similar purpose for some mentally ill persons?

I then vaguely recalled an episode in the Bible that seemed relevant. After much searching, I found the story in the fifth chapter of the Gospel of Mark, which tells the story of Jesus in the land of the Gadarenes. Jesus was presented with a disturbed man with an unclean spirit who lived in a cemetery. "No one could bind him, not even with chains . . . and always, night and day, he was in the mountains and in the tombs, crying out and cutting himself with stones." Here was the first reported "case" of a chronic self-mutilator. Jesus diagnosed demon possession and performed an exorcism. The spirit, named Legion, left the man and entered a herd of swine, which immediately committed suicide by drowning in the river.[1] Why didn't the demon-possessed man commit suicide? What kept him alive? We cannot be sure, but perhaps he was saved by repeatedly cutting himself with stones.

Intrigued by the possibility that some forms of self-mutilation represent an attempt at self-healing, I steadfastly began to review the world medical literature on self-mutilation and to gather case reports. In talking with other physicians both in the United States and abroad, I was provided with many cases of patients who had enucleated their eyes, castrated themselves, sliced open their skin, and so forth. Only rarely have these cases been published in the literature, leading me to believe that published reports represented a small proportion of actual cases. As my interest in the topic became known, I had the opportunity to become involved personally with

---

1. Homer Smith, in *Man and His Gods* (1952), noted that this story was the focus of a major controversy in 1890. Thomas Huxley, the great defender of evolution, attacked the notion of Christian "authority" in a debate with several British clergymen. He used the example of the Gadarene demon to state: "If Jesus taught the demonological system involved in the Gadarene story—then I, for my part unhesitatingly refuse to believe in that teaching and deny the reality of those spiritual convictions."

The prime minister of England, William Gladstone, entered the fray and wrote that since Gadara was a Jewish city, the Jewish swineherds were forbidden to raise pigs. The destruction of the swine by Jesus was a just punishment. Huxley clarified that he did not question Jesus' action but rather questioned the validity of the Gospel story. Gadara, he explained, was not a Jewish settlement. Yes, it was, Gladstone replied angrily.

Intellectuals throughout Europe were spellbound by the ludicrous debate over the pigs. However, Huxley felt that an important principle was at stake: it was a case of "savage superstition" versus "the ethical ideal of prophetic Israel." Gladstone's attention turned to a general election and the controversy ended without any formal conclusion.

many of the patients described in this book. Some were referrals from colleagues, while others sought me out on their own.

The more I examined the topic of self-mutilation, the clearer it became
that it is a significant clinical problem that might be studied best from the
perspective of cultural psychiatry. My resolve to carry out this study was
buttressed by Dr. Mansell Pattison's work in delineating a specific "deliberate self-harm" syndrome. His findings that this syndrome truly does exist,
and that its prevalence is much higher than anyone might have expected,
coincided with my own.

The more I examined self-mutilation, the more puzzling it seemed. The
behavior was surrounded by a mysterious aura. What could possibly motivate people to alter and destroy their body tissue or to consent to the mutilation of their bodies by others? Certainly there are culturally sanctioned
rituals in which self-mutilation is a key element. Among some aboriginal
groups, for example, boy's penises are sliced open during rites of passage to
adulthood. Shoulder and chest muscles are ripped apart in the Sun Dance
of the Plains Indians. Would an understanding of these rituals shed light
on the deviant self-mutilation of the mentally ill?

My attempt to answer these questions is found in the pages of this book,
which explores the many variations of self-mutilative acts across cultures
and through time, utilizing the perspective of cultural psychiatry. Just as
culture strives to organize a society into a logically integrated, functional,
sense-making whole, so too cultural psychiatry strives to integrate the components of complex, problematic behaviors such as self-mutilation and to
make sense of what may appear to be senseless. During the five years that
it took to complete the first edition of the book, I encountered a wide
variety of forces that may impel or compel people to mutilate themselves.
These forces ranged from congenital insensitivity to pain to hypersecretion
of adrenal hormones, from castration anxiety to intolerable guilt, from the
experience of child abuse to confused perceptions of maleness and femaleness. Further, I came to realize that an understanding of the behavior demanded an examination of the vast array of cultural practices, attitudes, and
beliefs—from religion and mythology to folk healing, from infibulation to
initiation rites, from artistic and literary depictions to blood customs—that
form the theater within which self-mutilation is performed.

Bodies under Siege presents information about self-mutilation from differing perspectives. Biological data are considered, as are psychological and
social data. Since biology, psychology, and social forces do not exist in a
vacuum, I attempt to place them within the overarching web of culture in

order to produce a meaningful synthesis. Self-mutilation is far too complicated a behavior to be understood by only one approach. It is clear that the
individual human body mirrors the collective social body, and each continually creates and sustains the other. Misperceptions of reality, feelings of
guilt, negative self-images, antisocial acts, and all the other symptoms we
associate with personal mental illness defy understanding without reference
to the psychological, social, cultural, and physical integrity of the communal "body."

The writing of the book was both exciting and lonely. As I worked with
patients and delved into a literature seldom visited by psychiatrists, the
mystery of self-mutilation melted away. Almost daily I seemed to learn
something new that seemed terribly significant. The thrill of discovery was
tempered by self-doubt. If self-mutilation was so important, why was the
last major psychiatric book on the topic written in 1938 (Karl Menninger's *Man against Himself*)? Of course, a number of individual cases and
studies had been published since then, and in 1979 two books had appeared. Edward Morgan's *Death Wishes?* dealt with some forms of deliberate self-harm in Great Britain, while Ross and McKay's *Self-Mutilation*
discussed teenage girls who carved their skin in a Canadian correctional
facility. Although both books were quite well done, they failed to impact a
seemingly disinterested audience.

Why the disinterest? Laypersons with whom I discussed self-mutilation
invariably thought it to be a grotesque act. The importance of cultural attitudes quickly became apparent to me, however, since parents who willingly
had their sons circumcised were revulsed at the widespread African practice
of female circumcision. Certainly the self-mutilative behavior of mentally
ill persons was regarded as meaningless and disgusting. A memorable telephone call illustrates this point.

The nasal voice of the caller seemed a bit tremulous as she asked, "Is this
Dr. Favazza?"

"Yes, it is," I replied.

"This is the Western Union operator, doctor, and I have a telegram for
you—but you're not going to believe it," she said. "Do you want me to read
it to you?"

"Please do," I answered.

"It says, 'Have current African patient whose eyes and testicles were removed for use in witchcraft. Come to London. Maurice.'" After a short
pause, she asked, "Is that true, doctor? Do people really do things like that?"

I calmly explained that I was writing a book on the topic and the sender of the telegram, Dr. Maurice Lipsedge, was a leading psychiatrist at Guy's Hospital in London. And I assured her that in fact people do engage in such activities.

"Doctor," she responded, "that's really disgusting."[2]

In talking with hospital staff on psychiatric and surgical wards, I was impressed by the anger, awe, and even fear that self-mutilative patients seem to elicit among caretakers. When I asked what could possibly motivate persons to mutilate themselves, I usually received unedifying, terse responses such as, "It must be a chemical imbalance" or "It's part of the borderline syndrome" or "It's a way to get attention." It is as if the presence of a self-mutilator threatens the sense of mental and physical integrity of those around him or her. What is it about a self-mutilator that is so unsettling for others? I believe Podvoll (1969) was correct in noting that

> the self-mutilator can incorporate into his actions patterns which, to a greater or lesser degree, remain unarticulated in most of us. That is, such patterns already exist in muted intensities within the patient's social field. As such, he may even perform a service to his culture in his dramatic expression of those patterns which are felt to be intolerable within the self. Still other patterns invoked are those which elicit silent levels of admiration and envy. The history of these images reaches at least as far back as the Passion of the Cross and has prevailed among some of the most respected members of our culture. (p. 219)

I was disturbed by the "bad press" given to self-mutilators in the mental health literature. They were portrayed as exasperating patients who demanded enormous amounts of professional attention. In fact, many of the articles about treatment focused on the therapist's struggles to maintain a sense of equilibrium in dealing with these patients. If everyone felt so

2. I came to learn through meetings with Dr. Lipsedge and through an article in a Nigerian newspaper that the patient was a well-trained physician who was suffering from schizophrenia. His family had taken him to a "healing compound," a sort of quasi hospital in which Western fundamentalist religious approaches were combined with native African healing methods. He had been chained to a post overnight; and when his family came in the morning, they found that his eye had been enucleated and his testicles cut off. The police were called, and the compound attendants swore that someone must have entered the compound and mutilated the patient in order to use the organs for *ju-ju* (magic). An alternative theory was that the attendants, for fear of legal reprisals, were covering up the fact that the patient had not been watched closely and had mutilated himself. Bewildered, the family brought him to London in hopes of an "eye transplant." When they appeared at the ophthalmology clinic with this strange request, the psychiatrists were consulted and the patient was admitted to a psychiatric unit. After careful scrutiny, Dr. Lipsedge determined that the patient "probably" had mutilated himself.

negatively about self-mutilation, what sort of reception awaited my book? Had I been deluding myself?

Because I believed that *Bodies under Siege* was unique, important, and deserving of a large audience, I sent it to one of the most prestigious publishers in the country. But I was not prepared for the reaction it received. It was accepted by the editors but rejected by the sales manager, who did not think it would have a very large market. At another top-rated publishing firm, I was told that the book was approved by a series of in-house committees but was turned down by the chief executive, who found it "disgusting." Another publisher joked that it would make a good diet book because he felt like vomiting whenever he tried to read it. In all, fifteen commercial publishing houses rejected the manuscript.

I also sent it to a university press. For the director of the press, a quick glance sufficed; he returned it to me the day he received it (a new world record!) with a brief note stating that he "wasn't interested." The acquisitions editor of an aggressive psychiatric publisher thought that I must be "somewhat strange" to pick self-mutilation as a topic and wouldn't even look at the manuscript.

With failing courage and rising depression, I showed the manuscript to a highly regarded literary agent. Fortunately, she shared my enthusiasm and feelings about the book. After careful consideration (she had never come across rejection letters such as mine), she advised submission to the Johns Hopkins University Press.

The editorial staff at Johns Hopkins immediately liked the book. But as is customary, they sent it to two expert reviewers. After a month of anxious waiting, I received their completely opposite findings. One reviewer wrote that the work was "packed with interesting information, well written, and comprehensive. The scholarship appears substantial and thorough, and this book clearly represents a significant contribution . . . organized in a logical and effective way. . . . Without reservation, I recommend publication of this book."

The other reviewer recommended against publication. He (or she) could not accept my finding that self-harm usually was an attempt to reduce troublesome symptoms. My discussion of animal models of self-mutilation was "not comprehensive," and my statements about the treatment of certain biologic symptoms were "in error." This reviewer didn't like the term *self-mutilation*, preferring *bodily disfiguration* instead.

The editors asked me to write a rebuttal to the second reviewer's comments. I prepared a twelve-page document, complete with copies of correspondence with self-mutilators, case reports, even several questionnaires that some patients completed by using their blood for ink, that carefully answered every objection. And then I waited.

After a while, the good news arrived. The manuscript had been accepted and would be published in September 1987. Several months later, after review by a professional copyeditor, the manuscript was sent to me for final corrections. To my surprise, I discovered numerous errors. When I called the copyeditor to discuss the matter, she was shocked by her failure to spot them and blamed it on my disturbing choice of subject matter.

My self-doubts returned. Self-mutilation is undeniably unsettling to everyone who comes into contact with it. What would the reviews of my book say? Would it even be reviewed, or was the topic too disgusting? Would others become interested in research on self-mutilation? What would patients think of it?

To my enormous relief, *Bodies under Siege* was reviewed by fourteen professional journals (I had been led to hope for four or five reviews), and all but one was positive. Linford Rees, one of Great Britain's most famous psychiatrists, wrote in the *British Journal of Psychiatry*, "A comprehensive, lucid, and interestingly written book which is likely to become a classic on the subject." Roland Littlewood, Europe's leading cultural psychiatrist, called it a "pioneering study" in the *British Medical Anthropology Newsletter* and noted that "the book's illustration of success and failure with the author's own patients prevents the work becoming a mere catalogue, almost inevitable in what is the first standard reference of its type." Bengt Jansson, a professor at Sweden's Karolinska Institution, writing in *Acta Psychiatrica Scandinavica*, praised the book for its "new psychiatric knowledge . . . and cultural insights." Joseph Westermeyer, an indefatigable researcher and professor of psychiatry, psychology, and anthropology at the University of Minnesota, wrote in *Contemporary Psychology* that "any clinician who has self-mutilating patients will gain from this well-written, informative, and helpful book." In *Psychosomatics*, Arthur Freeman, a psychiatrist who is dean of the Louisiana State University School of Medicine, described the book as "a successful elucidation of the grim clinical reality of self-mutilation within its cultural context." He also noted that "we will be reading much more about self-mutilative behavior in the coming years, and this book is the place to begin." Ronald Simons, a noted American cultural psychiatrist, wrote in the *Journal of Nervous and Mental Disease*, "A compendium of cultural and clinical reports of self-mutilation and a summary of what is and is not known about therapy, the book is a major contribution to both the anthropological and psychiatric literatures." Vincenzo di Nicola, a well-known Canadian psychiatrist, said in the *Canadian Jour-*

nal of Psychiatry, "Favazza examines the Deliberate Self-Harm syndrome, paving the way for defining a new syndrome. I had the sense of sharing in a clarifying discovery, as I imagine an early reader of Gull's description of anorexia nervosa might have felt." The *American Journal of Psychiatry* noted, "Dr. Favazza has brought a breadth of discussion and depth of review not found before regarding patients who harm themselves." The one negative review, written by Nancy Scheper-Hughes, an anthropologist, in *Medical Anthropology Quarterly,* took me to task for medicalizing self-mutilation. The author devoted most of her antipsychiatric review to describing her contact with a female repetitive self-mutilator who had been heavily medicated and restrained in an attempt to keep her from doing further physical damage to herself.

The favorable reaction to *Bodies under Siege* by psychiatrists and psychologists was matched by laypersons. I have appeared in numerous television and radio interviews, and have received invitations to lecture on the topic all over the world. Newspaper reporters used the book to support articles about self-mutilators in communities throughout the United States. As had happened with anorexia and bulimia nervosa a decade earlier, media publicity encouraged self-mutilating patients to speak publicly about their disorder and to seek professional help. The book also served to bring the issue of self-mutilation to the consciousness of mental health researchers. In short order, self-mutilation became a "hot" topic for study, and hundreds of papers have been published in the years following the book's appearance in 1987 (a softcover version came out in 1992).

Because so much new information on self-mutilation has become available, the publisher asked me to revise the book. This revised edition contains updated material on the place of self-mutilation in diagnosis, biological findings (especially those on the neurotransmitter serotonin), treatment, and the linkage of eating disorders with self-mutilation. The bibliography has been expanded. Since so much media attention has focused on body piercing, I asked Fakir Musafar to write an epilogue that deals with this social phenomenon. Fakir, the guru philosopher of the "modern primitives" movement, is a man with exceptional knowledge about body modification. He has experienced personally just about every type of body modification that has ever been thought of, and he has instructed many others about the possibilities, the rewards, and the dangers of modification practices.

Persons who know Fakir as the subject of startling photographs—the most famous one shows him hanging from a cottonwood tree by two gigantic hooks through his chest—can appreciate his earnestness. In conversation his intellect and spirituality are prominent. His esthetic sensibility is evident in the artistry of the journal that he founded in 1992, *Body Play and Modern Primitives Quarterly*. In fact, it is difficult to categorize Fakir. Among the words that come to mind are visionary, teacher, philosopher, artist. However, there are some persons who would dismiss him at a distance as weirdly exhibitionistic, the personification of masochism, bonkers, or even insane. He refers to himself as a shaman. At this point in his life, I suspect that his self-assessment is accurate. Not everyone will agree with his point of view, but I believe that it is well worth examining.

In a scholarly discussion, Graver (1995) noted that

> pain becomes for Fakir an interiority deeper than the self. By disciplining his attention to the pain, he feels it not as a foreign invasion of the body but as a sensation of the body that separates the body from the mind. . . . The pain lights up an interior scene in which the mind meets the body as protagonist meets antagonist in a play. Each has its own agenda of values and desires, and they must adjust to one another within the dramatic conflict of the ordeal. . . . Fakir affirms his identity and individuality through somatic baptisms of suffering rather than through immersion in language. . . . His rituals often involve a kind of hieroglyphic nomination in which the physical mark of the name is made permanently upon the body through a tattoo or piercing and the spirituality of the mark rests upon the painfulness of its creation. . . . Where Christianity is content to baptize souls with water and words, Fakir draws from cultures (and invents rituals of his own) that baptize the body by immersing it temporarily in pain.

Fakir follows a universally noble tradition in which spirituality is gained by taming the bonds of the flesh. By conquering pain and transforming his body, he walks on the path to enlightenment. He places his practices outside of Christian culture but, had he lived in earlier centuries, he very well might have found soul mates among the company of the Desert Fathers, the athletes of God who sought salvation through mortification. Properly speaking, Fakir does not truly mortify his body but rather attempts to transcend pain. Even with the proper spiritual training, those who would emulate him do so at grave personal peril. I for one cannot even think about putting holes in my body without shuddering, yet there are many persons who carve and cut themselves. As an uncontrollable behavior, the morbidity may be quite high. As a controlled behavior, however, it may have its rewards.

As a general orientation, readers should know that I define *self-mutilation* as the deliberate destruction or alteration of one's body tissue without conscious suicidal intent. There is no necessarily negative connotation to the term *self-mutilation* in this definition. I then divide selfmutilative behaviors into two major groups. The first, *culturally sanctioned* self-mutilation, is subdivided into rituals and practices. Everyone is familiar with ear piercing, a very common culturally sanctioned practice, but greater meaning is attached to rituals. The dynamics of performing the behavior oneself or allowing others to do it are similar in most relevant regards. The other major category is *deviant* self-mutilation, in which the behaviors are the product of mental disorder and anguish. This category is subdivided primarily on the basis of degree of tissue damage and the rate of self-mutilative acts into three types, namely, major, stereotypic, and moderate/superficial. Self-castration is an example of the major type, head banging the stereotypic type, and skin cutting the moderate/superficial type.

The short answer to the question "Why do patients deliberately harm themselves?" is that it provides temporary relief from a host of painful symptoms such as anxiety, depersonalization, and desperation. The long answer is that it also touches upon the very profound human experiences of salvation, healing, and orderliness. Self-mutilation is a morbid form of self-help. In the hands of special individuals who are able to control the behavior, it provides some benefits. However, the training, discipline, and courage needed to attain such positive results is not my cup of tea nor would it appeal to most people. Self-mutilation is nothing to trifle with. For individuals who cannot control the behavior, it provides short-term relief but at a great cost, such as the loss of an eye or unsightly scars.

The numerous examples of self-mutilation in this book are painful to comprehend. The culturally sanctioned mutilative rituals may seem strange at first glance, but they are no stranger than going to church and worshiping a crucified god. As I wrote down the litany of cases of deviant selfmutilation, I recalled Krafft-Ebing's *Psychopathia Sexualis*, published in 1868. Unlike that classic, *Bodies under Siege* goes beyond mere description to search for meaning. Ultimately, it celebrates not death but rather the will to live. It chronicles the struggle of humankind to maintain equilibrium. Therefore, dear reader, empathize if you can with the poor souls who are the victims of self-mutilation, but save your grieving for the dead.

MUTILATIVE BELIEFS, RELIGION, EATING, AND ETHOLOGY

I

To understand better the complex behavior of abnormal self-mutilation, it is important to examine beliefs, attitudes, practices, and images relating to mutilation in general. Many blood customs, for example, pertain to healing practices and to the sealing of pacts. Sexual mutilation provides opposing images of psychotic monsters and of pleasurable self-indulgence. Literary accounts range from uncontrolled mob violence to the exquisitely painful machinations of Kafka's famous penal colony.

Cosmogonic myths demonstrate the origins of social order from the body parts of dismembered primal beings. In Shamanism, imagined self-mutilation of the healer is a stepping stone to wisdom and to the development of the capacity to heal oneself and others. Mutilative images are central to disparate religions, as demonstrated by Tibetan Tantric meditation, North American Plains Indian mysticism, and the iconography of Christ's Passion. Indeed, the best known and most widely revered religious symbols are the cross upon which Christ was tortured and the stone lingam representing the phallus of Siva who castrated himself out of anger. The claims of some mentally ill self-mutilators that they are gods or godly agents become more understandable in light of the interconnectedness of religious sentiments and the concepts of sacrifice and the sacred, violence, and suffering.

The relationship between eating disorders and self-mutilation is a special one. From a clinical point of view it may be described in terms of impulsivity and issues of control over one's body. From a different stand, however, the very experience of learning to eat may underlie a basic propensity for self-mutilation. An examination of cannibalism, the fundamental form of institutionalized aggression, provides a unique, gut-level perspective on the inherent nature of self-harm.

In this section automutilation among animals is examined. Medical science often utilizes animal models, and it is not surprising that this approach is being tried in the study of self-mutilation. By environmental manipulation, surgical procedures, and administration of certain drugs, it is possible to induce laboratory animals to mutilate themselves. The complexity of the central nervous system and the difficulties associated with comparing animal and human nature impose limits on the relevance of ethology for understanding self-mutilation, but some of the leads from such studies hold promise.

1

Mutilative Beliefs, Attitudes, Practices, and Images

— — — — — — — — —

Beliefs, attitudes, practices, and images diffuse across latitudes and longitudes and centuries. Our perceptions of self-mutilation as grotesque or beautiful, heroic or cowardly, awesome or pitiful, meaningful or senseless, derive in great part from the perceptions of those who have lived before us. They are passed on in great paintings and statues and folk art, in novels and fairy tales, in history books and travelers' accounts, in religious rituals and secular customs, in the waging of war and the punishment of criminals, in popular songs and theatrical performances, in the ways we heal the sick and bury the dead, in the rearing of children and the handling of animals.

Self-mutilation cannot be totally divorced from the more general concept of mutilation directed against others; the perceptions and practices of the one are intimately linked to the other. However, the mutilation of unwilling victims is less intellectually troublesome because it usually can be explained or rationalized in fairly simple terms, such as revenge or a method of instilling fear in others. Even when a person mutilates others for idiosyncratic reasons, a reasonable response traditionally has been either to lock the person in a jail or mental hospital or to kill him or her. Self-mutilation, however, is a profound phenomenon that defies ready comprehension and rational response.

A major goal of this book is to strip away the mysterious aura that surrounds self-mutilation. Admittedly, this is not an easy task because our perceptions of self-mutilation are often unconsciously linked not only with the fear, revenge, mob violence, and governmental power associated with mutilation in general but also with concepts such as sacredness, self-knowledge, and the power of blood to heal and to bind individuals together. Let us, then, begin this task by examining some beliefs, attitudes, practices, and evocative images of mutilation and self-mutilation.

Decapitation and Scalping

Decapitation as a punishment has been popular throughout history and reached its apotheosis with the use of the guillotine in France. The ghoulish image of Salome dancing around the severed head of John the Baptist has long fascinated Westerners, the scene even being set to music in Strauss's popular opera. Lea (1973) recounted a most curious Chinese legal ritual in which a man was at liberty, upon surprising his wife in the act of adultery, to slay the couple. In order to substantiate the truthfulness of the situation, however, he had to cut off their heads and bring them to a magistrate. The heads were placed in a tub of water, which was then violently stirred so that they would revolve and meet in the middle. If the heads met back to back, the victims were pronounced innocent and the husband killed. If they met face to face the husband's story was accepted. He was then gently beaten to teach him to watch his wife more closely in the future and was given a small amount of money to assist in the purchase of a new wife.

Decapitation has long been used as a technique of terrorism in warfare. Victors would cut off the heads of the vanquished and display them on poles to demoralize remaining enemy forces. Such tactics were commonly employed during the Christian-Moslem wars. The biblical account of the Maccabean revolt ends with the mutilation of Nicanor. His vanquishers put his head on public display as evidence that the Lord had helped them.

Carroll (1982) gathered data on the "rolling head" myth among native Americans. He uncovered fifty-one stories from twenty-eight different tribes. The most common variant is a story in which a man lives with his wife and children, usually in isolation. The wife has illicit sexual relations, often with a snake lover. The husband then kills both the wife and the lover, severing the wife's head. The head pursues her children — predominantly her sons — who throw objects to delay the head and who eventually destroy it. Carroll interpreted these stories to be ultimately concerned with castration anxiety, the severed head symbolizing a severed penis.

Although decapitation has a lengthy tradition in Western history, head taking was a preoccupation among the Slavs, Turks, and Albanians. Sworn brethren would cut off the head of a dead or dying comrade to prevent it from being taken by the enemy. In the pan-Balkan custom of head shaving, persons left a large hairy lock intact so that, upon decapitation, their heads could be carried by using the lock of hair as a handle. Without this "handle," an enemy would have to carry the head by inserting a finger in the mouth. Christians shuddered at the thought of having an infidel Moslem finger in their mouths, and Moslems were repelled at the thought of having an unclean Christian finger in their mouths.

Serbian and Montenegrin ballads frequently praise heroes by enumerating the number of Turkish heads they cut off. In fact, in 1848 the British envoy to Montenegro, Sir Gardner Wilkinson, complained to the ruler that he found the sight of rotting Turkish heads on a tower to be disagreeable.

The ruler refused to change this custom, however, for fear of offending his subjects.

In border fights between the Montenegrins and Turks in 1912 a new fad emerged, that of taking noses instead of heads. This was possibly related to the fact that the Montenegrin soldiers were no longer issued the *handzhar*, a large knife well suited for head taking. Durham (1928) recounted a conversation with a professor who, at the news of the fighting, gleefully stated, "Now you will see plenty of noses! Even baskets full!" When told that such behavior would disgust all of Europe, the enraged professor declared that nose cutting was a national custom and that Turks were not human beings. "Just as heads were carried by the hair-lock, so noses were carried by the moustache. A woman, one of the camp followers, took them from her capacious pocket along with some other human fragments, which I will not particularize. Maybe British rule will have stopped head-hunting in New Guinea before the collecting of human fragments ceases in the Balkans."

North American Indians practiced scalping, as did the Visigoths, Anglo-Saxons, and Franks. Herodotus mentions it, as does the second book of the Maccabees. Among native Americans, warriors willingly engaged in activities that they knew would lead to the loss of their own or the gain of another's scalp. The scalp was removed to provide evidence of having killed an enemy even though the operation was not always fatal and many lived through the procedure (Nadeau 1941). Eastern tribes removed the entire scalp. Nadeau wrote: "They remove it as nicely as we would the skin of a rabbit. First they cut the skin to the bone all around the head with a knife. They start in front, in the middle of the forehead, follow around and behind one ear, then in back of the neck and around the other ear and finish in front where they started. Then often pulling a little on the hair to raise the edge of the skin, they throw the head backward on their knees, and peel off the scalp as easily as one would a glove from the hand" (p. 180).

The Chinooks practiced a more radical form, sometimes pulling off the ears, eyes, or all of the facial skin with the scalp. Plains Indians favored partial scalping, taking only a small portion of flesh. The nineteenth-century traveler George Catlin noted: "The scalp is procured by cutting out a piece of the skin of the head, the size of the palm of the hand or less, containing the very center or crown of the head, the place where the hair radiates from a point, and exactly over what the phrenologists call self-esteem" (Nadeau 1941, p. 183).

Scalping was also done by European settlers. Catlin noted that settlers paid for the scalp of their enemies, both Indian and Caucasian. In fact, a type of knife made in Sheffield, England, was quite popular for scalping and was traded to the Indians for horses.

The Zuni Indians of the American Southwest were scalp takers and had a scalp "house" in each town. In Zuni theology, dead persons are often considered rainmakers, thus the scalp ceremonial was performed not only to propitiate the dead enemy and to maintain the society but also to ensure rainfall and abundant crops.

Blood Customs, Healing, and Corpse Abuse

Blood customs are among the oldest known to mankind. Blood has awesome symbolic and physiologic powers, as evidenced by its role in religious sacrifice, healing, the formation of brotherhoods, and blood feuds. When harvested properly, it can alter the course of personal and communal history. It is my contention that some mentally ill persons mutilate themselves as a primitive method of drawing upon their blood's ability to foster bonds of loyalty and union among members of their social network, to demonstrate their hatred of and conquest over real and imaginary enemies, to heal their afflictions, and, as is discussed in chapter 2, to set right their relationship with God.

Although blood customs have a worldwide distribution, they were especially important in the everyday life of people living in the Balkans (Durham 1928). Union could be achieved, for example, by feasting on an enemy's blood. Thus one group of Balkan pirates displayed the mutilated corpse of the Holy Roman Emperor's envoy in a church. Wives then demonstrated solidarity with their husbands by licking the bloody body.

Blood feuds were common in areas such as Albania and Montenegro. The taking of blood was an almost sacred duty for the relatives of a murdered or seriously aggrieved person. A blood taker lost face and honor in his community until he fulfilled his obligation to kill his victim. Because of the popular belief that the soul of a slain person could find no peace until blood had been taken for it, people were fearful of dying by an unknown hand. If family members were dissatisfied with the course of vengeance, they saved the bloody clothing of the murdered person to remind his young sons that they needed to take more blood. Blood taking not only pacified the original victim but also, by replacing the blood lost by the group, ensured family unity.

Particularly in Europe human blood and fragments of flesh and bone have been prized as healing agents. In book 28 of his monumental *Natural History*, Pliny writes: "Thus epileptics even drink the blood of gladiators out of living goblets. . . . They consider it the most effective method of cure to swallow down the blood when it is still warm and bubbling out of the man himself, and thus simultaneously to swallow the very breath of life from the mouth of the wound." A belief in the efficacy of the blood of persons who died violently to cure epilepsy persevered into the nineteenth century. Hans Christian Andersen's autobiography, for example, describes an execution he witnessed in 1823: "I saw a poor sick man, whom his superstitious parents made drink a cup of the blood of an executed person, that he might be healed of epilepsy; after which they ran with him wildly until he sank to the ground."

In a large number of European legends and customs blood was used to treat leprosy. An ancient rabbinical commentary (Midrash Shemoth Exodus Rabba) on Exodus 2:23 — "A long time passed, during which the king of Egypt died" — states that the king was considered dead because he had contracted leprosy and that the Egyptian priests prescribed a grisly cure: the king had to bathe twice daily in the blood of three hundred Israelite children. One legend held that Richard, the king of England from 1189 to 1199, had leprosy. Since nothing seemed to help, he called upon a famous Jewish physician, who recommended that Richard bathe in the blood of a newborn child and eat the child's heart. It is interesting to note that great anti-Semitic animosity arose in the thirteenth and fourteenth centuries because of the appearance of red spots on consecrated communion wafers in some churches. These spots were thought to be Jesus's blood, the result of the secret piercing of the wafers by Jews. This incredible belief persisted until the German scientist Ehrenberg presented a paper at the Academy of Sciences at Berlin in 1848, demonstrating that the "blood" was really a bacterial growth that flourished under certain conditions.

Following the crusades, Europe was flooded with relics, such as the bones and body parts of saints, that were objects of veneration and in many cases were used in healing practices. In various European popular beliefs, afflicted persons have been urged to use corpse fragments; for example, pressing a corpse's finger on an aching tooth supposedly cured toothache. Pliny's *Natural History* describes the efficacy of a corpse hand: "Stroking with the hand of a person who has died early is supposed to cure goiter, glandular swellings near the ear, and throat complaints; nevertheless, a good many think that this can be effected by any corpse's hand, provided only that the dead person be of the same sex, and the thing is done with the left hand upturned."

Sadism and Murder

Donatien-Alphonse-François de Sade (1740–1814), better known as the Marquis de Sade, devoted his life and his writings to the glorification of sexual gratification associated with inflicting pain on others. He spent sixteen years in prison and eleven more years at the asylum for the criminally insane at Charenton, where he died. His first serious offense occurred when he trapped a woman, whipped her severely, and then superficially sliced the skin of her entire body with a knife. In 1772 he masterminded the "Cantharidic Bonbon Orgy" in which he placed Spanish fly (officially known as cantharides, this chemical was thought to be an aphrodisiac but in reality is a dangerous astringent) in the chocolate dessert served at a ball. According to some accounts the ball turned into a sexual orgy orchestrated by de Sade. Several people supposedly died as a result of esophageal strictures caused by eating the Spanish fly, and de Sade was charged with sodomy and murder.

Most of de Sade's writings were done in institutions and, until fairly recently, were universally reviled as repulsive and depraved. Jules Janin, a critic writing in *Revue de Paris*, 1834, wrote of de Sade's works, "What an indefatigable monster. . . . When he reaches the end of his crimes, when he has exhausted his fund of incests and bestialities, when at last he is there, panting over the bodies he has stabbed and violated, when there remains no church to be polluted, no child he has not butchered in his rage, not a single moral idea upon which he has not smeared the filth of his odious doctrines and language, only then is it that he halts . . . and looks at himself . . . and smiles" (cited in Gillette 1966).

Certainly de Sade cannot be accused of being a great writer. In his novella *Justine*, for example, a lecher shows Justine the realistic wax effigy of a woman in the same posture as the crucified Christ and then says, "This statue is the representation of my former mistress, who died nailed to this wall. I had it constructed to replace her real body when it began to decompose." *The One Hundred Twenty Days of Sodom, or, The Romance of the School of Libertinage* contains a catalog of sexual vices most of which are silly or improbable, for example, "A man extracts all of a woman's teeth, replacing them with red-hot nails which he secures in place with a hammer. This is done after he forces her to perform fellatio."

Count Leopold von Sacher-Masoch was de Sade's counterpart in that his literary writings depicted sexual pleasure derived from being the object of pain. Both sadism and masochism are, by definition, associated with sexual pleasure, while self-mutilation is usually not. In my study of 250 chronic self-mutilators, only 2 percent said they were often or always sexually aroused when they decided to harm themselves; 3 percent said self-harm often or always aroused sexual feelings in them. Twenty percent said they sometimes used self-harm as a method of ridding themselves of troublesome sexual feelings. There does exist, however, a definite subgroup of self-mutilators who are sexually excited by limb amputation, especially of the feet and toes. Additionally, some persons enjoy pain during sexual activity (hot wax dripped on their breasts, use of oversized dildos, pinching), and some like to engage in painful self-mutilation, such as sticking pins into their skin. While participation in bondage scenarios involving mild flagellation and being tied up with ropes and chains may be considered within the spectrum of normal sexual behavior nowadays, extensive tissue damage must be considered pathological. One patient, whose major sexual outlet is masturbation in front of a full-length mirror, was able to excite himself only through self-harm, such as whipping himself with wires (the cuts often took seven to fourteen days to heal), lacerating his penis with brush bristles, squeezing his testicles in a door jamb, and burning himself with candle wax. As a child, this patient was forced to engage in sexual acts with both parents in which he was whipped, had rubber probes stuck into his penis, had clamps placed on his testicles, and was given ice-water enemas.

Many murderers who mutilate their victims are psychotic and sadistic. Some, like Jack the Ripper, have gained enormous notoriety because of the multiple mutilative murders they have committed. Probably the most infamous mentally ill mutilator, however, was Gilles de Rais, a French nobleman born in 1404. He fought against the English along with Joan of Arc and was her military instructor. At the age of 26 he retired from public life to his castle in Brittany.

My suppositions are that he was schizophrenic and that the content of his illness was influenced by the Zeitgeist of his era. His was an era of witchcraft, demonology, and Satanism. It was an era of Black Masses, severe repression, and fabulous trials, for example, persons were accused of such sacrilegious acts as using communion wafers for sodomistic purposes and using children's blood in place of consecrated wine. Gilles de Rais turned to necromancy with a vengeance, abetted by an Italian ex-priest, Francesco Prelati, who taught that contact with Satan could best be achieved by performing the most brutal and sinful acts imaginable.

De Rais began by sodomizing young boys, but Prelati scoffed, saying that this was not enough to entice the devil. De Rais then kidnapped a little boy, cut the boy's throat, removed his hands, eyes, and heart, and offered the pieces to Satan in a mock religious ceremony. But still the devil did not materialize.

De Rais supposedly sodomized, mutilated, and murdered more than seven hundred children. At his trial he told of his usual procedure of sexually assaulting boys in the cellar of a tower, cutting open their chests and burying his face in their lungs, and opening their abdomens and handling their intestines. He also confessed to necrophilia with the dismembered bodies and to attempted intercourse with a fetus he cut out of a pregnant woman.

At his trial in 1440, de Rais repented, and the bishop of Nantes was forced to receive him back into the church saying, "Weep, you madman, that thy tears may wash away the pollutions of the charnel-house within you." De Rais and Prelati were then simultaneously hanged and burned to death.

Mutilative Imagery in Religion

Although chapter 2 is devoted to religion, here I focus on three totally different belief systems — Tibetan Tantrism, North American Indian mysticism, and Christianity — that contain exceedingly vivid images of mutilation. These powerful images are not superficial bits of drama but rather are intrinsic to the meaningfulness of the belief systems. Stripped of blood and torn flesh, most religions become no different from fairy tales. The True Cross is not sparkling clean and silver plated.

Tibetan Tantrism

The *Tibetan Book of the Dead*, or *The Great Liberation through Hearing in the Bardo*, describes a series of meditations on death and birth as experienced in six psychological states. During these states the meditator must deal with various deities who appear. "*Bar* means in between, and *do* means an island or mark; a sort of landmark that stands between two things. It is rather like an island in the middle of a lake. The concept of bardo is based on the period between sanity and insanity, or the period between confusion and . . . wisdom; . . . between death and birth. The past situation has just occurred and the future situation has not yet manifested itself so there is a gap between the two. This is basically the bardo experience" (Rinpoche 1975, pp. 10–11).

The bardo retreat, seven weeks in total darkness, is the most rewarding but dangerous form of meditation. The meditator experiences luminosity and visions accompanied by brilliant colors and sounds. The meditator feels detached from the world, like a gigantic head floating in space, and hears the sounds of a thousand claps of thunder yet there is nothing to vibrate.

The first visions are those of the peaceful divinities, who permit the meditator to experience the eternal peace of the cosmos. But then the terrifying, wrathful deities of mutilation appear as a sign of cosmic passion and aggression. Perfect instantaneous enlightenment occurs when the meditator understands that he is projecting these horrible images from within himself.

> With teeth biting the lower lip, glassy-eyed, their hair tied on top of their heads, with huge bellies and thin necks, holding the records of karma in their hands, chanting "Strike!" and "Kill!" licking up brains, tearing heads from bodies, pulling out internal organs: in this way they will come.
>
> When projections appear like this do not be afraid. You have a mental body of unconscious tendencies, so even if you are killed and cut into pieces, you cannot die.

After death comes rebirth. The reading of the *Bardo* is especially significant to dying persons because, with the insights gained, they can search out an appropriate womb to enter. But even if a person has died, the *Bardo* should be read in the presence of the corpse "until blood and pus come out of the nostrils. . . . This profound instruction leads great sinners on the secret path."

North American Indian Mysticism   book

The Sun Dance of the Plains Indians is a ritual Alexander (1967) describes as "the index of an entire culture, not merely in a material sense but especially with respect to the whole pattern of life, social and ideal, which guided into its development the particular genius of the hunters and warriors of the prairie. . . . The Sun Dance is essentially an interpretation [and] a philosophy of life" (p. 137). It is an eight-day ritual characteristic of buffalo-hunting tribes, such as the Arapahoe, Cheyenne, and Dakota. Although participants volunteer out of personal initiative, the entire tribe cooperates in its performance, for it is the entire tribe that benefits from the suffering and self-mutilation of the dancers.

The climax of the ceremony is the Gazing-at-the-Sun dance, which portrays the dangers of a warrior's life, namely, Capture, Torture, and Release. The dancers are "captured" by warriors while women sing songs of grief. In earlier times they were then tortured (although bloodletting is currently prohibited by federal law). Incisions were made on their backs and chests, and pieces of wood with attached leather thongs were inserted under the cut muscles. The thongs of some dancers were attached to buffalo skulls, but others had the thongs attached to the top of the Sacred Pole. They then danced; those who were attached to the Pole were hoisted into the air while they gazed at the sun. They then struggled to break free of their bonds. Some, unable to stand the pain, were cut free. Others successfully struggled until the wooden skewers ripped through their flesh; sometimes friends added their weight to the dancers and pulled hard until the flesh gave way. The pure in heart able to withstand this religious ordeal expected to receive a vision which, when understood, would make clear the meaning and course of their lives.

"Possibly, in a more mystical sense, here is shown the drama of all embodied human life—for more than one religion and philosophy, from the ancients onward, have depicted man as snared in the flesh, there to suffer and endure, and if by the prowess of his spirit enduring to the end, escaped and triumphant in a newer and more spiritual vision. Assuredly there is here an elemental coincidence between the essential elements of Indian and Neo-Platonic or even Christian thinking" (Alexander 1967, p. 169).

Christianity

The most enduring images central to Western cultural tradition are those of the Passion of Christ. The most powerful and intense images were developed during the fourteenth through seventeenth centuries and have been classified by art historians (Schiller 1972). Some are drawn directly from biblical accounts, while others are ahistorical images drawn from the imaginations of the artists. Without getting into abstruse theological arguments, suffice it to say that Christ willingly submitted to his Passion. His voluntary suffering, crucifixion, and resurrection both fulfilled and transcended the old prophesies.

The fourteenth century saw the rise of the flagellant cults, and many paintings of that period depict the *Flagellation* of Christ. He is shown tied to a column while his captors unmercifully whip him. His body is covered with multiple wounds as the surrounding crowd listens to Pilate's unsuccessful pleas for sympathy. In *Ecce Homo* (Behold the Man) scenes Pilate displays the wounded Christ to the angry crowd in the hope that the pitiful sight will satisfy its lust for blood. In many paintings Christ wears a robe but it is opened, the better to display his battered body.

Christ is shown *Nailed to the Cross*, wearing a crown of thorns while metal spikes are hammered through his outstretched arms and crossed feet. An interesting feminine variation of this theme was inspired by the mystical piety associated with convents. In these images Christ is nailed to the cross and stuck with a lance by women representing the Virtues, Ecclesia, Synagogue, and Caritas. Since humanity's salvation was made possible by Christ's, it was considered virtuous to assist Christ by torturing him.

Christ *Crucified on the Cross* is perhaps the most commonly painted scene in Western art. While some paintings portray Christ free of wounds, many others spare no details. These images echo the vision of Saint Bridget of Sweden (1303–73): "He was crowned with thorns. Blood trickled over his eyes, his ears, his beard; his mouth was open, his tongue bleeding, his cheeks hollow. His body was so greatly sunk that it seemed he no longer had any entrails."

In *Lamentation* scenes the body of Christ is mourned. In one of the most famous, by Andrea Mantegna (about 1500), Christ rests on a wooden bed. No spikes are visible, but Christ's hands and feet prominently display the jagged wounds. *Pietà* scenes portray Mary's grief at her son's death. Particularly gruesome yet touching are German wood carvings of the pietà in which a sorrowful, adoring Mary holds the emaciated and ravaged body of Christ in her lap. Another related devotional image is the *Man of Sorrows* in which Christ's suffering is emphasized, although it is not associated with any specific event in his life. Such scenes were invitations for viewers to fulfil themselves by imitating Christ.

Reformation art had its own special focus on the Passion. In Lucas Cranach's *Christ on the Cross, and the Risen Christ Slays Death and the Devil* (1553), for example, John the Baptist, Cranach himself, and Martin Luther stand at the foot of the cross. From a wound in Christ's side a jet of blood — representing the stream of grace — falls on the painter's head, while Luther holds open a Bible, his finger pointing to the words, "The Blood of Jesus Christ cleanseth us from all sin."

Arma Christi scenes focus single-mindedly on Christ's sufferings. *Arma* refers to the weapons with which Christ conquered death and Satan. These weapons symbolized triumph and were a sort of coat of arms. Typical *Arma Christi* images include the lance used to pierce Christ, the nails used to fasten Christ to the cross, instruments such as whips, pincers, and scourges used to torture Christ, a crown of thorns, and even the bloody knife used to circumcise Jesus. The *Arma Christi* image sometimes replaced the crucifixion as the center of Passion scenes. Instead of depicting Christ in his entirety, only his mutilated body parts were shown; sometimes the central image was a large crown of thorns containing four petal roses. Each rose framed either a wounded hand or foot of Christ. In the center of the crown was Jesus's heart, dripping blood, pierced by a lance. In fact, in the year 1354 the Feast of the Lance was proclaimed, and a Christian cult arose that meditated on and venerated the lance that was stuck into Christ's side by the Roman soldier Longinus.

Although for twelve centuries Jesus's heart was not especially venerated, it has become his most revered body part. In the thirteenth century, French and German nuns prone to mysticism declared visions of glory blazing from Christ's wounded heart. In these visions the heart was still firmly within Jesus's body; the blazing glory was interpreted as saving grace and, in paintings, became a stream of blood that gushed from Christ's side onto a person's head or into a chalice. These mystical visions were popularized by Carthusian monks in the fifteenth and sixteenth centuries.

In 1610, Saint Francis de Sales founded the Order of the Visitation for nuns. On the order's coat of arms was an image of Jesus's heart with arrows sticking out of it and with a crown of thorns and a cross at its top. From 1673 to 1675 a member of that order, Saint Marguerite-Marie Alacoque, had several widely publicized visions during periods of ecstasy: "The Heart of Jesus was represented to me as on a throne formed of fire and flames, surrounded by rays more brilliant than the sun and transparent as crystal. The wound which He received on the cross was clearly seen there. Around this Sacred Heart was a crown of thorns, and above it a cross which was planted in it" (Saint Margaret Mary 1931, p. 64). Her visions climaxed decades of attempts by a small group of priests to establish the Sacred Heart as an approved devotional image.

The Council of Trent (1545–63) had carefully considered the question of religious images and had produced a list of those that were acceptable. Jesus's heart was not on the approved list. Despite this prohibition the Sacred Heart image was commonly used in the imagery of the Catholic church in Mexico. Kehoe (1979) has demonstrated that this image diffused from Mexico to Europe. The heart of the Aztec death god, for example, was often portrayed through a wound in his chest. From this heart a dynamic "fluid" streamed out while the god held another heart crowned with flaming leaves in his hand. Thus, the Catholic church appropriated Mexican religious symbols and reinterpreted them to coincide with Christian beliefs. Under Pope Clement VIII in 1600 an investigation was held to examine adherence to the Council of Trent's proclamation on approved imagery. As a result a new edict prohibited many images once again. "Molds for pastry and sweets, however, in the shape of sacred hearts and other such symbols were allowed in Mexico" (Keleman 1967, p. 117). Mexican images of the Sacred Heart spread to Europe and were integrated into mainstream Christian iconography.

Christian art over the centuries has associated human body parts and instruments of torture with biblical figures and saints (Ferguson 1954). A severed head, depending upon the context, might refer to Goliath, or to Holofernes, or to Salome, or to John the Baptist. Saint Agatha, a third-century martyr, had her breasts cut off with shears; paintings of her show a dish with her mutilated breasts on it. Saint Catherine of Alexandria, another early martyr, was torn to death by the emperor Maximin; her special attribute is the spiked wheel. One of Saint Eustace's attributes is the instrument of his martyrdom, a life-sized, iron brazen bull into whose red-hot body he was placed. Saint Laurence's attribute is the gridiron, upon which he was roasted. Saint Lucy is often portrayed holding her self-enucleated eyes in her hand.

Devotional books, such as Gallonio's *De SS Martyrum Cruciatibus*, describe the gruesome fate of the martyrs not only in words but also in vivid drawings; martyrs are shown being flayed alive, dismembered, having their teeth and tongue cut off, being gored by bulls, cooked alive, and eaten by wild animals. Although many of the legends about the early Christian martyrs are clearly embellishments designed to impress the faithful, the actual torture and suffering they (and later on the Tudor martyrs in England) endured were quite real and quite horrible.

From a psychiatric perspective one of the most interesting and unusual martyrs was Saint Wilgefortis, who was the daughter of a cruel Portuguese king and supposedly lived around A.D. 800. Having made a vow of virginity, she was shocked when her father not only made sexual advances but also betrothed her to a Saracen Sicilian king. She prayed to God to stop the marriage by depriving her of her beauty. She became an ascetic, starved herself, developed an unattractive hairy body, and even grew a beard! The Sicilian king understandably refused to marry her, and her father, enraged, had her crucified. While on the cross, she spoke of "the passion that encumbrances all women" and urged women to pray that through her they would be similarly blessed and liberated from worldly care. From A.D. 1200 her cult spread, and she was known as Saint Liberata in Spain, Saint Ontkommena in the Netherlands, Saint Kummernis in Germany, and Saint Livrade in France. Lacey (1982) considers her to have suffered from anorexia nervosa as manifested by self-starvation, hair growth, high ethical and moral standards, and an inability to cope with the demands and fears of adult sexuality. She belonged to the upper social class, and her illness began in early adolescence, culminating "in Wilgefortis's crucifixion by her father with the support and encouragement of her family, the symbolism of which would not be lost on the anorectic patient of today" (p. 817).

Mutilative Imagery in Secular Art

Although it is beyond the scope of this volume to survey the artistic history of mutilation, the visual images of Hieronymus Bosch's Triptych of the *Garden of Delights* (sixteenth century) are among the most famous and incredible in Western art. The theme of the painting is man's fall from grace, his indulgence in sinful pursuits (especially lust), and the hellish punishments for his transgressions. Sinners are grouped together; gamblers, for example, are pictured with dice in their hands, but their hands have been cut off while dogs and rodents gnaw at their bodies. Men overly given to delight in music cry in agony because flutes have been shoved up their rectums. Two mutilated ears with a long dagger protruding between them (a bizarre phallic war machine) slash their way among those who have reveled in hearing evil. A central figure is known as the Tree-Man (some critics refer to the figure as Alchemical Man), a strange creature whose legs are lacerated tree trunks and whose egg-shaped torso is cracked open to reveal a tavern full of lost souls. Knights given to anger are ripped apart. A sinner with blackbirds flying out of his anus is devoured by a disgusting bird who, in turn, defecates his human meal into a cesspool full of vomit, feces, and gold coins. Similar themes are portrayed in another of Bosch's famous triptychs, *The Last Judgment*. Here we see some sinners sliced up and placed in a frying pan while others are impaled by spears and still others are ripped apart and tortured.

Bosch remains an enigmatic artist, for he left no letters, probably never traveled from his hometown, did not date his paintings, and inspired no early biographies. A complete understanding of all his images requires knowledge of the minutiae of medieval symbolism in general and of Dutch variants in particular. A person who painted such horrifying images today might very well be exhibiting schizophrenic pathology, but Bosch's images were well attuned to the cultural climate of his time. Mutilation and torture were regarded as the inevitable "rewards" of leading a sinful life. It was a time in which God's Eye saw every misdeed. Indeed, Bosch's painting *The Seven Deadly Sins* depicts a mutilated Christ as the pupil of God's Eye, which clearly sees humankind's transgressions. "Beware, Beware, God Sees" are the words inscribed around the pupil.

Certainly many of the most highly regarded twentieth-century artistic images reflect a peculiar type of mutilation. One thinks of surrealism, especially Dali's nightmarish figures, and of Picasso who has ripped apart the human body and reassembled it in bizarre ways in an attempt to clarify our perceptions through distortion. And perhaps it would be remiss not to mention two of the most enduring images of classical art—the headless *Winged Victory of Samothrace*, the essence of grace, and that epitome of feminine beauty, the mutilated torso of the Venus de Milo.

Mutilation in Literature

Throughout this book I refer to the famous, classical literary mutilation scenes found in Sophocles's *Oedipus Rex*, in Ovid's *Metamorphoses*, in Catullus's poem about the self-emasculation of Attis, and in Shakespeare's grisly drama *Titus Andronicus*. Although a complete survey of literary depictions of mutilation would constitute an entire large volume in itself, I present several examples that demonstrate mutilation and self-mutilation in differing contexts, namely, mental illness, theatricality, the judicial process, religion, and mob violence.

The oldest, fairly detailed literary example of self-mutilation associated with mental illness that I have found is in book 6 of Herodotus. Cleomenes was a Spartan leader who left the city and was involved in complicated political intrigues. He was brought back to Sparta and restored to a high position. However, "He had always been a little queer in the head, but no sooner had he returned to Sparta than he lost his wits completely, and began poking his staff into the face of everyone he met. As a result of this lunatic behavior his relatives put him in the stocks. As he was lying there, fast bound, he noticed that all his guards had left him except one. He asked this man, who was a serf, to lend him his knife. At first the fellow refused, but Cleomenes, by threats of what he would do to him when he recovered his liberty, so frightened him that he at last consented. As soon as the knife was in his hands, Cleomenes began to mutilate himself, beginning on his shins. He sliced his flesh into strips, working upwards to his thighs, hips, and sides until he reached his belly, which he chopped into mincemeat."

Franz Kafka, perhaps more than any other author, has succeeded in developing self-mutilation as a most peculiar and penetrating literary genre. *The Hunger Artist* is about a professional faster, a man who was booked by an impresario to sit in a cage and starve himself for forty days in full public view. In addition to casual onlookers, teams of permanent watchers (usually butchers) watched closely to ensure that the hunger artist did not secretly break his fast. Kafka's hunger artist found himself deserted as people sought other amusements, and he was reduced to working for a circus. He was neglected more and more until one day an overseer's eye fell on his cage. He asked why nothing was in it except dirty straw. The workmen poked into the straw with sticks and to their surprise found the hunger artist. When the overseer told the hunger artist that he admired his fasting, the reply was, "But you shouldn't admire it because I have to fast. I can't help it because I couldn't find the food I liked. If I had found it, believe me, I should have made no fuss and stuffed myself like you or anyone else." With that the overseer cleaned out the cage and buried the hunger artist, straw and all. And into the cage he placed a wild, young panther whose joy of life was a real crowd pleaser.

Kafka's *In the Penal Colony* begins with the portentious phrase, "It's a remarkable piece of apparatus." The apparatus in question is a machine upon which persons are mutilated and then executed. It consists of a bed, a control device called a designer, and a harrow or set of needles. A condemned man is strapped naked to the bed, and then, over the course of twelve hours, the harrow carves words into the prisoner's flesh. The prisoner is not told the nature of his crime or the sentence that has been passed on him. In fact, he learns of it only by deciphering the message that is carved on his body. An insubordinate soldier, for example, would have the words "Honor Thy Superiors!" carved on him. After the prisoner deciphers the message and is enlightened through his wounds, the harrow pierces him and casts him into a bloody pit, where he is buried.

A more contemporary depiction of self-mutilation is found in Flannery O'Connor's highly acclaimed novel *Wise Blood*. Amid a setting of rural southern poverty, the protagonist, Hazel Motes, "saw Jesus move from tree to tree in the back of his mind, a wild ragged figure motioning him to turn around and come off into the dark where he was not sure of his footing, where he might be walking on the water and not know it and then suddenly know it and drown." Following a family tradition he becomes a bizarre preacher of the Church-of-Christ-without-Christ, a church where the blind don't see, and the lame don't walk, and the dead stay dead, and the blood of Jesus doesn't save. Tortured by his struggles to reject or to accept Jesus, he finally pokes out both his eyes with a pointed stick, stops preaching, and lives in a small boarding home where he puts rocks in his shoes. When asked by his landlady why he walks on rocks, he answers, "To pay." She then discovers that he wears strands of barbed wire under his shirt and says, "It's not normal. It's like one of them gory stories, it's something that people have quit doing—like boiling in oil or being a saint or walling up cats. People have quit doing it. . . . What do you do it for?" "I'm not clean," he replies. Having finally found Christ, he contracts influenza and dies, the winter winds slashing at the boarding house, "making a sound like sharp knives swirling in the air."

Germinal (1885), Emile Zola's great novel about social injustice in the French mine pits, vividly demonstrates the theme of mob violence. The story recounts how starved mine workers revolted against management.

They cornered Maigrat, the hated shop owner, on a roof and yelled, "Look! Look! The tom-cat's up there! After the cat! After the cat! Go for him!" Maigrat fell, smashed his head on a stone wall, and his brains spouted out.

Then old Mother Brule yelled, "Cut him like a tom-cat!" The other women pulled off his trousers and raised his legs. Mother Brule separated his thighs, grabbed his genitals, and tore them off the corpse. "I've got it! I've got it," she laughed triumphantly. Another woman said, "Swine! You won't fill our daughters anymore! We don't have to offer you our backside in return for a loaf of bread anymore." The women shook with terrible gaiety and spat on the lump of hairy, bleeding flesh. "Mother Brule then planted the whole lump on the end of her stick, and holding it in the air, bore it about like a banner, rushing along the road, followed, helter-skelter, by the yelling troop of women. Drops of blood rained down, and that pitiful flesh hung like a waste piece of meat on a butcher's stall."

Zola's likening of the mutilation of a man to the mutilation of a cat is not a piece of literary bravado but rather an accurate reflection of European folk beliefs. Darnton (1984) shed light on this curious aspect of mutilation by examining ways of thinking in eighteenth-century France. One theme he developed is the mutilation and torture of animals, especially cats. In fact, his lead essay begins, "The funniest thing that ever happened in the printing shop of Jacques Vincent, according to a worker who witnessed it, was a riotous massacre of cats." The episode he examined is a revolt by printer's apprentices in Paris during the 1730s. The apprentices led a miserable existence, and even at night they were unable to sleep in their dingy bedroom because the wife of the printing shop's owner allowed her cats to sit on the roof and howl. When the howling became too much for even the shop owner, he asked the apprentices to get rid of the cats, except for the one favorite feline of his wife. The apprentices gleefully collected all of the cats, beginning with the one they were asked to save, and proceeded to massacre them by placing them in sacks and smashing them with iron bars. They then gathered the cats, some still barely alive, and held a mock trial. The cats were pronounced guilty, given last holy rites, and hanged on a small gallows. The shop owner and his wife, aroused by the men's laughter, flew into a rage, but the apprentices were delirious with "joy, disorder, and laughter." During the following days, the apprentices joked about the event and reenacted the scene in mime at least twenty times. Years later one of the participants noted that it was the most hilarious event of his life.

Why was the massacre thought to be so hilarious? Certainly the event allowed the apprentices to turn the tables on the bourgeois. They provoked the shop owner to authorize the massacre, and then they used it as a pretext to put him on trial symbolically. "They also used it as a witch hunt, which provided an excuse to kill his wife's cat and to insinuate that she herself was the witch. Finally, they transformed it into a charivari, which served as a means to insult her sexually while mocking him as a cuckold. . . . [They] ridiculed him in splendid Boccaccian style and got off scot free."

What was so special about cats? As Darnton points out, cats have long fascinated humankind in general, and artists and poets in particular. Their night howling sometimes sounds like a human scream. And cats are well suited for staging ceremonies: "You cannot make a charivari with a cow. You do it with cats: you decide to *faire le chat*, to make *Katzenmusik*." Torturing cats was a very popular form of amusement in Europe. In France, during the *dimanches des brandons* in Samur, children attached cats to poles and roasted them over bonfires. In Aix-en-Provence cats were smashed on the ground. People were described as being "patient as a cat whose claws are being grilled." Hogarth's drawings *The Stages of Cruelty* vividly depict the joyousness obtained from animal mutilation.

Cats were popularly associated with witchcraft in Europe. The devil himself was depicted often as a huge tomcat who presided over sexual orgies. The standard method of protecting oneself from sorcery was to maim a cat by smashing its legs, cutting its tail, or burning its fur, thus stripping it of its evil powers. Cats also had occult powers, both good and bad. A cat could keep yeast dough from rising in a bakery, for example, and a person could hasten recovery from a bad fall by sucking the blood from a cat's freshly amputated tail. Too, cats were closely associated with a household, and when a new house was built the French often placed a live cat in the walls. Finally, cats were, and are, connected with sex. The slang word *pussy* means the same in French as in English, and the shrieks of copulating cats sometimes refer to cuckoldry. Thus, the printer's apprentices "could hear a great deal in the wail of a cat . . . witchcraft, orgy, cuckoldry, charivari, and massacre."

2

Self-mutilation in Myths of Creation, Shamanism, and Religion

■ ■ ■ ■ ■ ■ ■ ■

"Et nos servasti . . . sanguine fuso"
And you saved us by shedding blood

Mithraic inscription in the Roman church
of Santa Prisca

Self-mutilation is a violent act associated with suffering, either immediate or delayed. However, there are many culturally sanctioned instances where persons willingly mutilate themselves or allow others to mutilate them. They engage in violence and endure suffering in the belief that their behavior serves a higher purpose beneficial to themselves or their community. Michael and Aubine Kirtley (1982), for example, photographed and described the New Year festival of the Abidji tribe (Ivory Coast). On the eve of the festival tribal members are required to attend meetings devoted to reconciling divisive personal and communal issues. On the day of the festival bad spirits are driven away, and some individuals, caught up in the pandemonium, enter a trance state to the accompaniment of rhythmic drumming. Guided by *sekes*, beneficent spirits that possess their bodies, they mutilate themselves by plunging a knife into the abdomen. These serious wounds are then treated with poultices made from kaolin, herbs, and raw eggs. Healing occurs, and the entranced mutilators say that their *seke* prescribes both the wound and the cure. Although the Abidji cannot explain clearly the reasons for this ritual, it probably serves as a physical demonstration of the social healing that has occurred within the entire community.

Most mentally ill persons are nonviolent and suffer because of their illness. Why should they wreak violence upon themselves and endure even more suffering through the act of self-mutilation? The most simple answer provided by patients is that self-mutilation reduces, at least temporarily, pathological symptoms such as anxiety, guilt, and hallucinations. The psychiatric theories that attempt to explain this process are discussed later in this book. Here, however, I examine the process from a different perspective, namely, that of religion and its offspring, shamanism.

22

The decision to examine self-mutilation in the context of religion stems from several observations. The first is that some forms of mental illness are characterized by symptoms such as shifting levels of consciousness, auditory and visual hallucinations, and altered perceptions of the body and of the environment that are similar to religious experiences; indeed, some mentally ill self-mutilators experience and articulate their condition in religious terms, for example, they claim to be a god or to have a special relationship with the spirit world. A second observation is that many religions have extolled the practice of bodily mortification. A third is that violence, according to some scholars, is at the core of religion; as stated by Girard (1977, p. 24), "Violence is the heart and secret soul of the sacred. . . . Religion shelters us from violence just as violence seeks shelter in religion." A fourth is that religion functions in great part to help individuals deal with the suffering inherent in life.

It is my contention that religious sentiments, albeit in varying degrees, are present among many mentally ill self-mutilators, especially those who experience psychosis, and that an understanding of religion helps us understand why such persons mutilate themselves. In this context self-mutilation may be regarded not only as a destructive act but also as a creative one. Let us, therefore, begin at the beginning when the world itself was created.

Myths of Creation

In 1923 a German scholar, Hermann Guntert, examined the primary Indo-European cosmogonic myth as told in the oldest Germanic and Indo-Iranian texts. He discovered a basic mythologem, namely, that the world was created as the result of the sacrifice and mutilation of the primordial hermaphroditic being. Lincoln (1975) provided the most definitive study of this important myth. He recognized that among those who tell and live myths, the greatest prestige is given to myths about the creation of the cosmos. He noted that the cosmogonic myth establishes the order of the world and thus has important social, material, and economic ramifications as well as deep religious significance. He reconstructed the basic Proto-Indo-European myth of the creation of the world from the dismembered body of a primordial being by examining three classic texts, Rigveda (India), the Greater Bundahisn (Iran), and the Prose Edda (Scandinavia).

The Rigveda states that the gods tied up Purusa, sacrificed him, and divided his body into portions. From his eye the sun was formed, from his mind the moon, from his navel the midair, and from his head the sky. Earth came from his feet, and from his ear came the regions of the earth. From the dripping fat were formed the creatures of the air and animals both wild and tame. His mouth became the Brahman, his arms the Rajanya, his thighs the Vaisya, his feet the Sudra.

The *Greater Bundahisn* tells how Ahriman, the Evil Spirit, dismembered both an ox and Gayomart. From the semen of the dead ox were created corn, medicinal herbs, and a pair of every species of animal. From Gayomart's head lead was fashioned; his blood became tin, his marrow silver, his feet iron, his bones copper, his fat glass, his arms steel, his life's departure (breath?) gold. As he lay dying, Gayomart's sperm spilled to the earth and from it came the ten species of humanity.

The Scandinavian *Prose Edda* states that both a cow and the giant Ymir were mutilated by the gods. From Ymir's body the world was made. His blood became the sea and lakes; his flesh became the earth; his bones became mountains; his teeth and jaw became rocks and pebbles; his skull became the sky.

Despite minor variation the three primordial victims are structurally similar. From semantic and phonological studies it is also apparent that they all derived from a Proto-Indo-European myth figure.

Even in China the giant figure of P'an-ku can be traced to the Indian Purusa. When P'an-ku was sliced up, his breath became the wind and clouds, his voice the thunder, his eyes the sun and moon, his limbs and fingers the earth and mountains, his blood the rivers, his sweat the rain, his skin and hair the plants and trees, his teeth and bones the metal and stones, and the parasites on his body became human beings.

In this most ancient myth, creation is born of violence in the form of sacrifice and mutilation. The first sacrifice of the Primordial Being was the origin of the world, and from the mutilation of this Being society and social order were established. Over the millennia this myth in its various elaborations has been, and continues to be, reenacted in countless religious rituals. With each reenactment the world and social order are re-created. Participants in these rituals experience the suffering and terror that come with sacrifice and mutilation, but they are rewarded for their participation in this mythic process by feelings of security, solace, well-being, and personal order.

The self-mutilative acts of some mentally ill persons may be understood in the light of this mythic process. Their bodies become a microcosm of the vaster cosmos, and the irresistible urge to self-mutilation becomes an unconscious reenactment of the cosmogonic myth in which chaos is averted and a new order established. Self-mutilation offers a temporary respite from illness rather than a permanent cure because the sacrificial death of the

Primordial Being is not emulated; the mentally ill person sacrifices a body part or a portion of blood in order to achieve a modicum of well-being. A partial sacrifice achieves only a partial peace.

Shamanism

From the earliest days of human history, special men and women have devoted their lives to healing the illnesses and reversing the misfortunes of the members of their community. One such group, known as shamans, attends to these difficult tasks through personal contact with the spirit world. Revered for their wisdom and granted a lofty status by their social groups, shamans hold special interest for us because they voluntarily participate in their own bodily mutilation in order to become healers.

Persons who receive a calling to shamanism enter into a crisis and endure an initiatory sickness. In order to become shamans they must go through a traditional sequence of mystical events, resolve their crisis, and emerge "resurrected" as new persons able to travel to the spirit world in order to protect and to heal the members of their tribe. According to Eliade (1975), shamanic initiation has five important moments: (1) torture and dismemberment of the body; (2) reduction of the body to a skeleton by scraping away the flesh; (3) substitution of the viscera and renewal of the blood; (4) time spent in Hell, during which the future shaman learns from demons and from the souls of dead shamans; and (5) an ascent to Heaven in order to be consecrated by God.

"The sufferings of the elected man are exactly like the tortures of initiation; just as in puberty rites or rites for entrance into a secret society, the novice is 'killed' by semi-divine or demonic Beings, so the future shaman sees in dreams his own body dismembered by demons; he watches them, for example, cutting off his head and tearing out his tongue" (Eliade 1975, p. 89). In the shamanic world these experiences of suffering and mutilation are intense and are perceived as totally real and very dangerous.

Would-be Yakut (Siberia) shamans "die" and lie silently for several days in a secluded place during their initiatory sickness. Demons scrape the flesh off their bones, remove the fluids from their bodies, and tear out their eyeballs. In this condition they are transported to Hell for three years, where their heads are cut off and their bodies are finely chopped and distributed to diseased spirits. In this process the would-be shamans endure great suffering and learn the secrets of healing. When their bones are covered with new flesh and their bodies given new blood, they emerge from the underworld with a new personality, that of a true shaman.

Similar stories are told by Australian aboriginal shamans. A medicine man of the Unmatjera tribe described how he became a healer. He stated that he was killed when an old tribal doctor threw stones at him; one went through his head, from ear to ear. The doctor then removed all of his internal organs, packed his body cavity with stones, and sang over him. He was given a new set of internal organs and brought back to life.

Araucanian shamans in South America must walk barefoot on hot coals. The masters then "exchange" their eyes and tongues with those of the initiates, who also have their bodies "pierced" by a rod that is passed through the stomach and out the spine. Would-be Dyak (Borneo) shamans assert that their heads are cut open. In order to achieve insight into healing, their brains are washed and restored into their heads. Gold dust is inserted into their eyes to empower them to see souls that might wander off. Their hearts are pierced with arrows to enhance their ability to sympathize with the sick and suffering.

These examples from disparate, ancient traditions point to bodily mutilation as a stepping stone to wisdom, special capacities for healing oneself and others, and a higher level of existence. The shaman allows his body to be dismembered painfully and stripped down to the bare bones. It is then reconstructed so that the shaman emerges as a wiser and healthier person. Shamans have discovered the therapeutic value of self-mutilation. Is it not possible that some mentally ill persons faced with suffering and misfortune have made the same discovery?

Religion

- A 46-year-old woman cut out her tongue with a razor. She said that she had "received a message from God to cut out my tongue . . . duty demanded it."

- A 26-year-old man believed that he possessed some of Jesus's features and that God had talked with him. He blinded himself by scratching out his eyes, stating that "God told me to, to prevent people suffering."

- A 32-year-old man had sought to purify his spirit for six years by preaching in public, carrying religious signs, shaving his head, and meditating in the hills. Burdened by guilt over episodes of drunkenness, aggression, and sexual transgressions, he cut off both his testicles "as a freewill offering to God." Following the death of his father five years later he entered into a brief homosexual relationship. Disgusted by this, he turned to the New Testament and read that "there be eunuchs who have made themselves eunuchs for the Kingdom of Heaven's sake." When he felt sexual desire two weeks later, he cut off his penis with a razor and burned it in a fire, stating, "Even if I do get certified [as legally insane] and in the eyes of the world I am mad, it is far better for me to have cleansed myself."

In each of these recent clinical cases the diagnosis of schizophrenia was made. However, in certain historical and cultural contexts these incidents of self-mutilation might have been regarded as socially meaningful or even inspired. Indeed, within the most profound religious traditions gods, prophets, martyrs, saints, and sinners in search of redemption have mortified, mutilated, and sacrificed themselves. That some mentally ill persons model their behavior on that of these spiritual heroes is clear and, at least on a superficial level, quite understandable. Identification with a conquering hero may permit psychotic persons to feel in control of a world that appears to be crumbling around them (the consolation of illusion). For self-mutilators, however, not any hero will do. Napoleon is never chosen, but Jesus frequently is. Even in non-Christian cultures self-mutilators tend to identify with religious rather than secular heroes. Is there, then, some special connection between self-mutilation and religion?

Religion means many things to many people and can be appreciated on various levels. Surely religion is love, compassion, purity, joy, and tranquillity. Yet at the very core of religion one finds violence, sacrifice, blood, suffering, martyrdom, and self-mutilation. Two of the most revered symbols, for example, are the cross of Christianity and the Siva lingam of Hinduism.[1] Others before me have reached the same conclusion (Bowker 1970; Burkert 1983; Girard 1977). This bloody violence is not purposeless but rather has from the earliest times served to establish and to preserve cosmological and personal order. It is my contention that, likewise, some modern-day mentally ill persons mutilate themselves to establish and to preserve order in their lives. I do not believe that they consciously understand the significance of their actions, however. Their self-mutilations rarely have commu-

---

1. The symbol of the cross on which Christ was willingly tortured and sacrificed is undoubtedly well known to readers. Less well known, perhaps, is the symbol of the Siva lingam. According to Hindu belief, Brahma the Creator was angry because he was unsuccessful in creating human beings and so commanded Siva to do so. Siva refused to create imperfect beings and responded to his father's command by castrating himself. Siva's severed penis or lingam sunk into the ground, penetrated the netherworld, and then shot up into the sky as a burning pillar of flames. His lingam is a most sacred object. Statues of it, some of them five feet tall, often have Siva's face carved on them as an indication of the relationship between procreation and creative thought. According to Kramrisch (1981): "In the world of Siva, the significance of the *linga* is comparable to that of the Cross in the Christian world, and that of Siva with the *linga*, or the faces of Siva together with the shape of the *linga*, to the figure of the Savior on the Cross."

nal consequences but rather are attempts to achieve personal salvation and well-being. Although the "religious" self-mutilations of the mentally ill are idiosyncratic and, unlike truly "sacred" mutilations, devoid of meaning for the community, they touch upon a profound, mythic process. The following somewhat lyrical scenario attempts to reveal the essence of the Sacred.

Let us imagine a group of travelers in search of the Sacred. They pass through consecrated grounds and enter the Holy Temple. As they penetrate the gilded antechambers sweet music fills their ears. Through the disorienting mist of incense they see the object of their quest, the True Altar. A blinding yet strangely peaceful light reflects off the altar's gold and pure-white marble sides. Bedazzled, most of the travelers feel no need to go further. They are satisfied with their sense of awe and refresh themselves with a little bread and wine given to them by the priests. But those brave souls who truly wish to experience the terror, bliss, and recognition of supreme authority (*mysterium temendum, fascinans, et augustum*) of the Holy go on bended knees to the True Altar's edge. The sound of hymns has disappeared, replaced by groans and muffled shrieks of agony from the Altar's center. Fearful, they peer over the top of the Holy Altar into the Well of Eternal Life. What they see disgusts them momentarily, but they are powerless to avert their eyes. The well is deep, so deep that it reaches the very center of the earth, and it is apparent it is the source of all the streams and rivers of the world. Should this well dry up, no crops would grow. It is apparent, too, that this well supplies humankind with a special type of sustenance called the Sacred. Without it Chaos would control the universe and people would exist in hopeless lawlessness, devouring one another like wolves.

There is no water in the Well of the One True Altar, only blood and bits of flesh and bone that pop to the surface. Look! There is Odin's eye, and Jesus's heart with a lance tip in it. Now Osiris's lost phallus floats by, and Attis's private parts. Now the breasts of Saint Agatha appear, and slices of Buddha's limbs. Here is the marrow of P'an-ku, the chest muscles of some courageous Sioux braves, and the charred skins of the Tudor martyrs. Although the violent commotion has comingled all of the blood, one can discern different textures and colors. The blood from blessed bulls and rams and oxen swirls to the top but is displaced by Dionysus's claret-colored blood and the crimson blood of Mithra.

Here, in the presence of the Sacred, the voyagers understand that everything in the universe—the crops, the forests, the rivers, the animals, the ordering of human groups, the moon, the sun, the stars—is dependent upon the continued beneficence of the Holy Well. And they understand that the blood and flesh in the Well must be periodically replenished, especially during those times when the forces of chaos and evil let loose the dogs of war and set locusts on the fields, when pestilence and plague run rampant, and the sun darkens the sky. But whose blood shall be shed, whose flesh shall be picked apart to save us all?

Sacrifice and Suffering

During several manic episodes over the course of twelve years, a woman bit off a large piece of her tongue, wounded her arms, badly lacerated her vagina with her hand, burned her skin, and blinded herself while trying to gouge out her eyes. She claimed that God had ordered her to purify herself by sacrificing parts of her body.

A 48-year-old widow accused herself of being a great sinner. She went naked into the street and asked a minister and other men to marry her. She felt that her eyes were sinful because they had looked at worldly things. After reading Matthew's words in the New Testament, she quietly took out both of her eyes and asked the doctors to cut off her legs and feet, stating that since Christ had sacrificed his blood she too must sacrifice her blood in order to become saintly.

A 25-year-old man removed both testicles with a razor blade and then cut into the base of his penis. He said he did this because he heard the voice of his mother, who told him that he would be denied entry into the kingdom of heaven unless he sacrificed his penis and testicles.

In these three cases as well as in many others described in this book, it is clear that the self-mutilations of some mentally ill persons occur in a context of religious sacrifice. True sacrifice demands the death of a consecrated object; throughout history persons who have consecrated their lives to a particular god and who have endured suffering and death willingly out of devotion to their god have been revered as martyrs. Few religious followers become martyrs but many choose to emulate their suffering and, indeed, may inflict suffering on themselves deliberately. They are, in effect, engaging in a partial sacrifice.

Why are sacrifice and a focus on suffering so important to religion? What purposes do they serve? Why do some mentally ill persons perceive their acts of self-mutilation as sacrificial? What do they gain by inflicting suffering upon themselves?[2]

The concept of sacrifice was an important concern of the founders of modern anthropology at the end of the nineteenth century (Bourdillon and

2. Among the best sources for a theoretical understanding of sacrifice and suffering are the books by Money-Kryle (1930), James (1962), Girard (1977), and Bourdillon and Fortes (1980).

Fortes 1980). Tylor's theory, based on the connection between sacrifice and prayer, is that a person who offers a valuable sacrificial gift to a deity anticipates that the deity will respond with a special favor, such as recovery from illness, or general beneficence. Frazer's theory holds that the blood and flesh of sacrificial victims serve to rejuvenate the gods and to keep them from dying. Smith's theory focuses on the communion that is established between a group and its deity as a result of eating the flesh of the sacrificial animal or human victim. Hubert and Mauss's theory defines sacrifice as "a religious act which, by consecration of a victim, modified the moral state of the sacrificer or of certain objects in which he is interested," and a sacrificial rite as "a procedure to establish a communion between a sacred world and the profane world through the intermediary of a victim." Some of these early anthropologists also noted that a powerful "energy" is released at the moment of sacrifice.

Perhaps the most astute modern student of sacred sacrifice is René Girard (1977). According to him, sacrifice is a religious act that protects a group from its own violence, restores harmony to a community, and reinforces the social fabric by focusing communal dissension onto a sacrificial victim. "There is no question of expiation. Rather, society is seeking to deflect upon a relatively indifferent victim, a sacrificeable victim, the violence that would otherwise be vented on its own members, the people it most desires to protect" (p. 4). Sacrificial victims have been primarily such persons as prisoners of war, slaves, small children, and the handicapped, persons who are not fully integrated into communal life and who do not share close social bonds with a broad cross section of citizens.

Religious sacrifice entails suffering, whether it be the suffering of an animal whose throat is slit, a person whose heart is ripped out, or a god who is crucified; certainly in Christianity Jesus' suffering is an integral component of his self-sacrifice. In addition to this linkage with sacrifice, suffering is the raison d'être of the widespread religious practice of self-mortification.

Hinduism, perhaps the most complex of all religious systems, presents fertile grounds for self-mortification and self-mutilation. We have already examined the cosmogonic myth in which Purusa was dismembered. As recounted in the holy Vedas, the world "is just food and the eater of food," an endless cycle of devouring and being devoured. Through sacrifice one identifies with this cycle of creation and destruction and attempts to gain some measure of control over it.

In the Hindu pantheon of gods, Siva personifies the forces of destruction and evil in the universe. Bowker (1970) noted that Siva must be propitiated and "on the basis of the threefold relationship of devourer, devoured, and devouring, the propitiation of the devourer sometimes took on frightening and awe-inspiring forms" (p. 204). Kali, the Dark Goddess, is a ferocious and bloodthirsty aspect of Siva. Her teeth are fangs, and she wears a necklace of skulls and a belt of amputated limbs. In her four hands she carries a sword and a decapitated head dripping blood. Campbell (1962) noted that "in the temples of the Black Goddess Kali, the terrible one of many names, whose stomach is a void and so can never be filled and whose womb is giving birth forever to all things, a river of blood has been pouring continuously for millenniums, from beheaded offerings, through channels carved to return it, still living, to its divine source" (p. 5). Human sacrifices to Kali were abundant until forbidden by law in 1835. Today her temples in India and Nepal are still the scene of animal sacrifices.

The Hindu gods represent opposite and complementary qualities. Siva is not only the force of destruction that demands sacrifice and suffering; he also is the force of creation. These seemingly disparate qualities represent different aspects of a unitary process.

In Hinduism, suffering is inherent to the tensions of the cosmos. Again, according to Bowker, "Basically suffering is an experience, a part of the universe of being, which needs to be seen in perspective. It may in fact be extremely beneficial, particularly if it is the foundation of better things, or if it is the knife which cuts humans off from their attachment to unworthy objects. . . . That explains why asceticism, privation voluntarily accepted, is so important in Hinduism. It is a part of the process of getting suffering in perspective. . . . Suffering is the process of being devoured, and as such it is the relationship between the two conflicting principles of the universe, the urge to life and the urge to death" (1970, p. 207).

Indeed, travelers to India cannot help but be impressed by the numbers of ascetic holy men, some of whom appear wasted and who twist their bodies into odd positions in order to free themselves from the bondage of attachment to worldly objects; also seen are numerous beggars, some of whom have deliberately mutilated their bodies. What is puzzling is that Indian psychiatrists rarely report instances of self-mutilation as a result of mental illness. One explanation is that self-mutilators in India are not necessarily considered by their family members and social group to be in need of psychiatric treatment; thus they are not brought to the attention of the rudimentary mental health system. Another explanation is that there are social groups and religious festivals in which persons given to self-mutilation are well accepted. *Hijras*, for example, are transvestites who often appear at marriage ceremonies and threaten to be disruptive unless they are given money. Some *hijras* are male homosexuals; others are men with anatomically deformed genitals; and still others are men who have voluntarily castrated themselves. Ronald Simons has produced an exceptional film called *Floating in the Air, Followed by the Wind*, which depicts a yearly Tamil festival in which devotees go into trance, pierce their tongues and cheeks with thick pins, and carry heavy religious objects that are anchored to their bodies by hundreds of fish hooks.

Within the mystical Islamic tradition of Sufism, asceticism and self-mortification are very prominent. The term *Sufism* derives from *suf* or wool and refers to the custom of wearing coarse and uncomfortable woolen garments as a sign of penitence and the renunciation of worldly pleasures. In Morocco, a Sufic brotherhood called the Hamadsha engage in head slashing during healing rituals. In describing this and similar brotherhoods Crapanzano (1973) noted their extreme behavior: "wild dances, including ecstatic, frenetic trances; drinking boiling water; eating spiny cactus and other defilements; charming poisonous snakes; and innumerable acts of self-mutilation. All of them attempt to produce some sort of extraordinary psychic state which may be interpreted as union with God or possession by a demon" (p. 3). Indeed, al-Hallāj (A.D. 858–922), the most revered Sufi martyr, advocated suffering as an important pathway to salvation, in emulation of Jesus's crucifixion, and many Sufic traditions are derived more from the Christian Desert Fathers than from mainstream Islam.

In Shia Islam (the Shiites are the second largest sect, the first being the Sunnis) great attention is given to the martyrdoms of the religious heroes Ali, Hasan, and especially Husain. During yearly passion plays the deaths of these martyrs are reenacted so fervently that both the actors and spectators inflict wounds on their bodies. During the festival of Husain thousands of Shiites flagellate themselves frenetically while recalling his words: "Trial, afflictions, and pains, the thicker they fall on man, the better do they prepare him for his journey heavenward."

Is self-mutilation encountered among mentally ill Moslems? Several British psychiatrists with experience in Arabic countries have told me that the prevalence of self-mutilation there is somewhat higher than in Europe. In questioning several leading Islamic psychiatrists from the Middle East, however, I was assured that self-mutilation is *never* encountered because suffering is forbidden by the Koran. Indeed, I vividly recall a conversation with an elderly and stately Moslem psychiatrist who became a bit irritated by my questions. He stated that no Moslem would ever mutilate himself and added, while pointing a finger at me and twisting it, "Remember that the Prophet said that even when you kill an infidel you should twist the knife rapidly so as to cause him no pain."

However, M. Fakhr El-Islam, professor at the University of Kuwait, recently sent me a case history of a 29-year-old chronically anxious Jordanian who had a four-year history of irritability and rage outbursts in response to minor frustrations at home and at work. Two months before his self-mutilation, he indulged rather excessively in religious practices, although his parents thought this to be a favorable development. He lost his driver's license because of reckless driving and withdrew for the fourth time from an arranged marriage ceremony. Then, one night he locked himself in the kitchen, cut himself on the scalp, and cut off his hand. Despite psychiatric investigation, the patient refused to disclose the motives for his behavior. Since he was not psychotic, he received a diagnosis of personality disorder, "in view of his social and occupational instability, gross acting-out behavior and lifelong impulsive acts that secured him secondary gain in his family." Interestingly, the *Kuwait Times* (July 26, 1984) published a story about the surgical operation in which the patient's hand was successfully reattached to his arm. No mention was made of the fact that he had cut off his own hand.

As pointed out by Bowker, "Of all religions, Buddhism is the one which concentrates most immediately and directly on suffering" (1970, p. 237). Indeed, the First Sermon of Buddha at Benares contains the essence of his wisdom. In his sermon, Buddha disavowed both devotion to the indulgence of sense pleasures and to self-mortification. Instead, he preached a middle path that gives knowledge and leads to calm, insight, enlightenment, and Nirvana. First, one must comprehend the Noble Truth of suffering: birth is suffering; aging is suffering; sickness is suffering; death is suffering; sorrow and lamentation, pain, grief, and despair are suffering; association with the unpleasant is suffering; disassociation from the pleasant is suffering; not to get what one wants is suffering; in sum, the five aggregates of attachment are suffering. Next, one must comprehend that the Noble Truth of the origin of suffering is a craving that produces a craving for sense pleasure, for existence and becoming, for nonexistence and self-annihilation. The Noble Truth of the cessation of suffering involves giving up and renouncing this craving, emancipating and detaching oneself from it. Finally, one is ready to follow the Noble Path leading to the cessation of suffering: right view, right thought, right speech, right action, right livelihood, right effort, right mindfulness, right concentration.

Buddhism downplays the concept of self and regards personal existence as a constantly changing flow of energy and matter. In this context, mortification of one's body is considered painful, unworthy, and unprofitable. From my correspondence with psychiatrists around the world it would appear that self-mutilation has a low incidence in Buddhist culture areas.

When it does occur it seems to take the form of self-castration in order to overcome sexual temptations.

The Judaic tradition and the Christian tradition that sprang from it cannot be comprehended accurately without reference to bloodshed, sacrifice, and suffering. Indeed, the sacred text of the Holy Bible, a book that has greatly influenced human behavior and the course of events for millennia, devotes many pages to these topics. And from the New Testament has come the most famous example of sacrifice and suffering in all history and the most potent of all religious symbols—the bloody cross of the crucifixion.

The ancient notion that suffering is a just punishment for sins is found in the Old Testament, but some of its writers were well aware that this is not invariably the case. Thus, Jeremiah (12:1) pleaded with God to answer, "Why is it that the wicked live so prosperously? Why do scoundrels enjoy peace?" The answer that emerged is described by Bowker as "perhaps the supreme contribution of Israel to a human response to suffering, that suffering can be made redemptive, that it can become the foundation of better things, collectively, if not individually" (1970, p. 51). Nowhere is this more poignantly expressed than in Isaiah's description of the Servant (a metaphor for the people of Israel).

> Ours were the sufferings he bore, ours the sorrows he carried. But we thought of him as someone punished, struck by God, and afflicted. Yet he was wounded for our transgressions, crushed for our sin. On him lies a punishment that brings us peace, and through his wounds we are healed. . . . Yahweh burdened him with the sins of us all. (53:4-6)

Traditionally for the Jews, the messiah that would come to rule in justice and in peace was an idealized version of King David. But then, according to James (1962), "The tribulation of the Jews during and after the fall of Jerusalem in A.D. 70 led to the Rabbinic interpretation of self-inflicted suffering as an atoning sacrifice in expiation of the national guilt, in preparation for the coming of the Messiah and the establishment of his righteous reign" (p. 116).

Enter Jesus, a man-god whose life assumed both unique meanings and linkages with older deities such as Mithra, Attis, and Dionysus.[3] Within the

---

3. Sinless Mithra was born on December 25, the old date of the winter solstice. His sacrifice of the primal bull was repeated by thousands of his initiates over the ages. From the bull's spinal cord grew wheat and from his blood grew grape vines—the prototypical bread and wine of the communion meal. Attis castrated himself and was resurrected. His love was Cybele, the great mother goddess whose shrines were converted into shrines to the Virgin Mary. Dionysus, born of a virgin, was mutilated as a child and eventually resurrected.

new Christian tradition, Jesus was both the glorious King David and the Suffering Servant. Indeed, 1 Peter 2 states: "Christ also suffered for you, leaving you an example, that you should follow in his steps. . . . He himself bore our sins in his body on the tree, that we might die to sin and live to righteousness. By his wounds you have been healed."

In the scriptures enormous emphasis was placed on Christ's suffering during the Passion, on the metaphor of the Christian congregation as the body of Christ, on the literal need for individuals to present their bodies to God, and on the redemptive value of suffering. A few quotes will suffice:

> It is now my happiness to suffer for you. This is my way of helping to complete, in my poor human flesh, the full tale of Christ's afflictions still to be endured; for the sake of his body which is the church. (Col. 1:24)
>
> My dear friends, do not be bewildered by the fiery ordeal that is upon you, as though it were something extraordinary. It gives you a share in Christ's sufferings, and that is cause for joy. (1 Pet. 4)
>
> According to the law almost everything is purified by the blood, and without the shedding of blood there is no forgiveness. . . . So Christ was offered up once to take away the sins of many. (Heb. 9:22, 28)
>
> All men have sinned and are deprived of the glory of God. All men are now undeservedly justified by the gift of God, through the redemption wrought in Jesus Christ. Through his blood, God made him the means of expiation for all who believe. (Rom. 3:24–25)

Thus, Christ's suffering and crucifixion were a true sacrifice involving consecration of the victim, spilling of blood, death, expiation of sins, and establishment of a sacramental meal in which believers could partake of a portion of divinity by eating the victim's flesh and blood. Christ was both priest and victim. His willing self-sacrifice, an act of redeeming love, was followed by his victorious resurrection, and it afforded humankind the opportunity to reestablish a right relationship with God. In order to enter into this relationship, humankind had to participate in certain rituals, hold certain beliefs, and follow certain rules of conduct. For our study of self-mutilation the one rule of conduct that has proven most portentous is the verse of Matthew 18:7–9 (almost identical words are used in Mark 4:43–48):

> What terrible things will come on the world through scandal! It is inevitable that scandal should occur. Nonetheless, woe to that man through whom scandal comes! If your hand or foot is your undoing, cut it off and throw it from you! Better to enter life maimed or crippled than be thrown with two hands or two feet into endless fire. If your eye is your downfall, gouge it out

[handwritten marginal note: Biblical exhortation to S-m]

and cast it from you! Better to enter life with one eye than be thrown with both into Gehenna.

Martyrs and the Company of Saints

The establishment of the early Christian church was distinguished by numerous martyrs who willingly died for their faith and endured incredible tortures. These men, women, and children epitomized the formation of a collective social body out of their individual bodies. Unlike gladiators who glistened with oil and fought for their lives, martyrs aggressively sought a passive death—the bloodier the better. Their model was Christ crucified on the cross. Martyrs did not whine at their fate but rather welcomed it. "In dying, the martyr's victory over Satan, instinct, and the world was confirmed; in suffering, his power was demonstrated" (Bradford 1990). The great theologian Tertullian, at the end of the second century A.D., wrote his impassioned tracts *On Flight in Persecution* and *The Antidote for the Scorpion*: "At this present moment, it is the very middle of the heat, the very dog-days of persecution. Some Christians have been tested by the fire, some by the sword, some by the beasts; some, lashed and torn with hooks, have just tasted martyrdom, and lie hungering for it in prison. . . . We say, and we say it openly while you are torturing us, torn and bleeding, we cry aloud, 'We worship God through Christ!' . . . Nothing whatever is achieved by each more exquisite cruelty you invent; on the contrary, it wins men for our school. We are made more as often as you mow us down. The blood of Christians is seed [*semen est sanguis Christianorum*]."

The *Acts of the Martyrs* by the Bollandists comprises fifty large folio tomes in which the lives of the martyrs are recorded to serve as models for all believers. The life of Saint Potitus serves as an example. As a child he was persecuted by his father because of his Christian beliefs. His father asked, "My child, do you not fear the punishments to be inflicted on Christians? If you are brought before the Emperor Antoninus, what will become of you? Those strange doctrines of yours will cause your flesh to be torn to pieces by hooks, and you will be eaten by the lions." Potitus responded, "Father, you can never frighten me with these things. In the name of the Father, and of the Son, and of the Holy Ghost, I am prepared to suffer everything for Jesus Christ."

Potitus went on to cure a rich woman with leprosy by invoking Christ's help. At that time Antoninus's daughter was possessed by a devil who caused her to scream. Sacrifices to the Roman gods did not help. Potitus was asked by the emperor to cure the girl. "If I cure your daughter, will you believe in the God I believe in?" asked Potitus. After a few moments' hesitation the emperor said, "I will." Potitus succeeded, in Christ's name, in exorcising the demon from the girl. The demon, in the shape of a dragon, left the room, leaving behind the stench of fire and brimstone. The emperor reneged on his promise, however, and tried to force Potitus to sacrifice to the Roman gods. When he refused, Antoninus brought him to the coliseum where, before a large crowd, he ordered the tortures to begin.

Although Potitus was stretched on the rack, for him it was like lying on a bed of roses. Several starved and ferocious beasts were let loose, but they merely licked Potitus's feet. Four armed gladiators entered the arena, but their weapons fell harmlessly to the ground. Horrible pincers with two large spikes were set on Potitus's head; when closed the spikes would pass through his brain. But, in response to Potitus's prayers, the pincers were lifted from his head and were set by an invisible hand on the emperor's head. He shrieked in agony; Potitus agreed to remove them only if the emperor agreed to allow his daughter to become a Christian. After Antoninus assented, Potitus announced that he, a servant of Christ, was victorious and that now he desired to be united with Christ, whereupon he was taken out of the city by Roman troops who cut off his head.

Obviously the hagiographers embellished the stories of the tribulations of the early martyrs, but these stories were widely read (e.g., Voragine's *Legenda Aurea*) and served as the focus of countless inspirational sermons over the centuries. More true to fact are the accounts in John Foxe's *Acts and Monuments* of the three hundred Protestant martyrs who were burned at the stake in Tudor England between 1531 and 1558. Especially interesting is an episode on the eve of the martyrdom of Thomas Bilney, the first Tudor martyr, in which he burned off a finger by placing it over the flame of a candle. Asked what he was doing Bilney replied, "Nothing but frying my flesh by God's grace, and burning one joint, when tomorrow God's rods shall burn the whole body in the fire."[4]

The ascendency of the Desert Fathers, holy men and women who sought salvation in the solitude of the Egyptian desert, in the fourth century A.D. was an event that made an enormous impact on Christianity. Large monasteries, some with ten thousand inhabitants, were established, and it was said that as many persons lived in the desert as lived in the towns of Egypt.

[margin note: Desert Fathers]

---

4. Byman (1978) interpreted Bilney's action as one of many counterphobic devices utilized by the martyrs to overcome their fears and the pain of the fire, just as Christ overcame pain and uncertainty in his Passion; other examples include embracing the stake upon which they were to be burned, lifting their hands to heaven while their bodies were being burned, and saying prayers. In fact, ritualistic acts and compulsive behaviors are performed by some self-mutilative patients, especially chronic self-cutters.

In their small cells these seekers of religion practiced severe asceticism, desiring to rid themselves of all passions of the flesh. Their lives represented the concepts found in Socrates' *Phaedo* and echoed the saying of Dorotheus the Theban: "I kill my body, for it kills me." Their ideal was *solus ad solum*, alone to the alone, and as Waddell (1957) points out, they gave the intellectual concept of eternity to Europe: "These men, by the very exaggeration of their lives, stamped infinity on the imagination of the West" (p. 23).

The first Desert Father was Saint Anthony (A.D. 251–356). The widely circulated book *Vita S. Antonii* was highly influential in the spread of the ascetic movement. After being orphaned at age 20, Anthony opted for a life of celibacy and went to live in empty tombs where he had visions of demons who whipped him. He then lived alone in an isolated deep pit for twenty years. His disciples lowered bread to him every six months. During this time he neither washed nor removed his only garment, a coarse animal skin. His fame spread widely, and his behavior served to inspire others (although centuries later the historian Gibbon described him as "a hideous, distorted emaciated maniac, without knowledge, without patriotism, without natural affection, spending his life in a long routine of useless and atrocious self-torture, and quailing before the phantoms of his deluded brain").

Perhaps the most fantastic of the desert hermits was Saint Simeon Stylites, whose odd behavior inspired a cult of imitators. At an early age he devoted himself to celibacy and to self-starvation. He went to a deserted mountain top and had his foot chained to a large rock. The chain sunk into his flesh, creating a large ulcer. The ulcer became infested with worms, and as the worms fell to the ground Simeon placed them back into the wound saying, "Eat what God has given you." He is best known, however, for climbing onto a small platform at the top of a sixty-foot pillar and living there for the last thirty years of his life. Sparse amounts of food were passed up to him in a basket.

With the development of the great monastic orders in Europe during the eleventh century, the spirit of asceticism and self-mortification once again became prominent, and in this spirit self-flagellation as a voluntary act of penance became widespread. Heinrich Suso, a German mystic, wrote the following famous third-person account of his flagellatory experience: "He shut himself in his cell and stripped himself naked, and took his scourge with the sharp spikes, and beat himself on the body and on the arms and on the legs, till blood poured off him as from a man who had been cupped. One of the spikes on the scourge was bent like a hook, and whatever flesh it caught tore off. He beat himself so hard that the scourge broke into three pieces and the points flew against the wall. He stood there bleeding and gazed at himself. It was such a wretched sight that he was reminded in many ways of the appearance of the beloved Christ, when he was fearfully beaten. Out of pity for himself, he began to weep bitterly. And he knelt down, naked and covered in blood, in the frosty air, and prayed to God to wipe out his sins from before his gentle eyes" (Cohn 1958, p. 124). It should be noted, however, that self-flagellation was not a Christian invention, but rather was widely practiced over the course of history in many circum-Mediterranean religions; for example, the priests of the cult of Attis scandalized the Romans because of such odd practices as self-flagellation, hearing confessions, and self-castration.

The first followers of Saint Francis were passionate flagellators, as were Saint Dominic and Peter Damian (who taught that one thousand lashes equaled the recitation of ten penitential psalms). Monastic self-scourging served as a model for a public that was undergoing severe social stresses in the thirteenth century. Politically, the Guelphs and the Ghibellines were at loggerheads. Spiritually, Joachim of Fiore preached that the year 1260 would usher in the age of "the Eternal Gospel," a time of peace and happiness. Public expectations were high and reached a fever pitch as the year progressed. Then, in November 1260, an epidemic of self-flagellation began.

Thousands of Perugians spontaneously beat themselves with small leather whips. The Italian historian Salimbene wrote an eyewitness account: "All men, both great and small, noble knights and men of the people, scourged themselves naked, in procession through the cities, with the Bishops and men of religion at their head; and peace was made in many places, and men restored what they had unlawfully taken away; and they confessed their sins so earnestly that the priests had scarce leisure to eat" (Jones 1961, p. 50).

The epidemic did not last very long in Italy but spread and took hold in the south of Germany. German flagellant leaders produced a Heavenly Letter, supposedly dictated by Christ in Jerusalem, which stated that God was angry because people neglected religion and practiced usury and adultery. God decided to punish humankind by sending disease, famine, and pagan invasions. Since people still did not change their evil ways, God decided to destroy them all. But the Virgin Mary begged God to give humankind one last chance, and an angel ordered mass flagellation if humanity was to save itself.

In the face of prolonged drought and poverty, the masses responded to the warning of the Heavenly Letter. Many priests and secular authorities were caught up in the movement. Then, in 1348, the bubonic plague spread from Hungary. The tremendous death rate and fears associated with

the plague gave renewed impetus to the cause of the flagellants. Itinerant bands of flagellators organized into highly disciplined groups of from
fifty to several hundred men, with uniforms reminiscent of those worn by
the crusaders and with lay leaders who, contrary to the church's orders,
heard confessions and granted absolution from sins. These groups flagellated themselves twice a day for thirty-three and a half days (a number
corresponding with the years of Jesus's life) and were received enthusiasti-
cally in the towns and cities they visited. They would march up to a church,
take off their clothes, don a special skirt, and pray and sing while they
whipped themselves before an admiring public who believed that the flagellants would protect them from the plague and from death. "It became a
privilege to welcome and assist such people. . . . People not only brought
the sick to be healed by these holy men, they dipped clothes in the flowing
blood and treasured them as sacred relics" (Cohn 1958, p. 134).

The influence of the flagellant cults, whose emphasis on self-prescribed
penance threatened the authority of the church and whose popularity
threatened the social order, led to secular and ecclesiastical suppression
highlighted by actions taken at the Council of Constance in 1417. Many of
the flagellants violently attacked the church, killed priests, and massacred
Jews, who, they claimed, spread the plague by poisoning wells. It took the
church and state authorities about fifteen years to control fully the flagellant
movement. A few sporadic epidemics occurred — for example in 1396 Saint
Vincent Ferrer had a vision of the Antichrist and organized mass flagella-
tions in southern Europe — but the practice died out everywhere except in
Thuringia, in central Germany. There, the cult remained secretly organized
and even adopted new practices, such as whipping babies and baptizing
them in their own blood. The last Thuringian flagellators were captured
and burned at the stake as heretics in the 1480s.

Although the movement waned, individual devotees continued to flagellate themselves. To this day public self-flagellation, particularly during
Eastertime, may be encountered, especially in areas influenced by the Spaniards, such as the Philippine Islands, Mexico, and the southwestern United
States.

In light of the Christian traditions of sacrifice, martyrdom, asceticism,
and penance it should not be surprising that a goodly number of the saints,
holy persons whose lives serve as models for the faithful, engaged in self-
mutilative practices. Pope Benedict XIV (1675–1758) discussed this issue
in great detail in *Heroic Virtue*. He wrote that "with the exception of the
martyrs, the Church venerates and gives the sanction of her authority to

the sanctity of those only whom she finds to have been zealous in the mortification of the flesh and senses."

An extreme example of a saint who was truly zealous in the mortification of her flesh and senses is Saint Mary Magdalene de'Pazzi. (Although many books about her have been written in Italian, I here rely on the account provided by the English scholar Eric Dingwall, in his book *Very Peculiar People*.)

Born in Florence in 1566 of an aristocratic family, Caterina de'Pazzi was a religiously precocious child. At age 10 she made a vow of perpetual chastity, secretly whipped herself, and wore a crown of thorns. Although her parents were unhappy with her behavior, they allowed her to enter a Carmelite convent where she chose the name of the holy harlot, Mary Magdalene. Due to the austerity of her life she soon gained a reputation for outstanding virtue. Frequently she experienced periods of "rapture" during which she made predictions about the future. She reportedly was able to cure diseases; one procedure she followed was to lick the skin lesions of afflicted nuns, including one who was thought to have leprosy, and to suck the maggots out of skin ulcers.

At age 20 she declared that God had ordered her to eat only bread and water. Because of swelling in her feet she often crawled around the convent on all fours and kissed the feet of the bewildered nuns. Claiming that she was being hounded by devils, she frenetically and publicly whipped her body to chase them away and threw herself naked on thorn bushes until she was covered with blood. She burned her skin with hot wax and cajoled the novices in the convent to whip her and to step on her mouth.

At about age 37, emaciated and racked with coughing and pain, she took to her bed and did not leave it until she died four years later in 1607. Her painful gums were so badly infected that she could not bear to close her jaw, until her teeth fell out, one by one. Her body was covered with putrefying bed sores, but when the sisters offered to move her she warned them off for fear that by touching her body they might experience sexual desires.

Because of her virtuous life, her miraculous healing, her clairvoyance, and the presence of a perfumed fragrance that emanated from her corpse, she was beatified by Pope Urban VIII in 1626. She was admitted to the company of the saints by Pope Clement IX, who issued a decree of canonization in 1668. A large statue of her holding a flagellant whip can be seen in her church in Florence where many people from around the world still come to pay her tribute.

Stigmatics

When St. Paul attempted to win converts for his yet unnamed religion, he was badly beaten. He said that the stigmata (marks) on his body were those of Jesus (Gal. 6:17), and he called for church members to share in Christ's suffering. For over a thousand years this call was generally heeded, and then a miraculous event in the history of Christianity supposedly occurred in 1224 during the day dedicated to the Holy Cross on the little mountain called La Verna, near the Italian town of Assisi.

As a young man Francis di Bernadone enjoyed the good life provided by his prosperous father. However, after he foolishly decided to join a military group on a raid against nearby Perugia, he was captured and imprisoned for a year, during which he contracted malaria. Upon his release he began to hear voices and to behave oddly, for example, he kissed the infected hands of lepers.

He visited a dilapidated country church and while praying before a crucifix heard Jesus tell him to restore the church. He went home, sold his father's possessions, and gave the money to the priest in charge of the church. Enraged, his father demanded restitution and even asked the local bishop to set up a church court. Francis appeared before a crowd at the hearing, returned the money, and then stripped off all his clothes; naked before the world, Francis answered that god in heaven was his only father.

He then devoted his life to praising god and winning souls. The pathway he chose was the renunciation of worldly pleasures. He consistently fasted and wore only a coarse tunic, even on the coldest days. His malaria stayed with him, and during a trip to Egypt he developed a serious disease of his eyes. St. Bonaventure's biography states that by 1224 Francis "began to suffer from diverse ailments so grievously that scarce one of his limbs was free from pain and sore suffering. At length, by diverse sickness, prolonged and continuous, he was brought to such a point that his flesh was wasted away and only as it were the skin clove to his bone."

In this weakened condition he prayed at a retreat on Mount LaVerna. According to the *Fioretti* (Little Flowers), a book about Francis written a century later, he contemplated Christ's Passion on September 14, "and his fervour grew so strong in him that he became wholly transformed into Jesus through love and compassion." He saw a vision of Christ crucified, and "in the hands and feet of St. Francis began to appear the marks of the nails in the same manner as he had seen them in the body of Jesus." Until his death two years later, his body carried the five wounds of Christ, which often trickled blood.

News of Francis's stigmatization spread rapidly throughout Europe. Thirty-one cases of the stigmata appeared in the next twenty-five years. In 1231 the body of Blessed Dodo, a Dutch monk who was accidentally killed, was found to have the five wounds (for accounts of this and other cases see Thurston 1952; Whitlock and Hynes 1978; Wilson 1992). The Belgian nun Elizabeth of Herkenrode (d. 1275) went into frequent ecstatic states while contemplating the Passion, during which she pummeled herself with her fists. She developed not only the stigmata but also a crown of thorns wound around her head.

About three hundred cases of the stigmata have been reported since the time of St. Francis. Most of these cases (271) have been women. Many are clearly the result of deliberately self-inflicted wounds, some are readily explained by psychological processes, and a few are problematic.

In 1869 Louise Lateau was seriously ill with throat abscesses and experienced mystical visions. A year later, at age 19, she developed the stigmata. Her wounds bled every Friday until her death at age 33 (the age of Jesus' death). She was studied by Dr. Warlomont (1875) under the auspices of the Belgian Royal Academy of Medicine. Lateau noted that every Thursday morning one-inch oval spots on her hands, feet, and chest turned pink and after several hours turned into vesicles. In the middle of the night, the vesicles would rupture, and blood would flow for a day. The lesions did not appear to be deliberately induced (at least at a conscious level), and on microscopic examination the blood was totally normal. During the period in which the blood was present, Lateau was in a state of "absorption and far-off contemplation," changing often to sadness, terror, and contrition. She claimed that during this ecstasy she saw Christ in person and that all the scenes of his Passion passed before her eyes.

The stigmatic wounds of Theresa Neumann, a Bavarian peasant, also bled every Friday, but hers persevered for thirty-six years, and blood also dripped from her eyes. She was examined for two weeks by the professor of psychiatry at Erlangen, Dr. G. Ewald. He noted that her medical history included episodes of blindness, deafness, and paralysis that suddenly remitted. During one of these episodes, a physician was prevented from examining her eyes when she had a timely, single, bizarre "convulsion." She was amenorrheic and had a long-standing conviction that she was medically ill. This conviction was probably strengthened by her parish priest, who continually pointed out the sufferings of Christ and the virtue of emulating the suffering of the martyrs. Neumann developed stigmata on her hands, feet, chest (over her heart), and scalp, as well as bloody tears. Some lesions bled continuously for a while, but then only on Fridays. No blood had flowed from her lesions for the three months before Ewald's examination. He found three small dark crusts on the back of her hands and on her chest, as well as four tiny crusts on her soles and palms. She claimed to be in an ecstasy when blood came from her lesions, during which she lived through the scenes of Christ's Passion. When she experienced his crucifixion, she extended her arms, stared blankly, spoke in an Aramaic dialect, and fell into a swoon. Ewald concluded that the stigmata were genuine (in the sense that they were not deliberately caused), although he considered her a hysteric.

Another German physician, F. Gerlich (1929), after examining Neumann for several weeks, believed she was not a hysteric. An American physician, Joseph Klauder (1938), also examined her several years later. Neumann impressed him as being "emotionally normal, plain, and humble. She did not exploit or talk about herself or the stigmas; on the contrary she was reticent and showed them reluctantly." He concluded that her stigmata were genuine, excluded medical conditions such as blood dyscrasia, and noted that even among some Muslims there are reported cases of stigmata appearing during periods of contemplation on the battle wounds of Muhammad. Klauder concluded that cases of genuine stigmata should be classified as an "exotic dermatosis," and he favored a psychological explanation for their pathophysiology, for example, autosuggestion, vasomotor lability, and "latent powers" associated with mysticism.[5]

Wilson (1992) listed nineteen stigmatics in the twentieth century, although the actual number is probably much greater. The most famous is Padre Pio, an Italian monk whose wounds stayed open from 1918 until his death in 1978. An 11-year-old African-American Baptist girl, Cloretta Robinson, in Oakland, California, bled from the palm while in a school classroom. She had just read a book about the crucifixion of Jesus. Stigmatic wounds on her hands, feet, and forehead, appeared during the period

5. Newspapers and magazines covered the case extensively, often showing gruesome photographs of Neumann's bloody face. In 1928 a German psychiatrist, Alfred Lechler, encountered a 26-year-old patient known as Elizabeth K (Lechler 1933; Wilson 1992). Her long list of symptoms included severe trembling, episodes of paralysis, bouts of anorexia, and urinary and fecal incontinence. Lechler treated her with hypnotherapy and hired her to serve as a maid in his home. She heard a sermon about Christ's crucifixion on Good Friday and told Lechler that she could literally feel nails being driven into her extremities. Lechler, who was cognizant of the Neumann case, made a hypnotic suggestion that Elizabeth concentrate on nails being hammered into her hands and feet. On the next day, wounds appeared. He then suggested that she concentrate on pictures of Neumann with bloody tears. Within hours Elizabeth bled from inside her eyelids. When Lechler suggested that the blood cease from flowing, quite quickly it stopped.

of Lent. Jane Hunt, a bus driver's wife in England, developed the stigmata in 1985 while shopping for groceries. The wounds disappeared two years later after she received a hysterectomy.

The appearance of bloody tears and sweat has been reported sporadically in the medical literature, and the expression "to sweat blood" is commonly used as a metaphor in many languages to indicate that a person has engaged in particularly difficult and stressful tasks. The biblical origin of this concept is found in Luke 22:44, "And being in an agony, he [Christ] prayed more earnestly: and his sweat was as it were great drops of blood falling down to the ground."

Most literary portrayals of stigmatics are rather forgettable. The one exception is Ron Hansen's *Mariette in Ecstasy* (1992), the story of a 17-year-old postulant at a priory of the Sisters of the Crucifixion. When Mariette develops the stigmata, life in the convent is turned topsy-turvy. One nun licks Mariette's wounds, while others accuse her of seeking attention, of fabricating everything, of contaminating everyone with her wiles. Mariette herself wonders if she hasn't made it all up in some way. She gets caught reading medical and religious books about the stigmata. She writes to a priest not to believe anything she says. When her father cleans the blood off her skin, he finds no lesions. Mariette declares that "Christ took back the wounds." Her father smirks and tells the nuns, "You have all been duped." But have they?

The Religious Context of Self-mutilation in the Mentally Ill

Self-mutilation — the hacking off of a hand or the gouging out of an eye or the slicing off of a penis — by a mentally ill person is a dramatically awesome act reminiscent of a sacrificial rite.[6]

The bodies of some mentally ill self-mutilators can be thought of as a stage upon which is enacted a personal drama that reflects, in varying proportions, personal psychopathology, social stresses, and cultural myths, especially those of a religious nature. The themes of these myths are suffering, dismemberment, blood sacrifice, resurrection, rebirth, and the establishment (or reestablishment) of a new, prosperous, healthy, and amicable order. Although an audience might regard the self-mutilative act as the tension-heightening conclusion of a tragedy, the actors — at least at the moment of their self-mutilation — might regard it as a tension-reducing, cathartic moment, or a moment of clarification, or a moment that harbingers

6. In his classic study of Nuer (African) sacrifice, Evans-Pritchard (1956) noted that the sacrificer is "acting a part in a drama" and that "we seem indeed to be watching a play or to be listening to someone's account of what he had dreamt" (p. 322).

a new, more joyous conclusion to the drama. For some, pain and blood are associated with death, but for others they are associated with birth.

Religious ritual and some acts of self-mutilation share an interesting interplay with time and reality. During religious rituals the continuing flow of normal, secular time is interrupted by intervals of sacred nontime (Leach 1976). Turner (1968) noted that "in the life of most communities, ancient and modern, there appear to be interludes in historical time, periods of timeless time, that are devoted to the celebration of certain basic postulates of human existence, biological and cultural . . . the moment when ritual is being performed" (p. 5). Some mentally ill persons suffer from frightening episodes of depersonalization, during which time and reality are distorted. The act of self-mutilation often serves to terminate these episodes. It allows self-mutilators to reexperience their biological existence and place in society.

depersonalization

While some mentally ill self-mutilators consciously believe and publicly declare themselves to be gods or members of the company of saints, others seem to tap unconsciously into such beliefs. In this context acts of self-mutilation and mortification may take on a sacrificial quality. At a personal level these sacrifices often have profound consequences. By gouging out an eye, for example, the self-selected victim may avert suicide (martyrdom) and may cause group members to reevaluate their relationships. The power of drama to influence the lives of both the actors and the audience cannot be underestimated.

The acts of mentally ill self-mutilators, however, have no transcendency. They have little meaning for the universe or the world or the community at large but rather affect only the self-mutilators and occasionally the members of their small social networks. Deviant self-mutilators are not liminal objects (Turner 1977) and the flow of their blood opens no significant channels between God and Man. Their use of religious symbolism is based on private rather than public delusions. Although therapists should try to utilize powerful religious and shamanic symbols in selected cases, the fact remains that self-mutilators are neither gods nor saints but rather frightened prophets manqué.

3

Self-mutilation, Eating Disorders, and Cannibalism

———————

Lillian Malcove (1933), a psychoanalyst, contends that the experience of learning to eat is the prototype of the fear of being dismembered or mutilated. A child sees food cut into pieces and mashed by special instruments (knives, forks, and spoons) and finally eats it. "Since the child's thinking is at this stage animistic, that food that he cuts and eats is endowed with attributes of human life, and can therefore easily be identified with himself or other persons. . . . The identification of the child's self with his food . . . is facilitated by fairy tales, or oral caresses and endearments, and by games improvised to expedite the feeding procedure. For the child, eating is literally a cannibalistic procedure which includes the ante-mortem tortures of cutting and crushing, and in which the table silver supplements the teeth and the hands."

Much evidence points to a relationship between self-mutilation and eating disorders (Favazza et al. 1989). Brenda and William Parry-Jones (1993) traced the earliest literary reference to a story in Ovid's *Metamorphoses*. Because he scorned the gods and violated the sacred groves of Ceres, Erysichthon was punished by an insatiable craving for food: "At last when . . . his grievous malady needed more food, the wretched man began to tear his limbs and rend them apart with his teeth and, by consuming his own body, fed himself." The authors also examine the case of the famous eighteenth-century author Dr. Samuel Johnson, who was a lifelong bulimic and ruminator given to melancholy, tormenting scruples, obsessive-compulsive rituals, and hypochondriasis: "His eating pattern was characterised by excesses of uncontrolled consumption, interspersed by attempts at abstinence or reduced intake. . . . His table manners were crude, his ingestion rapid like a cormorant, and mastication was perfunctory." His companion and biographer James Boswell wrote: "Such was the heat and insatiability of his blood that not only did he pare his nails to the quick; but scraped the joints of his fingers with a pen-knife, till they seemed quite red and raw" (quoted in Parry-Jones 1993). He also reportedly bit and rubbed his lips continually. It is likely that Johnson's self-mutilative behavior was a form of punishment for indulging his impulses as well as a way to relieve tension, perhaps in association with his intense fear of giving in to masturbation. Recent medical historians make a good case for Tourette syndrome, a neuropsychiatric disorder characterized by many of the behaviors, including minor self-mutilation, demonstrated by Dr. Johnson (Murray 1979; McHenry 1985).

The Parry-Jones (1993) article also describes three other historical cases from England of self-mutilation associated with bulimia. The first, reported in 1745, was of a 10-year-old boy who ate 55 to 78 pounds of food daily and immediately vomited. If not fed upon demand, "he would gnaw the very flesh off his own bones." The boy was described as cheerful and with a healthy-looking face. He died of emaciation within two years of the onset of his "extraordinary Boulimia." The second case (1786–1828) was of a girl with a voracious appetite; for example, she ate 10 pounds of bread daily at age 6. A year later her menses began, she was sexually attacked by her father, and she developed epilepsy. As an adult she had attacks of great hunger; it was reported that "if her wants are not satisfied . . . [she] bites her own flesh." She was thought to be normal mentally except during her paroxysms of hunger. The last case, reported in 1815, was of a 16-year-old boy who developed such an insatiable appetite during the course of typhus fever that he tried to eat his fingers.

In modern times the association between eating disorders and self-mutilation was noted in three articles that stressed female genital mutilation. French and Nelson (1972) reported on a 38-year-old housewife hospitalized for intractable binge eating and self-induced vomiting. After a marital argument, she slashed her genital area with a razor blade. Simpson (1973) discussed a 22-year-old patient with such problems as severe dieting, compulsive overeating, self-induced vomiting, wrist cutting, breast slashing, and cutting her vagina with a butcher knife. On the basis of three cases, Goldney and Simpson (1975) described a syndrome of female genital self-mutilation, eating disorders, and hysterical personality disorder.

Several studies of patients identified as self-mutilators note the presence of eating disorders. Of 15 adolescent female self-mutilators, "12 were moderately overweight to obese and 2 were extremely thin and exhibited some anorexic behavior in the hospital. . . . Several reported extreme and rapid fluctuations in weight" (Simpson and Porter 1981). Another study reported that 15 of 23 self-cutters described compulsive overeating or severe anorexia or periods of each; 7 had frequent nausea. Only 2 patients in the control group reported significant eating difficulties (Rosenthal et al. 1972). A study of 12 female self-mutilators who had slashed themselves an average of 38 times found that in "an early pubertal phase" 6 had had anorexia nervosa and 3 had had both anorexia nervosa and bulimia (Yaryura-

Tobias and Neziroglu 1978). Coid, Allolio, and Rees (1983) reported that 4 of 7 hospitalized female habitual self-mutilators demonstrated the "compulsive" behaviors of either anorexia or anorexia/bulimia and noted that "severely disturbed patients who habitually mutilate themselves show profound disturbances of appetite characterized by both bulimic and anorexic episodes." The case of a 22-year-old woman with a ten-year history of trichotillomania of the eyebrows, eyelashes, and pubic area and a one-year history of bulimia has been reported (Hall and McGill 1986).

Another body of literature describes self-mutilative behavior in patients identified as having anorexia nervosa and/or bulimia nervosa. Pierloot, Wellens, and Houben (1975) associated self-mutilation with poor outcome in 32 anorexic women. Garfinkel, Moldofsky, and Garner (1980) reported a 9.2 percent self-mutilation rate among 68 bulimics. Yellowlees (1985) found that 4 of 15 bulimics had deliberately injured themselves. Jacobs and Isaacs (1986) reported a 35 percent self-injury/suicide attempt rate in 40 subjects with pre- and postpubertal anorexia nervosa. A comparison of 84 laxative-abusing bulimics with 101 non-laxative-abusing bulimics recorded self-injurious behavior distinct from suicide attempts in 40.5 percent of the former group and 25.7 percent of the latter (Mitchell et al. 1986).

Favazza and Contério (1989) gathered data on 290 female self-mutilators. The typical subject was a 28-year-old single Caucasian female who had cut herself on more than fifty occasions. Half of the women reported the history of an eating disorder. Of the total sample, 22 percent listed bulimia nervosa, 15 percent listed anorexia nervosa, and 13 percent listed both. The same survey data was gathered on a large group of female undergraduate students enrolled in a basic psychology course; 14.5 percent had an eating disorder and 38 percent of this group also had a history of deliberate self-harm.

A typical and instructive case history demonstrating the self-mutilation and eating disorder linkage is the following.

Ms. C, aged 24 years, first cut herself at age 13 because she was angry with her alcoholic father, who had sexually abused her for many years: "I couldn't get back at him, so I cut myself and I felt better." From the ages of 17 to 19, she repeatedly cut herself because, she said, "it made me feel less depressed." During the next four years, Ms. C did not cut herself, but she became a severe alcoholic and abuser of a variety of street drugs; according to Ms. C, "drinking and drugs took the place of cutting for me." Although she had a history of not eating for brief periods of time since age 13, she was first hospitalized for anorexia nervosa at age 23 after a fifty-pound weight loss. This hospitalization occurred several months after she had markedly decreased her alcohol and drug use. Upon discharge, her weight slowly but steadily ballooned to the point of moderate obesity. She then resumed heavy use of alcohol and was hospitalized. She was placed on a diet and was denied access to alcohol on a locked ward, so she "had to start cutting again." On one occasion she escaped from the ward, went to a bus stop near the hospital, and proceeded to scream wildly and slash herself many times with a razor blade in front of a group of frightened onlookers. Ms. C stated that cutting herself, drinking alcohol, and not eating were "interchangeable ways of hurting myself." However, she felt that cutting herself was the best method because it prevented people from getting too close to her, helped her to get back at her father, let her feel that she was "in control" (although she admitted that most times she could not control her desire to cut herself), and brought her back to reality when she had "no feelings, like I'm hypnotized."

Ms. C's symptoms shifted over time. I met her when self-mutilation was the major symptom. Had I encountered her at another time during the course of her illness, the primary diagnosis might have been anorexia nervosa or substance abuse. German psychiatrists studied thirty-two females whom they termed "multi-impulsive bulimics"; a history of self-mutilation was found in 24 (75%) of the women, while 11 (34%) reported alcohol abuse and 7 (22%) drug abuse (Fichter et al. 1994). This shifting of impulsive symptomatology is characteristic of what I and Richard Rosenthal (1993) term the syndrome of repetitive self-mutilation.

Parkin and Eagles (1993) described an odd form of self-mutilation, namely, deliberate bloodletting by venipuncture, in three women who had lengthy histories of bulimia preceded by anorexia (a fourth case has been reported [Brown 1993]). All three had some medical training and proficiency in venipuncture that, like binging and purging, relieved feelings of anxiety, tension, and anger. One woman, for example, developed anorexia nervosa at age 17. This was followed by six years of bulimia nervosa during which she overdosed once, burned herself several times, and cut herself three times. She began her self-bloodletting in her senior year of medical school and claimed that it reduced tension and gave her a sense of control and satisfaction as she lost blood. She also believed that it helped her to lose weight (she usually removed a liter of blood each time).

Food for Thought

Cross (1993) related the finding that skin-cutting and eating disorders are present more often in females than in males to womens' perceptions of their bodies as functionally mysterious and prone to abrupt, profound transformations. The female genitalia, for example, are partially internal; menstruation cannot be controlled; changes in body contours at puberty may be dramatic; during pregnancy the fetus is experienced as the "other within"; the lactating breast belongs both to the child and to the mother. Thus, there are elements of ambiguity, paradox, and discontinuity in females' experiences of their bodies. Cross states that self-cutting and eating disorders are "attempts to own the body, to perceive it as self (not other), known (not uncharted and unpredictable), and impenetrable (not invaded or controlled from the outside)." Cross theorizes that certain girls who are reared in an environment of severe physical pain, sexual abuse, or extremely unempathetic parenting develop a developmental deficit. She says that a "psychological chasm between body and self" is erected. As adolescents, those girls try to overcontrol their unruly emotions, sexual feelings, and bodily changes by the seemingly simple and efficient maneuver of transforming "in a kind of internal projection" their psychological problems into concrete, physical ones. Their body becomes both their "whipping boy" and their solace. According to Cross, "the metaphorical destruction between body and self collapses: thinness is self-sufficiency, bleeding emotional catharsis, bingeing is the assuaging of loneliness, and purging is the moral purification of the self." The process ultimately fails because "the body comes to resent its task master . . . escapes control and inflicts its own persecution . . . as body and self constantly shift roles of victim and victimizer, master and slave."

The lyrical and wonderfully sympathetic conjectures of Cross do not explain the underlying, basic relationship between self-mutilation and eating disorders. Malcove's (1933) theory that a childhood fear of mutilation resulting from the practical experience of learning to eat makes psychological sense. Malcove notes children's identification with food. If this is true, then the act of eating, at least during the early stages of life, serves to make self-mutilation a palatable behavior in the sense that it is inherent in the human condition. The child's act of eating is rewarded by a primary gain because hunger is temporarily satisfied. In later life, self-mutilation also offers a primary gain, namely, temporary respite from unpleasant experiences such as anxiety, tension, depersonalization, and racing thoughts. Food, like self-mutilation, is a source of solace. Although psychoanalysis often focuses on a child's use of bowel control to frustrate others, every parent knows that a child can utilize eating in a similar manner. Children, for example, can express willful anger toward their parents either by refusing to eat or by spitting out their food. This behavior may be the prototype of self-mutilation as a retaliation against an abusive adult. By eating what their parents offer, children also are able to please their parents and win affection. This form of secondary gain may be the prototype of self-mutilation as manipulation of others.

Malcove's final point is that eating is a "cannibalistic procedure" to a child. The horrible truth of this insight is seen in repressed, psychotic persons who amputate a body part and then consume it. A mild derivative of this behavior is commonly encountered in nonpsychotic self-cutters who drink their own blood. Certainly, in Western societies cannibalism is thought of as the ultimate ghastly antisocial act of aggression. Idiosyncratic acts of murder and cannibalism, indeed, are totally repellant. Yet one scholar, Eli Sagan (1974), contends that cannibalism is the fundamental form of institutionalized aggression and that it is impossible to comprehend the true nature of human culture without understanding the role of cannibalism in human history. For our purposes it is important to note that the culturally sanctioned, "affectionate" cannibalism of mortuary customs embodies the same dynamics as the psychological processes of incorporation and introjection—processes that are significant in serious depression, a mental disorder often associated with self-mutilation.

Idiosyncratic Cannibalism

Judging from the thousands of references to cannibalism not only in the anthropological literature but also in popular novels and missionary-in-the-stewpot cartoons, a casual observer might conclude that the evidence for the existence of cannibalism is both overwhelming and clear. As we shall see, however, the issue is not a simple one.

Individual acts of cannibalism have certainly occurred throughout human history in times of extreme famine. There is excellent evidence that the stranded members of the Donner Pass group ate human flesh (Stewart 1960), as did the survivors of a much publicized air crash in the Andes (Read 1974). Starved inmates in Nazi concentration camps resorted to cannibalism (Russell 1954), and Roheim (1932) reported that famished Ngoli and Yuma Australian aborigines induced abortions to provide food for the rest of the family. Cannibalism within the context of starvation was even the topic of a famous literary essay. Jonathan Swift's political parody and censure of Irish helplessness and English voraciousness was titled *A Modest Proposal for preventing the Children of Poor People from being a Burthen to their Parents, or the Country, and for making them Beneficial to the Publick* (1729). Swift's modest proposal was that the impoverished and starving Irish sell their children at age 12 months to the rich of England, who would then eat them, thus improving the diet of one group and the wealth of the other.

Individual acts of cannibalism certainly have also occurred among psychotic persons, usually with a religious overlay. A psychiatrist in Papua New Guinea, for example, reported the case of a 30-year-old psychotic native who killed and ate his son (Burton-Bradley 1976). The patient had a family history of mental disorder, was a heavy betel nut chewer (the chemical arecoline in betel nuts induces euphoria) and spree drinker of alcohol, and was an avid reader of Christian literature provided by missionaries. He had read about the apostles, about Jesus' fast of forty days, and about Abraham and the sacrifice of Isaac. He then decided upon a course of action.

> I decided to kill my child. After I made up my mind, I fasted for 5 days. I then took my little boy into the bush and came to the place where I had decided to kill him. When I came to the spot, I prepared a small place for the child to sit and I spread a laplap on the ground for him, then I began to dig a grave. After that was finished, I struck him twice on the forehead with my axe. I then took my knife and cut him in the stomach and upward toward the chest through the bone. I then took his heart out. I chopped it up and ate some of it. I also made some cuts in my own body and mixed some of my son's blood with this. Then I put the body in the grave. I had brought some glue and petrol with me which I mixed with the remaining slices of my son's heart. I tried to boil it but was not successful. I had hoped that the steam and the rest of the mixture would go up to God and he would then send me the power in my dreams to do the right things for my people. The people's heads would also become clear, and they would then do the necessary things to bring about the white man's way of life. God would send many goods to the people and we would find money. Then I lay down in the grave and slept with my dead son. No dream came the first night. On the second, I dreamed that I saw a light go up to heaven. I then covered the grave and returned to my village. (quoted in Burton-Bradley 1976)

Burton-Bradley noted that native informants considered the man's act to be pathological. The official diagnosis was an acute schizophrenic reaction; a year later "the autism and ambitendencies of nuclear schizophrenia were well in evidence." The patient's bizarre act was probably also influenced by the effect of starvation-induced chemical changes as well as by the euphoria of arecolinism. Cannibalism had a tradition in Papua New Guinea (e.g., as a method of revenge or of absorbing a victim's life principle, as a way of facilitating conception, as part of warfare, and as an act of justice). Indeed, a Supreme Court judge in Melanesia had ruled that cannibalism per se was neither improper nor indecent but rather must be understood within a cultural context (Griffin 1971). In this case, however, the cultural context was overshadowed by the presence of mental illness.

A psychiatric case report of idiosyncratic cannibalism (Benezech et al. 1981) deals with a 41-year-old paranoid schizophrenic man whose wife was also suffering from the same illness. During a psychotic episode when he was 29, the man, with the help of his wife, tried to strangle a neighbor. The man was hospitalized two years later and then traveled across Europe because God's voice told him to undertake religious missions. These auditory hallucinations persisted and controlled much of his subsequent behavior. His wife died of an apparent drowning, but he later confessed to killing her. He said that his wife had planned to kill him and then herself, but since he did not want to die, he killed his wife first. His attempt to rape a young girl and drink her blood was subverted when the girl's mother appeared. He then murdered an elderly person, ate large pieces of the victim's thigh, and tried to suck the blood from his victim's femoral artery. The following day, the man killed a farmer and his wife with a pitchfork and beat their maid severely. He stated that God had told him to kill everyone. The killings proved that he was bad and, therefore, he ate the victim's flesh to be united with God. "I ate his flesh and drank his blood to obey the sentence: who will eat my body and drink my blood will live" (quoted in Benezech et al. 1981). His reference was to Jesus' words in John 6:54–56, "He who feeds on my flesh and drinks my blood has life eternal, and I will raise him up on the last day. For my flesh is real food, and my blood real drink. The man who feeds on my flesh and drinks my blood remains in me, and I in him."

From the examples just provided, it is clear that in *rare* instances cannibalism has existed. But has cannibalism ever been a custom or ritual practice among human groups?

Customary and Ritual Cannibalism

The first mention of cannibalism in Western culture is a single paragraph written by Herodotus about the Androphagi, a savage tribe that spoke a peculiar language, paid no regard to justice, lived in a far-off land beyond the eastern desert, and ate human flesh. Likewise, the ancient Greek geographer Strabo (64 B.C.–A.D. 21) described the Irish as man-eaters who thought it honorable to devour the bodies of their dead fathers, although he added, "I am saying this only with the understanding that I have no trustworthy witnesses for it." These two examples, although frequently cited over the ages to prove the existence of cannibalism, are best regarded as unsubstantiated anecdotes.

In fact, the first persons in classical times to be accused of ritual cannibalism and blood sacrifice were the Christians. This accusation was made during the first three centuries A.D. by the Romans, who even held official inquiries into the matter. Justin Martyr (100–165) responded angrily in his *Second Apologia* by denying the charges and then by accusing the Romans of cannibalism: "If you have extorted by means of tortures some single confessions from our slaves, wives, and children, they are no proofs of our guilt. It is not we who do that which is laid to our charge; but you who did it, and yet you do worse . . . We might, if we filled ourselves with blood, as talk goes, declare it to be a worship after the manner of your Jupiter Latiaris, and would be justified in your eyes." Tertullian, in his *Apologeticum* (written about 200) wrote: "We are called the most villainous of mortals because of the secret practice of killing and eating children. . . . Prove it then, if you believe it, or believe it not, as you have not proved it."

The early Christians, in turn, accused competing sects, such as the Gnostics and the Manicheans, of cannibalistic practices. Epiphanius (305–403) wrote that the Gnostics were lechers who ate human semen while saying, "This is the body of Christ and the Passover meal." Likewise, he said that the Gnostics drank menstrual blood while saying, "This is the body of Christ." He further stated that they prepared a perfect Passover meal by mixing a deliberately aborted human fetus with honey, pepper, and herbs and then ate the meal with their fingers. Saint Augustine, in his book *On the Customs of the Manicheans*, accused the Manicheans of eating sperm and menstrual blood in their religious rituals.

The New Testament contains numerous references to the feuds between the early Christians and competing sects. These feuds were characterized by charges and countercharges, some of which, by today's standards, seem absurd. Thus, in *The City of God* (completed in 426), Saint Augustine dealt with attacks made upon the concept of the resurrection of the body. Since Christ promised that not one hair on the head of his followers would be harmed (Luke 21), pagan scoffers wanted to know whether people would be resurrected with all the hair that barbers had ever cut from their heads. Likewise, would all the fingernail clippings rejoin their bodies? What shape would deformed children assume? But according to Augustine, the "most difficult question" that the pagans asked was "Whose flesh shall that man's be in the resurrection, which is eaten by another man through compulsion of hunger? For it is turned into the flesh of the person who eats it and fills that part that famine had made hungry and lean."

In the Middle Ages, Christians made charges of cannibalism and child sacrifice against heretical groups, such as the Cathars and the Waldensians. The last recorded proceedings against heretics on such charges were made in Italy in 1466. Members of the "Fraticelli de opinione" confessed under torture that they would pulverize the body of a child, burn and dry the remains, and mix them with wine, which was then consecrated as the true body of Christ and drunk in their rituals.

The many accusations of cannibalism that have been made against Jews are detailed in Strack's comprehensive study *The Jew and Human Sacrifice* (1909). These accusations began in earnest during the eleventh and twelfth centuries and seem to be related not only to fears about the great epidemic diseases that swept over Europe but also to the heightened religious enthusiasm associated with the Crusades.

The first "blood" case against Jews can be dated accurately to 1235 in Fulda, Germany. Through confessions made under torture, it was determined that on Christmas Day two Jews cruelly slaughtered the five sons of a miller, collected their blood in wax-coated bags, and burned their remains. As punishment, a group of crusaders killed thirty-four Jewish men and women. In 1236, Emperor Frederick II appointed an expert commission to determine the facts in the case and to report on the widespread popular belief that Jews needed Christian blood for their rituals. In their deliberations the commissioners paid special importance to the testimony of Jewish converts to Christianity. In July of that year, Frederick issued an edict, based on the commission's findings, in which he declared the Jews of Fulda "to be entirely acquitted of the crime attributed to them, and the rest of the Jews of Germany of so grave an accusation."

There is a dreary sameness in the many cases in which Jews have been accused of blood sacrifice and cannibalism over the centuries. It should be noted, however, that many people, political leaders and scholars among them, have publicly pronounced the innocence of Jews in these cases, although those testaments do not seem to have made a great impression on the European populace. In the mid–nineteenth century, anti-Semitic writers began to produce impressive studies. Pawlikowski's *Der Talmud in der Theorie und Praxis* (1866) gives seventy-three examples in which Jews were involved in human sacrifice "in order to eat the blood in their unleavened bread." *Der Talmudjude* (1871) of Professor August Rohling of Prague represents the apotheosis of charges against Jews. Even though many scholars of that time attacked the book for its pseudoscholarship and faulty conclusions, it fueled a fire that persists to current times. In fact, a young Brazilian psychiatrist recently told me of her childhood experiences in a large northern city in Brazil. She and all the neighborhood children who attended the local Catholic church were taught to take revenge on the Jews because they had crucified Christ. Thus, on Good Fridays they taunted and destroyed a straw effigy of a Jew, and they were warned that if caught by a Jew they would be killed and their livers eaten! According to my informant, this custom still prevails, although she added that adult Catholics had cordial relations with Jews in the city.

Unfortunately, accusations against Jews have served, and continue to serve, the apparent need of some groups to persecute others. In 1983 a government printing house in the U.S.S.R. published a book entitled *The Class Essence of Zionism*, by Lev Korneyev. This book resurrected a famous Russian trial of 1913 (the Mendel Beiliss case) in which Jews were accused of murdering Christian children in order to obtain blood, which, when mixed with matzo, formed an essential component of the ritual Passover meal. A virulent anti-Semite named Alexei Shmakov not only prosecuted the case with zeal but also proposed that Russian pogroms against Jews were instigated by "Zionist agents." Although Lenin himself proclaimed in March 1919, "Shame on accursed czarism which tortured and persecuted the Jews! Shame on those who foment hatred toward Jews," Korneyev's book cites Shmakov favorably and concludes that Russian anti-Semitism results from "disgust on the part of the native population for the peculiar psychological and behavioral traits of the Jewish bourgeoisie."

The Man-Eating Myth (1979), by the American anthropologist W. Arens, is a scathing attack on the notion of customary cannibalism. Arens believes that both scholars and laymen have embraced the exotic image of cannibalism because of a need to engage in "a never-ending search for the primitive in order to give meaning to the concept of civilization" (p. 184). Thus, just as one tribe may establish its moral superiority by charging another tribe with ritual cannibalism, so too Westerners have accepted the existence of ritual cannibalism in primitive groups as a justification both for colonization and for a sense of righteousness.

He points out that cannibals were persons who, like Herodotus's Androphagoi, traditionally lived on the fringes of Western civilization. When the boundaries of this civilization greatly expanded during the fifteenth century, however, cannibals were supposedly encountered. Thus, Christopher Columbus's journal notes that the Arawak Indians described their enemies, the Caribs, as "men with one eye, and others with dogs' noses, who ate men, and when they took a man, they cut off his head and drank his blood, and castrated him." A papal representative at the Spanish court, Peter d'Anghera, embellished Columbus's account and wrote fantastic dispatches that had great popularity. He described cannibals, mermaids, giants, and Amazon women.*

---

*The Amazons were a tribe of warrior women whose name derives from the Greek words meaning "without a breast"; in some Latin manuscripts the word *Amazon* is written *unimamma* (Schecter 1962). Homer's *Iliad* contains many references to these fierce women. In his

The Spaniards cruelly subjugated the Native Americans of the Caribbean islands and Mexico. The major rationalization for killing or enslaving the Indians was that they were subhuman beings who lacked rationality and morality, as evidenced by their indulgence in human sacrifice and the most horrible abomination of all, cannibalism. While it is undeniably true that some Native Americans, such as the Aztecs, practiced human sacrifice on a large scale, the evidence for cannibalism is quite conjectural. In fact, no European ever directly witnessed an act of Native American cannibalism, and the attempts of some modern scholars to explain Aztec cannibalism on the basis of nutritional needs are highly dubious.

Arens accurately points out that none of the voluminous literature on Africa includes mention of any European who actually witnessed a cannibal meal. According to Arens, when "the explorer David Livingstone considered the evidence for cannibalism among an African group he was familiar with, [he] concluded with the terse comment: 'A Scotch jury would say, Not Proven.'" Arens feels similarly about data from Papua New Guinea, and even accused another anthropologist, Ronald Berndt, of succumbing to sensationalism in accepting an informant's account of an unlikely cannibalistic episode.

Brief mention by Arens of this case struck me as beyond bizarre, so I went to Berndt's (1962) book for details. The action that Berndt describes supposedly takes place following a battle in which several men and women were killed:

> Here Unapi'na of Kogu selected the corpse of a young woman name Pazu'na; finding her attractive, he knelt between her legs and pulling them to this thighs began to copulate, cutting the body as he did so. A Kogu woman, Aria, came up, and said to him, "You are taking a long time. You are only pretend-

---

Judgements Derived from Heaven, Ptolemy states, "Such are the Amazons, who avoid having contact with men, who apply themselves to weapons, and who made their daughters hardy from childhood, cutting off their right breast in order that they may be better fitted to military exercises, and who uncover this portion of their bosom in exploits of war and in combats, so as to reveal their natural vigor and male courage." According to Hippocrates, the Amazons cauterized the right breast of their daughters with a hot copper instrument. By burning the breast, its development was arrested. Without this impediment, the Amazons were better able to handle weapons and to draw their bows when shooting arrows. According to several ancient commentators, the Amazons maimed male children by dislocating their knee and hip joints so that they would not try to conspire against the women when they grew up. Over the centuries, the term *Amazon* came to mean female warrior, without any reference to breast mutilation, and it was in this sense that Columbus used the term. In fact, the Amazon River in South America was named after a group of female warriors of the Tapuya tribe encountered by one of Pizarro's officers in 1541.

ing to cut. All the time you copulate." But having ejaculated he began again, at the same time slowly cutting off the woman's breasts. By this time Aria, a *nenafu* of his, became impatient and set to work on the corpse herself with her bamboo knife. She began to cut across the corpse's belly, but Unapi'na was so intent on copulating that he did not notice how near her knife was. Aria, for her part, was careless. She cut further in and across, hacking away at the flesh; and since Unapi'na's penis was in the woman's vagina, she cut most of it off. Unapi'na fell back crying, blood flowing from the stump of his penis. Aria blamed him for what had happened. "You sit there copulating, not bothering to cut her up properly. This women is dead, ready to be cut up for eating. I told you about it, but you continued copulating. Thus, I cut off your penis!" Unapi'na replied, "I looked at this Kamano woman; she was a good woman. I looked at her vulva, and I liked it; that is why I copulated. But now you have cut off my penis! What shall I do?" Aris removed the end of the penis she had cut off, popped it into her mouth, and ate it, and then continued with the cutting. Unapi'na was helped back to his house, where he rested. Ovens were made and the meat cooked, amid dancing and singing. Unapi'na was given the woman's vulva and surrounding flesh to eat. (p. 283)

Papua New Guinea is well known in the medical literature because of a puzzling disease called *kuru*, which is found only among members of the Fore tribe. The major symptom of *kuru* is progressive, uncontrollable trembling that invariably proves fatal. The Fore attribute the disease to sorcery; but, as shown especially by D. Carleton Gajdusek (who won a Nobel prize for his studies), we now know that *kuru* is a disease caused by a slow-acting virus. The controversy about *kuru* centers on its mode of transmission, which is popularly thought to be through cannibalism—that is, the virus-infested brain of the victim is eaten during a mourning ritual. The problems with this supposition are many. No European has ever seen any Fore tribesmen actually eating human flesh. Although Gajdusek (1977) has written, "We believe that contamination during the cannibalistic ritual was the sole source of transmission of *kuru* from man to man," he also published in the same article a picture of a Fore group preparing food which has as its caption: "Children participated in both the butchering and the handling of cooked meat, rubbing their soiled hands in their armpits or hair, and elsewhere on their body. They rarely or never washed. Infection with the *kuru* virus was probably through the cuts and abrasions of the skin, or from nose picking, eye rubbing, or mucosal injury." Without delving into the epidemiological details, I believe it is fair to state that the case for cannibalistic transmission is not totally convincing.

Finally, mention should be made of supposed cannibalism in North America. Ever since the 1930s, anthropological and psychiatric literature has made numerous references to a mental illness termed *windigo psychosis* among Algonkian Indians, such as the Ojibwa and Cree, in Northwestern Canada. The disorder is frequently classified as a "culture-bound psychosis" characterized by a compulsive desire to eat human flesh. However, as pointed out by Kennedy (1970), Preston (1980), and, most important, Marano (1982), windigo psychosis has never existed. In fact, Marano concluded that the situation is an example of mass suggestibility among anthropologists who, enticed by the exotic notion of cannibalism, fabricated the disorder in an attempt to explain certain events.

■

Although it is true that the vast majority of references to customary cannibalism are anecdotal or biased, it seems foolhardy to dismiss all the sources as unreliable. Let us examine the report of Andre Dupeyrat (1954), a missionary in Papua New Guinea. He befriended a chief who described how he had arranged for his own parents' death:

> They had got too old. You know what it's like. My father had become so feeble that he could no longer shake a spear. He had no teeth left, and he ate like a child. . . . As for my mother, her skin had got as wrinkled as an old lizard's and as black and flaccid as the wings of a bat. She could no longer go to the vegetable garden. Her eyes were full of filth. It was then that I realized that their time had come. . . . (The chief then said that he asked some close friends in a neighboring tribe to do him a favor.) They sent a delegation to invite my parents to a banquet at their village. On the way there, they brained them with clubs, strapped them on a branch and took them back to their village. Then they cut them up, cooked them in a stone oven, and ate them. Afterwards, they washed and cleaned the bones, and brought them back here. You can see what good care I take of them. . . . But then, I'm a dutiful son! (p. 206)

Dupeyrat also described his experiences at the funeral of another chief whose body was allowed to decompose in the jungle heat and humidity. The natives collected the greenish fluid that oozed from the decaying body and used it as a sauce for bits of taro. They then ate the taro in order to absorb the strength, virtues, and qualities of the dead chief.

A chief produced a skull for Dupeyrat and said that it belonged to a powerful enemy who had been killed: "I cut off his head while he was still alive. I gave my two elder sons—they will one day become chiefs—his eyes to eat. To my wife, I gave the thing that makes women fertile. To my warriors, I gave the heart, the liver, the entrails, so that they should become fearless. As for me, by this hole which you see here, I sucked out his brains, and I keep his skull in honor, for his valor has entered into me" (p. 244).

It is true that Dupeyrat's book is replete with the judgments of a Christian priest confronted by savages, yet it also demonstrates a high level of empathy with the natives. His informants do not use the charge of cannibalism to blacken the character of their enemies, but rather they willingly admit their own participation in the act.

Even if one dismisses Dupeyrat's report as fanciful, one cannot dismiss the reports found in the publication *The Ethnography of Cannibalism* (Brown and Tuzin 1983). I especially call attention to the claims of the anthropologist Fitzjohn Porter Poole that he actually witnessed eleven occasions of customary cannibalism during mortuary rites among the Bimin-Kuskumin of Papua New Guinea.

The Bimin-Kuskumin consider various body parts to possess either male or female substances, and the eating of specific parts obtained from a deceased person during funeral rites is thought to be appropriate. Thus, certain male relatives of a dead man consume morsels of his bone marrow (male substance) to honor him, to facilitate the movement of his spirit to the ancestral underworld, and to recycle his generative and ritual strength within his male descendants. Certain female relatives, however, eat small portions of his lower belly fat (female substance) to enhance their own reproductive and ritual power. Poole witnessed the former event on five occasions, and the latter event four times. If the wife of a deceased man is still capable of childbearing, she is expected to eat a tiny raw fragment from her dead husband's penis in order to enhance her fertility. Poole states that while he twice saw penis flesh presented to a widow, he never actually saw it being consumed. He further notes that many tribesmen consider this ritual to be disgusting and degrading, and they claim that the women often vomit up the penis flesh or only pretend to eat it.

Among the Bimin-Kuskumin, certain male relatives of a deceased woman eat her bone marrow to honor her reproductive capacity, while the woman's husband, if still sexually active, eats a small, raw portion from his dead wife's vagina to enhance his daughters' reproductive capabilities and to protect himself from witches. Poole saw this event on four occasions and notes that the man who eats such vaginal flesh is required to undergo extensive purification rites because he is considered to be extraordinarily polluted.

When a leading Bimin-Kuskumin male elder dies, parts of his raw heart tissue are eaten by other male elders in order to perpetuate his great ritual power and knowledge. When a leading female elder dies, parts of her uterus and vagina are eaten by her female relatives and by other female elders to perpetuate her ritual power and to diffuse her reproductive power. Poole observed the former practice twice, and the latter practice once; on each occasion he discerned marked ambivalence on the part of all those who participated in the cannibalistic rituals.

Totem, Taboo, and Transubstantiation

The notion that cannibalism is inherent in the human condition was set forth by Sir Thomas Browne in his lyrical *Religio Medici* (1634): "We are what we all abhor, Anthropophagi and Cannibals, devourers not onely of men, but of our selves; and that not in an allegory, but a positive truth; for all this mass of flesh which we behold, came in at our mouths; this frame we look upon, hath been upon our trenchers; in brief, we have devour'd our selves."

A modern version of this idea was developed by Freud in *Totem and Taboo* (1950). Freud theorized the existence of a primal horde in the earliest stage of the development of mankind. The leader of the horde was a powerful father who, in order to maintain his authority, drove out his rebellious sons:

> One day, the brothers who had been driven out came together, killed, and devoured their father and so made an end of the patriarchal horde. United, they had the courage to do and succeeded in doing what would have been impossible for them individually. . . . Cannibal savages as they were, it goes without saying that they devoured their victim as well as killing him . . . and in the act of devouring him they accompanied their identification with him, and each one of them acquired a portion of his strength. The totem meal, which is perhaps mankind's earliest festival, would thus be a repetition and a commemoration of this memorable and criminal deed, which was the beginning of so many things—of social organization, or moral restrictions, and of religion (p. 142).

Freud's scenario is based upon his reading of anthropological reports and on his observations during the psychoanalyses of neurotic patients (he reckoned that the psychological regression experienced by these patients sheds light on the primitive mentality of early man.) He asserted that the events in his scenario might have existed in fact or might have existed only in the imaginations of the primitive people, who nonetheless experienced them as real. Although the validity of Freud's scenario has been strongly challenged by many modern scholars, it contains a certain elegance and heuristic value. Freud contended that a cannibal feast gave rise to three elements of human life—namely, social organization, moral restrictions, and religion—that we know to be significant in both culturally sanctioned and pathological self-mutilation.

According to Freud's formulation, social organization in society arose because the brothers planned and carried out their act of murder and cannibalism and then established clan solidarity. Many culturally sanctioned mutilative rites serve this same purpose, for example, initiation rites often include mutilations (such as skin cutting, tooth removal, and circumcision) that serve to bind group members together and validate membership in the tribe and cults. The brothers' deeds also demonstrated acts of independence from authority and proof of masculinity. These same motives underlie some instances of self-mutilation, especially in institutionalized mental patients and prisoners. Not infrequently, for example, prison gang members cover their bodies with visible, grotesque, and often obscene tattoos to prove their masculinity, to assert their dislike of authority, and to enhance a sense of belonging among group members.

The origins of moral restrictions in society in Freud's scenario derive from the brothers' desire not to share the same fate as their father. Thus, they prohibited the killing and eating of each other. In time, these prohibitions were generalized to other clan members and eventually evolved into the simple injunction "Thou shalt not kill." Many mutilative rites are linked to moral restrictions; for example, the vaginas of young African girls are sewn closed in order to prevent sexual intercourse until marriage. Among the mentally ill, self-mutilation may serve as an alternative to suicide— a psychologically depressed patient begged staff to kill him, and then he plucked out both his eyes, stating that he did it so that he could continue living.

The link between cannibalism and religion is somewhat complicated but significant for our understanding of self-mutilation among some patients. For Freud, the talion law—an eye for an eye, a tooth for a tooth—is deeply rooted in human nature. Thus, when Christ redeemed mankind from the burden of original sin by sacrificing his own life, he was expiating the original murder of the primal father by the sons. Christ was the incarnation of the sons who displaced their father just as the son-religion of Christianity displaced the father-religion of Judaism. The original cannibalistic meal evolved into the rite of communion, a sacrament in which the company of brothers obtained sanctity by identifying with the primal sons as Christ and then by devouring the flesh and blood of god.

Many anthropologists have attempted to account for *ritual* cannibalism in an evolutionary format. Thus, it has been hypothesized that primitive man ate human flesh simply because it was available as a food source. As mankind developed, cannibalism became part of religious rituals, especially in the complex non-Western civilizations, while it was replaced by animal sacrifice, especially in Western (Judeo-Christian) cultures. With further cultural evolution, cannibalism and animal sacrifice were superseded when the religious belief in transubstantiation was developed. According to this belief, cereals and other substances could be transformed into flesh by the recitation of certain prayers and the performance of ritualistic acts. In Christian practice, for example, a priest is thought to be able to convert bread and wine into the flesh and blood of Jesus. The communicant who ingests these transformed substances does not do so because they are symbols but rather because they supposedly are the actual body tissue of God.

The transubstantiation of bread into the flesh of a god is popularly associated with Christianity, where it was ecclesiastically established at the fourth Lateran synod in 1215, but a chapter entitled "Eating the God" in Frazer's *Golden Bough* (1958) provides examples of the practice both in pre-Christian and non-Christian cultures. The Aryans of ancient India, for example, believed in the transubstantiation of rice cakes into flesh during holy sacrificial rites. Thus, "When it (the rice cake) still consists of rice-meal it is the hair. When he (the Brahman priest) pours water on it, it becomes skin. When he mixes it, it becomes flesh; for then it becomes consistent; and consistent also in the flesh. When it is baked, it becomes bone. . . . And when he is about to take it off (the fire) and sprinkles it with butter, he changes it into marrow" (vol. 2, p. 81). Spanish priests who came to Mexico with the conquistadors discovered that the Aztecs practiced a transubstantiation ritual twice a year. At the festival of the winter solstice in December, for example, the Aztecs made an image of the god Huitzilopochtli out of dough mixed with the blood of children. The image was venerated and then cut into pieces by a priest. This ritual was called "killing the God Huitzilopochtli so that his body might be eaten." The Aztec king was given a piece of dough cut out from the heart area of the image while all the males attending the ceremony were given a crumb from the image. The ceremony was called *teoquado*, which means "god is eaten."

Depression

Severely depressed persons are at high risk for self-mutilation (many cases are included in this book). On one level this association may be understood as the depressed person's need to punish himself or herself for real or imaginary crimes and sins. However, on another, more profound, level it may be understood as a derivative of cannibalism. As Freud first showed in

Mourning and Melancholia (1917), the psychological processes of mourning and of severe depression are qualitatively similar and are modeled upon the earliest infantile interaction within reality, namely, taking in food. As expressed by Cameron (1963), in the mourning process "the mourner tends to take over some of the characteristics of the lost one and to act like him, speak as he did, even to look like him and live as he did. It is as though the mourner were saying to the world, 'He lives again in me!' . . . It seems to be a normal defense against crushing loss, a process of taking onto oneself parts of the behavior and appearance of the lost persons, in that they are in a sense preserved alive." In psychodynamic terms, the mourner *identifies* with, or feels like, the deceased. This process is based on the mechanism of *introjection* (the internalization of the deceased).

The vast majority of cannibalistic acts occur during mortuary rites. In fact, Sagan defines "affectionate" cannibalism as the eating of body parts of kinsmen who have died a natural death and notes that the emotions associated with this form of cannibalism "are very similar to our own feelings toward dead relatives — affection, sorrow, and the desire to preserve and remember the virtues of the deceased." We have already discussed the Bimin-Kuskumin, who practice affectionate cannibalism in order to assume the generative and ritual strength of a deceased kinsman. Their belief is that by eating a dead person's flesh, some characteristics of the deceased will be kept alive and recycled. One wonders during the course of human development whether such cannibalistic mortuary rites developed as a concrete expression of the emotions associated with the mourning process or whether the psychological process of mourning that we now experience (often associated in many cultures with a feast or special meal) evolved from primitive cannibalism.

The relationship between mourning and cannibalism is clearly demonstrated by the Wari' tribe of western Brazil, which practiced cannibalism until the 1960s. When enemy flesh was eaten, obvious hostility was demonstrated, and the body parts were abused and treated disrespectfully; but when the flesh of a Wari' was eaten at funerals, great honor and respect was demonstrated. Unlike the Bimin-Kuskumin, the Wari' did not believe that eating human flesh recycles the characteristics of the dead person. Instead, they ate the flesh of tribal members to help the mourners' "gradual detachment from thinking about and remembering the dead . . . for prolonged sadness is believed to endanger individual health and productivity" (Conklin 1995). By devouring the corpse instead of putting it in the ground to rot, the dead person's spirit was free to become a Water Spirit and then to return as a peccary (a piglike, hoofed animal), which could be hunted and eaten. For the Wari', mourning lasted about ten months. At that time the mourners went on an extended hunt and killed as many animals as possible. A successful hunt signified that the spirit of the deceased was prospering in the afterworld. Amid feasting and singing, the Wari' said, "Sadness has ended; now happiness begins."

Many depressed persons overuse the psychological mechanism of introjection and enter into dependent relationships. In Cameron's (1963) words, "The depressive adult is a person who has had to meet implacable demands for compliance during infancy by the overuse of introjection. Introjection is a symbolic engulfing, a perceptual taking in, the primitive forerunner of social role organization. The infant incorporates his mother symbolically, as he has previously incorporated his food, and sets her up inside as a regulating image. Instead of internalizing merely the role . . . he internalizes the whole frightening image, which then controls what he does" (p. 553). Depressive persons typically have much repressed anger over their situation and regard the controlling maternal image with ambivalence. Because they overuse introjection, the anger they experience at the loss of a loved one or a prize possession is turned inward, thus potentiating the repressed anger. The result may be psychotic decompensation, replete with feelings of great guilt and sometimes with self-mutilation. The cultural prototype of this process is apparent in cannibalistic and self-mutilative mortuary rites. The eating of a dead person's flesh, with no matter how much affection, contains elements of aggression and of ambivalence. Anthropophagy during mourning satisfies at some level the feeling of anger at the deceased for having abandoned the mourner, and it is quite common in many cultural groups for mourners to mutilate themselves, especially by chopping off a finger. In some cultures this activity has become symbolic. Mourners, for example, may wear black clothing, cut off their hair, and put ashes on their body. Among patients we find some who mutilate themselves upon the death of a loved one. For example, a 24-year-old man became depressed after his father died; he then attempted to circumcise himself with a pair of scissors, saying that this might lift him out of his depression.

Sagan (1974) states that "if the relatives of a dead person cut off a finger joint or spill their blood on the face of a corpse, it is logical to assume, knowing what we know about the practice of eating the corpse, that these relatives are offering parts of their own bodies to the deceased so that they may be eaten by him. . . . There is a basic polarization in anthropophagy between affection and aggression. It may well be that lying in back of this is a more basic ambivalence—whether to eat or be eaten" (p. 33). The construct of cannibalism contains both feast and famine, chaos and order, evil destruction and beneficial regeneration (Sanday 1986). This polarization and ambivalence reflect a common theme of religious and political rituals in which a victim is transformed into a killer, and a prey into a hunter (Bloch 1992). The "affection" of cannibalism restores social order. The deceased continues to live symbolically in the bodies of the group, which in turn will be devoured. The mourner endures a period of necessary sadness but then resumes a normal life when happiness begins. However, the aggression of cannibalism directed against nonkin enemies is motivated by hostility and revenge. In this regard, I believe that aggressive cannibalism serves as the prototype not only for religious self-mortification and some cases of anorexia nervosa in which one's body is treated as an enemy but also for habitual self-mutilation among the mentally ill.

The conquering cannibal literally tastes the fruits of his victory, but victory can also be achieved by exactly the opposite action, namely, self-starvation. In many religious traditions, enlightenment and victory over the forces of evil come after a period of prolonged fasting. Cannibalism and self-starvation appear to be linked poles representing the opposite sides of revenge-victory. Political activists in India and more recently in Northern Ireland attempted to overthrow British rule by starving themselves. The metaphor for their actions is clear: the British have devoured our country and now we will demonstrate vividly how this devouring leads to weakness and to total destruction.

In like manner, anorexia nervosa is an object lesson. It is a form of indirect self-mutilation in which the patient achieves victory over real and fantastic enemies through fasting. To eat is to accept the status quo. To eat is to partake of a regenerative cannibalistic ritual. To eat is to open one's self to the possibility of being devoured and to participate in the cycle of life. The episodic gorging often accompanying anorexia is a sign of weakness, a dent in the anorectic's armor, and must be undone by self-induced vomiting. Anorexia is tragic because it overshoots the mark. Once a certain point is reached, the catabolic process relentlessly feeds upon itself until the anorectic's body and will to live are shrunken. The therapist's task is to reverse the process of decay and to convince the patient that victory may be won short of fasting unto death.

4

Animals and Automutilation

—————————

Much of what we know about the cause and treatment of human diseases derives from studies of animals. In psychiatry, for example, basic knowledge of brain physiology has come from experiments done with squids and snails; many basic psychological principles have resulted from laboratory work with dogs, rats, and mice; an illness much like major depression in humans can be induced in monkeys. In this chapter reports of animal automutilation (I use the prefix *auto* instead of *self* because no one knows whether an animal has a true sense of self) are examined in an attempt to understand better human self-mutilation.

Through experiments with automutilation in animals, scientists hope to explain the pathophysiological mechanisms underlying the self-mutilation found in certain human diseases with a strong biological component. Such experiments involve strategically placed surgical lesions and the administration of drugs that alter brain chemistry. In order to learn about social factors influencing human self-mutilation, scientists are experimenting with restrictive environments that cause automutilation in animals. Some theorists believe that self- and automutilation derive from an innate aggressive drive and that an understanding of human self-mutilative behavior is enhanced by ethological observations.

The earliest medical reference I have found to animal automutilation is contained in the February 13, 1855, "Proceedings of the Pathological Section of the Irish College of Surgeons." Discussion focused on a case of automutilation in a 12-year-old lioness that lived in the Dublin Zoological Gardens. The animal had been in good health and had given birth to four litters of cubs. She had a history of regular menstrual periods except for the year previous when she had not been "in season." One morning she was discovered to have bitten off six inches of her tail. Shortly, she bit off another large piece and finally demolished the remainder. After a brief interval, she began to eat one of her paws. Despite attempts to treat her by changing her diet, applying topical medicines, and other means, she continued to mutilate herself. She presented such a pitiful sight that the staff decided to destroy her. The only finding on autopsy was some ovarian degeneration.

The secretary of the Zoological Gardens stated that he found it necessary to drown animals that incessantly bit their tails, and he linked tail biting with the tendency of female animals to destroy their offspring.[1] The surgeons noted that animal automutilators were almost always females who appeared to have some interruption or disturbance of their sexual functioning, and they suggested that automutilation was due "to something akin to mental derangement, or as one of the manifestations in the lower animals of the protean hysteria" (p. 211). The condition was likened to the nail biting and occasional destruction of finger tips that occurred as an early manifestation of hysteria in women.

Although the Irish surgeons' comment likening animal automutilation to hysteria in humans seems far-fetched, patients (predominantly women) with hysterical personality disorder are, in fact, prone to self-injurious "gestures," one of the most common being wrist slashing. Additionally, persons with this disorder are typically quite attentive to their physical appearance and grooming. Interestingly, the majority of automutilative lesions in monkeys, such as hair pulling and scratching, are "aberrations of normal grooming behavior" (Jones, Congiv, and Stevenson 1979).

Biochemical Lesions

From the study of neural tissue in animals much as been learned about how human brains function. Nerve cells (neurons) in the brain generate measurable impulses that transfer information to other neurons. The point of transfer is called a synapse, or cleft, where one neuron makes contact with other neurons. An impulse that travels along a neuron reaches a synapse (typically each neuron may have from 1,000 to 10,000 synapses) and either excites or inhibits connecting neurons. The propagation of an impulse across a synapse occurs as a result of a voltage difference or as a result of chemical "transmitters" released at one side of a synapse that affect

1. Konrad Lorenz (1954) reported on the instinctive reactions of female animals who have just given birth. Normally, the mother sucks, lifts, bites, removes, and eats the fetal membranes, placenta, and umbilical cord from her offspring. Sometimes, however, the impulse to devour the fetal wrappings goes awry, and the mother will rip open the abdomen of, and even eat, her offspring. Lorenz stated that this occurs in domestic mammals, such as pigs and rabbits. If the offspring are removed immediately from their mother and are returned to her, cleaned and dried, several hours later when her devouring impulses have passed, they are in no further danger. Among feral animals, however, mothers destroy their young only if they are diseased. He recounted the story of a 2-month-old sickly jaguar at an Austrian zoo. Its mother was seen licking it nervously and shoving her mouth under its belly near the umbilicus. Spectators at the zoo interpreted the action as maternal solicitude for a sick baby, but Lorenz noted, "Beginning of conflict between brood-tending reaction and impulse to devour dead young." The next morning the young jaguar had disappeared, having been eaten by its mother.

the receptor neuron. It is thought that imbalances of chemical transmitters such as dopamine, norepinephrine, serotonin, and GABA (gamma-aminobutyric acid) play a significant role in various psychiatric and neurological disorders. Among the human disorders in which neurotransmitter imbalances have been implicated are three possibly related syndromes characterized by self-mutilation, namely, the Lesch-Nyhan syndrome (severe mutilation), and the deLange and Tourette syndromes (moderate mutilation). These syndromes are discussed in later chapters. Scientists are currently attempting to better understand the self-mutilative components of these syndromes by developing models in which animals are given drugs that cause neurotransmitter changes and lead to automutilation. The obvious value of producing an animal model is that it might then be possible to develop medications that would eliminate mutilative behaviors.

A classic observation of animal automutilation was made by Peters (1967) when testing the response of rats to caffeine. After administering high doses of caffeine he observed that 90 percent of semistarved rats demonstrated a sequence of behaviors that progressed to stereotyped acts, such as running backward or in circles and tail chasing, and culminated in biting of their legs and tails. The mutilation was so intense that some rats died from hemorrhage. "A ball of wire put in the cage served as a temporary substitute for self-aggression but ultimately the animal would turn upon itself.... Attacks came intermittently. When biting itself, the animal would shriek and then stop biting" (pp. 141–42). Interestingly, when the rats were aggregated, the amount of automutilation declined since the rats' "aggressive behavior appeared to be satisfied to a large extent by chasing and biting neighbor rats which usually ran away before they had become severely mutilated."

Utilizing Peters's observations, Lloyd and Stone (1981) were able to induce automutilation in a certain strain of rats on a normal diet by giving them caffeine and similar drugs. The active ingredient in all of these drugs was methylxanthine, a chemical that increases the amount of neurotransmitters such as dopamine and norepinephrine in the brain. Based on behavioral observations of the mutilating rats, the authors felt that the use of methylxanthine in rats was a step forward in the development of an animal model for the Lesch-Nyhan syndrome.

A second proposed model is based on the administration of the drug pemoline to rats. Pemoline is an amphetaminelike central nervous system stimulant that selectively increases levels of the neurotransmitter dopamine. When given to rats, it causes hyperactivity, highly repetitive behaviors (stereotypes), avoidance of physical contact with others, abnormal social behavior, and automutilation such as foot biting (sometimes to the point of amputation) that appears to be a fragmented, exaggerated grooming response. The behavioral similarities between pemoline-treated rats and humans with the deLange syndrome (who often indulge in acts suggestive of exaggerated grooming behavior such as hand licking, hair stroking, and eye picking) have led researchers to speculate that the two conditions also share neurochemical similarities (Mueller and Hsiao 1980).

Another animal model is based on the observation that very high doses of amphetamine in rats cause occasional automutilation as well as marked stereotypic behavior. Researchers are now able to induce automutilation without stereotypy in rats by implanting silicone pellets that continuously release small doses of amphetamine (Mueller et al. 1982). This new model is superior to the caffeine and pemoline models in that it produces more specific behavior effects at lower doses and also appears to affect selectively dopamine transmitter levels in a specific area of the brain (the caudate nucleus).

A newly reported finding concerns clonidine, a drug used in humans to treat hypertension and also to reduce the symptoms of opiate withdrawal. Clonidine's major action seems to be the stimulation of certain brain neurotransmitters (a recent report presents cases of clonidine abuse by patients who claimed it provided a euphoric effect). Mueller and Nyhan (1983) found that automutilation in rats induced by caffeine and amphetamine is potentiated by clonidine, while other behaviors caused by the drugs are reduced. Since caffeine and amphetamine produce very different behavioral effects in rats, this experiment indicates that the automutilation effect of the two drugs seems to be mediated by a common mechanism.

Of possibly very great significance in understanding human self-mutilation is the finding that clonidine produces severe autobiting in isolated and food-deprived mice (Bhattacharya et al. 1988). The larger the dose, the greater the biting and gnawing off of their forelimb digits. This behavior is worsened when the mice additionally receive drugs that reduce the activity of serotonin in the brain and is lessened by drugs that increase serotonin activity. Lowered serotonin activity appears to be a feature of the Lesch-Nyhan, deLange, and Tourette syndromes. It also is thought to be a major factor in self-cutting, the most commonly encountered form of self-mutilation. In the case of the experimental mice, the manipulation of various drugs indicates that enhanced dopamine activity has a permissive mediating effect on the clonidine-induced automutilation. Studies of human self-mutilation have emphasized primarily the role of lowered brain serotonin activity, but it is becoming more apparent that other neurotransmitters (dopamine as well as norepinephrine) also are significant. They very well may play a permissive or mediating role, for example, they might be responsible for irritability and hyperarousal, which are traits that facilitate self-mutilative and impulsively aggressive behaviors (Markowitz and Coccaro 1995).

Animal models for human self-mutilation based on the study of brain neurotransmitters have not yet provided any therapeutic breakthroughs. They have, however, provided laboratory justification for the use of medications such as haloperidol and pimozide (drugs that lower the brain levels of neurotransmitters such as dopamine and norepinephrine) for the treatment of some human self-mutilative syndromes. These drugs are able to curtail or eliminate automutilation in specially prepared animals.

Localized Biological Lesions

Some animals will gnaw off a trapped limb in order to free themselves. Foxes are especially known for such behavior; in fact, a fox will bite off an injured limb even when the injury is less serious than that sustained by being caught in a trap. Of more interest is the observation that animals will lick, gnaw, and scratch parts of their bodies that are abnormally sensitive, for example, as a result of infections, skin irritations, vitamin deficiencies, parasite and flea infestation, and poor blood supply. This pathological "cleaning behavior" may cause severe tissue damage. Opossums, long-tailed monkeys, small South American monkeys, and carnivorous mammals are especially prone to such automutilation. Meyer-Holzapfel (1968) provided examples from zoos of an opossum that gnawed away its hind leg, of a hyena that gnawed away both hind paws, of a Moor macaque monkey that ate its penis, scrotum, and testes, and of lions that gnawed their paws and tails.

A study of a large mouse production colony found that 8.5 percent of the males mutilated themselves by biting off their penises. Evidently the vigorous sexual activity of the mice resulted in spontaneous incomplete ejaculations and consequent formation of acellular, mucuslike plugs that blocked the urethra. Urinary retention ensued, causing such pain that the mice bit off their penises (Hong and Ediger 1978).

Although it seems unlikely that localized lesions play a role in most human self-mutilation, two observations come to mind. First, some mentally ill humans excoriate their skin severely, often under the delusion that insects or parasites are present. As noted in chapter 6, these patients may seriously gouge their skin with knives and needles in an attempt to dig out these imaginary invaders. They may even bring bags with pieces of skin, dried blood, and dirt to the physician for inspection. Second, some patients mutilate body parts that are abnormal, for example, some self-castrators have a history of testicular pathology, such as undescended testicles or mumps orchitis. In these cases it seems likely that both psychological and biological factors operate to focus the patient's attention on the abnormal body part and make it a target for destruction. The memory of pain in a body part may persist even though the original lesion is no longer "really" painful, especially if the body part — such as the testicles — is heavily associated with symbolic meanings. The importance of pain memory to mutilation has been demonstrated in experiments with rats (Dennis and Melzack 1979). If the sensory fibers from a rat's forelimb are surgically cut, the rat will mutilate the organ. If the forelimb is painfully irritated prior to the destruction of the sensory fibers, the automutilation of the organ is accelerated, often to the point of amputation by chewing. Since the surgical cut makes it impossible for the rat to receive sensations from its forelimb, it is thought that the memory of the pain operates through brain mechanisms to accelerate an automutilative chewing response. Administration of the antiepileptic drug phenytoin (Dilantin) prevents the automutilative response, presumably by affecting the neural circuits that process pain memory.

Mutilation in Captive Animals

In an attempt to understand better the role of environmental and social factors in human self-mutilation, many experiments have been performed utilizing animals, namely, monkeys, that are high on the evolutionary scale. It is clear that animals placed in artificial environments, such as zoos or laboratories, are predisposed to automutilation, that social isolation increases this predisposition, and that stressful events, such as a frustrated sex act, threatening stimuli, or thwarted aggression, may precipitate this behavior (Jones and Barraclough 1978).

Tinklepaugh's complicated case of a male monkey named Cupid is the best-known early report on automutilation (1928). Cupid established a relationship with a female monkey named Psyche. He reacted violently and attacked two other female monkeys, Topsy and Eva, when they replaced Psyche in his cage. Through various experimental manipulations Cupid developed a relationship with Topsy. When Topsy was then replaced by Psyche, Cupid seemed fine. After two weeks Topsy replaced Psyche. Just as Cupid was about to copulate with Topsy, "he jumped away and began biting his hind feet." For three days he repeated this behavior, never completing copulation, so that his hind feet became badly torn. As he was being attended to medically, Psyche shrieked from her nearby cage and threatened Topsy, who was in Cupid's cage. Without warning, Cupid viciously bit his

Autoinjurious behavior in a monkey. (Photo courtesy of Drs. Arnold S. Chamove and J. R. Anderson)

feet, jumped down, ripped open his scrotum, mutilated the end of his tail, and tore a three-inch gash in his hip. During the following four months he appeared to be in a "state comparable to the depression of some psychoses." He eventually was able to interact normally with both Psyche and Topsy, but whenever Tinklepaugh approached the cage Cupid began to bite his own paws and scrotum.

Although Tinklepaugh did not draw any firm conclusions from this case, he suggested that the automutilation may have resulted from the frustrations of disturbed sexual bonding. Similar behavior in monkeys frustrated by incomplete copulation has been reported by Sackett (1968).

Time and again it has been shown that automutilation in adult laboratory monkeys is highly associated with social isolation during the first year of life; other behaviors associated with early social isolation include social withdrawal, rocking, huddling, clasping, excessive fearfulness or arousal, stereotyped actions, and inappropriate heterosexual and maternal reactions. These behaviors are most severe and persistent when the isolation is total, begins at birth, and continues for at least six months. In general, automutilation increases in isolation-reared monkeys under conditions of frustration, such as when a human experimenter interferes with a monkey's cage, although it may occur even without human interference (Cross and Harlow 1965).

Two British scientists, Arnold Chamove and James Anderson, are actively studying the social context of aggressive behavior in captive monkeys who spent the first year of life either in isolation or in varying degrees of social contact with other monkeys. All captive monkeys during their second year of life demonstrate social aggression (biting, grabbing, threatening, and chasing other monkeys) three times more frequently than autoaggression. During autoaggression a monkey may bite its arm, knee, or foot, slap itself in the face, attempt to "surprise" itself, and threaten or attack the limb that "surprised" it. Upon reaching maturity (the fifth year of life), however, monkeys raised with social contacts no longer engage in autoaggression while monkeys raised in isolation demonstrate increasing levels of autoaggression (see appendix to this chapter).

It appears that inadequate social input leads to the appearance and continuance of autoaggression in monkeys raised in isolation. Behaviors such as clasping, sucking, and brief vigorous biting begin during the first three months of isolation and may be a precursor of autoaggression. The normal behavior of play fighting among monkey peers is subverted during isolation. The socially deprived monkeys may learn to use themselves as targets for aggression as a means of stimulating themselves. The monkeys may also learn that autoaggression is more controllable and safer than social aggression, for example, a dominant male will not interfere with a monkey that is hurting itself but will threaten or attack socially aggressive monkeys. This tendency to autoaggression is established during the first two months of isolation and can be decreased or eliminated if soon after the first two months the monkey is placed in consistent contact with peers or, better still, with a receptive adult female monkey.

Comparisons between Animal Automutilation and Human Self-mutilation

In considering the comparability of automutilation in animals with self-mutilation in humans, the question of similarities in the behavior itself must be addressed. Clearly some mutilative behaviors appear identically in animals and humans. Mild acts such as hair pulling, head hitting, and skin scratching, for example, are seen in confined monkeys as well as in about 17 percent of normal children. More severe acts such as head banging, face slapping, eye and ear digging, and self-biting are seen in laboratory monkeys as well as in severely mentally retarded humans. Both humans and animals scratch, gouge, and bite accessible body tissue. Animals use their claws and large incisor teeth for automutilation; during the course of evolution humans have substituted tools, such as knives and razor blades. Thus, the behaviors appear to be comparable.

Some conditions that affect chemical and physiological functioning in the brain cause or facilitate auto- and self-mutilation. Both animals and humans may mutilate themselves as a response to drugs that affect the brain. Especially implicated are addictive drugs such as alcohol, amphetamine, caffeine, and heroin (human heroin addicts often become fascinated with the process of injecting themselves with a needle and sometimes can get "high" merely by sticking a needle into their arms). The mechanisms through which drugs cause or facilitate auto- and self-mutilation are unknown, but it is thought that they affect levels of neurotransmitters in various regions of the brain. The Lesch-Nyhan syndrome and, to a lesser degree, psychotic conditions such as schizophrenia, manic-depressive disorder, and major depression are associated with severe self-mutilation, and there is some evidence that neurotransmitter abnormalities also play a major role in these disorders.[2]

Although research on human brain functioning has advanced greatly through new technology, it is still far easier to conduct experiments on animals. Researchers hope eventually to discover the neurophysiological mechanisms that unleash mutilative behavior. It is very likely that the animal mechanisms will be comparable to those in humans. An interesting anecdote in this regard was told to me by a researcher working on anorexia nervosa, a syndrome in which persons starve themselves and, as is being reported more frequently, may indulge in self-mutilation. In an attempt to create an animal model for this disorder in rats the researcher destroyed a bit of brain tissue known as the locus cereuleus, a small, epinephrine-rich cluster of neurons in the brain stem (an abnormality of the locus cereuleus has been implicated in human anxiety disorders). The rats did, indeed, become anorexic but, in addition, displayed much automutilation.

Automutilation seems to be a device to increase or decrease levels of arousal. Monkeys that are highly aroused as manifested by agitation and

2. Although no animal models have been developed for schizophrenia or manic-depressive disorder, claims have been made that animals may develop severe depression although many authors are careful to use very precise language. Thus Moran and McKinney (1975) state that "assorted techniques have been developed by various researchers in an attempt to reproduce in non-human primates that state of despair and withdrawal that is labeled depression in human primates." One such technique is to confine monkeys in a steel vertical chamber designed to induce feelings of helplessness and hopelessness.

rage become calm following an act of automutilation. This sequence of events also occurs in many cases of human self-mutilation — persons report mounting tension and anger before the act and lowering of tension, even calmness, after it.

Monkeys, especially in isolation settings, may automutilate by engaging in "self-fighting" behavior and by attacking a limb that has "surprised" them. This behavior has been interpreted as autostimulation used to counteract low levels of arousal. As will be discussed in greater detail in subsequent chapters, human self-mutilation often serves to increase low arousal levels; for example, head banging in the mentally retarded and in sensory-deprived children may serve this purpose. Sociopaths may engage in stimulus-seeking behavior, including self-mutilation, in an attempt to counteract low cortical arousal levels. Human prisoners are especially prone to self-mutilation, although the social isolation of a prison cannot fully compare with the total isolation of experimental monkeys. Convicts frequently experience loneliness, alienation, and frustration in social relationships while living in overcrowded prisons. The notion that people can feel isolated even while in the company of other persons has been popularized in the concept of "the lonely crowd."

Many monkeys reared in social isolation become adult automutilators. The behavioral effects of early social isolation are probably due to a variety of mechanisms that include impaired learning of social skills, impaired ability to adapt to change (a consequence of perceptual-motor deficits resulting from a lack of critical experiences in early life), increased frustration, a tendency toward depression, and general developmental lag (McKinney 1974; Jones 1982). A large number of human self-mutilators report pathological childhood experiences, including physical and psychological abuse by parents and inadequate supplies of parental love, nurturance, and comforting physical contact. As children, self-mutilators often experience a sense of abandonment, of loneliness, and of unlovability, and they may carry these traits into adolescence and adult life. Loneliness is a common complaint among psychiatric patients, and relative social isolation during childhood along with a current inability to form close relationships is often reported by persons who deliberately injure themselves. According to Jones (1982), "This series of events — developmental isolation, bonding disturbance, and later predominant feelings of social isolation, loneliness, and anomie, with consequent frustration in interpersonal situations — is the sort of sequence that might be predicted from the animal model" (p. 146).

Many of the inferences we make about animal behavior indicate that it often may be identical to or very similar to human behavior, but the human capacity to utilize symbols and to communicate information about thoughts, emotions, and perceptions bespeaks a major problem in comparing human and animal behavior. Thus, comparative environmental and social studies, while instructive, are handicapped by the complexity of the human situation. It is in the area of animal biological studies that we can learn much about human self-mutilation. Here the problem does not rest so much in the differences between animals and humans but rather in the anatomical and functional complexity of the central nervous system itself.

Appendix

A number of publicly acclaimed books, such as Konrad Lorenz's *On Aggression* (1966), Desmond Morris's *The Naked Ape* (1967) and *The Human Zoo* (1969), and Eibl-Eibelsfeldt's *On Love and Hate* (1972), address animal aggression and its relationship to human aggression. As neatly summarized by Fromm (1973), these books draw a similar conclusion, namely, that "man's aggressive behavior as manifested in war, crime, personal quarrels, and all kinds of destructive and sadistic behavior is due to a phylogenetically programmed, innate instinct which seeks for discharge and waits for the proper occasion to be expressed" (p. 23). Presumably self-mutilation can be added to this list of humanity's aggressive behaviors.

Lorenz's work is of interest since so many subsequent ethological studies derive from his observations. Lorenz holds that animals are innately aggressive but not destructive, that an animal's aggression is predominantly directed toward competitive members of its own species, and that aggression is a positive force. The aggressive drive has important value for survival in that it functions to balance the distribution of animals of the same species over the environment and thus ensures an adequate food supply. Therefore, animals will claim a territory sufficient to meet their nutritional and other needs and will aggressively protect this territory from competitive animals. The aggressive drive also affects sexual selection; the strongest and fittest males will chase away their weaker rivals during the breeding season, gain access to females, and protect their offspring from predators. Another function of the aggressive drive is the development of a ranking order, "a principle of organization without which a more advanced social life cannot develop in high vertebrates. . . . Under this rule every individual in the society knows which one is stronger and which weaker than itself, so that everyone can retreat from the stronger and expect submission from the weaker if they should get in each other's way" (p. 40). The establishment of a ranking order provides peace and order within a group in that the dominant animals use their force to control intragroup fighting, to provide leadership against attacks by predators, to diminish group tensions by ensuring some sort of consistency, and even to serve as role models.

For Lorenz the aggressive drive is a species-preserving instinct, but the spontaneity of the instinct is what makes it dangerous, especially in humans. Aggression sometimes is a reaction to external factors, but it also may explode without demonstrable external stimulation; for example, when the central nervous system lowers the aggression threshold, or when the stimuli that normally release aggression fail to operate for an appreciable period of time, then an organism will search actively for a "missing stimulus" against which aggression can be unleashed. Lorenz holds that this process of unleashing dammed-up aggression becomes especially dangerous in situations where group members know each other well. He provides an example: a person sneezes in the presence of a close friend with dammed-up aggression. The friend may overreact to this trivial stimulus. In rare instances the friend may kill the person who sneezed; usually, however, the overreaction takes the form of a redirected activity in which the aggression is expressed by smashing some object. Likewise, one could develop a scenario in which a mentally ill person with dammed-up aggression responds to an irritating stimulus by redirecting aggression through the process of self-mutilation. Redirection of aggression is an evolutionary expedient for neutralizing aggression. A related mechanism is the display of an appeasing attitude; for example, a strong attacking animal will stop its attack if a weaker animal adopts a submissive, vulnerable posture. The ritualization of appeasement attitudes results in social bonding among animals. Lorenz notes that the personal bond of an individual friendship is formed only in animals with highly developed intraspecific aggression, that in many cases love develops through ritualization of a redirected attack, and that these rituals eventually assume an autonomous existence in which an aggressive animal's partner becomes highly valued. In the case of an imaginary stimulus such as a threatening auditory hallucination, the redirection of aggression onto the self (certainly the aggression cannot be directed physically against a hallucination) through self-mutilation may also be a type of appeasement attitude. By demonstrating their wounds and vulnerability, self-mutilators may hope to forestall further attacks against themselves. In some cases repetitive self-mutilation may represent an attempt to form a social bond with a perceived attacker such as a vicious cell mate in a prison. On an unconscious level, it may even represent an attempt to obtain a loving relationship with a parent.

While most scientists would agree that animals possess an aggressive instinct, a great many would not agree that irrational behavior in humans has phylogenetic origins or that behavioral principles derived from the study of animal instincts have any application to humans. Ashley Montagu's *Man and Aggression* (1973) contains twenty chapters by noted scholars, each of whom debunks the ethological concept of aggression as applied to humans. In Montagu's words, "There is, in fact, not the slightest evidence or ground for assuming that the alleged 'phylogenetically adapted instinctive' behavior of other animals is in any way relevant to the discussion of the motive-forces of human behavior. The fact is, that with the exception of the instinctoid reactions in infants to sudden withdrawals of support and to sudden loud noises, the human being is entirely instinctless. . . . That is not to say that man is born a *tabula rasa*. Clearly, the reason why man is not an ape is that he possesses genetic capacities, the result of a long and unique evolutionary history, which, under the appropriate environmental stimulation, enable him to function as a human being. The most important of these genetic capacities is that for learning, educability, literally the species trait of *Homo sapiens*. Man is capable of learning virtually anything" (p. 11). These critics go on to attack the concept of innate human depravity and aggressiveness and put forth the concept that human aggression is learned behavior. In Leon Eisenberg's eloquent words, "To believe that man's aggressiveness or territoriality is in the nature of the beast is to mistake all men for some men, contemporary societies for all societies, and, by a remarkable transformation, to justify what is as what needs must be; social repression becomes a response to, rather than a cause of, human violence" (p. 56).

The concept of a human aggressive instinct and, indeed, of aggression in general has been extremely problematic for psychiatrists. Alfred Adler first mentioned *Aggressionstrieb* (aggressive instinct) in 1908 in "The Aggressive Instinct in Life and in Neurosis," but Freud, in 1909, noted in his famous case of Little Hans that "I cannot bring myself to assume the existence of a special aggressive instinct alongside of the familiar instinct of self-preservation and sex, and on an equal footing with them." For a full explication of the Freudian concept of aggression I refer the reader to Fromm's *The Anatomy of Human Destructiveness* (1973). Suffice it to say that Freud adopted the term *Aggressionstrieb* and, in fact, used it as well as the terms *Destruktionstrieb* (destructive instinct) and *Todestrieb* (death instinct) with his dualistic theory of life and death instincts. In *Civilization and Its Discontents* he wrote, "Starting with speculations on the beginning of life and from biological parallels I drew the conclusion that, besides the instinct to preserve living substance, there must exist another, contrary instinct seeking to dissolve those units and to bring them back to their primaeval, inorganic state. That is to say, as well as Eros there was an instinct of death."

Freud placed the source of the death instinct within the individual constitution; that is, aggression is not reactive but innate. Thus life itself is a conflict and a compromise between the continuance of life and a striving toward death, between metabolism and catabolism. Although both Lorenz and Freud have proposed an innate aggressive (destructive) instinct, Fromm is correct in pointing out that the former's aggressive drive serves life, while the latter's death instinct serves death. Both Lorenz and Freud believed that failure to express aggression in action may result in pathology.

Most contemporary psychiatrists have discounted the Freudian notion of a death instinct, and the few that have written about ethology are quite cautious about drawing parallels with human behavior. One psychiatrist who has attempted to explain human aggressiveness on the basis of ethological concepts is Anthony Storr (1968). He notes that we now tend to "accept the idea that sex is an internal force which has to be satisfied." Satisfaction—the release of sexual tension—may be achieved best with the help of a partner but may also be obtained through masturbation. Since the physiological state of the body in both sexual and aggressive arousal is quite similar and since the sexual and aggressive instincts share certain components, Storr proposes the notion that, like sex, aggression is an internal force that has to be satisfied. The reduction of aggressive tension may be obtained through activities such as war, hunting, sports competition, initiation rites, and religious sacrifice. It seems to me that this argument could be extended to include self-mutilation. In fact, many persons describe themselves as filled with unbearable tension; an act of self-mutilation may lead to dissipation of this tension and to a feeling of relief. Thus, as a tension-relieving device, self-mutilation may be analogous to masturbation.

MUTILATION OF BODY PARTS:
CULTURAL AND CLINICAL CASES

II

—— —— —— —— —— —— —— —— ——

In this section, data on culturally sanctioned and deviant self-mutilation are presented according to the various body parts that are mutilated—the head and its subdivisions, the limbs, the skin and body, and the genitals. Using an anatomical model is more than a device that allows us to make sense of a wide array of mutilative practices. In fact, most culturally sanctioned self-mutilation focuses on a specific body area such as the skull or genitals. Similarly, most self-mutilative mentally ill persons tend to damage one body part such as the eye or the skin.

From a cultural perspective, rituals and practices involving the sanctioned destruction or alteration of specific body parts are examined. In some instances the mutilation is self-inflicted while in others individuals voluntarily allow themselves to be mutilated. In the case of infants and young children, parental consent is given in accord with social expectations. Relevant folkloric, literary, and mythological references to body parts are presented in addition to native and scientific explanations for the mutilative behavior. As will be seen, the selection of a specific anatomical part for mutilation is often intertwined with cultural concerns such as beauty and social status.

From a psychiatric perspective, cases are described in which self-mutilation is the product of mental illness. Whenever possible the self-mutilators' own statements about their behavior are presented, as well as psychiatric understandings of the behavior.

It is my contention that deviant self-mutilation can be understood most fully by examining the cultural context (historical and contemporary) in which it occurs. This section presents the data upon which the conclusions of the third section of this book are based.

5

The Head and Its Parts

The head is importantly associated with two major facets of human life: aesthetics and control. Although our perception of physical beauty involves the total human body, the head holds a preeminent place. A minor anatomical rearrangement, such as the crossing of an eye, the elongation of a nose, or an alteration in hairstyle, can change a person's appearance drastically and turn beauty into ugliness. It is not surprising that a number of cultural practices (head molding, ear piercing, lip stretching, etc.) are linked with aesthetics. Facial plastic surgery for reasons of vanity is a common practice in Western cultures.

The notion of the head as the locus of control of the body is probably related both to the presence of the brain within the skull and to the head's position atop the body. In a commonly used social metaphor a king, president, or chief is the head of his or her people and controls them just as the human head controls its body. The power to control others emanates from the mouth and eyes. From the mouth come words that can entreat, cajole, flatter, deceive, persuade, bless, and curse. From the eyes, according to a widespread and remarkably persistent folk belief, comes a potent evil force. When propelled by a glance, this evil force can cause sickness and misfortune in the person it strikes.

The mouth, nose, eyes, and brain are head parts that play a special role in the prevention and treatment of illnesses and in the remediation of sinful thoughts and deeds. The mouth can be used to confess sins and pathogenic secrets, to pray for forgiveness and deliverance, to invoke the healing intercession of beneficent spirits, to name and to cast out harmful spirits, and to engage in a talk cure with a therapist. Nose bleeding can be induced, often in imitation of female menstruation, in order to rid the body of deleterious poisons. Self-inflicted destruction of the eyes — perhaps the most highly prized body part — is a time-honored and efficacious method of obtaining relief from the guilt associated with a terrible thought or deed. In modern thought mental illness is, to a great extent, linked with chemical and structural defects in the brain. Among the procedures used to correct such defects are the administration of drugs and, more rarely, the surgical destruction of brain tissue. In past centuries mental illness was sometimes thought to result from pathological forces, such as evil spirits or humors, in the cranial cavity. One method of treatment was to drill holes into the skull in order to allow these forces to exit.

The Skull and Head

In this section three examples of culturally sanctioned mutilative practices involving the skull and head, namely, head molding, trephination, and head slashing, are presented. This is followed by a discussion of the most common form of deviant head self-mutilative behavior, head banging.

Head Molding

In ancient Egypt a powerful king, probably Akhenaton, was born with a distinctive head shape. In imitation, the Egyptian aristocracy placed constricting bandages around the heads of their infants to produce a head shape similar to that of the king. In fact, an infant's skull is quite soft and can be molded by techniques such as massage and the application of pressure with bandages, boards, and stones. Head shaping was a prerogative of the upper classes in Egypt, and it created an ideal of beauty and a mark of social status that was imitated for thousands of years. The skull shape of the beautiful Queen Nefertiti was clearly the product of molding. The process of head molding appears to have spread from Egypt throughout much of the world. In modern times the Nazis encouraged German parents to massage their children's heads in order to produce an "Aryan" type skull.

References to head molding are found in classical Greek literature. Zenobius described a group, the Syrakoi, who chose as their leader the man with the longest head. This group may have been the same as the Macrocephali, who were described by Hippocrates in *On Air, Land, and Water*. Hippocrates wrote, "There is no other race of men which have heads in the least resembling theirs. They think those the most noble who have the longest heads. . . . Immediately after the child is born, and while its head is still tender, they fashion it with their hands, and constrain it to assume a lengthened shape by applying bandages and other suitable contrivances whereby the spherical form of the head is destroyed, and it is made to increase in length."

Head molding was practiced throughout much of Europe, especially in Holland and France, until the middle of the nineteenth century. Although primarily a rural practice, it affected the urban population as well because of the custom of sending city children to the country to be reared.

In Normandy, handkerchiefs were tightly and painfully wound around the heads of children. Because these constricting bandages were rarely removed, they served as breeding grounds for lice and many of the children developed skin ulcers. In the regions of Limousin and Languedoc the molded heads of women were quite distinctive; the molding was caused by tight-fitting bonnets that produced a pleasing head shape and supposedly enhanced the development of those parts of the skull linked with intelligence and memory.

European head molding was greatly influenced by phrenology. In order to increase desired mental functioning, parents reshaped infants' heads. Thus, one advocate wrote, "Let it [the infant's head] therefore be longer, so that behind it may be elongated like the end of a gourd and then indeed a spacious court is opened where memory can rest" (Brain 1979, p. 100).

Achille Foville, a nineteenth-century physician who worked in several mental asylums in France, found that 247 out of 431 patients had deformed heads as a result of being forced to wear a constricting bandeau that flattened the upper part of the skull and deformed ear tissue. Foville pointed to a correlation between the severity of head deformation and the severity and intractability of mental symptoms in the patients. Many French physicians regarded head molding as medically dangerous and condemned the practice. They thought it played a part in the development of epilepsy, mental retardation, and chronic insanity (Dingwall 1931).

Various Asian groups have engaged in head molding, primarily for aesthetic reasons; for example, some Pathan groups in the Punjab flattened the back of children's heads and also tried to elongate their noses. Statues of Buddha often demonstrate a protuberance on the top of his skull. This protuberance is known as the Ushnisha and represents the bump of intelligence. Indian sculptors, such as those in Gandhara, were influenced by Greek artists in their portrayal of Buddha's head. Buddha's hair was portrayed as a type of chignon on the top of his head and eventually came to represent an actual part of his skull. This strange lump was revered as a manifestation of Supreme Enlightenment.

In Africa, head molding appears to have been influenced most directly by the Egyptian concept of beauty and social status. Many African statues of elongated heads are not the result of artistic conceits but rather reflect the actual shape (albeit somewhat stylized) of admired models. Head molding is still carried out in some areas of Africa, especially on female infants.

There are many reports of head shaping in the Pacific Islands. The natives of the southern part of Malekula developed a most peculiar circular, small head shape with a double depression in the upper part of the skull.

Capt. James Cook described these natives as "the most ugly, ill proportioned people I ever saw, and in every respect different from any we had met within this sea." Some early anthropologists, unaware that the natives deliberately created the head shapes by applying constricting bands, initially thought the Malekula skulls represented a special racial type. The Samoans used stones wrapped in cloth to flatten the foreheads and noses of children; for them, Western noses were quite ugly and were referred to as canoes.

The Maya Indians in Central America practiced head molding. By applying a flat board to the forehead they were able to cause the frontal bone to slant backward to such a degree that the nose and forehead formed a straight line. Head deformation was also found in Peru. In the late sixteenth century, the Spanish provincial governments in Peru passed many decrees forbidding the practice on the grounds that it was physically damaging to children. Myth has it that the custom of forming tapering, high, elongated heads arose from a native desire to resemble a holy volcano from which the tribes supposedly originated.

In North America the Chinook, or Flathead, Indians were the leading practitioners of head shaping. Immediately after birth infants were strapped on a board; a flat piece of wood was placed on their foreheads and tied tightly to the plank. A variation was to place a large board that extended from the infant's shoulders to a point above the skull and to tie it tightly to a smaller board that pressed on the forehead, thus flattening the forehead and forcing the head to rise at the top. The boards were kept in place for a year. A European observer described a child on such a contraption: "Its little black eyes, forced out by tightness of the bandages, resembled those of a mouse choked in a trap" (Dingwall 1931, p. 166). Another observer described a child whose head had just been removed from the apparatus as the most frightful and disgusting object he had ever seen. The frontal part of the skull was completely flattened, and the child's inflamed eyes protruded half an inch from the sockets. As the children grew up their heads did not appear to be grotesquely abnormal, except for a broad face. The Chinooks bought and captured many slaves who were readily distinguishable by their "ugly," round, natural heads.

Trephination

Trephination, the deliberate removal of bone from the skull, is an ancient surgical procedure that has persisted to current times. In posthumous trephination a circular portion of bone is removed from the skull, polished, and worn on a necklace as an amulet against evil spirits. This practice was popular in prehistoric Europe and has been reported in some parts of

Africa today. The vast majority of trephinations, however, were and are performed on living subjects. The antiquity of the procedure is established in
the writings of Hippocrates. Paleopathologists have recently uncovered an
Egyptian skull from early dynastic times as well as one from ancient Iran
that show evidence of trephine openings. Over one thousand trephined
skulls have been found in South America, especially in Bolivia and Peru.
Trephined skulls have been found throughout much of the world—the
islands of Oceania, France, Russia, Sweden, North Africa, and the Balkans.

The most common procedure was for a surgeon to cut through the scalp
and scrape the skull with a sharp tool. This is a relatively safe procedure as
long as the dura, the covering of the brain, is not exposed. More dangerous
and less frequently used procedures included sawing, cutting, or drilling directly into the skull and then breaking off the bone to remove a plug. From
evidence of healing in the area of the trephination, various estimates have
been made about the mortality rate of the procedure. Two large studies involving 214 and 400 Peruvian skulls demonstrated healing in 55.6 percent
and 62.5 percent, respectively. One skull showed healing from seven distinct operations. It is not uncommon today for persons in eastern Africa to
survive several trephinations.

In a variation of the procedure, known as the sincipital T, a groove was
cut in the skull along the sagittal suture. Most of the skulls showing evidence of this procedure have been found near Nantes, France. In the Middle
Ages in Europe the heads of some psychotic women were scarified to release noxious humors; the wound was then cauterized with a hot blade that
burned a T into the skull. In the sixteenth century, Paracelsus advocated
surgical opening of the head as a last resort to cure mania; the procedure
was designed to allow an exit for hot humors that caused insanity by touching the particles of the brain. It is interesting to note that itinerant char-
latans known as stone cutters flourished in Holland and Belgium in the
fifteenth and sixteenth centuries. They made small incisions in the heads of
the mentally ill and by sleight of hand pretended to remove head stones or
stones of folly, as demonstrated in paintings by Bosch and Breughel.

How and why humans first thought of putting holes in their heads are
unknown. One theory is that the practice arose from an ancient method of
treating sheep for the disease called "staggers," namely, opening the sheep's
skull and removing worm larvae from the brain of the animal. There are
Yugoslavian folkloric accounts of the removal of beetles from the human
brain and Tibetan stories about the removal of centipedes. A simpler explanation is that trephination was devised as a cure for headache, perhaps by
allowing evil spirits to exit. The primary indication for trephination among

the present-day Gusii of Kenya is posttraumatic headache. The Gusii "head surgeon" incises the patient's scalp, removes any bone fragments, foreign bodies, or clotted blood, and scrapes the skull with a sharp knife over areas of discolored bone or fracture line until the brain membranes are exposed. Some patients have multiple operations; these usually involve the enlargement of the first hole.

Coxon (1962) reported on trephination among the Kisii, a small, remote African tribe of cattle farmers. About thirty elders who have served an apprenticeship with tribal "surgeons" perform trephination as a hobby. A clear history of head trauma must be present, with or without subsequent severe headaches. The surgeons use centuries-old instruments, such as chisels and saws, and are careful neither to cross cranial suture lines nor to cut into the dura. Anesthesia consists of diverting patients' attention by poking their ears with thorns while relatives hold them down during the six-hour ordeal. The operation is performed without any ritual, and the surgeon receives a nominal fee, payable only if the patient is satisfied with the procedure. Some patients have multiple operations. "The Kisii must have set a record in one man who has survived thirty-five trephinings. Although he has little cranium left, with a tin hat and an unlimited supply of aspirins he is free from headache and a successful farmer" (p. 264). By carefully selecting their patients and by adhering closely to empirically derived surgical techniques, the surgeons rarely have any complications. In fact, should the patient die or become seriously ill, the surgeon faces imprisonment and even capital punishment because it is presupposed that he acted out of carelessness or stupidity.

A number of trephined skulls show evidence of fracture lines, thus indicating that the procedure was also used to relieve pressure on the brain. In fact, trephination was used by European surgeons to relieve pressure until better surgical methods were devised in the late eleventh century. In the mining districts of Cornwall, in England, surgeons continued to trephine until the late nineteenth century. Evidently many miners suffered head injuries in the narrow shafts (the caps they wore did not offer sufficient protection, and blasting devices to loosen the earth were quite crude), and surgeons there considered it good practice to drill holes in the skull even before symptoms of compression were present. Other therapeutic indications for trephination throughout the world include epilepsy, mental illness, vertigo, coma, and delirium. It reportedly was done in Melanesia to promote longevity.

In *Eccentric Lives and Peculiar Notions* (1984), John Mitchell recounts the story of a Dutchman, Dr. Bart Hughes, who developed a small following. In 1962, Hughes advocated trephination as a means of achieving a transcendent state. He theorized that a consequence of the evolutionary process of adopting an upright stance was a reduction in the flow of blood to the brain because of gravity; as a result humans have reduced the range of their consciousness and lost touch with the dreams and intense perceptions of childhood (a child's skull does not enclose the brain as tightly as an adult's). Hughes' solution was to drill a small hole in his head to allow for increased blood flow. Although he claimed a more complete and satisfying state of consciousness as a result of the procedure, he was involuntarily committed to a Dutch mental institution. His cause was taken up by a man named Joseph Mellen and his girlfriend, Amanda Fielding, who ran for Parliament in London; her political plank called for free trephination for everyone under the National Health Service plan. They both put holes in their heads but Amanda had the foresight to make a movie, called *Heartbeat in the Brain*, of her self-operation. In it she calmly applies an electric drill to her skull in order to remove a plug of bone. According to Mitchell the couple has lived and worked together in harmony ever since. They bought an art gallery, and "there is nothing apparently abnormal about them." They frequently lecture about the benefits of trephination and show the film of Amanda's self-operation to the accompaniment of a soothing musical soundtrack.

Head Slashing

As reported by Crapanzano (1973), the Hamadsha is a lower-social-class, religious, healing brotherhood in Morocco whose rituals are considered extreme by most other Muslim mystic groups. Their healing ritual includes drinking boiling water, eating spiny cactus, charming poisonous snakes, and head slashing with razors and knives during ecstatic trances induced by wild dancing.

The Hamadsha are curers of persons who are struck or possessed by Jinn spirits. The Jinn are capricious, quick-tempered, despotic, and dangerous spirits who sometimes assume human or animal forms. When insulted or injured, even inadvertently, they may retaliate by striking a person blind, deaf, mute, or paralyzed. Alternatively, they may enter and possess a person as manifested by symptoms such as unconsciousness, fainting, convulsions, tremors, talking in tongues, flights of thought, and abrupt, meaningless changes in activity or talk. Aisha Qandisha is a libidinous, quick-tempered Jinn who is extremely important to the Hamadsha. She strangles and scratches anyone who disobeys her; because of her fondness for blood she compels her followers to mutilate themselves.

The *hadra*, or healing ceremony, is designed to cure Jinn illness and to promote health through the acquisition of a miraculous saintly force called *baraka*. *Baraka* enables adepts, devotees, and patients to perform the healing ceremony, to enter a trance, and to slash their heads to please the spirits. The saint's *baraka* may be acquired when a patient eats or is smeared by the blood of an adept who is in a trance state.

The ceremony lasts from four to twelve hours and may be attended by forty-five to eighty men, women, and children. After invoking Allah, several musicians play loud, fast, violent music, and the men form a dance line. They jump up and down, hyperventilate, and punch themselves until a trance state is achieved. Occasionally a woman will enter a frenetic trance, screaming and charging around the dance area. She may convulse, scratch or slash her head with a knife, or even try to cut off a breast. Severe head mutilation, however, is more common among the men who enter a frenetic trance. With a pocketknife a man will slash his head until his face and shoulders are drenched with blood. Sometimes the gashes reach the skull, although usually the cuts are superficial. On special occasions, such as the healing ceremony that takes place on the sixth and seventh days after Muhammad's birthday, the Hamadsha slash their heads with single- or double-bladed axes and hit their heads with heavy iron balls and massive nail-studded clubs. They may see a vision of Aisha Qandisha slashing at her head, compelling the dancers to slash theirs and to calm the spirit by making their blood flow. They smear the blood from their head wounds on the ailing parts of a patient's body, or they may dip sugar cubes or bread in their blood and give it to the sick to eat. The dancers claim to feel no pain and to be unaware of their wounds until they have emerged from the trance.

Crapanzano's explication of how patients are cured by the Hamadsha details such factors as group support and cult membership, which afford the patient explanations of illness, new social status, an increased social network, and changed self-image and social identity. Achievement of a trance state increases suggestibility, allows partial erasure of old, learned behavior, and facilitates catharsis. The author interprets the mutilation as a symbolic castration. The men, he claims, conceive of illness at some level of consciousness as an inability to live up to the standards of male conduct. In order to be cured, a man becomes a woman through symbolic castration. Thanks to the *baraka* of the saint, he passes through a feminization stage, is revitalized, revirilized, and able to become a man again. In the process, Aisha Qandisha is transformed from a socially and morally disruptive force into one that preserves order and morality. That most Hamadsha patients periodically continue to perform the *hadra* and to slash their heads suggests, however, that cures are temporary and that there is no personality change of long standing.

Deviant Self-mutilation of the Skull

Although head banging is the most common form of self-mutilation involving the skull, mild head banging of a self-limited nature may be demonstrated by up to 6 percent of normal children, especially boys. It is often preceded by transient crib rocking or head-body rolling, behaviors thought to provide some reassurance to the frustrated child who is attempting to master a new stage of development. This "normal" head banging coincides with tooth eruption and with the change from sitting to crawling (ages 8 to 12 months). It may last for one to three years. Head banging past the age of 4 years is almost always pathological, is primarily found in psychotic or severely mentally retarded children, and may be associated with head punching and slapping, recurrent vomiting, and self-induced seizures.

Many reasons have been proposed to explain head banging, the most fanciful being that it is done to reexperience the comfort of hearing mother's heartbeat when being held in her arms. Other theories regard it as a means of obtaining adult attention, a response to fatigue, an autoerotic response to understimulation, and an expression of frustration and impotent anger. A traditional psychoanalytic concept holds that head banging is a form of aggression-turned-inward that is channeled and directed by the superego. There are, however, many reports of children who engage in head banging at an age prior to the development of the superego. Freud and Burlingham (1944) described a 14-month-old child who knocked her head violently when isolated in the empty sickroom. At 15 months, "when put into her crib for a nap against her wishes, she threw herself against the bars and banged her whole body as well as her head repeatedly. When other children took her toys or attacked her, she always banged her head in despair. At 16 months she threw herself on the floor and banged her head over and over again when not allowed to take another child's toy" (p. 74).

Collins (1965) described the case of a 26-year-old severely retarded man whose head banging had persisted since the age of 4. By the age of 22 he was confined to bed, where he wore a thick rubber collar and was fully restrained. When the restraints were removed, he would immediately attempt to smash his head on any available object or to hit it with his fist or knee. Even when wearing a football helmet with a face guard he would manage to contuse and lacerate his head. He demonstrated a monotonous, bland affect. The author interpreted the patient's head banging as "an effort to maintain a self-identity through constant reinforcement of the perception of the extent of his body—a most primitive and basic level of existence" (p. 209). Thus, the patient's perceptual world may have been diffuse, unintegrated with reality, and meaningless. It was thought that he was able to differentiate himself momentarily from the external world and to experience himself as a separate entity by banging his head. A treatment program was devised in which he was exposed to many stimuli, such as sound from a bedside radio, mobiles hung over his bed, perfumed soaps and lotions, spiced candy and gum, and regularly scheduled trips to the toilet. Two attendants spent time with him on walks and played and spoke with him. Within weeks his intense head banging subsided, and in a year he no longer required restraints. After four years he was able to participate in simple group games, to follow simple instructions, to withdraw from painful stimuli, and to show obvious joy and affection when visited by his mother.

Bates and Smeltzer (1982) reported the interesting case of a 25-year-old severely retarded man whose intense head banging began at age 2. Since age 9 he had been in a state mental institution. Every few years he suffered through prolonged episodes of insomnia, weight loss, hyperactivity, and terrible head banging. For unknown reasons he would fling aside his protective helmet and suddenly bang his head against a wall in a staccato frenzy (once measured at three hundred blows in five minutes); often he bloodied his head before being restrained, and twice he knocked himself unconscious. Medications including sedatives, major tranquilizers, and lithium were ineffective, as were behavioral extinction programs. At age 21 his behavior and other symptoms were life threatening. He flung himself against walls and floors, butted staff with his head, bit his lips, lacerated himself with his fingernails, and beat his knees together until they bled. He developed a staggering gait, a Babinski sign, a loss of fine motor control in his hands, a rapid pulse rate of 120/minute, a marked weight decrease, and rapid fluctuations in the size of his pupils. Comprehensive tests were all within normal limits. Since nothing seemed to help and since he had a family history of manic-depressive illness, electroconvulsive therapy was performed. After six treatments over a two-week period the patient's symptoms came under control, as did his attempts at self-mutilation. Maximum benefits were achieved after six more treatments, and the patient did quite well. When symptoms returned in several months, they were then controlled by lithium and a major tranquilizer. At the time of the report the patient had been under control for three years, although his symptoms reemerged whenever attempts were made to lower the dose of either medication.

Baroff and Tate (1968) described the case of a 9-year-old psychotic boy with a five-year history of head hitting so severe that he suffered a detached retina and blindness. Treatment consisted of jolting him with an aversive stimulus—an electric cattle prod—whenever he banged his head. The results were dramatic: "In short, a pattern of self-injurious behavior which had existed for more than five years, had resulted in blindness in one eye, and had been completely refractory to standard forms of treatment, was interrupted literally in minutes, reduced to non-injurious minimum within days, and all but disappeared in five months" (p. 464).

Although these cases had successful long-term therapeutic outcomes, most reported cases of severe head banging record limited therapeutic successes. A discussion of behavioral treatment approaches for head banging and other behaviors is presented in chapter 11.

Although most reports of self-mutilation of the head by the mentally ill deal with specific organs, such as the eye or the tongue, rather than the head itself, a case described by Sinclair (1886–87) tells of a 25-year-old delusional man who had "recurring attacks of acute insanity" manifested especially by self-mutilative tendencies. While in the hospital he cut out his left testicle with a nail, claiming that it belonged to another patient. Five months later he excised his remaining testicle and ate it "to prevent anyone else getting it." Whenever possible he would scratch himself with pieces of wood, stone, or glass. He placed a nail against his forehead, hit it in with his hand, and drove it all the way into his skull by banging his head against the wall. Hospital staff noticed only a superficial scratch which he said was caused by a belt buckle. Two months later he became very ill and told the staff about the nail. It was surgically removed with difficulty, but the patient died the next day. On autopsy it was discovered that the nail had reached the frontal lobe, resulting in a large cavity filled with blood, pus, and broken-down brain tissue.

The Eyes

The only organs of the human body that have not been subjected to voluntary, ritual mutilation are the anus and the eyes. The anus probably has been spared because it responds to wounds angrily, and its refusal to heal often results in chronic inanition. The eye probably has been spared because it is the most intellectually valuable and magically endowed human organ. Anatomically the eye is unique in that it grows out from the brain, and thus it is the only portion of the central nervous system directly in contact with the outside world.

In mythology, folklore, and literature a host of often contradictory attributes are linked to the eyes. Thus, the eyes may be associated with creativity or with destruction, with purity or with shame and guilt, with love or with sexual transgression. As will be shown in the clinical section, these attributes of the eyes often are significant factors in deviant self-mutilation.

The eye was a potent force in Egyptian mythology. From the eyes of Ptah, the gods were created. Ra, the supreme sun god, rested with his eyes shut in the primordial ocean. He then arose, opened his eyes, and created the universe. When he grew old and senile, ambitious men plotted against him. In anger he sent his Divine Eye to slaughter them.

Horus was the name given to over twenty Egyptian gods. The earliest Horus was a falcon-headed god whose eyes were the sun and the moon (the hieroglyph for *god* is a falcon). Horus the Elder was the god of the sky. He was the son of Ra and brother of the evil Set. In the horrible battles between Horus and Set, between the forces of good and those of evil, Set plucked out Horus's eye and plunged humankind into chaos. Horus retaliated by emasculating Set. Horus the Younger was a god who eventually took over all the attributes of the previous Horuses. As the final conqueror of Set, Horus the Younger, with his powerful eye in place, restored order to the universe and brought peace to the world.

Siva is a major Hindu god worshiped both for his strict asceticism and for his generative powers. His character is one of contrasts between creation and destruction, good and evil. When Siva was meditating on a mountain, his wife playfully placed her hands over his eyes. The world immediately became dark, and its inhabitants shook with fear. But then a third eye appeared flaming in Siva's forehead and relit the world.

Hindu mythology contains one of the most bizarre stories about the eye. The god Indra desired the beautiful wife of Gotama. He obtained the help of Chandra, the moon, who took the form of a cock and crowed at midnight. Gotama thought it was time for his morning devotions and went to the riverside, leaving his wife alone. Indra sneaked into her bedroom and had intercourse with her. Upon discovering the deception, Gotama cursed Indra, and Indra's body was covered with a thousand openings like the female vulva to remind him of his sinful deed. Later, these openings were changed into eyes. Indra's eye-covered body is frequently depicted in drawings.

Another interesting Indian legend, this one of Buddhist origin, concerns Kunala, the son of the great king Asoka. After Asoka's wife died, he married a dissolute and unprincipled young woman. She lusted for Kunala, a handsome young man who was famous for the beauty of his eyes. When he rejected her advances, she became hateful and arranged to have him sent to a distant province. She forged the king's seal and sent a dispatch ordering that Kunala's eyes be plucked out. The order was obeyed, and the prince wandered the countryside as a beggar and minstrel. He eventually traveled to his father's court, where he was recognized. When King Asoka discovered what had happened, he burned his wife alive, punished all officials associated with the outrage, and either massacred all of the common people or transported them to the desert. He called upon a saint and prayed that Kunala's sight be restored. The saint assembled a great congregation and collected their tears in a vase. He said that if everything he had expounded about Buddha's writings was true, Kunala's sight would be restored after washing his eyes in the vase full of tears. Kunala washed his eyes in the tears and received back his sight.

I am indebted to B. B. Sethi, professor at King George's Medical College, in Lucknow, India, for providing two more examples from Hindu mythology in which religious figures enucleated an eye in order to please a god. Lord Rama wished to offer one hundred lotus flowers to the goddess Durga. He had only ninety-nine flowers, however, so he removed one of his eyes and offered it in place of the missing flower. Another story involves Soordas, a devotee of Lord Krishna. Once he actually saw Lord Krishna, and in order to preserve that wonderful sight in his mind he enucleated both his eyes. Soordas, in fact, literally means "blind disciple."

In Greek mythology the Cyclopes were one-eyed creatures. Homer portrayed them as lawless, ugly giants who killed and ate any stranger who dared come near their caverns in Sicily. The Cyclops named Polyphemus captured Odysseus and his companions, who escaped by blinding the giant with a hot stake. Medusa (also known as Gorgo) was a hideous monster with snakes instead of hair. Anyone who looked into her eyes immediately turned to stone. She was beheaded by Perseus. The blood from one of her veins was used by Asclepius to revive the dead; the blood from another of her veins was used to harm men.

The myth of Oedipus, especially as told by Sophocles, is the most famous of all self-mutilation stories. Oedipus unwittingly killed his father and married and sired children by his mother, Jocasta. When the truth became known, Jocasta hanged herself, and Oedipus blinded himself by sticking her golden brooches through his eyes:

> "Wicked, wicked eyes!" he gasps,
> "You shall not see me nor my shame—
> Not see my present crime.
> Go dark, for all time blind

To what you should have never seen. . . ."
And the bleeding eyeballs gushed and stained his beard.

In the Old Testament, Lot was rescued from the barbaric lust of the Sodomites when angels struck them blind (Gen. 19:11). In another story, the king of the Ammonites would spare his enemies only if they agreed to let him bore out their right eyes (1 Sam. 11:2); their blindness would then serve as a badge of slavery and would prevent them from fighting effectively. Eye mutilation within the Christian tradition has been granted legitimacy by several New Testament admonitions. Mark 9:47-48 notes: "If your eye is your downfall, tear it out! Better for you to enter the kingdom of God with one eye than to be thrown with both eyes into Gehenna, where the worm dies not and the fire is never extinguished." Matthew 5:28-29 states the same theme: "What I say to you is: anyone who looks lustfully at a woman has already committed adultery with her in his thoughts. If your right eye is your trouble, gouge it out and throw it away! Better to lose part of your body than to have it all cast into Gehenna." Matthew continues, in 6:22-23: "The eye is the body's lamp. If your eyes are good, your body will be filled with light: if your eyes are bad, your body will be in darkness. And if your light is darkness, how deep will the darkness be."

The oldest story of a person who removed an eye in accordance with Mark's and Matthew's admonitions is told in book 1, chapter 9, of Marco Polo's *Travels* (circa A.D. 1300). The Calif of Baghdad threatened Christians in that city. Unless they could literally move a certain mountain by virtue of their faith, they could choose either to be put to death or to convert to Islam. They turned to a pious, one-eyed Christian cobbler who proceeded to save their lives by causing the mountain to move. Years earlier the cobbler had voluntarily scooped out his eye in obedience to Matthew's injunction because he experienced lustful thoughts when he accidentally viewed the leg of a beautiful woman who had come to his shop. Marco Polo then commented: "By this act you can judge the excellence of his Faith."

In Christian tradition the lives of the saints, often embellished by regional folklore, were presented as models of comportment. Gradually saints with special characteristics were selected as patrons for specific diseases. Saint Lucy became the patron saint of eyes. She was born in Syracuse, Sicily, in about A.D. 283. She decided to consecrate her chastity to God and to disperse her wealth among the poor, much to the displeasure of her mother. Her mother finally accepted Lucy's wishes, but unfortunately she had already betrothed Lucy to a pagan youth. He was angered and reported

Lucy as a Christian to the governor of Sicily. She was found guilty and sentenced to a life of prostitution. When she refused to comply she was tortured, possibly blinded, and finally killed. Several centuries later a legend about her eyes became popular. In this legend a young man fell deeply in love with her and was especially attracted by her beautiful eyes. Mindful of her vow of chastity she cooled the young man's ardor by cutting out her eyes and sending them to him on a plate, a scene depicted by many artists. Her suitor was converted to Christianity, and Lucy's eyes were restored to her, more beautiful than ever.

The concept of the evil eye—the belief that a harmful force may be projected from the eye of a person or an animal—is frequently alluded to in the Bible. Proverbs 23:6, for example, notes: "Eat not thou the bread of him that hath an evil eye, neither desire thou his dainty meats." The origins of the belief in the evil eye, however, are prebiblical and widespread throughout Europe, the Near East, and the Indian subcontinent. Among the disorders attributed to the evil eye are disrupted social relationships, diarrhea, vomiting, anorexia, insomnia, impotence, sudden death, hypochondriasis, depression, headaches, malformed fetuses, colic, cataracts, nystagmus, failure to thrive in children, persistent yawning and hiccups, inflammation of the eye, ophthalmia in newborn children, fevers, and epidemic diseases such as plague, smallpox, and cholera. Additionally, the evil eye supposedly can cause spoilage of crops, accidental injuries, and illness in animals. In fact, the fourth century Council of Elvira in Spain prohibited Jews from staring at Christian crops for fear the crops would wither (a German word for evil eye is *Judenblick*, or Jew's glance).

Persons thought to be particularly susceptible to injury by the evil eye are pregnant women, children, nursing mothers, the wealthy, and anyone who is admired. Persons considered most likely to possess the evil eye are strangers, hunchbacks and others with physical deformities, eccentrics, and anyone who is envious of others. A literary portrayal of a *jettatore* (a person who possesses the lifelong ability to inflict the evil eye) can be found in *Le Corricole*, a minor novel by Alexander Dumas *fils*. Protection against the evil eye often takes the form of amulets, such as the red chili-horn, red ribbons, and pieces of metal. In some groups, children have dirt rubbed on their faces to detract from their beauty, thus making them less likely targets of the evil eye. A person afflicted by the evil eye may remove it by participating in rituals, for example, dropping oil in water and reciting, "Who has fascinated you? The eye, the thought, and the evil desire. Who will remove the fascination? The Father, the Son, and the Holy Ghost." A most unneighborly type of treatment is to throw the oil-water mixture onto a path in the hope that the evil eye will be removed from the afflicted person by attaching itself to the next person who walks along the path.

For thousands of years the concept of the evil eye was thought to be based upon scientific fact. The Greeks, for example, believed that vision flowed out from the eyes just as lantern light flows out from a candle. Plutarch drew an analogy between the voice that emanates from the mouth and the rays that emanate from the eyes; just as words can influence others for better or worse, so too can the eyes' rays. Montaigne's essay "The Power of Imagination" contains the following statement: "Imagination not only acts on one's own body but on the bodies of others, and thus one body may inflict injuries on his neighbor, as is apparent from the plague, smallpox, and the evil eye, which are sent from one to another." The "scientific" theory that one can emit poison from one's eyes and cause it to enter another's eyes by uttering words of praise was proposed in 1550 by Hieronymus Fracastorius: "For praise creates a peculiar pleasure and pleasure in turn opens the heart, the face and especially the eyes so that the closed doors are opened to receive the poison. . . . Therefore, it is most proper whenever we intend to praise a person, we add, 'May it be of no injury to you!'" In *Minor Morals*, Francis Bacon noted, "It seems some have been so curious as to note the times when the stroke or percussion of an envious eye does hurt, and particularly when the party envied is beheld in glory and triumph."

Although legends about eyes abound throughout the world, the English story of Lady Godiva and Peeping Tom is paradigmatic of stories in which lust is punished by blindness. In this legend, Lady Godiva of Coventry begged her husband to lower the high taxes that caused the townspeople so much suffering. He agreed to do so only if his wife would ride naked on her horse through the town. To his surprise, she agreed to his condition. She then ordered the populace to shutter their windows and not look upon her during the ride. Tom the tailor, however, peeped at her and was immediately struck blind.

Clinical Cases of Eye Mutilation

Quoi qu'il en soit, l'automutilation oculaire, si l'on en croit les confidences des aliénistes, est moins rares qu'elle ne le paraît.

A. Terson, 1911

Deliberate eye mutilation is not a common event, but neither is it rare. In talking with psychiatrists and ophthalmologists I have come to believe that the actual number of cases of deviant eye mutilation is much greater than the number of published cases. During a two-year period in the 1980s, for example, I interviewed four psychotic persons at the University of Missouri Hospital who had enucleated an eye. Assuming my experience is not unique, I estimate that about five hundred cases of eye enucleation occur each year in the United States. I also estimate that the incidence of milder forms of eye mutilation, such as the deliberate placing of noxious substances into an eye, greatly exceeds that of self-enucleation.

In tracing case reports from 1846 to the present, I found that eye mutilation is associated with many different psychiatric conditions. What follows is a presentation of cases that have been reported in the medical literature as well as of cases that have not been published. Beginning with organic mental disorders, I examine schizophrenic, affective, anxiety, somatoform, factitious, and personality disorders. In these cases I have tried to deduce the most appropriate diagnosis, a task complicated by changing symptomatology and methods of reporting over the years. Also, I have categorized cases with multiple diagnoses under what the author of the original article or I considered to be the principal one.

The term *organic mental disorder* implies a transient or permanent change in brain tissue and neurochemical or neurophysiological processes that results in symptoms such as disordered behavior, thoughts, and emotions. The expression of these symptoms is influenced by a person's psychological condition as well as by the social and cultural milieus. The basic syndromes associated with organic mental disorders are delirium, dementia, memory impairment, persistent or recurrent hallucinations, delusional thinking, major mood disturbances, and marked personality changes. As demonstrated by the following cases, the reported causes of organic mental disorders involving eye mutilation include syphilis of the central nervous system, encephalitis, drug and alcohol withdrawal and intoxication, encephalopathy, and dementia. (For cases in addition to those described here, see Fulton 1887; Despagnet 1893; Axenfeld 1899; Soebo 1948; Gerhard 1968; Rosen 1972.)

A 52-year-old man ordered his wife and children to dance, pray, and act in a religious manner. He then went to a convent, said God ordered him to do so, and refused to leave. He was forcibly taken to a hospital, where he demonstrated delusions of grandeur, religious exaltation, irritability, and excited behavior. He stuck his fingers in his eyes and displaced them out of their sockets. He said the voice of God told him that he had sinned and demanded that he tear out his eyes because he had seen the nakedness of his daughter. The rapid onset of dementia ensued (Goffin 1887).

A 16-year-old girl with an eight-year history of chronic encephalitis was found holding her right eye in her hand. She told the nurse that the eye had spontaneously fallen out of her head while she was sleeping. The patient seemed indifferent to the incident and did not complain of pain. Two hours later, she shouted and said that her left eye, which was found on her bed, had also fallen out. She initially denied gouging out her eyes, but several months later she said she felt "hypnotized" at the time and that an irresistible urge made her do it. She also admitted that some peculiar force had caused her to extract some of her teeth over the years and to bite her tongue (Goodhart and Savitsky 1933).

A 36-year-old man was thrown into jail because he had been on an alcoholic debauch for several days. On the first night he tore both eyeballs from their sockets. Until a few months prior to the episode he had been a man of good habits (Fulton 1887).

A 34-year-old chronic alcoholic felt sick from drinking too heavily and demanded that his mother get some medicine for him. When she left to go to the store, the patient was alone for fifteen minutes with his 8-year-old niece. He sexually assaulted the girl, killed her, and then shot himself in the eye with a pistol. He developed total amnesia for his actions. The author concluded that "his own right eye was shot out as a self-castration punishment for his sexual and homicidal crime" (Lewis 1928, p. 180).

A 21-year-old woman was hospitalized because of agitation, auditory hallucinations, and ideas of reference. She gashed her left cornea with a piece of glass and burned her right cornea with a cigarette. She repeatedly said, "I'm evil because my eyes can hurt you." In the years prior to hospitalization she changed her life-style from that of an "all-American girl" to one of macrobiotics, illicit drug use, and Eastern philosophies. In the week prior to her eye mutilation she used amphetamines and marijuana heavily (Westermeyer and Serposs 1972).

An 18-year-old youth with no previous psychiatric history was found wandering in the street nude with his right eyeball in his hand. He had taken LSD for four consecutive days, during which he was forced into a homosexual episode. He then felt that he was going to die, that the devil controlled his mind, and that he should obey the Bible and pluck out his eye because he had offended God. He said, "My mind was so weak because of the LSD that the devil possessed me. Now I've got the devil out of my mind since I plucked my right eye out" (Rosen 1972, p. 1109).

A 35-year-old man blinded himself during a cocaine-induced psychotic episode in order to rid himself of terrifying visual hallucinations (Wurfler 1956).

A 16-year-old boy with a two-year history of heavy, mixed drug abuse was in an automobile with his mother on his way to admission at a psychiatric hospital. During the lengthy trip, the boy purchased a number of nasal inhalers and swallowed the medication in them in order to feel "high." They stopped at a restaurant, but the boy remained in the car where he masturbated while his mother went to eat. When she returned ten minutes later, he screamed, "I did it, I did it! I have to get my balls out." A few seconds later he gouged out his eyeball shouting, "I have to get my eyeball out." At the hospital he was judged psychotic. Although amnesic for the event, the boy remembered a voice telling him, "If thy right eye offend thee, pluck it out." The hospital staff thought that his mother was also "presumably psychotic" and that the boy had a symbiotic relationship with her. It was assumed that the boy developed sexual fantasies about his mother while in the close confines of the car. Because these fantasies were totally unacceptable to him, he displaced them to his eyeball. By removing his eye he was able to remove his fantasy (Carson and Lewis 1971).

A 20-year-old man, who had abused various street drugs in his teens (and who had a probable borderline personality), became preoccupied with lustful thoughts and with the Bible for several weeks prior to hospitalization. One night he ingested phencyclidine, and he experienced dysphoria, hallucinations, altered perception and judgment, and loss of motor control for several hours. Early the next morning he decided that the text of Matthew 5:28–30 applied to him, and he proceeded to rupture the globe and severely damage the ocular tissue and optic nerve of his right eye with his fingers. He assumed a Christlike physical appearance and maintained that since losing his eye he had improved his self-control and no longer had lustful thoughts (Moskovitz and Byrd 1983).

A 56-year-old man with severe diabetic renal damage and retinopathy experienced severe pain in his left eye. As a result of marked uremia, his mental capacity was impaired, and he slashed his left eye with a knife in an attempt to control the pain (Brown 1970).

An 85-year-old demented woman who was hospitalized for gastritis and anemia suddenly gouged out her eyes. In response to questions she simply replied, "Why are you bothering me?" (Malavitis, Arapis, and Stamatinis 1967).

Schizophrenic disorders are characterized by deterioration in functioning and by symptoms such as delusions, illogical thinking, loosening of associations between one thought and another, hallucinations, blunted or inappropriate affect, disturbed sense of self, impairment in goal-directed activity, decreased involvement with the external world, and unusual behaviors including stupor, rigid posture, purposeless excited movements, and grimacing. No single symptom is invariably present or seen only in schizophrenia. The following is a sample of cases of eye mutilation in schizophrenic patients, many of whom admitted to being inspired by the Bible and were preoccupied with the supernatural and with sexuality. (For cases in addition to those described here, see Nettleship 1886; Kayser 1918; Lewis 1928; Marx and Brocheriou 1961; Gorin 1964; Brown 1970; Shore, Anderson, and Cutler 1978; Yang, Brown, and Magargal 1981; Arons 1981; Stannard et al. 1984.)

A middle-aged woman who thought that she came from heaven and that Jesus Christ was her father was hospitalized. She often had auditory hallucinations, and she imagined that electrical impulses were passing through the wall into her body. In subsequent years she had periods in which she soiled herself, destroyed clothing and shoes, and threw things out of the window. She then developed ideas of death. She tried to cut out her womb, but failed. She repeatedly quoted, "If thine eye offend thee, pluck it out," and tried to enucleate her eyes with her fingers and a nail file. She also tried to tear out her umbilicus and one of her teeth (Lewis 1928).

A 24-year-old man was in jail for parole violation. He claimed that he saw differently from each eye and that his left eye offended him. After reading Matthew's words in the Bible and seeing a vision of Christ and a "gold ball" in front of his left eye, he pulled the eye out in order to "purify himself." He stated that he belonged to the "youthful cosmically enlightened movement." Although he had planned to cut off his arm "to quiet his mother," he decided to take out his eye because hate rays were emanating from it. After the act he developed a Christlike affect and claimed that he was cleansed, at peace, and happy. He dated the onset of his problem to a period two and a half years earlier when he freely used LSD and marijuana (Brown 1970).

A 19-year-old girl had become psychotic three years earlier when she was rejected by a young man with whom she fell in love at a transcendental meditation camp. She thought that he was following her and that her parents were plotting against her. She started wearing dark glasses with reflecting lenses to hide her eyes. Despite psychiatric treatment she slashed her throat in a suicide attempt and beat her face in order to destroy her eyes. During hospitalization she proclaimed that something was wrong with her parents and jabbed at her eyes with a pen. She stated, "The radio said people would be better off if I were blinded." She intermittently attacked her eyes, saying such things as, "Everything I do is bad," and "Don't torture anybody but me." She said voices were controlling her. When a violent patient on the ward was put in seclusion, she again began to scratch her eyes. During the next seven months her condition improved, and she made no further attempts to harm herself (unpublished case of Dr. Paul Horton 1971).

A 36-year-old man with a history of chronic schizophrenia appeared before a nurse on the hospital ward holding his neatly dissected left eye in his hand. He stated that he had enucleated the eye because he wanted to "change" and to "save" the world, and because he could not find instruments for cutting off his genitals. At age 23 he had begun to deteriorate psychologically as manifested by restlessness, anxiety, numerous physical complaints, threats toward his sister, and fears that people could read his thoughts, especially his thoughts about homosexuality. He had several hospitalizations for psychosis and was constantly bothered by religious, philosophical, and sexual thoughts; for example, he feared he was turning into a woman. Through a woman friend he became involved with a religious sect. He became convinced that he heard the voice of the Lord and that he would be able to talk with his dead father if he devoted his life to God. In discussing this case, the authors equated the patient's eye enucleation with symbolic castration (MacLean and Robertson 1976).

An 18-year-old college freshman with no previous psychiatric history became increasingly withdrawn and preoccupied with religious ideas. He proclaimed himself an evangelist and began to sell his possessions. He ineptly acted out his homosexual fantasies within the dormitory, causing anxiety among the other students. When they rejected him, he felt guilty and became obsessed with a desire to expiate his sins. He drove to an isolated place, tied a tourniquet around his arm, and sawed off his hand with a hacksaw. He threw the hand into the lake and then removed his eye with a screwdriver. He walked back to the dormitory and was taken to a hospital where he described his emotional state as free of pain, at peace with himself, and Christlike. He said that his actions were a mission for God. He was successfully treated and two months later was discharged from the hospital (Goldenberg and Sata 1978).

A 24-year-old man had served time in prison for arson, rape, and other crimes. He said that he had been sodomized by an inmate in prison and that he had cut his wrists and blinded one eye in order to get transferred to a psychiatric hospital. He was hospitalized because he had slashed his remaining eye with a razor blade in the belief that blindness would eliminate his anxiety about looking at people and would allow him to be a successful musical entertainer. On the ward he claimed that he was Jesus, and he was preoccupied with the size of his penis (Crowder et al. 1979).

A 25-year-old man blinded himself by attempting to scratch out his eyes while sitting quietly in a park. He calmly stated that "God told me to, to prevent people suffering." He claimed that God had talked with him, and he believed that he possessed some of the features of Jesus. During hospitalization he was restless, heard voices, tried to grasp "white birds flying around my head," and claimed that his eyes were healed. He improved with treatment but was unwilling to talk about his self-injury. Three months earlier he had received treatment because he was eating his feces and acting belligerently (Tapper, Bland, and Danyluk 1979).

A 39-year-old single man took out his right eye with his fingernail in obedience to Matthew's biblical injunction. He claimed that voices of devils, angels, and persons he had formerly known commented on his behavior in an accusatory tone and commanded him to injure his remaining eye. He believed that he had stolen the soul of a nurse seven years previously and that she exerted great control over him. He also believed that he possessed both male and female sexual organs and that he produced numerous babies daily (Ananth, Kaplan, and Lin 1984).

Major depression and manic-depressive illness are *affective disorders*. Major depression is characterized by symptoms such as depressed mood, appetite and sleep disturbances, feelings of worthlessness and excessive, inappropriate guilt, agitation or psychomotor retardation, and recurrent thoughts about death and suicide. Delusions and hallucinations may be present that often focus on themes of guilt, punishment, disease, and death. The following is a sample of cases of major depression involving eye-mutilation. (For additional cases, see Ideler 1871; Adam 1883; Martinenq and Cortyl 1884; MacKinlay 1887; Axenfeld 1899; Lafon 1907; Holloway 1911; Gifford 1955; Byrnes 1949; Wackenheim, Becker, and Nevers 1956; Wilson 1955; Dollfus and Michaux 1957; Brown 1970; Bowen 1971; Arons 1981.)

A 48-year-old widow with a melancholy temperament wanted people to atone for their sins, and she accused herself of being a great sinner. She was hospitalized after acting bizarrely; for example, she went naked into the street and asked various men, including her minister, to marry her. While in the hospital she felt that her eyes were sinful because they had looked at worldly things. After reading Matthew's words in the Bible she took out both of her eyes and asked the doctor to cut off her legs and feet. She felt that since Christ shed his blood she must shed her blood in order to become saintly (Bergmann 1846).

A 41-year-old woman with a sad temperament had burned herself with candles and had tried to throw herself out of a window several years earlier. Following discovery of her husband's conjugal deceptions, she became profoundly depressed and developed a desire to suffer and to offer her sufferings to God. She was hospitalized, and while in a delirious state she ablated both of her eyes. One eye was found under her bed, the other eye on it. She was incoherent for two days, then she became calm and affable and regretted her actions (Terson 1911). In discussing the case, Terson referred to Blondel's thesis on self-mutilation (1906) in which seven cases of eye enucleation were listed. In five of the cases, the mutilation was performed by middle-aged women with a psychiatric diagnosis of Cotard's syndrome, which is characterized by melancholy, anxiety, thoughts of damnation and madness, propensity toward suicide and self-mutilation, and thoughts of negation, nonexistence, and annihilation. Terson noted that his patient did not have Cotard's syndrome; rather, he stressed the importance of paroxysmal delirium and of eye mutilators' need for expiation and martyrdom. He further noted that Blondel's use of the term *oedipism* to describe self-enucleators was not precise because Oedipus was not mentally ill when he took out his eyes.

A 50-year-old man became depressed with paranoid ideas following the death of his mother. He claimed that he saw the devil and that he had to atone for the sin of committing incest. He then took out an eye with his fingers (Harrer and Urban 1950; this article contains an interesting bibliography, especially of German works on self-mutilation).

A 44-year-old Egyptian immigrant from a strict Christian culture tried to scratch out his eyes because of guilt over going to topless nightclubs. Three years later he became agitated and preoccupied with religious thoughts. He said that a statue of Saint Mary commanded him to cleanse himself of sin by taking out his eyes. He was hospitalized after attempting to remove his eyes with a forceps. During psychological testing the next day, he shoved the test pencil into his left eye. He repeatedly attempted to take out his eyes for a week. He gradually improved with treatment, however, and was discharged six weeks later (Crowder et al. 1979).

A 28-year-old man was jailed for parole violations. During the two previous months he had become increasingly depressed and guilty over his antisocial behavior and over his mother's death (he felt responsible for her lung cancer). His woman friend had become increasingly religious, had threatened to leave him if he did not stop drinking, and had recently visited her ex-husband. In jail he did not interact much with his cell mates, and his depression deepened. He felt that he was the world's worst sinner and was Satan incarnate. He thought about having killed birds as a youngster, using his right eye to focus the gun, and about having sexually abused his sisters. He read the Bible constantly. After reading Matthew's words, he believed that God was telling him to remove his eyes to atone for his sins. While contemplating this he noticed a bird outside the window; for him this was confirmation of God's will that he remove his eye. He inserted his fingers into his socket, pushed out his eye, threw it on the floor, and fainted (unpublished case of Drs. A. Favazza and M. Jayaratna 1982).

Manic-depressive illness (bipolar disorder) is another affective disorder characterized by symptoms such as elated mood, increased activity, distractibility, and inflated self-esteem. Delusions and hallucinations may be present that often focus on themes of power, privileged knowledge, and a special relationship with a deity or famous person. These manic symptoms may alternate with symptoms of major depression. The following cases demonstrate eye mutilation during mania. (For additional cases, see Dehn 1894; Axenfeld 1899.)

A 26-year-old woman bit a large piece out of her tongue and was hospitalized for acute mania. She claimed God had ordered her to mutilate herself. A year earlier her 22-year-old brother was hospitalized with similar symptoms; additionally, he had gouged out his eye. Over the next twelve years she was hospitalized several times for mania and for mutilative tendencies. She claimed on various occasions that God ordered her to purify herself by tearing out her tongue, by fasting, and by burning herself. During a manic episode she deliberately wounded her arms, badly lacerated her vagina with her hand, and attempted to gouge out both her eyes, with resulting blindness in one eye (Howden 1882).

An 18-year-old girl became excited, rolled naked on the floor, screamed, sang nonsensical songs, and quoted the Bible. Her mood was happy even though she smeared herself with spit and urine. She imagined that she was in a castle and that a painter wanted to seduce her. In a calm moment she pulled her right eye out of its socket and twisted it, saying, "I have to die" (Axenfeld 1899).

During a manic episode, a 33-year-old woman tore up a picture of Christ, kissed it fervently, and proceeded to gouge out her left eye. She then cried, beat herself, spoke to imaginary persons, claimed that she was in a convent instead of a hospital, and insisted that she had to take out her remaining eye. She said that since she had always been bad, especially to her parents, and no longer believed in God, she needed to make a sacrifice. Her choice of an eye was made after reading the Bible. She had several more manic episodes and made further attempts to remove her right eye. During hospitalization at age 56 she recounted her earlier enucleation. She admitted to sinning with her eyes and recounted that she used to sleep in the same bedroom as her parents, frequently saw her father's genitals, and often heard her parents' bed creak. On her wedding day she dedicated candles to Saint

Joseph rather than to Mary. She thought that a statue of Joseph had nodded to her just before she took out her eye. She admitted that "looking" at a man always excited her sexually. The author of this case believed the major psychological determinant to be the patient's premature hypersexuality and her tendency "to look" (which derived from her witnessing her parents in bed). She substituted Joseph for her father, and during her psychosis supposedly experienced the same affective states she had originally associated with her father (Hartmann 1926).

Obsessive compulsive disorder is characterized by persistent and unwelcome thoughts, images, or impulses and by repetitive ritualistic or stereotyped acts. The following two cases demonstrate eye mutilation associated with this disorder (also see Scullica 1962).

A 50-year-old Italian woman totally blinded herself and grotesquely disfigured her face by compulsively punching herself. Since the age of 16 she had been obsessed with irresistible impulses to touch, press, and hit parts of her head and neck. She battered herself so much that she felt no pain. She believed she had two conflicting personalities, one that forced her into absurd actions and another that tried to lead her back to reality. She noticed certain "rhythms" of her eyes, teeth, and nose. She was able to identify life events that called her attention to these "rhythms"; for example, after her cousin developed a sore throat, the patient became obsessed with the position of her own tonsils. Her destructive actions were linked to these "rhythms." She was never psychotic. Her compulsive self-destructive behavior was finally controlled following a transorbital leukotomy. As a result of this operation, however, her thoughts and behavior became rigid and, in some ways, infantile; for example, she often held a doll in her arms and pretended that it was a baby (Balduzzi 1961).

A 30-year-old Jewish man was hospitalized because he impaired the vision in both of his eyes by banging them repeatedly with his fists. He first exhibited ritualistic behavior at the age of 10. His parents had a stormy marriage, and he slept with his mother until he was an adolescent. At the age of 13 he masturbated after he saw his mother naked and then began to press his eyeballs in order to relieve his feelings of guilt. He developed a compulsive eye-touching ritual. At the age of 21 he was operated on for a congenital cataract in his left eye. Postoperatively he began to hit his face and eyes compulsively. He was helped somewhat by psychotherapy, and he married a psychiatric nurse. Following the death of his grandmother and the pregnancy of his wife, he again started hitting his eyes. He sustained a detached retina and eventual blindness in his left eye. He was hospitalized several times and had to be restrained from hitting his face and eyes.

He gained some control over his actions, especially after developing a relationship with a rabbi. He separated from his wife and was operated on for a traumatic cataract in his right eye. He recognized the absurdity of his behavior but felt powerless to change (Stinnett and Hollender 1970).

Hypochondriasis is a disorder characterized by an unrealistic fear or belief of having a disease despite medical reassurance. Desoff (1943) reported the case of a hypochondriacal patient who was convinced that his eye was cancerous. On several occasions he popped the eye out of its orbit with his thumb but each time was able to have it pushed back in place. The eye became so damaged because of this trauma, however, that it had to be removed surgically.

The concept of *personality disorders* is complicated but basically refers to engrained, inflexible, and maladaptive characterological flaws that impair social or economic functioning and cause subjective distress. Borderline personality disorder is the only mental illness in which, according to the official psychiatric nomenclature, the occurrence of physically self-damaging acts is a major diagnostic criterion. Additionally this disorder is characterized by impulsivity, unstable relationships, inappropriately intense anger, brief mood swings, loneliness, chronic boredom, and uncertainty about one's self-image, values, loyalties, and gender identity. The following case demonstrates eye mutilation in this disorder (see also Goldsmith 1973).

An 18-year-old youth was hospitalized because of inexplicable stealing, occasional fainting fits, and frequent subjective "attacks." The "attacks" were characterized by a sensation of fear which seemed to originate in his abdomen and by the thought that his left eye was evil. Although the right side of his body was "good," he felt that someone evil was looking through his left eye and influencing his behavior. He begged the doctors to remove his eyes and relieve him of his symptoms. He began to cut his wrists and savagely cut his forearms and abdomen. Nineteen months later he began to cut the conjunctiva and skin around his left eye. In the following months he made further cuts with a razor blade to his eyelid, cornea, and sclera. He said that he cut his eyes to gain relief from "attacks" and to demonstrate his suffering to the staff. Staff members noted that his episodes of self-mutilation were often related to active planning for discharge from the hospital and to attempts to discuss his relationship difficulties (Griffin, Webb, and Parker 1982).

Antisocial personality disorder is characterized by continuous behavior in which the rights of others are violated. Persons with this disorder typically demonstrate criminal behavior, disregard for the truth, irritability, aggressiveness, recklessness, and impulsivity. Especially when placed in a restrictive prison setting, persons with this disorder are at high risk for self-mutilation. Segal et al. (1963), for example, reported on twenty-two young male prisoners in a Polish jail with "distinct pathologic personalities" who deliberately damaged their eyes. There were a total of 166 injuries to forty-three eyes. The most frequent method of injury was the placing of a toxic compound (ground-up, violet-colored, indelible pencil lead) into the eye. This compound often produced severe, chronic tissue damage and led to blindness, leukomas, and glaucoma. Other methods of injury included placing chlorinated lime, ground glass, or wood slivers into the conjunctival sac. Occasionally a lighted cigarette was stuck into an open eye. As a rule the prisoners injured their eyes on Saturday afternoons or on holiday evenings to delay detection and medical assistance. Some men inflicted their injuries within a few weeks of their scheduled discharge from prison. Many of the prisoners were terrified by the effects of their injuries, and they complied with medical treatment. Once they came under the influence of their fellow inmates again, however, they often repeated their injuries; nineteen prisoners mutilated themselves more than once, the maximum being seventeen times.

Factitious disorder is a fascinating mental illness. Persons with this disorder deliberately display physical or mental symptoms. Their motivation is not readily understandable and appears to be linked to their need to assume a patient role, to have contacts with physicians, and to undergo medical procedures such as diagnostic tests and operations. A typical case involving factitious eye damage is that of a 32-year-old nursing aide who reported that a fragment of glass had struck her right eye when she dropped a water glass into a sink. On ten different occasions over the next three months she had glass fragments removed from her eye, claiming that they all came from the initial accident. A nurse then saw her break a glass eyedropper and put tiny slivers of glass into her eye. The woman was popular with her co-workers, had a good work history, and appeared to be a very reasonable person, working to help her husband get through medical school. She had a 12-year-old daughter and "all in all seemed to be a happy, adjusted person" (Wilson 1955).

A malingerer, similar to a person with a factitious disorder, will deliberately produce and present symptoms. The major difference, however, is that the malingerer's goals for feigning illness are obviously recognizable, for example, to avoid an unpleasant assignment.

The literature on self-inflicted eye injuries by malingerers primarily deals with epidemics among soldiers. Cooper (1859, pp. 291–92) noted:

It was scarcely possible to imagine a more humiliating picture of depravity than was presented by a ward filled with soldiers, labouring under ophthalmia, deliberately produced by their own hands. A regular correspondence had been detected, between these ophthalmics and their friends, requesting that corrosive sublimate, lime, and blue stone, might be forwarded to them through which and good luck, they hoped to get their eyes in such a state as would enable them to procure their discharge with a pension. . . . Ophthalmia, when counterfeit, is generally confined to privates of indifferent character, and does not extend to officers, women, or children, which is not the case with true ophthalmia.

Cooper also related a situation in 1809 when three hundred soldiers became affected with ophthalmia. The sick men were placed in a hospital. The commanding officer became suspicious when he learned that one of the hospital nurses often went to a druggist's shop to purchase medicines. He devised a plan, and at midnight all of the men on a ward "were roused from their beds, and forthwith marched in a state of nudity" to another place. The ward was searched, and small parcels of corrosive sublimate were found concealed in the beds. "Means were taken to prevent a supply of this article, and in a very short time 250 of the men had recovered, and were then marched to their respective corps" (p. 293).

In 1945, Somerset provided references to seven World War I studies on military malingerers who put substances, such as jequirity and castor oil seeds, in their eyes. He also reported on thirty-one such cases among Indian troops serving under the British. He noted the low military rank of the soldiers and the high incidence of bilateral lesions. "Typically the patient keeps the eye closed and frequently shows a very guilty and sulky appearance. He is unco-operative in responding to his vision test and will refuse to count the dots on the illiterate tests or says the wrong number of dots all the way down the board" (p. 200).

In 1947, Somerville-Large reported on 375 cases of self-inflicted eye injuries among both British and Indian troops serving in India (these constituted 2.07% of all ophthalmic cases, excluding battle casualties). The most commonly used irritants were jequirity and castor oil seeds; other substances that were used included urine, tobacco, sand, and leaves. In his opinion "the ocular self-inflicted injury was considered to be a trivial thing among the Sepoys, and it was employed to escape for a few days from some unpleasant situation, perhaps following a rebuke or the refusal of permission to do some desired thing" (p. 188). It was also noted that French workers in Germany who wanted to escape penal servitude were able to simulate the symptoms of trachoma by rubbing a certain compound in their eyes. "The Germans were so afraid of trachoma that many French workers were able to go back home owing to that trick" (p. 197).

As seen in these examples as well as in the previously mentioned report on Polish prisoners, epidemics of self-inflicted eye damage seem to be limited to persons in total-care institutions. Another example of such an epidemic is found in Anaclerio and Wicker's report in 1970 on twenty-seven chronic schizophrenic inpatients in a federal mental hospital who injured their eyes by frequently gazing at the sun. Most stated that they sun gazed only when they were "sick" and that they did so in order to see or communicate with God or to make their eyes stronger. This behavior may have represented an institutional fad among patients at that time. However, sun gazing may be a more widespread phenomenon to which little attention has been paid. An ophthalmologist who has been examining eyes for twenty-five years at a large state mental hospital in Missouri told me that he has encountered only four cases of sun-gazing retinopathy; all were psychotic men who wanted to gain power from the sun. I am familiar with the recent case of a 42-year-old schizophrenic man with severe mutilative tendencies (self-amputation of his fingers and foot) who sustained bilateral macular burns as a result of staring at the sun. He thought himself to be God and wanted to blind himself as an act of atonement to save the world. Deliberate sun gazing with an intent to cause blindness has also been reported in a "neurotic" 17-year-old girl (Eigner 1966).

From an examination of the preceding cases it is clear that self-inflicted eye damage does not constitute a specific syndrome but rather occurs among persons with a variety of diagnoses and a variety of motives. With the exception of one patient (a demented 85-year-old woman who enucleated an eye), the eye mutilators presented here range in age from 15 to 56 years. The average age of the male mutilators is 26 years, while the average age of the female eye mutilators is 28 years. Although most eye mutilators do not damage other parts of their body, the case reports contain instances of additional mutilations to organs such as the tongue, head, ear, fingers, hand, abdomen, umbilicus, vagina, and penis.

Eye mutilation may be associated with many different diagnostic categories, but in its most severe form it is most commonly encountered in psychotically depressed or schizophrenic persons. The reasons given by these mutilators for their actions sometimes are highly idiosyncratic, for example, an attempt to dig out the brain through the eye or to decrease social anxiety and become a better musician. But much more often the stated reasons deal with the religious themes of atonement for sins, the casting out of evil spirits, the salvation of the world (frequently associated with an easily recognized identification with Christ), and obedience to God's will as expressed in Matthew's words in the Bible. The real or imaginary sins that must be atoned for become greatly magnified, especially in the minds of depressed patients. Examples of such "sins" listed in the case reports include murder, incestuous desires, hostility toward parents, sexual abuse by others, physical abuse of others, and economic failure. Self-blinding is a suitable method of atonement because the eye is such a valuable organ.

Self-enucleation in order to rid the body of an evil spirit represents an extension of the ancient, widespread folk belief in the evil eye. The "spirit-infested" eye of a psychotic person becomes a terrifying, aggressive organ that can change the course of events, maim and kill others, and force one to look at tempting or forbidden persons and things. By isolating the evil spirit in an eye, the psychotic person gains some control over terror and aggression; should all other attempts fail to control the spirit, the desperate act of enucleation can remove it from the patient's body. In normal religious life the struggle with devils may be won through prayer and healing rituals, but the demon of psychosis demands a more radical tactic.

Most psychotic patients report a certain tranquility following self-enucleation, either because they have received the severe punishment they believe they deserve or because they have successfully rid their bodies of an evil spirit. In nine of the case reports, these patients assumed an identity with Christ-the-Sufferer and often stated that their enucleation served to save the world, thus identifying with Christ-the-Healer. (In fact, Christ's healings mainly consisted of the casting out of demons from mentally ill persons.) Thus, self-enucleators' identification with Christ is understandable because they believe they have followed in Christ's footsteps and that, through their sacrifice and suffering, they have saved not only themselves but the world.

By far the most common motive expressed by self-enucleators is the need to adhere to Matthew's biblical injunction that one who has looked lustfully at a woman already has committed adultery in his heart, and he should, therefore, cut out his eye and throw it away to save his entire body from perdition. The purpose of the mutilation in this notion is clear. As stated in psychiatric terms by Menninger in 1938: "a mutilation is, therefore, an attempt at self-healing, or at least self-preservation. . . . Local self-destruction is a form of partial suicide to avert total suicide" (p. 271). Undoubtedly, self-enucleation in many psychotic persons substitutes for suicide.

The tendency for many psychotic persons to rationalize the mutilation of their eyes on the basis of a biblical admonition reflects the finding that deviant eye enucleation appears to occur only in Christian cultural areas. I have written to a host of psychiatric colleagues in China, Singapore, Hong Kong, India, and Japan, but I have been unable to find even one case of self-enucleation in those countries. Both Dr. John Cawte, an Australian professor of psychiatry who has worked intensively with aborigines, and Dr. Burton Burton-Bradley, a distinguished psychiatrist who has worked intensively with natives in Papua New Guinea, have informed me that they have never seen or heard of a case of enucleation in those populations. Dr. Wolfgang Jilek of Vancouver, Canada, told me of a case of enucleation in a Chinese immigrant woman with a history of postpartum psychosis. At first I thought this case was unique because of the patient's Chinese background. But on review of her records I learned that she was a religious convert to a fundamentalist Protestant church. Thus, it appears that eye enucleation is closely related to Christian beliefs, and it has been reported predominantly, if not exclusively, in Christian cultural areas of the world.

The Link between the Eyes and the Genitals

Menninger (1938) articulated the classic psychoanalytic position that self-castration is the prototype of all self-mutilation and that any substituted organ is invariably an unconscious representation of the genital. In commenting about the eye, Freud noted in his essay "The Uncanny" that "a study of dreams, fantasies, and myths has taught us that anxiety about one's eyes, the fear of going blind, is often enough a substitute for the dread of being castrated." The notion that the eye may represent the phallus supposedly originates in the belief that a vital fluid emanates from the eye just as sperm is emitted from the phallus; the glance of an eye then represents the male sexual function. Some amulets that counter-balance the force of the evil eye, such as the red chili-horn, are thought to symbolize the erect penis.

After a thorough review of both the psychoanalytic literature and that of eye mutilation it seems evident that in some cases the damaged eye clearly has been substituted for the genitals; in other cases the linkage between the two organs appears nonexistent. The psychoanalysts' error of overgeneralization stems from the fact that most of their case reports deal with neurotic disorders in which patients manifest eye symptoms such as blurred vision, hysterical blindness, and tics. Although many psychoanalytic cases deal with mutilative fantasies, for example, "a woman who had a strong desire for a penis had a dream in which a man appears with legs cut off, her own feet cut off, and an eye bleeding copiously" (Hart 1949, p. 264), they rarely deal with actual ocular self-mutilation.

Greenacre (1926) found a "constant linkage of the eye-complex with disorders and conflicts of the sex life" (p. 557), but one might argue that the coexistence of sexual conflicts (which are frequently present in the mentally ill) and eye disorders does not always imply a linkage. One of Greenacre's most astute observations was that "the eye may be held guilty for its own function, and the desire or fear of self-blinding appears as a wish on the part of the individual to punish himself for sexual looking, rather than as a direct self-castration wish. . . . The eye which is psychotically dimmed or blinded is generally the eye which has offended in its own right, rather than merely as a genital symbol" (p. 558).

Some psychoanalysts have interpreted mythological stories to illustrate the genital symbolism of the eyes. In the Egyptian myth of the battle between Horus and Set, for example, Set took out Horus's eyes and Horus retaliated by emasculating Set. In this story the eye might be interpreted as symbolic of the genital (or vice versa), or the two organs might represent highly valued but not necessarily linked parts of the body.

Interpreters of the Oedipus myth, as retold by Sophocles, have focused exclusively on the sexual linkage between Oedipus' self-blinding and his discovery that he had bedded his mother, that is, the eye mutilation symbolizes self-castration. One could argue, however, that Oedipus' greater crime was that he caused the death of both parents. In the play's beginning, Oedipus invokes a curse upon the king's (his father's) murderer: "May he wear out his life in misery to miserable doom" (lines 245–49). Later on, Oedipus learns that Queen Jocasta had given up her child for fear of the evil oracle that "he should kill his parents" (line 1183). The chorus then tells us that Oedipus rushed to find Jocasta. By the time he found her, she had committed suicide by hanging. He cut the dangling noose and proceeded to stick his eyes with the brooches from her robe, "shrieking out such things as: they will never see the crime I have committed or had done upon me!" (lines 1268–72). The Greeks (and most peoples until fairly recently in human history) regarded blindness as a terrible event. The blind seer who could perceive the future was a rare, paradoxical figure. Thus, Oedipus' self-blinding need not necessarily be interpreted symbolically. By causing the death of his parents he became a victim of his own curse, and by his self-blinding he resigned himself to a life of miserable doom.

Although Freud was the first person to develop the eye-genital link and the concept of the Oedipus complex, the great French author Marcel Proust independently discovered the oedipal complex (see Zilboorg 1939). In "The Filial Feelings of a Matricide," Proust tells the story of an acquaintance, Henri van Blarenbergh, whose father had recently died. Proust learned that his friend Henri had murdered his mother by sticking a dagger into her heart. "Soon afterwards," writes Proust, "four policemen, responding to an alarm, forced the bolted door and entered the murderer's room. He had inflicted wounds upon himself with the dagger, and the left side of his face was lacerated by a pistol shot. His left eyeball hung from its socket and rested on the pillow. . . . In this eye-ball on the pillow I recognize the most frightful torment that the history of human suffering has relegated to us. It is the eye of the unfortunate Oedipus that I see" (Zilboorg 1939, p. 293). Proust did not consider Henri a brutal criminal but rather a pious and tender son, an enlightened spirit driven by fate to crime and expiation "which will always remain both worthy and glorious." For Proust the matricidal act demonstrated a certain purity and a religious atmosphere of spiritual beauty such as can be found in the Greek tragedies. Henri's mutilated eye was not linked with any sexual symbolism.

Although the eye sometimes is clearly a symbolic substitute for a genital organ, this is not invariably the case. As stated by Crowder et al. (1979): "We suspect that self-mutilation of the eyes, like most other psychiatric symptoms, signs, and syndromes, will prove to be a non-specific entity or final common pathway for patients whose judgment is disturbed for a variety of psychotic and non-psychotic, organic and functional, learned and inspired reasons" (p. 423). Each case must be approached individually, and attempts must be made to understand the patients' desperate actions in the context of cultural, psychological, and biological forces. Although frequently grotesque, severe eye mutilation may in some cases be life saving in that it serves as a substitute for suicide.

The Ears

Piercing of the earlobe in order to display jewelry is the most common form of mild mutilation in the world. In one variation that is widely practiced in India and Southeast Asia, the earlobe is stretched in ribbonlike segments until it reaches shoulder length.

The ancient Egyptians pierced and stretched their earlobes, as can be seen in drawings of Queen Nefertiti and King Akhenaton. Many mummies have been found with mutilated ears, including one whose fleshy lobules were drawn into long strings. In the Old Testament book of Exodus, chapter 21, reference is made to the piercing of the ears of faithful slaves: "If the slave declares, 'I am devoted to my master and my wife and children; I will not go free,' his master shall bring him to God and there, at the door of the doorpost, he shall pierce his ear with an awl, thus keeping him as his slave forever." Even the Romans perforated and stretched their earlobes to accommodate jewelry. Celsus, the most famous Roman physician, devised surgical procedures for both men and women who wanted to repair the holes.

Sushutra, the Hippocrates of India, codified surgical procedures around 400 B.C. He described the procedure for piercing children's earlobes, which was done routinely for protection of children against evil spirits as well as for beautification. After both earlobes were pierced with an awl or needle, cotton-lint plugs were inserted into the holes: "If all goes well, you will bring the child to me every third day; each time I will remove the lint, lubricate the hole with oil, and stretch it with a thicker plug. When the bodily humours in the ear will have settled down, I will then begin to expand the hole with rods of wood, or with lead weights." The lobes were then stretched to accommodate heavy ornaments.

Majno (1975) concluded that plastic surgery was highly developed in ancient India for three major reasons: (1) unlike Greeks, Hindu warriors fought without helmets and were apt to have their noses and ears cut off; (2) the harsh laws of Manu prescribed amputation of body parts for offenders (a citizen who broke wind in the presence of the king was liable to be punished by having his anus mutilated); and (3) the use of heavy ornaments often resulted in torn earlobes. An elaborate system of classifying earlobes deformed by earrings was devised by Sushutra and gave rise to pedicle-flap reconstructive surgery.

According to psychoanalytic theory the ear, like the eye, may symbolically represent either the male or female genital. Although one might, therefore, anticipate the frequent occurrence of instances of ear mutilation, the medical literature on ear mutilation is quite small. The most famous case is that of the artist, Vincent van Gogh, who cut off his earlobe and presented it to a prostitute. Van Gogh's case is instructive because the forces that compelled his mutilation can be inferred from his paintings and his letters.

Vincent van Gogh was born on March 30, 1853, and died in infancy. Exactly one year later, on March 30, 1854, another child was born to the van Gogh family. He too was named Vincent, and he developed into one of the greatest artists in the world. It seems likely that the circumstances of his birth compromised his sense of identity. His mother idolized her dead child, and van Gogh became a substitute for his dead brother. Van Gogh additionally became fascinated with the idea of resurrection, and he identified with Jesus. He often painted a halo around his head in self-portraits, and in his painting the *Pietà* he substituted his image for that of Christ. His father was a minister, and, before devoting himself to art, van Gogh spent several years as a fervent evangelist preacher.

The event that precipitated van Gogh's ear cutting was the threat of his housemate, the painter Paul Gauguin, to leave him. Van Gogh had invited Gauguin to share a house with him, but the two men often argued bitterly. On December 24 Gauguin left the house. Van Gogh, armed with a razor, followed him. Gauguin turned and looked at him, whereupon van Gogh went back inside, cut off his earlobe, wrapped it up, and gave it as a present to a prostitute he had frequented. The prostitute's name was Rachel, whose biblical namesake "mourns her children." Just as the biblical Rachel mourned her dead children, so too did van Gogh's mother mourn her dead infant. By presenting his earlobe to Rachel, van Gogh may have wanted her to grieve for and to love him. If one accepts the notion that a mutilated organ may be a genital substitute, then van Gogh's act was tantamount to a castration that left him helpless, wounded, nonthreatening, and in need of maternal comfort.

Another force that influenced van Gogh's self-mutilation was the news of his brother Theo's engagement to Johanna Bonger. Theo was much more than a brother to van Gogh; he was also the provider of money, of friendship, and of love. They spent every Christmas together, but when van Gogh cut off his earlobe on Christmas Eve of 1888, Theo was with his fiancée. The mutilation was not only an expression of his anger at Theo for abandoning him but also a successful, albeit desperate, method of effecting a family reunion. Theo came to see him as soon as he learned of the act.

Several months before cutting off his earlobe van Gogh painted and then destroyed two pictures of Christ at Gethsemane in the Garden of Olives. With his religious background he surely knew the biblical scene at Gethsemane in which Judas betrayed Christ: "At that moment they stepped forward to lay hands on Jesus, and arrested him. Suddenly one of those who accompanied Jesus put his hand to his sword, drew it, and slashed at the high priest's servant, cutting off his ear" (Matt. 26:51).

Clinical cases of ear mutilation are quite rare (Weinstock 1988). In one case a 34-year-old man manually ripped off his right ear, saying that voices commanded him to do so in order to atone for his childhood sins. Before this event he repeatedly removed small sections of skin from his arms, face, and ear, and had been hospitalized for many serious infections, including one so severe that maggots were removed from his right ear canal. He reported relief from tension and depression after removing the skin. He believed that his mother and relatives wanted him to suffer and that he deserved to be a famous world political leader because he had suffered through self-mutilation. He started cutting himself at age 12; shortly afterward he reported auditory hallucinations and persecuting and self-depreciating thoughts. His diagnosis was paranoid schizophrenia (Silva et al. 1989). There also are a few articles in the literature on ear stuffing; for example, a psychotic man stuffed pieces of cooked chicken into both his auditory canals because he felt "empty" and wanted to replace missing tissue (Weiser et al. 1993). Lauerma (1994) believes that the behavior may represent an attempt to reduce auditory hallucinations.

The Nose

Self-mutilation of the nose is not common. However, plastic surgeons perform numerous rhinoplasties, thus affording a culturally approved procedure for individuals desirous of changing the shape of their noses. That so many persons are willing to undergo such operations, often at great expense, is understandable in light of the contribution of the nose to our perception of beauty. Indeed, the French essayist Pascal once observed that the history of the world might have changed totally if Cleopatra's nose had been a little longer!

While surgical procedures performed in Western cultures serve to reduce the size of the nose, the Polynesians used to break and flatten their noses. Some Australian aborigines still pierce the nasal septum and insert a piece of bone in order to flatten and widen the nose. Nowadays the outer wings of women's noses are sometimes pierced in some Eastern cultures to accommodate jewelry, a practice that has been a popular fad among male "punks," especially in England and the United States. Historically, the nose has been cut off or slashed as judicial punishment for adultery, and still today it is not unheard of for jealous husbands in circum-Mediterranean cultures to bite off the nose of an unfaithful wife.

Physicians have long been aware that nasal tissue has some of the properties of vaginal tissue in that it may become congested and even bleed as a form of "vicarious menstruation." Ritual nasal mutilation among males in Papua New Guinea is thought by the natives to serve the same purposes as female menstruation. In fact, Hogbin's book (1970) on this topic is titled *The Island of Menstruating Men* (also see Lidz and Lidz 1977; Read 1965; and Newman 1965).

The Gahuka-Gana and the Gururumba tribes of the Asaro Valley of Papua New Guinea practice nasal mutilation in their initiation rituals for male adolescents. The ritual marks the crossing over of young boys from the care of their mothers into the adult male division of society; during the ritual the mothers of the initiates smear their sons' bodies with clay in mourning. The boys are brought to a river amid the shouts, chants, and flute music of warriors. There they are confronted by a group of masturbating men who wade into the river and stick sharp leaves up their own noses until they hemorrhage profusely. The initiates also induce nasal hemorrhage. Weakened and tired, each person then inserts a cane of reeds down his esophagus into his stomach to induce vomiting. The initiates spend six weeks secluded in the men's hut where they learn the secret of the tribe's magic flutes. They then spend a year in the men's hut, have little contact with women, and practice nose bleeding, vomiting, and flute playing. Several years later they achieve full male status after a period of severe dietary restriction, intense flute playing, and instruction in the duties and rights of manhood.

The tribal men refer to the nasal bleeding as male menstruation. They are extremely frightened of a woman's menstrual blood, which they regard as a malignant force. They believe that each fetus is composed of womb blood and semen and that nasal bleeding rids the child of this womb blood and of menstrual contamination. Likewise, the induced vomiting is thought to get rid of any swallowed womb blood as well as any menstrual blood that may have been inadvertently eaten. Just as a young girl's hymen is broken ritually at the first menstruation, so too the vomiting cane is thought to break a membrane in a boy's body, permitting him to develop the sexual characteristics of a man. The men envy women's monthly, natural self-purification; therefore, they periodically induce nasal bleeding to maintain their health, strength, and attractiveness.

Tribesmen on Wojeo, an island off the coast of Papua New Guinea, have beliefs about the dangers of women's menstrual blood similar to those previously described. In their male initiation ceremonies the tongue, rather than the nose, is the bleeding site. It is believed that a boy absorbs pollution during nursing through the inadvertent ingestion of menstrual blood. Abrasion of the tongue is thought to rid the body of pollution, and it makes the tongue more sensitive for flute playing. Each initiate thrusts his tongue out over a small fire; it is then scraped with rough leaves until blood drops steadily into the fire. At the age of 18 or 19 another ceremony takes place — the inducing of artificial menstruation. In this ritual the boy wades into the ocean, where he deeply gashes the head of his penis with a sharp crab claw. Throughout their lives the men of Wojeo periodically "menstruate" by gashing themselves, especially when they are ill with a sickness blamed on female pollution.

The nose-bleeding rites of the Sambia, a hunting and horticultural people of the New Guinea Highlands, have been detailed by Herdt (1982). The Sambia place great emphasis on the nose in regard to aesthetics, body appearance, and gender symbolism (the words for the glans penis contain the generic term for nose). They believe that menstrual-womb blood is both a life-giving female elixir and a fluid lethal for male functioning; since men's circulatory blood originates from the mother's womb, it may be purged through initiatory nose bleeding. It is thought that a woman's air stream, emitted when speaking (especially during angry outbursts), carries harmful elements from her blood-filled caverns that enter and defile a boy's nasal orifice and interfere with the flow of blood and other bodily fluids. Even during coitus men wear nose plugs to avoid absorbing foul vaginal odors. Nose bleeding is considered to be the most effective method of ridding the male body of these dangerous materials. The most common method of inducing bleeding is to thrust stiff, sharp cane grass into the nostrils; alternatively, a strong salt solution may be injected into the nose. Both methods are very painful and efficacious. Nose bleeding occurs during differing stages of developmental rites for boys, and it is followed by indoctrination in tribal lore, customs, and secrets such as the dangers of intercourse, vaginal pollution, and menstruation. Men continue to practice nose bleeding privately in later life when their wives go off to the menstrual hut.

The nose-bleeding practices serve important social functions. By ridding himself of maternal blood, the boy separates from his mother. He is then free to displace female essences and to absorb "maleness" by engaging in fellatio and filling up his body with semen. The aggression associated with the nose bleeding instills fear and avoidance of women, obedience to male authority, and bravado in battle. Nose bleeding results in a series of constraints upon male-female relationships, and the practice provides contexts for self-identity at different stages of the life cycle. But as the social environment changes among the Sambia, especially as a result of pacification and a decreased need for men to be seen as fierce warriors, nose bleeding is gradually being eliminated as a ritual practice.

The Ndumba, another Highlands group in New Guinea, have separate transition rites for young men and women (Hays and Hays 1982). As a result of the 'ummansa ceremony, young boys receive special knowledge and enter into male company for life. As a result of the kwassi ceremony, young women who have reached menarche learn to control their natural power. Both ceremonies are stepping stones in preparation for marriage and for male-female relations.

In the 'ummansa ceremony the novice males endure mock attacks as they walk to a stream where they bathe. Sponsors hold the arms and heads of the boys while other sponsors repeatedly shove bundles of sharp-edged, stiff leaves into the boys' nostrils until they hemorrhage and the boys cry out for their mothers. Stinging nettles along with ginger root and salt are pushed into their nostrils to control the bleeding. The boys' bodies are rubbed raw with thorns until, finally, they bathe again. Later that day they are made to lick rough leaves until their tongues bleed. After a nap they are instructed in proper masculine behavior, especially sexual behavior. Groups of men visit the boys to provide further instruction and to rub their bodies with thorns, concentrating particularly on the boys' penises. The bloodletting in the ceremony is not done in imitation of menstruation but rather to make boys "strong" and to rid them of their "mother's blood." Thus, the nose bleeding is an act of purification and a prerequisite for entering into the men's house, learning the men's secrets, and participating in men's affairs.

Interestingly, girls also must endure nose bleeding during the *kwassi* ceremony. This ceremony, performed on an individual basis following a girl's first menstruation, lasts for several days. There is much dancing and singing, a repeated refrain being, "Men are the enemy." Toward the end of the ceremony, the girl is led to a stream where her mother's brother shoves sharp leaves into her nostrils to induce hemorrhage. Why is this done? One interpretation is that it is a way for men to assert their own social dominance. Even the nose bleeding of boys may be "a symbolic statement of control over society instead of merely a physical purification" (Hays and Hays 1982, p. 235), that is, ridding the boy of his mother's blood may represent freedom from women's power.

Young boys of the Awa tribe in New Guinea develop into men by engaging for ten to fifteen years in a series of rituals that include body purging and penis cutting. The purging ritual includes being beaten with a cudgel, inducing nasal hemorrhage and vomiting, having incisions made on the penis, and being stuck with stinging nettles. The Awa regard physical growth as a process in which a basically amorphous and watery body is transformed into a well-formed, firm body by the removal of liquid, for example, by purgation. "Bleeding, then, directly stimulates the drying, strengthening processes of tissue growth" (Newman and Boyd 1982, p. 257). Vomiting is another way of removing liquid from the body.

The ritual of severe penis cutting is associated with betrothal. In this ritual the young men first go through intense nose bleeding in which the sharp leaves are pounded into their nostrils with a stone or wooden hammer to cause copious bleeding. Their penises are then gashed open with a knife. Wedges of flesh are removed, and sometimes the urethra is penetrated. The wounded organ is repeatedly struck with a knife and vigorously rubbed with salt or nettles. The profuse bleeding and intense pain endured during this ritual are thought to enhance the life force in the initiates' bodies, to strengthen them against the dangerous and powerful female substances that are contacted during intercourse, and to induce the production of semen. After the initiates have been bled, all of the married men attending the ritual are invigorated by having their own penises bled. The glans penis is punctured by a stone-tipped arrow shot from a tiny bow. This procedure (penis shooting) is undertaken several times yearly by adult men to prevent and to treat illness and "to combat simple lethargy." The men then gather to instruct the initiates in the details of proper sexual conduct.

Young Awa women must also go through a special ritual at the time of their betrothal. Their noses are bled by their mothers' brothers to strengthen them and to stimulate their life force, and they are instructed about their sexual obligations and responsibilities. The intended bride waits in the house of her future female in-law. After the betrothed young man has completed his ritual, he joins his bride in public. The completion of the ceremony takes place at night. The bride is taken to a special ritual site where she engages in intercourse with a group of her husband's relatives while a group of older women (their wives) look on. The men copulate with her one after the other, as often as they wish. The copulations are to force harmful fluids out of the bride's vagina and to increase her reproductive potential.

The most famous psychiatric case of nasal self-mutilation is that of Freud's complicated, obsessive patient known as the Wolfman (a name given to him because of a dream he had). One of the Wolfman's chief complaints was the fixed idea that he was the victim of a nasal injury caused by electrolytic treatment of obstructed sebaceous glands. He claimed that he had a scar, hole, or groove in the tissue and that the contour of his nose was ruined. Dr. Ruth Brunswick, another psychoanalyst who treated him, stated that "nothing whatsoever was visible on the small, snub, typically Russian nose of the patient" (Gardiner 1971, p. 264). In 1923 he observed a black wart on his mother's nose. The following year he had two teeth extracted and began to have queer thoughts about his nose. When his mother returned to Europe he noticed an odd, small pimple on his nose. Eventually he scratched it out, looked in a mirror, and saw a "deep hole" where the pimple had been. He became obsessed with the hole and felt obliged to stare at it with a mirror every few minutes to observe the progress of healing. His life was embittered because, according to his perception, the hole never healed. His misery continued, and he consulted numerous dermatologists. When a physician told him that nothing could be done, he was seized by despair and was on the verge of suicide: "thus mutilated he could not go on living." When another physician used an instrument to press the spot on the Wolfman's nose, he experienced "an acute ecstasy" at the sight of his own blood. But he was not satisfied with the outcome and sought more medical opinions. His nose was treated with electrolysis, and when he complained of a scar he was told that scars never disappear. He looked constantly in his pocket mirror, attempting to establish the degree of his mutilation. Brunswick felt that his nasal symptoms represented a mother identification and an expression of his repressed, bisexual femininity. She noted that he purchased a woman's compact case and used it, as would a woman, to observe and powder his nose. She recognized sadomasochistic trends in his character and linked his demands for treatment of his nose with a castration complex (Gardiner 1971).

The Mouth

Self-mutilation of the mouth, particularly lip and tongue biting, is often seen in children with relatively rare organic disorders such as Lesch-Nyhan syndrome, deLange syndrome, autism, neuroacanthosis, and Tourette syndrome (these disorders are discussed in chap. 9 in the section on stereotypic self-mutilation; animal models have been presented in chap. 4).

Congenital indifference to pain with anhidrosis (markedly decreased sweating), congenital sensory neuropathy with anhidrosis, and familial dysautonomia (Riley-Day syndrome) are autosomal recessive disorders in which self-mutilation results from an inability to perceive pain normally. Such children with deficient pain perception accidentally may chew off parts of their tongues, lips, or fingers; they may pick off part of their noses, extract teeth, break bones, and sustain numerous bruises and ulcerations. Shelley (1962) described a girl with insensitivity to pain "who painlessly enucleated herself one night and then in the morning told the nurse nonchalantly that her eyeballs had 'dropped out' during the night" (p. 339). Needless to say, the management of such patients is highly problematic. Some recent studies suggest that decreased norepinephrine activity in both the central and peripheral nervous systems plays a role in these syndromes.

The dental literature contains a few brief case reports of various types of oral self-mutilation in which psychological factors were paramount (Goldstein and Dragan 1967; Golden and Chosack 1964). Hoffman and Baer's psychiatric study (1968) of three children who indulged in gingival self-mutilation revealed that the children developed organic lesions during a time when they experienced a strong sense of deprivation, for example, the birth of a sibling, abandonment by parents. The presence of the oral lesions affected family dynamics in that the children became the center of attention. Upon discovering that the lesions brought both attention and gratification of dependency needs, the children continued to aggravate the lesions by scratching and denuding their gingiva.

Culturally sanctioned mutilation of the teeth is done for a variety of reasons, the most common being beautification. In some African, South American, and Pacific Island cultures, teeth are blackened with burnt oil and filed. One Celebes Island myth tells of a queen who ordered the teeth of a rival filed to make her unattractive. The king, however, found the filed teeth extremely attractive; thenceforth, tooth filing became a common practice. The incisors may be filed or broken to create a desired shape or inlaid with metal. Certainly in Western culture many models and actresses have their teeth straightened, whitened, and treated to fulfill an ideal of beauty.

Teeth taken from captives have often been worn on necklaces. Loss of teeth was a sign of slavery, as among the African Ashantee. The ancient Peruvian ruler Huayna Ccapac punished a disobedient tribe by decreeing that they and all of their descendants should have three of their teeth pulled from each jaw. The knocking out of teeth has also been associated with mourning and with the propitiation of the ghost of a dead ruler, as among the Sandwich Islanders. An African Bantu myth holds that death enters the human body through the teeth; in order to allow death a chance to exit, a triangular gap or notch is created by filing the teeth.

Many Australian aborigines include tooth evulsion among the physical ordeals of male initiation rites. The removed tooth may be associated with contagious magic. It may, for example, be placed under some tree bark near a water hole; if ants run over it, then it is believed the child will suffer from a mouth disease.

Based on interpretations of dental folklore as well as on clinical cases, psychoanalysts have noted that the teeth may be associated with sexual symbolism. In *General Introduction to Psychoanalysis*, Freud wrote: "A particularly remarkable dream symbol is that of having one's teeth fall out, or having them pulled. Certainly its most immediate representation is castration as a punishment for onanism." The concept of the *vagina dentata* refers to a rarely held male fantasy that the penis may be mutilated during intercourse by teeth hidden within a woman's vagina.

Although the phallic symbolism of head parts such as the eyes, ears, nose, and teeth is certainly not obvious from a commonsense point of view, the possible phallic symbolism of the tongue is a more readily comprehensible notion. The tongue, like the phallus, is a vascular organ that can be protruded and used intrusively during sexual acts. The following two cases of self-mutilation of the tongue demonstrate sexual symbolism.

A 23-year-old woman who immigrated to the United States claimed that a physician told her she needed throat surgery to cure her stutter. At the age of 26 she had episodes of nervousness and uncontrollable slurping and had trouble holding food in her mouth. After four minor auto accidents she lost her job because of problems with auto insurance coverage. She started to bite her lips which became infected. She was hospitalized for three months for severe depression to the point of stupor. At the age of 29, single, unemployed, and very unhappy, she appeared at a psychiatric emergency room saying, "I keep biting my tongue!" She stuffed a bloody, saliva-soaked rag in her mouth and gnashed her teeth in it. She had bitten off the tip of her quivering, macerated, beefy-red tongue. She explained that her teeth were trying to destroy her tongue and that she used the rag to keep her teeth away from her tongue. Her speech was garbled. The accumulation of saliva caused lip smacking and drooling, and she was malnourished and dehydrated. Her fingers, used as wedges to pry apart her teeth, were sore and denuded of skin. Each time she bit her tongue she cried out in pain, protruded it, and exposed chunks of freshly lacerated, bleeding tissue. She begged for help and fell to the floor in agony. Many types of therapy were tried including electroshock, medication, hypnosis, and psychotherapy. None proved successful.

The psychiatrists who reported the case (Slawson and Davidson 1964) considered the patient to be immature because she rejected marriage. Since marriage "involves acceptance of the genital role and the reality of a penis," her tongue mutilation symbolized rejection of the penis and implied "an unconscious wish to destroy that threatening organ" (p. 587). Additionally, they noted that the mouth may symbolize the female genitalia; there are some anatomical similarities in that they are both cavities lined with moist, mucosal tissue surrounded by muscle, and both have lips (or labia) at the mucocutaneous junction. Both may possess teeth—the one in fact, the other in fantasy (*vagina dentata*). The bloody rag in the patient's mouth may represent a sanitary napkin that controls the blood of a fantasized castration. Thus tongue, penis, mouth, and vagina may all be equated symbolically, and the mutilation may demonstrate "an oral sadistic attack on the incorporation of an organ both feared and desired" (p. 588).

Michael and Beck (1973) described a 33-year-old divorced schizophrenic man who cut out his tongue during a psychotic episode. As a child the patient did not speak clearly until the age of 9 when his teacher "showed me how to use my tongue." At the age of 22 he married a school teacher; one year later he began exposing his genitals in public frequently. He spent many of the following years in a state mental hospital (he once tried to electrocute himself as punishment for exposing himself). His wife divorced him, and he took up with a woman patient. He was confused over wishes to be with his ex-wife. When he went to see her he feared that his son would say he loved him, and he would then be "forced" to have sexual relations with him "unconsciously" in his sleep. He decided to "correct" his bad decision of choosing the woman patient over his wife by purchasing a knife with the intention of cutting off his hands, then his feet, then his tongue, and finally gouging out his eyes. Instead, he cut off two-thirds of his tongue over a two-hour period and flushed it down the toilet. He felt relieved and asked his brother to call his wife to see what he had done. The brother took him to the hospital instead.

The psychiatrists believed that the patient's exhibitionism resulted from profound feelings of rejection and that the tongue mutilation resulted from fear of emerging homosexual impulses. They equated the mutilation with symbolic self-castration in that it was an attempt to correct a defect (exhibitionism) that caused his wife to leave him and to accomplish a merging with his mother, who apparently cared for him more when he had a speech impediment. In fact, his mother said that after the mutilation he sounded very much the way he did as a child.

Book 6 of Ovid's *Metamorphoses* contains a frightening story of tongue mutilation linked with sexual violence. The Greek hero Tereus married the beautiful Procne, and they had a child named Itys. At Procne's flirtatious insistence, Tereus traveled to Athens to bring her sister, Philomela, for a visit. With one look Tereus fell madly in love with Philomela. On the journey home he raped her. She pleaded to be killed, but Tereus instead cut out her tongue: "He thrust sharp tongs between her teeth, her tongue still crying out her father's name. Then as the forceps caught the tongue, his steel sliced through it, its roots still beating while the rest turned, moaning on black earth. As the bruised tail of a dying serpent lashes, so her tongue crept, throbbed, and whimpered at his feet. This done, the tyrant renewed his pleasure on her wounded body."

Tereus kept Philomela locked up and told Procne that she had died. Philomela, however, wove a coarse tapestry depicting her fate and had it delivered to her sister. Procne freed her and said, "Now is no time for tears; we need good steel. . . . This is my day for crime, to take a torch to all rooms of the palace and to push Tereus into its flames, or chip away his tongue, tear out his eyes, cut off the genitals that injured you." Just then her son, Itys, appeared, and she noticed how much he looked like his father. With tears in her eyes and despite Itys's pleading, she slaughtered him, cooked his body parts, and served them to Tereus for dinner. After he had eaten, she tossed the boy's bloody head into his face. The women escaped the anger of Tereus by changing into birds with red spots among their feathers. Shakespeare's gruesome play *Titus Andronicus* is based on Ovid's story and additionally contains instances of self-mutilation; for example, one character chops off his hand.

Not all tongue self-mutilation occurs within a sexual setting. Prince (1960) described several strange and fatal cases of self-mutilation of the tongue among the Yoruba of Nigeria. The first case was that of an 18-year-old student who acted strangely in school by trying to take the place of the teacher and creating a disturbance. He became involved in politics somewhat inappropriately and would not return to his studies. When brought to the hospital he held his head in an odd posture and kept protruding his tongue. He began biting his tongue so severely that he was given electroshock treatments and large doses of a major tranquilizer. He subverted all attempts to keep him from destroying his tongue, which turned into a necrotic mass from the constant, savage biting. The dead tissue was removed surgically, and he was given antibiotics and was fed through a tube. He did not hemorrhage much, and his blood pressure stayed within normal limits. He lost a great deal of weight, however, and his temperature rose; within ten days he was dead.

The second case involved an 18-year-old female student. When hospitalized she was quite psychotic as manifested by shouting, obstreperousness, auditory hallucinations, and the delusion that she had eaten her parents and her girlfriend. She was given a major tranquilizer. After two days she began to posture her head oddly and then bit off her tongue. She died within three more days in a manner similar to the previous case. A third case, about which little was known, was that of a psychotic young man who bit his tongue and almost totally severed it. He was brought to a hospital, and his tongue was sewn back in place. He pulled out the stitches, continued to bite his tongue, and died shortly afterward.

According to Prince (1960), in these cases a curse or invocation was the most likely factor precipitating the patients' psychoses and influencing their symptomatology. Among the Yoruba, words may be omnipotent: "To utter the name of something may draw that something into actual existence . . . not only within the mind and body of he who utters and he who hears the word, but also in the physical world as well" (p. 66). So many Yoruba patients believe in the power of a curse or invocation to cause all sorts of illness and misfortune that the cases of fatal tongue mutilation appear to be related to curses, "especially in view of the fact that this type of curse is not unknown in Yoruba land." For example, if someone is verbally abused by another or laughed at, he or she may retaliate by saying, "You will bite off your tongue and never speak again," or "You will laugh yourself to death." Since curses can be effective only when words are spoken, the destruction of a person's tongue is a particularly effective method; the victim no longer possesses the physical capacity to utter a retaliatory curse.

The Tlingit Indians of the Northwest Coast (North America) had a custom described by a French traveler in 1799 as "the most disgusting perhaps that exists on the face of the earth. . . . [Women] have the lower lip slit close to the gum the whole width of the mouth, and wear in it a kind of wooden bowl without handles which rests against the gum, and which the slit lip serves as a collar to confine, so that the lower part of the mouth projects two or three inches. . . . This whimsical ornament not only disfigures the look, but causes an involuntary flow of saliva, as inconvenient as it is disgusting." The initial ritual slitting occurred at menarche and was a rite of passage signifying that a girl was available for marriage. The piercer was the girl's future mother-in-law, who always was a member of a different clan from the girl (marriages were designed to interconnect tribal clans). When the girl married, a larger labret (the ornament that was inserted into the slit lip) was provided; each change in a woman's status was accompanied by a different labret. The symbolism of this custom is very rich and refers to social relations, eating, the potlatch ritual, and sexuality. The sliced lip represents a vagina, which is filled by a labret representing a tongue-phallus. In Tlingit art, figures "often unite with each other by sharing a tongue in what might be interpreted as a symbolic representation of sexual union . . . maleness and femaleness are united by the appearance of the labret when worn" (Jonaitis 1988). The custom also relates to the complex myth of Lenaxxidaq, the Tlingit female wealth bringer. In brief, the myth tells of the kidnapping of Lenaxxidaq's child by a man whose face was deeply wounded by the mothers' copper fingernails. The man became rich by returning the child; he became wealthy because the scar of his wound had the power to bring him coppers. The original Lenaxxidaq also had her child kidnapped. The child mutilated and then ate the eyes both of his abductor and one of the villagers. A woman survivor killed the child by poking a hole in the child's eye-filled stomach; she then was transformed into Lenaxxidaq. Orifices are important in this myth. Just as a young girl's lip is split, so too does Lenaxxidaq scratch her assailant's face. The scab that seals this orifice provides the victim with wealth and enough to attain a better social status. Just as lip splitting signifies a girl's new social role, and the insertion of labrets her status, so too the "myth suggests the perpetuation of social stability by the interaction of newly found orifices and symbols of wealth" (Jonaitis 1988). By the mid-1800s large labrets were no longer used by the Tlingit, largely because of negative reactions by European visitors. They were replaced by small silver or bone pins that were inserted into the lower lip.

6

The Limbs

The arms, legs, hands, feet, toes, and especially the fingers are body parts well suited anatomically for self-mutilation. The amputation of a finger joint, for example, can be accomplished rapidly and accurately with minimal loss of blood, with little loss of function for many tasks, and with good healing of the wound. Further, the deformed finger stump is readily available for public display. In fact, the most ancient form of ritual mutilation is finger amputation. It was practiced twenty thousand years ago (Aurignacian age) and continues to be practiced today. The first graphic evidence of finger mutilation is found in late Paleolithic imprints in the cave at Gargas in southern France. Although hand imprints have been found in many caves in the area, only in the Gargas cave do the imprints show finger mutilation. Of ninety-two recognizable imprints, the most common mutilation seen is the absence of the tip of the four fingers, with the thumb being spared. Several theories have been proposed to explain the missing fingertips; one holds that it is the result of Raynaud's disease, acting in concert with cold weather, to cause gangrene. This is unlikely since similar imprints of mutilated hands have been found in warmer regions, such as in the Maltravieses cave in central Spain. Another theory holds that the fingers may have been bent back so that the resulting imprints were a form of sign language to represent animal heads. Yet another theory holds that the finger mutilation was a cannibalistic custom. The most plausible explanation, however, is that the amputations were part of religious rituals associated with mourning or healing.

The antiquity of finger mutilation is also demonstrated by its presence in aboriginal populations. In 1886 an African Bushman family was "exhibited" in Berlin. Four of the six family members had one or more digit tips amputated. Virchow made drawings of their hands and noted that "in every sickness of what kind soever it is usual with them to take off extreme joints of the fingers, beginning with the little finger of the left hand." Gardner and Heider (1968) described and presented striking photographs of current finger mutilation among the Dugum Dani tribe of New Guinea. In this group young girls have their fingers cut off as a sacrifice at funerals; after a hard blow to the elbow to deaden the pain, the fingers are chopped off with a stone adze. Many Dani women fondle their children "with hands that are mostly thumbs."

Two Swedish anthropologists, Lagercrantz (1935) and Soderstrom (1938), wrote lengthy articles on finger mutilation. Some of their material is based on reports of travelers and explorers and *may* be exaggerated, although a host of studies, often with startling photographs, by respected nineteenth- and early twentieth-century anthropologists are included in their references.

In West Africa finger amputation was sometimes performed on corpses. If the deceased had been impotent, his little finger was cut off and inserted in his anus to horrify the dead man so much that his spirit would seek reincarnation as a woman so as to have children in a new life. The Bushmen amputated a corpse's finger in order to make passage into a blessed afterlife more smooth. Among the Ashanti parental love turned to anger if an infant died in the first week of life. The dead body was beaten, and a finger was cut off. The body was wrapped in sharp, cutting, spear grass and buried in the village garbage dump. When a first-born child died among the BaBoyes, all subsequent children underwent amputation of the first joint of the little finger. The severed finger was then buried in the grave of the deceased child to placate the evil spirit who killed the child.

Among the Xhosa a sickly child might be treated by amputation of a finger joint. Sometimes the operation was performed as a prophylactic measure to help the child "grow up strong and brave." Schambaa mothers cut off the fingertip of a child with eye problems and dropped blood from the severed fingertip into the affected eye. An interesting Mashona legend tells of ogres whose job was to prepare medicines for the chiefs. The ogres would kill a boy and a girl by choking them with grass seeds, then cut off parts of the genitals, the lips, and the first joints of the little fingers. These parts were taken by the chief, who secretly prepared medicine from them. The medicine was eaten at a feast to ensure a fruitful harvest.

The Hottentots amputated fingers as a sign of engagement and marriage. A widow, for example, would cut off a finger upon remarriage, thus releasing herself from all bonds with her dead husband. A number of tribes cut off specific fingers as a sort of surname or badge of the clan. In Africa finger amputation was performed also as punishment for adultery and robbery, as a way to sanctify sacrifices to the spirits, and for use in legal trials. Among the Zande a person accused of magically willing another's death was forced to eat a dish that contained a small-finger joint from the deceased. Further, amputated fingers were used as a sign of conquest and as jewelry.

A woman from Chimbu
Province, New Guinea highlands, who chopped her
fingertips according to local
custom in mourning for deceased male relatives. (Photo
courtesy of Dr. Wolfgang
Jilek)

In Oceania and the Pacific Islands finger mutilation was endemic, and it
persists in a few remote places. One reporter in New Guinea noted in 1900
that "the custom of amputating in some cases the first, in others the second,
joints of the index and middle fingers is very common after the death of a
near relative. . . . A mother will cut off the first joint for her children and
the second for her husband, father, or mother" (Soderstrom 1938, p. 26).
Finger amputation was performed, sometimes on a large scale, at times of
mourning; one hundred fingers might be amputated for a king's burial. If
the deceased belonged to a rich family, tribesmen sent their fingers to the
survivors, who were expected to reward such signs of mourning. In Hawaii
the mutilations were especially fierce; survivors of the deceased might, in
addition to finger amputation, pull out their teeth, burn themselves, tattoo
their tongues, and cut off their ears.

In Polynesia, Captain Cook reported finding many natives with amputated fingers and wrote that "this operation is performed when they labour
under some grievous disease and think themselves in danger of dying."
The same observations and interpretations were made by other observers:
"When a person became ill he was carried to Maatu's god's house and laid

outside. If the person's sickness did not yield to medicines, a consultation of the family settled who would sacrifice a little finger for the sick person. This was done in the sick person's house and the blood caught in a banana leaf and two outer finger joints placed in it. These were carried to the god's house" (Soderstrom 1938, p. 31).

Among some aboriginal groups in Australia, the tip of a woman's left little finger was bitten off at the time of her engagement to warn off suitors. In order to bring luck in fishing and to make winding of the fishing lines easier, the girls had their fingers removed. The procedure was to tie a band around a finger, tightening it daily until the joint dropped off. Another procedure was to bind the fingers with coarse spiders' webs until the joint started to die. The girl then placed her mutilated hand in an anthill until the ants ate off the joint.

Finger mutilation was also prevalent among North American Indians. At the death of a young Crow Indian warrior, for example, his relatives would plunge into a violent and prolonged mourning. They would sever finger joints, wail, cut off their hair, and gash their bodies until blood flowed freely. The Mandan Indians cut off the first and fourth fingers of the left hand during religious rites. In their quest for a guardian-spirit protector, many Plains Indians underwent a period of fasting, exposure to the elements, constant wailing, and amputation of a finger as an offering to the sun.

The Hands and Arms

Both in history and folklore the human hand has been associated with special powers. In Athens the hand of a person who committed suicide was cut off and buried separate from the rest of the body to prevent the ghost of the deceased from haunting the living. Biblical accounts of Jesus's ability to heal the sick by touching them led to the common European belief that the touch of a king could cure persons of diseases, especially of a form of tuberculosis called scrofula. The "hand of glory" refers to the folkloric belief that the severed hand of a hanged man possessed healing qualities. In eighteenth-century France, thieves often carried such a hand with them because it supposedly had the power to put people to sleep, thus making burglary easier. The Bloody Hand of Ulster, one of the older heraldic symbols, consists of an erect, red palm of a severed left hand on a silver background. It represents the hand of the brave O'Neill, the forefather of the Irish princes of Ulster. The legendary story of the hand states that several Celtic warlords were on an expedition when they sighted land. They raced for the land since the first to touch it could claim it for his clan. When

O'Neill's ship fell behind, he chopped off his left hand and flung it to the shore a moment before his competitors landed.

A legend reminiscent of Saint Lucy, who cut out her eyes to cool the passions of a suitor, is that of the tenth-century British saint Wilfreda. King Edgar was in love with her. He pursued her to the door of a church where, on bended knee, he grasped her hand and proposed marriage. She refused, however, and fled into the church, leaving behind her hand in the king's grasp. Unnerved, he honored her wishes and pursued her no longer.

In European jurisprudence during the eighth to twelfth centuries the use of a sworn oath to determine guilt and innocence was superseded by the ordeal, a procedure in which the accused was forced to undergo a test whose outcome depended upon divine intervention. It was believed that God protected the innocent from injury during an ordeal. The ordeal of boiling water was used by both secular and ecclesiastical courts. The accused put his or her hand into a caldron of boiling water and tried to retrieve a small stone or ring at the bottom. The more serious the crime, the deeper the water. The hand (or arm) was then carefully wrapped in a bandage and sealed with the signet of the judge. After three days the bandage was removed, and guilt or innocence was determined by the physical condition of the limb. The water was thought by Christians to represent the biblical deluge in which the wicked were punished, while the fire under the caldron represented Judgment Day. Actually, this form of ordeal has a lengthy history in the Near and Far East that predates its use in Europe. As late as 1867 this ordeal was used in Bombay, India, although the local official who ordered it was punished.

The most widespread European ordeal was one in which an accused person carried a red-hot iron bar and walked nine feet; the more serious the crime, the heavier the iron. The hands were then wrapped and examined for evidence of healing or injury after three days. It was not uncommon for persons of high rank to request this ordeal voluntarily to prove their innocence. A famous story involves Bishop Poppo, who went as a missionary to Denmark in A.D. 962. The pagan Danish king Harold Blaatland dared him to prove his faith in God. Poppo underwent an ordeal of red-hot iron before the royal court (a varying legend recounts that Poppo put on a red-hot gauntlet up to the elbow). His hands were not injured, and as a result of this miracle the Danes converted to Christianity.

During the trials of the Inquisition an accused person was presumed guilty, was usually not told the charges, and was tortured as a means of forcing a confession. Perhaps the most popular torture was the use of the strappado. The accused person's hands were tied behind his or her back. A cord was fastened to the wrists, and a 125-pound weight was attached to the feet (the weight was increased to 250 pounds during "extraordinary" torture). With the aid of a pulley the accused was lifted into the air and dropped rapidly. The rope was secured before the feet touched the ground, thus dislocating the joints of the person's arms. The procedure was usually repeated three times. Insane persons, children, and pregnant women were exempt from the strappado, and Inquisitors also were supposed to stop the torture if the accused's life or limb was endangered. It was practically impossible, however, not to dislocate the arm joints. The accused were warned that if they died or were crippled by the strappado they had only themselves to blame for not spontaneously confessing the truth.

The Feet

In 1882, Dr. R. A. Jamieson, of Shanghai, presented a pair of feet to the British Royal College of Surgeons. The feet belonged to a Chinese beggar who extracted much pity and made a profitable business in Shanghai's foreign settlement by displaying the mutilated stumps of his legs while carrying his feet on a string around his neck. After being run over by a carriage, he was carried to a hospital where he admitted that he removed the feet himself. In order to make himself as attractive as possible to the charitably disposed, he had fastened cords around his ankles, tightening them every two days. After two weeks he felt no pain; after six weeks he was able to remove the feet by partly cutting and partly snapping the bones. The stumps healed, and the feet became black and mummified. When the police threatened to confiscate his feet, he sold them to a hospital attendant. Jamieson noted that such instances of self-mutilation were frequent in China and added that "they throw a light on that singular mixture of courage, deceit, and sacrifice of almost anything to advance low enterprise, which characterizes the low orders in that country" (Jamieson 1882, p. 398).

In ancient China a severe method of ensuring feminine virtue was developed: women's feet were deliberately mutilated (Levy 1968). As a result Chinese women of beauty were confined to the bedrooms of their husbands. Literally and figuratively, Chinese men made sure that their wives and mistresses would not "run around."

Chinese foot binding started out fairly innocuously during the eleventh century A.D. when court dancers bound their feet with tight shoes. Their tiny feet became objects of admiration, and a more effective binding procedure for creating tiny feet was soon developed. Following an old palace tradition, a beautiful and elaborate pedestal in the shape of a lotus served as a dance floor; the term *golden lotus* became synonymous with bound feet.

At that time Chinese attitudes toward women were relatively liberal. Widows and divorcees were allowed to remarry, and courtesans wrote frank poems about their feelings. A conservative backlash developed during the Sung dynasty. Education for women was drastically curtailed. The "total" woman of this period was the one who stayed at home, was docile, worshiped her husband, and had tiny feet. Foot binding became a visible sign of the upper classes, signifying that a woman was so refined that she was incapable of doing anything useful except satisfying her husband. Officials sometimes ordered excessive foot binding to enforce morality among the lower classes. In the Fukien area, for example, one governor ordered that all women's feet were to be crippled to change their unchaste behavior. These women could hardly move, and when they attended celebrations or funerals the gatherings were referred to as "A Forest of Canes."

The process of foot binding began in early childhood. A bandage two inches wide and ten feet long was tightly wrapped around each foot, sparing only the large toe. The object of foot binding was to break many of the bones in the foot, to bend the toes into the sole of the foot, and to bring the sole and heel as close together as possible. The flesh often became putrescent during the binding, and sometimes one or more toes sloughed off. The pain continued for about a year and then diminished, until the feet became numb.

Children who attempted to loosen the wrappings were beaten, and every few weeks the bound feet were compressed into new and smaller shoes. The following was written by a woman who endured the bindings:

> In the summer, my feet smelled offensively because of pus and blood; in winter, my feet felt cold because of lack of circulation and hurt if they got too near heat. Four of the toes were curled in like so many dead caterpillars; no outsider would ever have believed that they belonged to a human being. It took two years to achieve the three inch model. My toenails pressed against the flesh like thin paper. The heavily creased plantar couldn't be scratched when it itched or soothed when it ached. My shanks were thin, my feet became humped, ugly, and odiferous; how I envied the natural-footed! (Levy 1968, pp. 27–28)

Deformed, tiny feet became a major standard of beauty. Poets praised them; men demanded them in their wives; courtesans without them were shunned. It was said that the tiny foot contained the beauty of the entire body: it glistened like the skin; it arched like the eyebrow; it pointed like jade fingers; it was soft and rounded (the deformed heel) like the breasts; it was small like the mouth, mysterious like the vagina, and its odor was more seductive than that of the armpits or glands. Lotus lovers reveled in smelling, rubbing, chewing, licking, and washing tiny feet. "Eating Steamed Dumplings in Pure Water" was the Chinese term once used to describe foot licking. One connoisseur noted that the flavor of the lotus foot was "the greatest flavor of mankind, beyond sweet and sour, unnameable." Another wrote: "Every night I smell her feet, placing the tip of my nose in the deepest recesses of her plantar. I am extremely excited by the smell. I only regret that I cannot swallow down the white chestnut with one mouthful. But I can still place it in my mouth and chew the plantar" (Levy 1968, p. 142).

The ecstasy experienced by Chinese men upon seeing or fondling a lotus foot was the equivalent of that experienced by Western men upon seeing or fondling a female breast. The Chinese also believed, however, that foot binding had a special bonus; namely, it caused layer after layer of folds to develop in the vagina, resulting in a "supernatural exaltation" during intercourse. The inability to walk supposedly also caused women's thighs to become sensuously heavier and caused the genital region to tighten.

Foot binding was no fad; it persisted for a thousand years. The Manchu conquerors of China in the seventeenth century passed laws against it, but these had little effect. It was not until the end of the nineteenth century that attacks against foot binding became widespread. Western travelers criticized the custom as barbarous. This had a great effect on Chinese intellectuals, who demanded that foot binding be ended because of the loss of face and prestige it engendered internationally. In 1894 an Unbound Foot Association was started in Canton, and branches emerged in many cities.

Christian missionaries zealously denounced the custom. Some refused to let women with bound feet enter a church; others would accept only girls with natural feet into boarding schools. A missionary named Gladys Alward worked as a provincial foot inspector, attacking the custom everywhere she went. A group of prominent Western women living in the Far East influenced the Empress Dowager Tz'u-ksi to issue an anti–foot binding edict in 1902.

Resistance to change was stubborn; for a millennium the Chinese people equated tiny lotus feet with perfect beauty. Laws against foot binding were not enough. Millions of leaflets and placards were distributed, and writers produced poems and popular songs that attacked the custom and proclaimed the beauty and virtue of natural feet. In 1911 the great Chinese revolutionary leader and physician Sun Yat-sen prohibited foot binding and ordered offenders to be fined. In many areas officials forcibly removed women with bound feet from their homes and publicly ridiculed them. Bounties were paid to women who turned in their bindings. The Japanese vigorously prohibited foot binding on Taiwan. Because women with bound feet often hid at home, the Japanese did house-to-house searches and destroyed all chamber pots, thus forcing women to be seen when they went to a public toilet.

Foot binding was finally eliminated in the 1930s. Chinese attitudes toward women had changed drastically in the face of liberal reforms. Women with bound feet were divorced and deserted by their husbands. Many who tried to "let out" their feet found that they were unalterably crippled. It is still possible today to see some elderly women in China who hobble along with canes, the permanent victims of a terribly cruel custom.

Clinical Cases

Deviant self-mutilation of only the upper limbs is associated mainly with organic disorders of the nervous system, with major depression, and with schizophrenia (wrist slashing is discussed in chap. 7). Religious delusions often are prominent. In contrast, deviant self-mutilation of the lower limbs is associated mainly with personality disorders and psychosexual disorders such as the paraphilias in which sexual excitement is linked with unusual or bizarre imagery and acts.

Urechia (1931) described the case of a 39-year-old alcoholic man who was admitted to the hospital with symptoms of syphilitic dementia. He was treated by innoculation with malaria (the high fever caused by malaria is effective in destroying the spirochete of syphilis). He proceeded to develop convulsions, however, and in his confusion he bit off and ate several of his fingers without feeling the slightest pain. When asked why he did it, his response was that they itched. He died within several days. An organized meningeal hemorrhage was found on autopsy.

Conn (1932) reported the case of a 21-year-old woman who complained of sharp, penetrating, shooting pains in various parts of her body and of visual and auditory hallucinations that accused her of autoerotic practices. Her pains were relieved by the injection of a placebo. While at home one week later, she placed her right hand under the bed spring and deliberately fractured the phalangeal articulations. At the same time she fractured the bones in her left hand and the proximal phalanx of the left little toe, and then she dislocated both thumbs. The next morning she displayed her malformed, bleeding hands to her mother, who fainted. The patient explained that she mutilated her limbs to relieve the terrible pains. Over the next six months she pulled out several fingernails, lacerated her ear, and kept banging her hands. In the hospital she proudly displayed her hands to anyone who was interested. She had several neurological signs, such as unequal, irregular pupils and a passive tremor of her left arm. Conn concluded that her symptomatology, observed over an eight-year period, strongly resembled an organic syndrome (an acute, descending, radicular type of encephalitis). He felt that her autoerotic conflicts resulted in mutilative acting out, conflicts that came "to the surface" because her organic pathology weakened her protective psychological inhibitions.

Self-mutilation of the hands and feet is associated with a number of neurological diseases characterized by a sensory deficit. Patients with congenital indifference to pain, for example, often accidentally injure themselves severely and may present with marked skeletal and soft tissue damage in their hands and feet. Their inability to perceive pain may stem from a cortical lesion. Landwirth (1964) described the case of an 8-year-old boy with sensory radicular neuropathy and retinitis pigmentosa. The child had a loss of pain, temperature, and touch sensation in both his legs and hands. Vibratory and position sense were also impaired. As a result of trauma his fingertips and toes were shortened, scarred, and blunted. The distal phalanx of his right thumb was absent. In another case a 22-year-old man had a congenital sensory neuropathy manifested by an inability to appreciate pain, temperature, proprioceptive stimuli, and other surface sensations. Several of his fingers and toes were surgically amputated because he was often unaware that he had injured them, resulting in chronic infections. Since he ignored his wounds, picked at them, and refused to change dressings, an irate surgical staff sent him to a psychiatrist. The patient explained that he felt overwhelming disappointment and anger when attempts to heal his wounds failed; by deliberately making his wounds worse he at least could predict the outcome with certainty. By the age of 21 his right leg had been amputated, and he had developed a chronic osteomyelitis in his left leg, which was sure to lead to another amputation. He began to cut his wrists and forearms in different locations. He first said the cuts were suicide attempts but later confessed his true motive; his arm cutting was a sort of experiment to determine the ability of his body to heal itself. He developed chronic osteomyelitis of his left index finger and asked that it be amputated. When the surgeon refused, the patient stuck his infected finger through a hole in a shoe box, calmly cut it off with a hacksaw, and put it in a plastic bag in a freezer for later "study." Feeling helpless and victimized by his untreatable medical condition, he mutilated himself in an attempt to establish control over part of his body. Instead of waiting passively to lose his finger, he actively destroyed it. "He could then feel that he was losing body parts because this was his wish" (Dubovsky 1978).

Religious delusions are prominent in all of the reported cases of hand mutilation by psychotically depressed or schizophrenic persons. Lewis (1928) described the case of a widow who came from a highly educated and cultured family. She had a happy marriage, a fine career, and no history of mental illness. Then, at the age of 57, she told her son that "the end of the age" was here and that the Second Coming of Christ would take place at Christmas. Several days later she cried and said that the rest of the world was going to be lost. She had dinner, obtained a knife, and almost severed her left hand at the wrist. At the hospital, surgeons found it necessary to amputate her hand. She declared that she "must have been misled by Satan," and she regarded the hospital staff as devils. She had lucid moments interspersed with confused ones. She groaned and prayed continually, spat on the floor, refused food, and drank water from a bucket to wash away her sins. She died suddenly. A complete autopsy showed no lesions except for "an appearance of exhaustion in the adrenals"; it was surmised that her death must have been due to a profound psychic or endocrine disturbance. Lewis concluded that "since this self-amputation was evidently done as a punishment for sin . . . the incident may be classified with those symbolizing self-castration at the somatic level" (p. 194).

Mintz (1964) reported the case of a 37-year-old man with a history of poor childhood adjustment, a bad conduct discharge from the military, and several psychiatric hospitalizations. While on a ship he developed delusions that his shipmates were going to torture and kill him. After a number of abortive suicide attempts, he began to identify with Christ. Since Easter was approaching, he decided to overcome his torturers by emulating Christ, who overcame adversity by enduring the torments of his captors. The patient burned his index finger to a crisp to prove he could withstand pain. Then he ate the distal and middle phalanx. When he discovered the difficulties involved in burning his wrist (he intended to eat his hand) and armpit, he abandoned the attempt, now confident that he was capable of vanquishing his tormentors. His behavior can be understood as an attempt to retain control over his aggression by identifying with the powerful figure of Christ and by destroying a part of his body rather than committing suicide. Eating his finger may have reflected the gratification of frightening homosexual impulses—the finger symbolizing a phallus—which were, in part, the source of his psychological decompensation.

In the section on eye mutilation in chapter 5, I described the case of an 18-year-old schizophrenic college student who felt guilty about his homosexual interests; he sawed off his right hand with a hacksaw and removed an eye with a screwdriver. He was a self-proclaimed evangelist and regarded his mutilation as a special mission for God. In the same article the authors,

Goldenberg and Sata (1978), also reported the case of a young man who became increasingly preoccupied with religious thoughts. This occurred after he participated in a Bible study group that discussed Matthew's famous injunction. He made several abortive attempts to saw off his hand and to chop it off with an ax. He finally shot his right hand with a rifle and repeatedly requested surgical amputation, "saying that he was acting on God's commandments."

Arons (1981) told of a 30-year-old schizophrenic man who sawed off his right hand and hid it in a wooded area of the hospital grounds. He had been preoccupied with Matthew's biblical passage and considered the amputation to be "a necessary act." His history was one of difficulty with schooling and of short-lived menial jobs. He considered removing his right eye but decided upon the hand amputation instead. He had attempted suicide previously and was subject to feelings of hopelessness. He admitted to derogatory auditory hallucinations about his homosexuality and to paranoid delusions of persecution. He spent the next twelve years in the hospital with little improvement and continued his homosexual activities with other patients. While on a pass he deliberately stood in front of a moving train and was killed instantly.

I am indebted to Dr. M. K. Au of Kowloon Hospital, Hong Kong, for the following interesting case of a 32-year-old schizophrenic Chinese man whose self-amputation of a hand was related to his participation in a martial art cult known as god-sent kung-fu, or magic boxing. This cult believes that fighters who master the mystic power of being possessed by a god (usually the Monkey God) become immune to injury.

The patient and a woman friend were devout followers of the cult. One day, after swallowing some charm papers, they believed evil spirits were after them. Confused, they ran naked through the countryside, where the police arrested them. They posted bail and were released. The next day, while at a restaurant, the patient chopped off his left hand at the wrist. He fainted and was rushed to a hospital where he was treated. Against medical advice he fled the hospital, leaving his hand behind. That afternoon the couple, certain that they were being chased by evil spirits, jumped out of the window of their third-story apartment. Because they were god-sent kung-fu fighters, they did not believe they would be injured by the fall. Both were brought to a mental hospital where they admitted to ideas of reference, auditory hallucinations, and paranoid delusions. When asked why he had chopped off his hand the man stated, "I wanted to show my determination to abstain from gambling. . . . I could not be harmed because of protection by the god-sent kung-fu." The woman responded well to treatment and was discharged within two months. The patient made a much slower recovery. His hand was surgically reimplanted and worked fairly well, although there was a loss of power and an angular deformity. The couple married. The woman's mental condition was stable, but the patient deteriorated. He gave up magic boxing and frequented various Christian churches. He hoarded rubbish at home, often walked backward, neglected his personal hygiene, and continued to have persecutory delusions and auditory hallucinations. He was not very compliant with treatment recommendations. The situation was one of a folie à deux in which the patient, who was clearly schizophrenic, "induced" psychotic symptoms in his mate.

Apotemnophilia, or "amputation love," is a word coined by Money, Jobaris, and Furth (1977) to describe a type of paraphilia in which a person is sexually obsessed with the stump. Two cases were described in which men demanded that they have a leg amputated. Neither man was psychotic, and their conditions were thought to be conceptually related, but not identical, to transsexualism, bisexuality, Munchausen syndrome, and masochism.

The first case was that of a man who telephoned the psychohormonal research unit at Johns Hopkins Hospital. He stated that he was a "cryptic transsexual" but that his problem centered on his leg rather than his genitals. He requested referral to a surgeon who might be willing to amputate his leg. Even though he was told that this could not be done, he maintained contact with the unit through letters and telephone calls.

He wrote: "Since my 13th year, my conscious life has been absorbed, with varying intensity, in a bizarre and prepotent obsessive wish, need, desire to have my leg amputated above the knee; the image of myself as an amputee has as an erotic fantasy (each one different) accompanied EVERY sexual experience of my life: auto-, homo-, and heterosexual, since, and beginning with, puberty." He had had sexual experiences with two amputees; the first, with an older man, was satisfactory while the second, with a woman, was not pleasurable. He used pictures of amputees as a visual aid during masturbation. Between his two marriages he admitted to "promiscuous sexual activity," especially with adolescent males. He loathed himself on those occasions when he felt "like a woman" and noted that he wanted "to make real the fantasy that I am an amputated homosexual adolescent, for in possessing my stump I can, concurrently, possess my penis."

Since he could not find a surgeon willing to amputate his leg, he deliberately injured himself in the hope of forcing an amputation. He hammered a steel pin into his left tibia and infected the wound by placing facial acne pus and nasal and anal mucus in it. He did this repeatedly, and he also tried to get rid of his leg by placing a tourniquet on his thigh. He told the physicians that his wounds were the result of an occupational injury. Unfortunately, from his point of view, his leg healed with medical treatment. He eventually sought counseling for his problems and took courses that would enable him to have a career fitting amputees with prostheses. Although he thought psychotherapy was helpful, he was frequently depressed over his inability to rid himself of his leg. He thought his condition resulted from pathological family relationships (he described his mother as extremely overprotective, his father as repressive and hypercritical of his relationship with his mother, his adult older brother as a chronic bedwetter, and his younger sister as a lesbian) and from early childhood incidents. When he was 2 years old, his left foot and leg were so severely burned in a kitchen accident that he was unable to walk for almost a year. When he was 5 years old, his mother was severely burned in another domestic accident. He wrote that he had a savagely forbidden wish to be like a girl and that an amputation might both secure his father's love and sympathy and establish his male identity: "One of the anticipated 'pleasures' [for me] of being an amputee is the possibility of a genuine experience of identification."

The second case also involved a man who contacted the unit to obtain a surgical referral for amputation of his right leg. Although he had had no sexual experiences with amputees, he thought it would be sexually pleasurable to rub and to fondle a man's stump. During sexual activity he fantasized both himself and his partner as amputees. He also had frequent fantasies about amputees engaging in activities in which they overcame their handicaps, for example, waterskiing. He was quite frustrated that no surgeon would cut off his leg and wrote that "it is interesting to note that transsexuals can obtain sex change [operations], people obtain cosmetic surgery to meet the norms of society, and I cannot obtain my fulfillment legitimately." Through "underground" ads in newspapers he was able to contact persons who had the same desires but who were successful in obtaining amputations. Their method was to contrive a leg injury that required subsequent surgical amputation. He rejected this approach as too brutal and painful. He was able to gain some gratification by doing highly regarded volunteer work with amputees. He considered three reasons for his apotemnophilia. The first was that the amputation might represent a sacrifice of atonement (presumably for his sexual activities) based on his early childhood experience as a devout church member. The second was that the amputation might represent a way to avoid homosexuality because "most amputees, one way or the other, do get married." The third, and most significant, stemmed from childhood experiences. He was born with a mildly clubbed right foot and was severely criticized by his father for his faulty gait. The condition was corrected surgically, but he received no praise for walking correctly. At the age of 15 he fractured his right leg: "I didn't mind the pain at all. I didn't mind the cast. In fact, I rather enjoyed this experience of cast, crutches, and means of mobility."

Wakefield, Frank, and Meyers (1977) reported the case of a 28-year-old married man who was sexually excited by the sight (or photograph) of female amputees, who was fascinated by men who had lost a digit or a limb, and who wished to undergo an amputation. Two years earlier he had experimented with amputation to see if it would be enjoyable. He deadened a finger by submerging it in dry ice. After it became necrotic he told a physician that it had been damaged at work. He experienced pleasure during "the ultimate act" of amputation by the surgeon. A few months prior to seeking treatment he put a rubber band around a toe and amputated it with a razor blade. As a child he used to tie strings around his fingers, toes, and hands; he felt pleasure when they became discolored and fantasized about their amputation. At the age of 13, intrigued by a photograph of a boy who had lost a leg, he constructed and wore a peg leg. While wearing this apparatus he experienced his first orgasm. He felt sexual excitement in cutting the hand or leg off photographs of women as a prelude to masturbation. He established contact with other men who liked to share photographs of and correspondence about amputees and mutilations. Members of this underground group also indulged in self-amputation and referred to themselves as "hobbyists." On one occasion both the patient and a fellow hobbyist put on sandals to expose their amputated toes and walked through a shopping center for signs of public reaction.

The patient said he was happily married and had a "normal" sexual relationship with his wife, who accepted his "hobby" even if she did not understand it. His mental status examination was within normal limits. He recognized the bizarre nature of his symptoms even though he described them in a matter-of-fact, almost blasé manner. He remained in weekly therapy for nine months but never really established an effective therapeutic alliance. In fact, his stated motive for entering treatment was exhibitionistic: "I think I might be contributing to the body of medical knowledge." Once during therapy he thought of his desire for amputation as "doing to myself what I might have wanted to do to her [mother]." The examining psychiatrists concluded that his self-mutilative acts were counterphobic responses to castration anxiety and that his reaction to the stump of female amputees belied an unconscious belief that women possessed a penis. Further, they felt that his "crippled woman fetish" was linked to hostility toward women and that his symptoms served as a safety valve for his unconscious rage and destructiveness. They also reported that between May 1973 and January 1975 the widely distributed erotic magazine *Penthouse* published twenty letters on "monopede mania," in which readers described their sexual experiences with amputees. They also cited a popular comic book called *Amputee Love* which contained ambiguous drawings that made it difficult to distinguish a woman's stump from a penis.

Beresford (1980) reported the case of a 29-year-old man who was hospitalized for an elective amputation of his right lower leg. Two years earlier he had shot himself in his right foot and calf. Although he described the shooting as an accident, both his stepfather and the emergency room physicians believed that it was done purposefully. When the patient was 5 years old his mother remarried, and from that time he began to regard his right leg as bad and alien. Periodically he tried to injure his leg, and once during adolescence he put his leg in a plaster cast he had constructed. As a child his favorite playmate was a young girl whose right leg was severely crippled from polio. The patient's current complaint was that his leg was extremely painful. He sought a complete amputation even though the surgeon recommended only a below-the-knee amputation.

During a psychiatric consultation the patient described himself as a loner who lived in a cabin in the woods with a dog as his main companion. His hair was shoulder length, and he wore a shirt with the picture of a rifle being broken below the words of an antidraft slogan. He described an episode in which he angrily threw a man out of a third-story window as the most frightening time in his life. The psychiatrist diagnosed him as having a schizoid personality. He noticed that the patient used counterphobic mechanisms as well as isolation, fantasy, hypochondria, and projection to defend against his feelings of aggression. He felt that the patient projected his aggressive impulses onto his right leg and desired to have the aggression removed surgically. After much discussion the patient agreed to a below-the-knee amputation. Surgery was performed without complications, and although he did not accept the recommendation for psychotherapy, the patient reported no pain at a six-month follow-up and ambulated well with a permanent prosthesis.

7

The Skin

▬ ▬ ▬ ▬ ▬ ▬ ▬ ▬

The skin is a thin layer of tissue that encloses the body. Physiologically it is a fairly simple organ; socially and psychologically, however, it is highly complex. Persons may be judged and much of their fate determined, for example, by the color of their skin. Throughout much of the world great amounts of time and money are devoted to achieving a skin type that is thought to be beautiful.

Although we sometimes merge our sense of self-identity with that of another person or entity when we fall in love, participate in an intense group experience, or achieve some sort of mystical state, we normally live within our skins. All that is enclosed by my skin is me; everything else is not me. The skin is a border between the outer world and the inner world, the environment and the personal self. Certain psychopathological conditions such as acute psychosis or hallucinogenic drug intoxication may cause the skin/self border to rupture, with the result being an inability to perceive where the body ends and the outside world begins. During the experience of a phenomenon known as depersonalization, persons may retain a grip on reality yet feel that something strange is happening to their sense of self. To terminate this frightening and numbing feeling they may deliberately slice open their skin. At first glance this act may seem paradoxical since skin cutting might be thought to open a portal through which the inner self and outer world might flow into each other. In fact, a very different process occurs. The cutting causes blood to appear and stimulates nerve endings in the skin. When this occurs cutters first are able to verify that they are alive, and then are able to focus attention on their skin border and to perceive the limits of their bodies. The efficacy of this process is startling; skin cutting almost always terminates episodes of depersonalization.

The skin may also be thought of as a sort of message center or billboard. Through scarification and tattooing, for example, permanent messages about one's beliefs and social status are communicated. Temporary emotional states are also often communicated via the skin. Rage, for example, may be displayed by flushing, embarrassment or shame by blushing, and fear by blanching. Some neurotic persons persistently excoriate their skin by digging into it with their fingernails. They tend to focus their gouging on insignificant bumps or minor irregularities on their skin. Once such a focus is found, the individual experiences mounting tension, which is temporarily alleviated by scratching and removing the irregularity. Such individuals often try not to scratch but eventually succumb to tension. The persistent scratching has been interpreted psychodynamically as an attempt to express repressed rage toward authority figures and as a mechanism for ridding the body of badness and contamination, such as sexual conflicts.

A more serious type of skin mutilation occurs in persons with delusions of parasitosis. These individuals are convinced that their skin is infested with parasites, insects, or tiny organisms. To rid themselves of these imaginary bugs they gouge their skin with fingernails, knives, and needles, and even caustic solutions. Examination of the skin may reveal discrete lesions or linear tracks where "parasites" have been pursued. The typical patient is a middle-aged or older woman who, when she seeks help, brings a bag with pieces of her skin, dried blood, and dirt for the physician to inspect. Unlike neurotics, these patients do not experience relief from excoriation. Psychological assessment reveals delusions of persecution as well as concern over sexual contamination (Zaidens 1951). Guilt and resentment, often stemming from a fantasized relationship with a parent, are projected onto the skin. This focusing on the skin — a circumscribed delusion — may be, in fact, a defense against more global psychological deterioration.

There exists a group of patients, mainly female, who deliberately cause eruptions or lesions by placing chemical or mechanical irritants on their skin. They then go to a physician, claiming that their skin disorder suddenly appeared, and they strenuously deny causing the disorder. In some cases the motivation for such behavior is to gain financial compensation or to avoid an unpleasant situation; for example, a teenage girl who detested school secretly put concentrated lye on her hands (Gandy 1936). In the majority of cases, however, the motivation for this form of self-harm is unclear. The diagnosis of this condition, known as dermatitis factitia, may be quite difficult, and misdiagnosis may have disastrous consequences. As noted by Hollender and Abram (1973, p. 1284), "The extreme occurs when the diagnosis is missed and a consulting surgeon, intending to be helpful, adds his mutilating procedures to the patient's own." Perhaps the most dramatic of these cases is that of a 31-year-old woman who suddenly developed gangrene of her left little finger, resulting in its amputation. Tricking her physicians, she was able to produce more gangrenous lesions and underwent thirty-three surgical amputations until her entire left arm had been removed (Thomas 1937).

Tattoos

Although tattooing is a universal practice of great antiquity, it reached its apotheosis in the Pacific Islands. Charles Darwin noted, "Not one great country can be named, from the Polar region in the north to New Zealand in the south, in which the aborigines do not tatoo themselves." The word *tatoo* was first recorded by Captain Cook and derives from a Polynesian word for knocking or striking (a sharp needle was dipped into pigment and was knocked into the skin).

Polynesian tattooing, or *moko*, was done by a professional artist and symbolized social rank. A design was carved into the skin, and black pigment was rubbed into the cuts. Although the entire body was tattooed, special attention was given to the face, which was covered with circles, curved lines, and scroll-type patterns extending from the throat to the hairline. The facial tattoo of a chief or of a freeman was unique to that person. Indeed, when Maori chiefs were asked to sign land deeds by Europeans, they drew their face patterns on the paper in lieu of a signature or a cross. After death the heads of beautifully tattooed men were sometimes cut off and displayed on a pole, cured over a fire and kept as a memorial, or sold to admirers. *Moko* was also thought to be useful in battle because a warrior might terrify and confuse an enemy by grimacing, thus turning "the dark lines of the *moko* into a quivering network of aggression."

Specific styles and techniques of tattooing were associated with island cultures, and they served different purposes. On Hawaii, for example, women's tongues were tattooed to mourn the death of a chief. Among the Motu of New Guinea, girls are tattooed at certain life stages. The earliest tattoos are placed on the hands and arms. As the girls grow older, their bellies, chests, and backs are done. When they become eligible for marriage, their buttocks, legs, and faces are tattooed. The Roro tattoo a betrothed girl's breast and, at the time of marriage, the navel. Among the Kajang of Borneo full-fledged headhunters were allowed to have whole-hand tattoos; a man who had merely participated in the killing of an enemy was allowed to have only one finger tattooed.

Under the influence of Christian missionaries tattooing greatly decreased in the Pacific. In Japan, however, the art of *irezumi* is still practiced, although its greatest period was in the seventeenth and eighteenth centuries. In the nineteenth century, tattooing in Japan was associated with the lower social classes. Criminals were sometimes punished by having their faces tattooed. Classical *irezumi* tattooing was probably preserved by geishas, whose beauty was enhanced by the procedure. *Irezumi* artists traditionally cover the client's entire body with extremely colorful designs of dragons, fish, gods, flowers, snakes, and famous lovers. As noted by Brain (1979), *irezumi* enthusiasts have their own art galleries and art museums devoted to the display of fine skins; they have even "bought the skin off a man's back, making a down payment and collecting the skin at his death" (p. 52).

McCallum (1988) writes that tattoos in modern Japan are "a highly unusual manifestation within a society that more or less rigidly enforces conformity to a standard way of life." Most Japanese dislike tattoos so profoundly that marginal groups, such as criminals, deliberately get tattoos as a sign of solidarity against cultural norms. McCallum considers "on a deeper psychological level" a Japanese fascination with the perverse, erotic, and sado-masochistic aspect of tattoos. He notes as a unique phenomenon in twentieth-century literature that many of the best Japanese authors have written about tattoos. The most famous story, "The Tatooer," written in 1910 by Tanizaki Junichirō, is about a master tattooer who enjoys inflicting pain on his clients and whose secret desire is to tattoo a masterpiece on the body of a perfect woman. After years of searching he finds the ideal candidate, an adolescent girl. He attempts to seduce her through exposure to decadent paintings. In one painting, a beautiful woman gloats over the dead bodies of men whom she has killed. The girl admits her arousal but begs to leave. The tattooer forcibly anesthetizes her and creates his masterpiece—a black-widow spider that covers her back. When she awakens and sees it, she is transformed into a spider-woman. The tattooer begs to see his creation once more. "Silently the girl nodded and slipped the kimono off her shoulder. Just then her resplendently tattooed back caught a ray of sunlight and the spider was wreathed in flames."

Captain Cook's discovery of tattooing was really a re-discovery, since tattooed Egyptian mummies have been found and mention of tattooing as a mark of noble birth among the Thracians was made by Herodotus. The biblical injunction of Leviticus (19:28) — "Ye shall not make cuttings in your flesh for the dead, nor print any marks upon you" — indicates that tattooing was practiced in the Near East. Julius Caesar noted that "all the Britons stain themselves with wood which produces a blue color." Roman soldiers often had themselves tattooed until Constantine forbade it in A.D. 325 on the grounds that it disfigured what had been fashioned in God's image. Despite Christian disapproval (Pope Hadrian also decreed against it in A.D. 787), tattooing survived among the Saxons; at the battle of Hastings the body of Harold was identified by his tattoos, one of which was the name *Edith* written over his heart. The anthropologist Durham (1928) reported on the high prevalence of tattooing on the hands of Catholic women in some Balkan areas. The tattoos portrayed multiple variations on the themes of the sun, moon, and cross. Although the people of the region explained that the tattoos were done for beauty and as a mark of Christianity, Durham was able to demonstrate that they were derived from ancient mithraic and sun cults. The Catholic church modified the ancient symbols and reinterpreted them to fit into a Christian context.

One of the first psychiatrists interested in tattooing was Parry (1934), who wrote about the practice "among prostitutes and perverts." He noted that prostitutes indulged in tattoos to enhance their sense of self-pity. He thought that a woman who put the name or likeness of her pimp on her arm might be trying unconsciously to evoke the jealousy and wrath of her customers, so as to encourage mistreatment and further justification for self-pity. Parry believed that male homosexuals got tattooed as a method of admitting or even extolling their "perversion." He reported, for example, that one man had the words *Open All Night* and *Pay as You Enter* inscribed on his buttocks. He also discovered that some men tattooed their penises in the belief that it facilitated seduction. He noted that Asian prostitutes tattooed their sexual organs as amulets to ward off venereal disease. Sailors were another group for whom tattoos served a magical function; the pain of flogging was thought to be lessened if a sailor had a Christian cross tattooed on his back. Similarly, the tattoo of a pig on the left foot supposedly protected against drowning.

Tattooing became a limited social rage in the West as access to Japan became possible in the nineteenth century. In fact, Czar Nicholas II of Russia and George V of England (then the Duke of York) were tattooed by the famous Japanese artist Hori Chiyo. In 1870 the first professional tattoo shop was opened in London, and the first tattoo machine was patented there in 1891. A number of fashionable Londoners, including Lady Randolph Churchill, had patriotic tattoos done at the royal coronation in 1901. This marked the end of the Victorian era with its prohibitions against facial painting. Lower-class women then started to use cosmetics, while some upper-class women had their lips tattooed red and their eyebrows a dark color.

Since tattoos are meant to be permanent (some, of course, can be removed using modern medical techniques), they have been used by governmental bodies to brand people, especially those thought to be criminals. Throughout most of the nineteenth century, for example, deserters from the British army had a *D* tattooed on their wrist, and bad characters had a *BC* put on theirs. Jews, Gypsies, and other "enemies of the state" had identifying numbers tattooed on their arms when they entered Nazi concentration camps.

Some nineteenth-century criminologists, such as Lombroso and Lacassagne, felt that tattooing was an atavistic trait of primitive man that persisted among the lower social classes and criminals. Current thinking holds that many people—especially those belonging to nonconformist groups—get tattoos to demonstrate their defiance of traditional authority, to display a stereotyped symbol of physical strength and aggressiveness, and to provide a sense of identity and solidarity with other group members. The majority of prisoners in jails (in Western cultures) eventually get tattoos despite prison rules against it. Hoffman and McCoy's profile of prisoners (1981) contains many photographs of inmates and their tattoos. Inmates may get similar tattoos to indicate that they belong to a certain group and that they have shared experiences; for example, members of the Walla Walla (Washington) inmates' motorcycle club all have tattoos of the club's name, swastikas, and curse words. Many studies link multiple tattoos with antisocial personality, an increased incidence of assaultive behavior, impulsivity, and difficulties in heterosexual adjustment.

Ferguson-Rayport, Griffith, and Straus (1955), in comparing tattoo constellations with Rorschach responses, considered tattoos to be akin to a spontaneous, projective psychological test. Personality disordered patients were more apt to have multiple tattoos, often crudely executed, that dealt with pornographic, sentimental, bombastic, and pseudoheroic themes, for example, tattoos of cartoon characters or of words, such as *Death before Dishonor* or *Fuck the Army* on the hand used to salute superiors. Schizophrenic patients were more apt to have solitary tattoos, sometimes placed on unusual sites, that dealt with idealistic or magical themes, for example, a woman draped in a flag or a star with a steer's head in the center and with a letter, such as *p* or *x*, in each of the star's points.

Scarification

Scarification, the process of deliberately cutting the skin in order to produce scars, is performed both for aesthetic and social reasons. While the traditions of Christianity, Islam, and Hinduism accept mortification of the flesh as a worthwhile and holy practice, they do not encourage permanent lesions. Scarification is especially prevalent among persons whose darkly pigmented skin is not particularly suitable for tattooing. The tendency of pigmented skin to form keloids, or hypertrophied scars, accentuates the scarification process. To produce keloids, cutters lift the skin with a hooked thorn and cut it with a small blade; the higher the skin is pulled before cutting, the higher the keloid.

While scarification is less common in Africa now than in the past — many governments have passed laws prohibiting it — it is still practiced. The Bateke tribe's flat facial scars are among the most intricate and delicately wrought. Scarification was done by the Bangwa of Cameroon to enhance beauty and to indicate social status. Scarification also served medical purposes. A star cut on the skin over the liver was thought to prevent hepatic disease, and cuts all over the body were thought to free a person from illness-producing spirits within the body. Brain (1979) reported that scarification had ceased among the Bangwa by the 1960s, although he still saw "a few fine examples of the art."

Unlike some tribes which produce scars as distinctive tribal marks, the Tiv of Nigeria scarify themselves, at least on a conscious level, primarily for aesthetic reasons (Bohannon 1956). The procedure is revered not only for its beautiful results but also for its indication of a willingness to endure pain. Some scar designs on Tiv females are characteristic and immutable over generations, while others change just as Western clothing fashions do.

Although scarification among the Tiv clearly serves aesthetic purposes, Lincoln (1981) has uncovered another extremely significant purpose. The key to Tiv social organization is genealogy; it determines territorial rights, suitability of marriage partners, land usage, and many aspects of personal behavior. All of the Tiv who live in a territorial segment (called a *tar*) consider themselves to be descended from a common patrilineal ancestor. When a *tar* is threatened by conflicts, certain rituals involving a decorated sacred object (called an *Imborivungu*) are performed by a secret group of learned elders. The fertility of the land and the well-being of the *tar* depend upon this sacred object, which is seen by only a few select Tiv. On those occasions when the sacred object must be replaced or repaired, the elders use sacrificial blood from an aborted fetus. The woman undergoing the abortion must be pregnant for the first time, as her fertility is thus concentrated in the fetus. The blood is poured through the central hole of the sacred object and then is scattered onto the fields and into wells, thus ensuring a good harvest.

The sacred objects of the Tiv are carved statues of women. The decorations on the objects roughly duplicate the scarification patterns inscribed on females at puberty. These scars represent Tiv family, heritage, land, traditions, genealogy, and myths. Thus, according to Lincoln, the scarification "may represent the structure of time, placing the pubescent girl at the intersection of past and future. Beyond that, it may be taken as a picture of genealogical descent, whereby she is shown to be heir of the ancestors, bearer of descendents, and guarantor of the lineage's continuity" (p. 48). The scarification is not merely a didactic device but rather a ritual that truly transforms the girl into a woman and, inasmuch as scars mirror the designs on the *Imborivungu*, into a sacred object upon whom the *tar*'s fertility depends. Thus, the scars serve to anchor time and space and to ensure the continuity of life.

A somewhat similar function of scarification has been found among the Guyaki (Ache), a South American group. When young boys are considered attractive to women and knowledgeable about hunting, they participate in an initiation ceremony during which they undergo a symbolic death and have their lips pierced by the tibia bone of a monkey. The ceremony celebrates mythically the origin of the true Ache, and the "reborn" boys pass into a new age-group. After six to eight years they grow a small beard and are eligible for marriage. They then go through an excruciating ordeal in which deep cuts are made down the entire length of their backs. Honey and ashes are rubbed into the wounds to control bleeding and to enhance scar formation.

In Ache thought, the order of the cosmos is threatened at various times by a supernatural blue jaguar, which is able to devour the markers of time, the sun and the moon. By ritually "splitting" the earth with their axes the Ache impose order on the chaotic earth and thus protect it from the jaguar. They liken this splitting of the earth to the splitting of the skin on the boys' backs. Both acts serve to promote a safe passage of time and to prevent the world from falling into destructive chaos.

Scarification is associated with rebirth and with the development of masculinity during initiation ceremonies among the Kagoro on Papua New Guinea. Teenage boys first endure a period of fasting and preparation. On the day of the ritual they are beaten with sticks as a reminder of their submission to the tribal elders (among the Elema tribe, submission is expressed by the initiates' willingness to let the chief urinate in their mouths). The painful skin-cutting ritual is held in the darkened men's ceremonial house, where the boys chew plant leaves that may have analgesic properties. According to two psychiatrists who recently witnessed the ceremony, the initiators used razor blades to "cut double circles around the boy's nipples and continued to make a wide band of incisions in a curved serpent-like pattern symmetrically on the right and left side of the body, first on the upper arms, chest, and abdomen, then from the shoulders down the back to the lateral aspect of the thigh" (Jilek and Jilek-Aall 1978, p. 255). A crocodilelike skin pattern is formed over much of their bodies which are then covered with oil and mud to produce raised scars; such a pattern is associated with the belief in huge, reptilian monsters that embody the masculine-aggressive principle. Amid the noise of drums and bull-roarers, the boys' pet dogs are clubbed to death and "carried off dangling from a pole like slaughtered pigs." When the wounds are healed the boys emerge from the ceremonial house and, fully decorated, go on public display while the women of the village rejoice and dance around them. The boys are reborn as men and are strengthened by bloody ordeals to compensate for the perceived lesser biological endurance of the male sex. They also are rid of the polluting female blood that accumulated in their bodies during gestation and suckling.

Chapter 2 in this volume on religion, shamanism, and cosmogonic myths developed the concept that deviant self-mutilation may sometimes be a creative act linked with the restructuring of chaos into a prosperous, healthy, and amicable order. Psychiatric studies have focused traditionally on the act of self-mutilation with little consideration of the fact of scar formation. From the cultural examples I have presented, it seems likely that the scars resulting from self-mutilation may themselves have a symbolic significance related to the notions of rebirth, the continuity of the life process, and the stability of relationships. The presence of scar tissue is a physiological indication of wound healing. In cases of deviant self-cutting, the formation of scar tissue may sometimes symbolize psychological healing.

Human Pincushions

Gould and Pyle (1896) compiled medical reports on a nineteenth-century European phenomenon, namely, the practice by "hysterical" women of sticking pins into their bodies. In one case 217 needles were removed from the abdomen of a young woman during an eighteen-month period. Her physician first thought that she swallowed the needles during an epileptic seizure, but after removing one hundred additional needles from a tumor on her shoulder he discovered that she was sticking them into herself. Another case described a 26-year-old woman who, while in prison awaiting trial, pressed thirty pins and needles into her chest. She used her prayerbook as a hammer. On autopsy, needles were found in her lungs, mediastinum, and liver. Her descending vena cava was perforated, and her left ventricle had a needle sticking in it.

There were probably two cultural influences on the behavior of these "needle girls." The first was a fascination with media reports from the Near East about holy men who placed their bodies on beds of nails. The second and more immediate influence was the popularity of European entertainers who called themselves human pincushions. The best known of these was Edward H. Gibson, a vaudeville performer whose act consisted of inviting members of the audience to thrust pins into any part of his body except his abdomen and groin. He offered $5,000 to any physician able to detect signs of pain. On one occasion he erected a wooden cross on the stage and prepared to have himself crucified. An assistant hammered a gold-plated spike through the palm of Gibson's hand, but the act was stopped when some people in the audience collapsed. Gibson was not a hysteric; rather, he had a congenital indifference to pain (Dearborn 1932).

The practice of sticking needles into the skin is still encountered although not written about very much. A colleague in England told me of a 32-year-old man whom he saw recently in a hospital emergency room. The patient went there because "one of his needles" had become embedded in his chest wall. At the age of 10 he used to sew his fingers together with needle and thread. He progressed to sticking sewing needles into his body, especially his chest, in a compulsive manner. To accomplish this he had constructed a sort of catapult made of a pair of metal compasses and an elastic band. Although he struggled to resist the impulse—at times throwing away both the apparatus and the needles—ultimately he would give in. The needle sticking was described as painful and bloody. It caused his nipples to become erect and was followed by genital erection and masturbation. The patient had a history of marked problems in interpersonal relationships, especially with women, of long-standing anxiety, of obsessive tendencies, and of sexual guilt. All of the needle-sticking patients I have encountered personally also cut and burned their skin. Their usual practice is to stick sewing needles under the skin of their arms, legs, chest, and abdomen. They then massage the area so that the needles migrate from the point of entry, thus hampering any attempts to remove the needles surgically.

"Needle freaks" are well known within the drug subculture. These are individuals who seem to derive so much gratification from injecting themselves that the act of sticking themselves with a needle is as important as the drug itself. Some heroin addicts, for example, are able to obtain pleasure and to reduce withdrawal symptoms merely by sticking a needle into their arms. The psychological significance of needles was apparent during my visit to a Free Medical Clinic in San Francisco. There I learned of groups of heroin addicts who shared needles, even though clean ones were available and even though the addicts were aware of the dangers of contracting hepatitis. One addict told me that his group's safety precautions consisted of making sure that anyone who was jaundiced used the communal needle last! Some therapists at the clinic noted that many addicts requested acupuncture as part of their treatment. Regardless of what physiological process (if any) took place, the needle sticking itself gratified some basic need in these addicts.

Case Studies of Skin Cutters

The case of Helen Miller is among the best-documented modern cases of self-cutting (Channing 1877–78). At the age of 29, after two years of incarceration, Miller was discharged from the New York Asylum for Insane Criminals. A few months later she was sentenced to jail for grand larceny (she had stolen a stuffed canary and a microscope lens from a physician). She was well known to at least a dozen physicians and was being treated both for opiate addiction and for dysmenorrhea. To gain admittance to the asylum she began to "cut up." Once in the asylum she periodically slashed herself; at final count ninety-four pieces of glass, thirty-four splinters, four shoe nails, one pin, and one needle had been removed from her arms. On one occasion, "the skin and superficial fascia were cut in a straight line and as cleanly as if done by a surgeon, but the muscular tissue below was hacked in every direction and nearly to the bone" (pp. 370–71). She felt no pain when inflicting her wounds and seemed to experience erotic pleasure whenever the doctors were forced to probe her flesh to remove objects. She experienced paroxysmal episodes during which she cursed and abused other patients, neither ate nor slept, and begged to be left alone. These outbursts terminated after several days either in self-mutilation or utter exhaustion. At the age of 30 her delusions of persecution became more intense; indications of dementia began to manifest themselves. While it is very likely that Helen Miller was suffering from neurosyphilis (years earlier she had what were thought to be syphilitic skin lesions), her self-mutilation was diagnosed as hysterical in origin. More important, her psychiatrist considered her self-mutilative acts to be a manifestation of attempted suicide. Even today some professionals associate skin cutting with suicide; I contend, however, that it has little to do with suicide but is an attempt at self-treatment. This important theme is discussed in chapter 10.

The early psychoanalytic literature viewed self-cutting as symbolic castration in order to avoid real castration, as Rado (1933) put it, "the choice of the lesser evil." Novotny (1972) was impressed by the frequency of alcoholism and of the borderline state in habitual self-cutters. He interpreted the fear of penetration by any object, such as a hypodermic needle, in some of these patients as representing symbolically "the wished for and feared penetration by father." Since cutting offers direct libidinal gratification, he regarded it as a masochistic phenomenon. Since both rage and sexual grati-

X-ray of the arm of a woman who inserted sewing needles under her skin.

The arm of a 39-year-old man, much of whose life has been spent in institutions, including orphanages, prisons, and mental hospitals. He said, "I reach out for help by cutting myself. It may be stupid, but I get results. People help me when I cut."

Self-inflicted lesions on the
legs of a patient with Addison disease. (Photo courtesy
of Dr. B. I. Chazan)

fication result from the cutting, Novotny surmised that guilt may follow,
which, at least in part, is atoned for by the injury (much in the same way
Sioux warriors cut their chest muscles to atone for the unconscious wish to
bite the breast of the frustrating mother, according to Erickson). Novotny
found that many cutters are unable to separate fantasy from reality when
stress is intense and that they project "oral rage" onto the environment.
Rather than suffer passively from some fantasized attack, cutters take control and mutilate themselves, reconstituting their ego functions to a certain
degree; for example, cutting helps patients distinguish between reality and
fantasy, between what is "inside" and what is "outside."

   Winnicott (1958) presented the case of a woman who was fascinated by
autocannibalism, as exemplified by her fantasies about lost Arctic explorers
who ate parts of their bodies in order to survive. The woman mutilated
herself by eating pieces of her fingers. Winnicott considered her act to be
one of "experiencing." He noted that each person who reaches "the stage
of being a unit with a limiting membrane and an outside and an inside . . .
[has] an inner reality . . . an inner world which can be rich and poor or can

be at peace or in a state of war" (p. 230). An intermediate part of the life of a human being is "experiencing . . . [which] exists as a resting place for the individual engaged in the perpetual human task of keeping inner and outer reality separate yet interrelated" (p. 230). Kafka (1969) developed the theme of experiencing in a psychoanalytic study of a young woman who had the "exquisite border experience of sharply becoming alive" at the moment of cutting herself. She described the flow of blood as being like a voluptuous bath whose pleasant warmth spread over her body, molding its contour and sculpting its form. She was at a loss to understand why everyone did not indulge in blood baths, especially since they were readily accessible simply by "unzipping" one's skin. The patient described her blood to Kafka as a transitional object, "a potential security blanket capable of giving warmth and comforting envelopment," which was linked to her internalized mother. Since the patient did not always consider her skin to be her own, cutting it was a "transitional choice between the sadistic and masochistic object." Kafka felt that the elimination of skin cutting might result when the patient re-formed a more bodily-ego-syntonic skin membrane. The process he recommended was the working through of the transference and, especially, of the countertransference; for example, the patient decreased her self-mutilation when Kafka "experienced fully my inability to save her life."

Kwawer (1980) reported on his intensive psychotherapy with a hospitalized 23-year-old woman with borderline personality disorder who was prone to self-cutting. In childhood her family was exceptionally attentive to her physical appearance. Her parents fought, sometimes to the point of physical violence and separation. When the patient left home at the age of 18, her parents' marriage improved significantly. She began to overeat and entered therapy because of fears of nighttime intruders. Her first cutting episode, at the age of 21, came in response to her therapist's vacation. Subsequently, she worked with several therapists, who treated her with medications but were unable to help her stop cutting herself, pulling out her sutures, and setting fire to her bandages. When she entered the hospital, all medications were stopped, and treatment was exclusively psychotherapy. She cut herself badly when her therapist went on vacation. She experienced shame over her bodily functions and described her menses as disgusting. She collected her blood and saved it; in stressful times the jar of blood had a calming effect on her. Therapy focused on her feelings and fears of being alone and abandoned and on her sexual identity: "Becoming more openly erotic in her attachment to me, she stared at my groin in treatment hours, trying to visualize my genitals, and had fantasies about my sexual relationships" (p. 212). Nursing staff dealt with her mutilations matter-of-factly. Her injuries were treated as medical problems, and staff members did not capitulate to her demands for "caring." Kwawer felt that her angry demands for demonstrations of his concern were an insistence that he "take responsibility for behavior we both knew only she could control." As the cutting abated, she developed a vampiristic ritual — sipping or drinking her blood every night, mixing dried blood with water if no fresh blood were available. Her requests for medication were denied, and she became more open in psychotherapy, where her fantasies about homosexuality, prostitution, masturbation, and abnormal sexual urges were explored. She was elected chairman of the patient community group, learned to drive, bought a car, secured a part-time job, actively pursued her interest in pottery, and planned for her discharge. She went to live in a halfway house, continued outpatient therapy, and stopped cutting. Kwawer concluded that "only after a direct confrontation in the treatment with her self-mutilation, vampiristic rituals, and psychotic mother, was it possible to carry on a therapeutic inquiry into the developmental issue of womanhood around which [her] adult life had faltered" (p. 215).

The importance of depersonalization in some instances of skin cutting is clear in the case of a 20-year-old man who was hospitalized for the first time after cutting his wrists (Miller and Baskhin 1974). His symptoms of mutism, negativism, confusion, disorientation, and marked psycho-motor retardation resulted in a diagnosis of catatonic schizophrenia. Three weeks after discharge he went on a drinking binge and awoke in a jail to learn that he had assaulted, robbed, and nearly killed a man the evening before. He spent the next four years in prison, where he cut himself a dozen times. Upon release from prison he planned to marry, but at the last moment his fiancée changed her mind. The patient decompensated and was hospitalized for two years (which is when the article was written). During the period he incessantly cut himself on the arms, legs, chest, and abdomen. His chest cuts exposed his ribs, while the limb cuts went deep into muscle; once he even cut into his peritoneum. His psychiatrists determined that the patient "mutilated himself to terminate states of acute depersonalization characterized by feelings of unreality, deadness, and depression, of being outside himself and not in full control of his actions" (p. 641). He was unable to recount the events of his life in a meaningful chronology; because of innumerable episodes of depersonalization, he experienced life as a series of discontinuous episodes. His "claim that he could tell when each wound was inflicted and what the circumstances were surrounding the mutilation leads to the conclusion that he preserved in the flesh, in a dramatic and conspicuous manner, the history of events he could not integrate into the fabric of his personality" (p. 647).

Bliss (1980) reported on self-cutting among women with the rare diagnosis of multiple personality. The cuttings—sometimes brutal ones—were done by alter egos. One patient reported while hypnotized: "When I was 19, Sarah [a personality] cut my foot [a deep gash with a broken piece of glass]. She couldn't hurt my stepfather so she hurt me. She just gets angry, and I get hurt. . . . She cut my wrist with a big long knife to punish me because I'm weak" (p. 1392). Bliss had only female cutters in his sample. He felt that while women usually direct their rage against themselves, men direct their anger against others who presumably symbolize brutal relatives in early life. He felt that some of the strange assaultive and lethal crimes are committed by men with multiple personalities. Another study of 100 patients with this disorder found that 71 had a history of suicidal gestures. "Internal homicide" behavior in which one personality attempted to kill an alternate personality was found in 53 patients, while self-mutilation, which was usually inflicted on one personality as punishment by another, was observed in 34 patients (Putnam et al. 1986).

Siomopoulos (1974) regarded skin cutting as an impulse neurosis strongly linked with sexual symbolism; for example, skin cutting supposedly represents the creation of multiple little female genitalia on the skin, "which become available for uninhibited touching, handling, and all sorts of manipulations" (p. 90). One of his case reports tells of a young woman with a history of intense masturbatory activity in childhood. At the age of 14 she reached menarche, and she became preoccupied with religious ideas. She was sent to a convent school where she began to cut herself on unexposed body areas, such as the breasts and abdomen. The impulse to cut followed periods of extreme tension and was irresistible. She cut herself frequently, "with mixed feelings of pleasure and guilt." She dreaded sexual contacts and avoided dating. She was hospitalized but continued to mutilate herself. The self-cutting became less frequent as she participated in therapy that dealt with her fears about sexual relationships and her early masturbatory activity.

Epidemiological and Group Studies of Skin Cutters

Self-cutting, especially wrist cutting, became a focus of psychiatric interest in the 1960s, in both the United States and Great Britain. It seems likely that the incidence of self-cutting increased at that time, although no hard data are available to support this impression. A number of studies (Pao 1969;

Grunebaum and Klerman 1967; Burnham 1969; Asch 1971) portray the typical wrist slasher as "an attractive, intelligent, unmarried young woman, who is either promiscuous or overtly afraid of sex, easily addicted and unable to relate to others. . . . She slashes her wrists indiscriminately and repeatedly at the slightest provocation, but she does not commit suicide. She feels relief with the commission of her act" (Graff and Mallin 1967, p. 41). These investigators consider most self-cutters diagnostically to be schizophrenic or borderline.

Nelson and Grunebaum (1971) reported on twenty-three wrist slashers, mainly white females, who were contacted for follow-up five to six years after the initial contact. Six were diagnosed as psychotic, eight borderline, and two neurotic. Three patients who had been intermittently psychotic over the years, often while under the influence of alcohol, had committed suicide. Two of the six psychotic patients still alive had worsened; three had improved; and one improved for a long while but then continued cutting. Four of the borderline patients had improved, while four had continued cutting. Both neurotic patients had improved. The improved patients attributed their decline or cessation in cutting mainly to increased ability to cope with sexual and angry feelings, to marriage with its responsibilities, and to therapy. Improvement was associated with increased verbal expression of feelings, with ability to use constructive behavior, and with control of psychotic symptoms; insight into the genesis of slashing behavior usually was not helpful.

Twenty-four hospitalized women who repeatedly cut their wrists were found to have the following characteristics: (1) a history of self-mutilation, such as rubbing glass fragments into their faces, carving initials in their skin, repeatedly traumatizing fresh fractures, and cutting themselves on the legs, abdomen, and face; (2) a history of surgery, hospitalization for serious illness, or lacerations requiring multiple sutures before the age of 5; (3) irregular menstrual periods, frequent amenorrhea, and a negative reaction to menarche; (4) confused sexual identity; and (5) complaints of depression, chronic feelings of emptiness, and eating disorders such as anorexia and/or bulimia. Most of the wrist cutting done in the hospital was a reaction to separation or rejection; for example, it occurred during active planning for discharge or just before the therapist's vacation. The patients described themselves as numb, unreal, or empty immediately prior to cutting. During and after the cutting episodes they felt satisfied, relieved, and even happy and fascinated at the sight and warmth of their blood. Rosenthal et al. (1972) interpreted these findings to mean that the patients experienced mounting anxiety that led to frightening depersonalization; cutting terminated the depersonalization — "a primitive way of combating the feelings of unreality and emptiness." Further, since the cutters had histories of menstrual problems and 60 percent of the episodes occurred during menses, wrist cutting was possibly a means of dealing with supposed genital trauma and conflicts about menstruation. The cutting thus represented a form of vicarious menstruation that was regulated and predictable rather than passive and frightening.

In England the Gardners (1975) did a controlled study of female habitual self-cutters. The most common experience leading to self-cutting was an unpleasant feeling of tension that intensified until the patients experienced relief by cutting their skins. Only seven of twenty-two patients suffered depersonalization before cutting. The cutting group was similar to the control group, for a higher prevalence of psychosexual disorder (frigidity or lesbianism) and obsessionality.

Yaryura-Tobias and Neziroglu (1978) identified twelve female patients who suffered from severe obsessive-compulsive symptoms, aggressivity (verbal or physical), insomnia, severe sexual disorders, family discord, and self-mutilation. Ten of the women cut their arms, legs, chest, abdomen, and vagina; one excoriated her skin; one cut her cornea. The average number of slashes was thirty-eight. Their diagnoses included psychosis with paranoid symptoms (four patients) and Tourette syndrome (one patient), while nine patients had had anorexia nervosa in the past. Eight patients had abnormal five-hour oral glucose-tolerance tests. The investigators identified two phases of illness, in both of which obsessive-compulsive symptoms predominated: the first phase occurred during early puberty and was usually characterized by anorexia nervosa and secondary amenorrhea; the second phase was characterized by self-mutilation and aggression.

Simpson (1975) compared twenty-four Canadian wrist cutters with a control group of persons who had attempted suicide by self-poisoning. Each group had twenty females and four males, all of whom were referred for psychiatric evaluation. On a scale of lethality both groups were judged to be quite low; nine self-cutters and ten self-poisoners had made previous suicide attempts. The cutters differed significantly from the controls in having major mood instability; complaints of "emptiness"; a strong interest and/or job in a paramedical field; excessive use of alcohol and drugs; a history of compulsive overeating and/or anorexia; negative reactions to menarche and menstruation; a history of surgery or hospitalization in early childhood and of a home broken by divorce, death, and parental deprivation; difficulties in verbalizing emotions and needs; a tendency to "abscond from hospital"; and a pattern of painless cutting and bleeding after a period of depersonalization, followed by relaxation and repersonalization.

Another English study (Roy 1978) compared twenty nonpsychotic inpatients, who had cut themselves at least twice, with a control group. The cutters (thirteen women and seven men) were significantly more introverted, neurotic, and hostile, had more sadomasochistic fantasies, made more suicide attempts, and reported excessive physical punishment in childhood. The predominant diagnosis among the cutters (eighteen patients) was personality disorder. The main reasons given for cutting were self-anger (seven patients) and a need to relieve tension (six patients).

Simpson and Porter (1981) studied twenty children and adolescents (sixteen girls and four boys) hospitalized for self-mutilation. Their average age was 15 years. Although all of the subjects were periodically suicidal, none intended to commit suicide through mutilation. Most of the girls cut their arms or wrists; several cut their breasts, burned themselves with cigarettes, or punched themselves until bloody or bruised. The boys typically cut their arms and/or penises. General characteristics of the group included eating disorders, abuse of alcohol and drugs, a history of physical abuse by family members (often including sexual abuse), and a sense of abandonment, isolation, and unlovability. The inability during childhood to develop reliable dependency relationships with stable parental figures apparently resulted in an inability to establish separate, independent personalities during adolescence. Simpson and Porter felt that the acts of self-mutilation were (1) a form of stimulation that enabled the person to "feel something" other than terrifying isolation; (2) a method of satisfying physical and sexual needs that historically were met through violent and bizarre activity; (3) an outlet for anger and rage; (4) a means of self-punishment for real or imagined transgressions or for loving fantasies toward parental figures; (5) a dramatic request for help; and (6) a relatively safe, controlled method of reducing painful emotional trauma. Self-mutilation neither killed the patient, as would suicide, nor physically harmed others who contributed to the patient's survival.

Self-cutting in Institutions

Patients in mental hospitals and inmates in correctional facilities are high-risk groups for self-mutilation, of which the most common form is skin cutting. A good predictor of such behavior among prisoners is the presence of scars on the wrists and arms upon entering prison (Jones 1986). Major self-mutilation is rare. A seventeen-year case review of inmates at a

Canadian regional penitentiary uncovered only seven cases of attempted or successful self-castration. Four were transsexuals who had been refused sex-reassignment surgery because of their disturbed personalities. Only one case carried a diagnosis of psychosis (Conacher and Westwood 1987).

The increased incidence of self-mutilation is due to both the presence of psychopathology among institutionalized persons and the nature of institutional life. Living where behavior is closely scrutinized by staff and where basic functions such as eating and sleeping are regulated encourages regression and thus may worsen individual psychopathology. Forced institutionalization, such as commitment to a mental hospital or imprisonment, often creates feelings of desperation, demoralization, despair, and boredom among inmates, who may resort to self-mutilation to deal with these feelings. Also, the crowding together of persons over extended periods of time facilitates the outbreak of all sorts of epidemics, including epidemics of self-mutilation.

An epidemic of self-cutting occurred on a psychiatric inpatient unit for twenty-five emotionally disturbed adolescents. The epidemic began when a girl cut herself, possibly because of troublesome sexual thoughts. She then tried to make her thumb fall off by wrapping a rubber band around it and also began to push numerous pins into her body. After eight months she was discharged from the unit when she inserted pins near her eyes. Another girl began to cut herself at the same time. After she began to swallow pins, nails, and glass she too was discharged. One month after the second girl started cutting, a boy cut criss-cross designs on his hands. All in all, eleven adolescents were caught up in the cutting. Eventually, it was discovered that several of the boys had cut secretly a month before the girl cutters were discovered. The adolescents took their cutting patterns from the first boy and girl who initiated the behavior. The epidemic was prolonged by two girls who vied with each other to produce the more severe symptoms; it ended with the transfer to another unit of those cutters who had antiadult feelings. The four transferred patients did well. "It would appear that each needed a period of acting out to be followed by a more controlling environment, and it proved impossible to provide both situations in the same unit" (Matthews 1968, p. 132).

In one Canadian correctional institution for adolescent girls, 86 percent of the inmates carved their skin. The average number of carvings was 8.9 per girl, with a range from 1 to 33. Most of the episodes (71%) involved carving initials in the skin, for example, the initials of a parent or a "lovelight" (a term used by the girls to refer to a close and intimate girlfriend; the term did not necessarily have any sexual connotation). Most of the carvers said they cut themselves when they were alone and feeling angry or depressed. Forty-eight percent reported that the carving was related to the lovelight system, where the act was regarded as a demonstration of affection, a sealing of a pact, a demonstration of anger over rejection by a lovelight, a jealous response to a lovelight's behavior, or a method of getting more attention from a lovelight. Girls who carved were thought by their peers to be "sharper" and more popular than noncarvers. On psychological tests, one-time carvers scored as less seriously disturbed than noncarvers or girls who were multiple carvers. "Carving was the girl's way of expressing independence, autonomy, and personal freedom. It was more than just a symbol of adolescent striving for independence or their way of opposing adult infringement on their personal freedom. It was a very adequate way of controlling their social environment. Through this behavior they could imitate and control adult intervention" (Ross and McKay 1979, p. 134). Carving thus provided the girls with a sense of power, satisfaction, and control over their lives.

Podvoll (1969) argued that self-mutilators in a hospital quickly assume an identity equated with their acts. The label *cutter* or *slasher* confirms a distinctive, functional role for the patient. Although self-cutting may lead to a personal sense of calmness, it evokes "feelings of unbearable intensity" in caretakers and challenges staff roles and hospital structure. The hospital unit that contains a cutter must engage in a struggle of caring versus punishment. There is little doubt that the presence of a self-mutilator often affects dynamic interactions of both staff and patients. As noted by Kroll (1978), relationships exist among self-mutilative behavior, the rituals and ceremonies of a hospital unit, the meaning and coherency of its social organization, and its therapeutic effectiveness. He demonstrated that a marked reduction in the incidence of self-mutilation on a psychiatric ward occurred only after "problems were dealt with from a consistent framework, and the staff pulled together as a unit" (p. 433).

Prisons are notorious hotbeds of self-mutilation. One reason seems to be the high number of psychopaths (persons with a diagnosis of antisocial personality disorder) who end up in prisons. Psychopaths seem to have a heightened need for excitement, novel experiences, and stimulation. Hare (1970) presented evidence that psychopaths have a lowered state of cortical arousal and a chronic need for stimulation. Psychopathy has been associated with poor performance in monotonous tasks, with slow-wave EEG abnormalities (a probable indication of cortical underarousal), with avoidance of drugs that reduce arousal, and with a preference for novel and complex stimulation. When thrust into prison, psychopaths are denied opportunities for excitement that exist in the outside world, and they may seek extra stimulation because of their inability to tolerate the routine and boredom of prison life. In many cases self-mutilation serves to provide extra stimulation. In his classic book, *The Mask of Sanity* (1964), Cleckley noted of the sociopath that "being bored, he will seek to cut up more than the ordinary person to relieve the tedium of his existence . . . [and will] eventually turn to hazardous, self-damaging, outlandish, antisocial, and even destructive exploits in order to find something fresh and stimulating."

Virkkunen (1976) examined forty self-cutters in Finland who had antisocial personalities. He found that thirty-five men had slashed themselves in prison; nine of these men had also slashed at least once outside prison, often in "prisonlike" closed spaces. The slashings usually occurred during quiet times at night when the prisoner was alone in his cell or in solitary confinement. The reasons given for the slashings were that "the closed space was oppressive" or that the prisoner "wanted to create some diversion," for example, to obtain drugs or a transfer to the psychiatric unit. Virkkunen's interpretation was that the inmates had a "poor ability to feel" and resorted to slashing themselves as a method of self-stimulation.

Johnson and Britt (1967) examined self-mutilators in a prison and found that very few were motivated by factors external to prison life, such as relationships with family or loved ones. "Normal" motivations resulted in 42 percent of self-mutilating acts. These motivations were normal in the special sense that they were consistent with the inmate value system that rewards behaviors intended to outwit officials or to disrupt usual administrative procedures. Most normal motives involved a desire for reassignment; the self-mutilative acts were intended to manipulate a transfer to or away from a particular prison, to obtain assignments to a certain cell block (sometimes to establish a homosexual relationship), to gain access to narcotics, and so forth. Normal self-mutilators typically resided in areas where manipulation of officials would be most successful, such as in regular inmate quarters and punitive segregation units.

Fifty-eight percent of self-mutilative acts resulted from "abnormal" motivations, that is, motivations not consistent with prison culture in that they reflected efforts to evade pressures from other inmates and an inability to withstand the stresses of prison life. Inmates with these motivations were more likely to mutilate themselves while in the hospital or in nonpunitive, segregation settings, thus highlighting their maladjustment to the prison environment. Most abnormal motives included desire for medical or psychiatric attention, desire to avoid homosexual attack, anxiety over admission to prison or subsequent reassignment, and wish for reclassification. A secondary class of abnormal motives was related to anxieties over relationships with particular inmates, such as the fear of being killed if one was suspected of informing on other prisoners.

Mutilations done in anger typically involved two to four deep lacerations over the fleshy parts of the arms or legs. The cuts did not hurt. The mutilator was somewhat relieved by the sight of his blood and the wound and called for help. The manipulative inmate typically made a small, single, painful, horizontal cut requiring a few sutures. If the manipulation did not work the inmate might escalate his mutilation, even to the point of sawing off toes or cutting his heel cords with razor blades. The fearful inmate typically made one or two small, painful cuts on his arms. If this "cry for help" did not produce results, he might injure himself more severely. Inmates who were in mental turmoil displayed a wide variety of self-mutilative acts, ranging from superficial cuts to facial lacerations. The cutting was not painful and, in fact, often gave a pleasant sensation of relief.

One of the most sympathetic studies of self-destructive behavior, especially self-cutting, among prisoners is Toch's *Men in Crisis* (1975). His book is a catalog of the feelings, thoughts, and behaviors of prisoners caught up in a spectrum of despair. It considers self-mutilation a unique index of "breakdowns" among prisoners. In an institution for youthful offenders Toch found a self-mutilation rate of 7.7 percent; in adult male prisons the rate was 6.5 percent; in a women's prison the rate was 10.8 percent. He noted that most acts of self-mutilation are not officially recorded in prison files; they are recorded only when severe medical problems arise, when changes in discipline are needed, and when bizarre, psychotic patterns emerge. In most instances the "inmates are disinfected, bandaged, and discreetly sent back to their cells."

Toch interviewed prisoners in the New York penal system and categorized his findings into themes or major concerns of the inmates, for example, themes of coping, self-perception, and impulse management. In general the dilemmas facing the inmates were existential questions about dependence, mastery over fate, and the capacity to endure pressure.

Toch considered self-mutilation by prisoners to be a form of coping. Some prisoners, for example, regarded the world in general and the prison in particular as overpowering, unfair, and malevolently arbitrary. Problems were viewed as predestined by some greater power, and self-mutilation became an expression of disengagement or self-exoneration. Prisoners placed in solitary confinement sometimes panicked; for them self-mutilation became a demand for release or escape. Some inmates felt a desperate need for support, understanding, or help that could not be provided by untrusted, unsympathetic, or incapable peers or staff. Self-mutilation served to bring such inmates to the attention of medical staff, who were often perceived to possess magical powers. As stated by one prisoner: "I didn't really have my mind made up. I thought if I asked for the razor blade, like, one of the dudes might not give me the razor blade, call the man and tell him I'm asking for razor blades; and the man might come. But the razor came instead of the man, you know? So I got the razor blade, and I cut on my bed. This was about eleven o'clock at night, and I cut my arms. I cut my arms pretty bad. I cut them, and I cut them again. I cut on the inside, and then I cut my throat. I cut my throat three times and then I laid down and went to sleep" (p. 48).

Toch also explored the role of negative self-assessments; for example, self-mutilation was a simple statement of bankruptcy among prisoners who perceived themselves as "inescapably relegated to the junk heap of life." For some prisoners self-cutting was a form of moral or psychological surgery that removed the basis for feelings of shame and guilt. As one inmate said: "It might sound strange to you, but after I done it, the next day I felt different. For some reason . . . it made me feel better. It made me feel that I had cut something out of myself, I started making a new thing" (p. 61). Inmates who thought that an important relationship was dissolving sometimes cut themselves as a demonstration of the depth, sincerity, and intensity of their affection. One male inmate stated, "Well, we got these sexual relations going, and things didn't exactly work out my way. He got angry with me because he was trying to be a woman, and I was already one. . . . I told my husband that I would cut up if he didn't straighten up, and he said, 'Go ahead, I don't think you've got the heart.' So I figured, 'We'll see.' So that night I actually cut up" (p. 80). As a child this inmate first cut himself after witnessing his father's attack on his mother in which her arm and leg were broken. "I thought if I tried to cut up or something like this, maybe someone in the family would start loving me and baby me." His sister saw the cuts on his arms and told his father, who responded by stripping him and beating him with a belt.

The psychosocial backgrounds of eight inmates at a special facility for habitually violent prisoners were the focus of a study by Bach-Y-Rita (1974). These men were self-mutilators and averaged ninety-three scars each. With one exception, all of the cuts were self-inflicted while the men were in prison. The men were characterized as having alcoholic fathers, depression and loneliness during adolescence, early family instability, and confused sexuality. They frequently cut themselves without feeling pain while in isolation. The cutting was preceded by a feeling of depression and mounting tension and was followed by a sense of relief. Bach-Y-Rita felt that "the constellation of withdrawal, depressive reaction, hyperexcitability, hyper-reactivity, stimulus-seeking behavior, impaired pain perception, and violent aggressive behavior directed at self or others may be the consequence of having been reared under conditions of maternal social deprivation" (p. 1020).

Hillbrand et al. (1994) compared fifty-three self-mutilating male forensic inpatients in a maximum security hospital with a control group of non-mutilators at the same institution. During the two-year study, 17 percent of patients engaged in self-mutilation. The self-harm group was younger, more verbally and physically aggressive across a range of severity of violence, received higher doses of neuroleptics, had more diagnoses of personality disorder or mental retardation, and had more civil and correctional patients. "Self-mutilation was less frequent among insanity acquittees. Unlike civil and correctional patients who stand to gain secondary benefits from self-mutilation in the form of a desirable transfer (i.e., return to civil hospitals and jail or prison, respectively), insanity acquittees are less likely to gain secondary benefits from self-mutilation." Almost half the cases were confined to one incident. More than two incidents were an indication that the behavior would be repeated, and the more the incidents, the greater the likelihood of severe self-mutilation. "Thus, there appears to be a window of opportunity for treatment after the first incident. . . . After that time, self-mutilation appears to be refractory to treatment." Some patients self-mutilated more than fifty times.

To test Turner and Toffler's hypothesis (1986) that self-mutilation in prisoners indicates severe psychiatric morbidity rather than reflects the institutional environment alone, Wilkins and Coid (1991) examined women when they were admitted to a London prison: a 7.5 percent previous history of self-mutilation was found. Cutting was by far the most common form of self-injury; 27 percent had injured themselves two to five times, 32 percent six to ten times, 19 percent more than ten times, and 15 percent more than fifty times. About a quarter of the women said that their self-harm was entirely precipitated by the stress of life events (arrests, arguments, loss of property, etc.), while another quarter said that their urges for self-harm had no explicable reason; half offered both reasons. Most (76%) planned or considered their behavior for less than an hour; many said it was a sudden impulse; 69 percent said that the self-harm relieved their symptoms of tension, dysphoria, and irritability; and 26 percent felt relief from depersonalization. In comparison with a control group, the women with a preprison history of self-mutilation had a high incidence of both personality disorder and impulsive disorder diagnoses; they also had "a depressing picture of early deprivation, family disruption, and physical and sexual abuse . . . poor adjustments in their sexual development, uncertainty in later sexual orientation and identity, failure to develop stable relationships, and evidence of polymorphous perversity."

In a second paper (Coid et al. 1992), a statistical cluster analysis identified two groups. One group was characterized by five or more episodes of self-harm; teenage onset of the behavior; no identified external precipitant for the behavior; multiple body areas affected; symptom relief achieved; history of overdoses, alcohol abuse, fire setting, and other impulsive behaviors; personality disorder diagnosis (especially antisocial and borderline); multiple previous convictions with first court appearance as a teenager. Another group had fewer than five episodes of self-harm; onset at age 20 or later; frequently identified precipitants for their behavior; little symptom relief; uncommon history of overdoses, alcohol abuse, fire setting, impulsive behaviors, or personality disorder diagnosis; few previous convictions with first court appearance as an adult. The authors concluded that the poor prognosis of the first group was due to a deficit in impulse control combined with a severe underlying affective disorder. This conclusion was based primarily on an association between borderline personality disorder (the most common diagnosis given to women in the first group) and depression. The authors note, "however, there is disagreement between researchers as to whether BPD predisposes to affective disorders, represents an attenuated form of affective disorder, is an atypical variant of affective disorder, or is a 'common pathway' to several psychiatric conditions including affective disorder." In dealing with the most disturbed and antisocial patients within "the spectrum of BPD," the authors believe that the depressive symptomatology might be considered "an affective disorder in its own right."

In 1939 Dollard et al. hypothesized that persons who are frustrated are more likely to demonstrate aggression when certain internal characteristics and external factors are present. The results of a study of male inmates at medium/maximum security prisons who had been referred for mental health services upheld this frustration-aggression hypothesis. Shea (1993) found that self-mutilators had higher levels of internal characteristics that increased the likelihood of self-harm than did non-self-mutilators, for example, higher levels of subjective distress, social alienation, and impulsivity, as well as poorer insight and coping skills. Among the external factors present were a highly restrictive environment, the prevalence of sharp objects and matches that could be used for self-harm, substance abuse, changes in relationships or living quarters, real or perceived losses, extremes in temperature, and a reaction of staff that facilitated secondary gain from self-harm. In addition, "MMPI data from this study suggest that self-mutilators are hypersensitive to environmental stressors and respond to frustration more intensely than do non-mutilators." Utilizing this model, points for interpretation and treatment were identified. Environmental policies might be more amenable to change than prisoners' internal characteristics, but perhaps the most useful approach would be to improve inmates' coping skills, assertiveness, and communication in order to decrease the intensity of their responses to stressors and to frustration.

Although exposés of prison conditions and prisoner behaviors appear frequently in the media, the high prevalence of self-mutilation is rarely reported. A remarkable example of such a report is the forty-eight-page article "Rock-a-Bye-Baby: The Life and Death of Marlene Moore," written by Anne Kerhsaw and Mary Lasovitch and published in the Kingston, Ontario, *Whig-Standard Magazine* (Nov. 25, 1989). A victim of childhood physical and sexual abuse, Marlene became a bully and was placed at the age of 13 in a juvenile corrections facility, where she was introduced to self-mutilation; 86 percent of the girls there were skin carvers. The majority of her adult years were spent in correctional and mental health institutions. Her life was marked by aggression, assaults, thefts, rape, alcohol and drug abuse, lesbian encounters, and at least a thousand episodes of self-cutting. Her body became a mass of scars. Many well-intentioned persons, including social workers, psychiatrists, lawyers, and parole supervisors, tried to help but without success. At the age of 32, during her final stay in jail, Marlene joined other prisoners in cutting themselves. While in a punitive segregation cell, she collected her blood, threw it at the guards, and hanged herself. Her story shocked the sensibility of an entire nation.

An interesting report on self-mutilation in a "labor correcting camp" in the Soviet Union was provided by Yaroshevsky (1975), himself an inmate who worked as a prison surgeon. Although he did not describe the "unbearable" and "inhumanly hard" conditions in the prison or note the incidence of self-mutilation, he wrote that he had treated inmates "who cut their veins, sewed up their mouths, sewed buttons on their bodies, disemboweled themselves, slashed off their fingers, toes, genitals and ears, swallowed foreign objects, and so on" (p. 443). One young prisoner urinated on his feet and put them through a broken window until they froze. Yaroshevsky regarded these self-mutilative acts as a way of both expressing grievances and gaining transfer to the medical unit. Political prisoners did not mutilate themselves, despite the fact that their conditions were much worse than those of the other prisoners. Rather, they went on hunger strikes, a passive mode of protest by which they asserted control over their own fates and bodies. Breyten Breytenbach, an Afrikaner poet and novelist, recently published a book (1985) about his experiences in a maximum security South African prison where he was incarcerated because of his underground work against apartheid. According to him, murder, rape, and cannibalism were rampant in the prison, and inmates often decorated their bodies by embedding bits of colored glass in their penises. A study of prisoners in Japan revealed that members of organized racketeer groups, or *yakuza*, distinguished themselves by special tattoos, by amputating one or more fingers, and by inserting objects such as small buttons, pieces of plastic, and pearls under the skin of their penises (Tsunenari et al. 1981). The tattoos symbolized manliness, the finger amputation showed apology or loyalty to the boss of the group, and the penile balls supposedly served to keep a parasitic hold over women because the balls allegedly enhanced sexual gratification.

8

The Genitals

This chapter considers the many forms of male and female genital mutilation found in culturally sanctioned practices and among mentally ill persons. Self-mutilation of the genitals has played an important role in psychiatry. Psychoanalytic theory holds that the mutilation of other body parts is symbolic of or a substitute for genital injury.

Castration

In the beginning there was Chaos. Then Gaea, deep-breasted Earth, appeared, as did Eros, who influenced the creation of beings and things. Gaea gave birth to Uranus, the sky, whom she made her equal. The Sky covered the Earth, and Gaea and Uranus produced the twelve Titans, the first race. Uranus kept the children captive in the depths of the earth. Gaea, an angered mother, fashioned a sickle and planned vengeance against Uranus. The children refused to take part in the plot except for Cronus, the last born Titan. With Gaea's help, Cronus took the sickle and castrated his father Uranus, casting his genitals into the sea. They splashed into the water; from the resulting sea foam Aphrodite was born, and from the wound blood that dropped to the earth the Furies were born. Cronus released his siblings and ruled the new dynasty. He married his sister, Rhea, and they produced six children. Fearful of being deposed, Cronus ate the first five children as soon as they were born. When she was pregnant with her sixth child, Rhea went to her parents (Uranus and Gaea) for help. She gave birth in a secret cave and fooled Cronus by wrapping a stone in swaddling clothes. He ate the stone thinking it was his child. Rhea reared the child, who grew up and vanquished his father, Cronus. The child's name was Zeus.

This famous story from Greek mythology demonstrates several themes associated with castration that have been incorporated into Western psychological perceptions. A son deposes his father by castrating him, thus establishing a prototype of adolescent rebellion against tyrannical authority. When the father's mutilated genitals were cast into the sea, the sea foam formed into Aphrodite, the goddess of fertility and the personification of the power of love, thus demonstrating the linkage between the sexual and aggressive drives. The blood from the father's genital wound fell to earth and gave rise to the Furies, the terrible forces that can drive a person to madness.

It is generally thought that castration originated at least five thousand years ago when humans learned that the procedure made some animals more docile, larger, and tastier to eat. The Caribs, fierce Indians for whom the Caribbean area was named, are the only known group suspected of applying this reasoning to other humans. They reportedly castrated prisoners and kept them in stockades for fattening and tenderizing before being eaten. Culturally accepted castration of men throughout the world tends to fall into several major categories, namely, punishment and prevention of sexual misconduct, enhanced religious spirituality, and institutionalized eunuchism.

Adultery has been punished by castration in a wide variety of cultures from the most simple to the most complex. The Babylonian Code of Hammurabi, produced in about 2000 B.C., provided the first written narration of castration. The code listed it as a punishment for sexual crimes; it also forbade the adopted children of eunuchs to leave home or fail to provide for their parents when they grew old. Other early references to castration as a punishment for adultery can be found in Egypt, beginning with the Twentieth Dynasty (1200 B.C.), and in China from about 1000 B.C.

In Western nations during modern times castration has sometimes been employed as therapy for sex offenders and as a means of preventing the propagation of criminal rapists and mentally retarded persons. One of the most virulent proponents of preventive castration (Barr 1920) noted that "the very life blood of the nation is being poisoned by the rapid production of mental and moral defectives, and the only thing that will dam the flood of degeneracy and ensure the survival of the fittest, is abrogation of all power to procreate" (p. 234). Barr called for mandatory castration of "the scum and dregs of mankind . . . the hereditary irresponsible . . . degenerates, imbeciles, defective delinquents, and epileptics—the very nightmare of the human race, ever with sexual impulses exaggerated" (p. 234).

Bowman and Engle reported in 1957 on the use of castration for the treatment of sex offenders in various countries. In Denmark 600 male sex offenders were castrated between 1929 and 1952 with the consent of the prisoner, his wife, and close relatives. In Norway 243 men were castrated between 1934 and 1950: "If the patient fully realized the purpose of the operation and accepted it voluntarily, the results were good" (p. 81). The authors noted that psychiatric opinion in England and the United States was largely against castration because it had not been shown to be effective and because of a fear that "it might get out of hand."

To understand the linkage between religion and castration we must turn to Phrygia in Asia Minor. It was here that the cult of Cybele was formed during the fifth century B.C., and it extended into the early Christian era (Engle 1936; Frazer 1922; Hays 1964; Vermasseren 1977). Cybele was the Great Mother goddess, Mother of Men, Mother of Beasts, the mysterious power that awakens everything to life. She had many different names, including Aphrodite, Artemis, Persephone, and Demeter. She was compared with Isis and was known as the "life-giving, frenzy-loving, joyful one, gratified with acts of piety." Her cult spread throughout Asia Minor and into Greece where she was described in the Homeric hymns as being surrounded by howling wolves and roaring lions.

Only one man consorted with Cybele. His name was Attis, and he was, according to differing legends, either a prince or a shepherd. One popular version of Attis's miraculous birth held that the sperm of Jupiter (Zeus) accidentally spilled to the earth, and a wild hermaphrodite named Adgistis was born. The gods were terrified of this brutish creature, and Bacchus (Dionysus) volunteered to deal with him. Bacchus added wine to Adgistis's water, and when he fell asleep the god tied the brute's genitals to a tree. When Adgistis awoke he found himself deprived of his genitals. From the blood of this wound a fruit-bearing tree arose. A king's daughter ate a piece of fruit from this tree and found herself pregnant. She gave birth, but her father ordered the child abandoned in shame. The child, Attis, was reared by a goat and by shepherds (as was his grandfather Zeus), and he grew up to be an attractive youth.

Cybele fell in love with Attis, and he pledged eternal fidelity to her. But then he had an affair with a nymph. Enraged, Cybele killed the nymph. Attis became insane and, thinking himself pursued by the Furies, emasculated himself, whereupon he was changed into a pine tree.

Attis's emasculation was immortalized by the great Roman poet Catullus (first century B.C.). He described how Attis, moved by madness,

> Lopped off the load of his loins with a sharp flint.
> Woman now, and aware of her wasted manhood,
> Still bleeding, the blood bedaubing the ground still,
> With feminine fingers she fetched the light drum
> That makes the music, Great Mother, at your mysteries.
> (*Poems of Catullus* 1969)

Festivals in honor of Attis were held in the month of March. On the Day of Blood (March 24) the cult priests, in mourning for Attis, flagellated themselves and cut off their genitals. Just as the priests of the Syrian goddess Astarte had done in centuries past, the priests of Cybele ran through the streets proudly holding their bloody genitals, which they eventually threw into a house. The honored household was then duty bound to supply the emasculated priests with women's clothing and ornaments, which they would wear for the rest of their lives. Many spectators, caught up in the intense emotionality, the frenetic music of cymbals and drums, and the sight of flowing blood, followed the priests' example and castrated themselves. This day of sorrow and irrevocable sacrifice was followed by the Day of Joy, the Hilaria, which celebrated Attis's resurrection. Secret ceremonies were also held, the most famous being a baptismal rite in which a devotee climbed into a pit. A bull was placed on a grating over the pit (the taurobolium) and was slaughtered. The bull's blood fell through the grating and covered the person in the pit, washing away his sins and granting him a new life. Some historians believe that the bull's testicles were eaten in the ceremony. The main sanctuary of Cybele, where this bloody baptismal was performed, was located in Rome on the grounds of the Vatican Hill, near what is now Saint Peter's Cathedral.

About 204 B.C. the statue of Cybele was carried to Rome, where she was worshiped as Mother of the Trojans, the founders of Rome, and where she protected the Roman state. As the Roman Empire expanded, so did her cult, and temples dedicated to her were erected in Spain, France, Germany, Britain, and all the Roman provinces. When the Romans accepted the statue of Cybele into their city they knew little of these wild rites. In fact, they were shocked by the strange appearance of the priests of Cybele who flocked to Rome. The priests had long, bleached hair. They wore ornaments and walked like women. They told fortunes for money, engaged in trance dancing, and flagellated themselves. Although the emperor Julian called emasculation "that holy harvest," most Romans thought the priests were insane and mocked their effeminacy. But some Romans were fascinated by their burning faith, ascetic life, and austere discipline. According to the French historian Graillot (1912), "Many troubled souls were drawn toward these interpreters of the divine word who appeared superior to other men, who listened to companions and examined consciences and gave consolation and divine hope."

The growth of the early Christian church coincided with the period of cult worship of Cybele and Attis, and Christian priests assumed some of the higher characteristics of the eunuch-priests. The flagellatory practices of some Desert Fathers also appear to have been derived from the eunuch-priests. Many of the temples devoted to Cybele were taken over by Christians, who converted them into shrines of the Virgin Mary. And, as Hays (1964) pointed out, "the carefully desexualized figure of Christ is more than a little reminiscent of Attis."

Although the Christian church did not encourage castration, some followers interpreted literally the words of Matthew 19:12: "For there are some eunuchs which were so born from their mother's womb: and there are some eunuchs which were made eunuchs of men: and there be eunuchs which have made themselves eunuchs for the kingdom of heaven's sake."

The most famous castrate was the theologian Origen (A.D. 185–254), who later lamented his action. Another was the presbyter Leontius, who castrated himself so that he could continue his relationship with the virgin Eustolium. His act angered the church hierarchy, who deposed him from his high office and protested when the Arian Christian sect ordained him bishop of Antioch. There is some evidence, too, that a sect of self-mutilators known as the Valesians zealously followed Origen's example. Active during the first half of the third century, this sect supposedly castrated themselves and also forcibly castrated others. In A.D. 325, the Church Council of Nicea prohibited priests from becoming eunuchs, and this became the official position of the Roman church forever after. A singular exception was the tradition of castrating young boys to preserve their voices for performing in the church choirs. It was thought that the sweet singing of the castrati rendered great public good. A number of theologians, such as St. Alphonsus Liguori, and popes, such as Benedict XIV, objected to the practice, which finally was stopped in 1880 by Pope Leo XIII.

Castration for religious reasons among Western Christians has occurred infrequently over the centuries. One of the most famous religious castrates of the nineteenth century was George Rapp, founder of the utopian, Christian, Harmony Society (1785–1847) in Pennsylvania. Rapp was troubled by sexuality and strongly encouraged the members of his community to live in celibacy. He castrated himself and was accused of castrating his son and several men who were unable to control their sexual urges.

Within the Eastern Orthodox tradition, the secret sect known as the Skoptsi, or eunuchs, included castration as a central religious practice. The sect, which flourished in Russia throughout the nineteenth and even into the twentieth century, was founded in 1757 by a runaway peasant named André Ivanov Blochin. He cut off his testicles because he could not follow his ideal of complete sexual abstinence. He was exiled but reemerged in Petrograd, using the name Kondrati Selivanov. He was recognized as

Christ by a small band of disciples, was again exiled by the authorities, and achieved "perfection" by cutting off his penis with a red-hot knife. He interpreted Matthew 5:27–30 (the text referring to cutting off one's hand and gouging out one's eyes) to mean that the genitals should be cut off so that a person would not be tempted to commit adultery. Selivanov believed that Adam and Eve were created sexless and that after the Fall, Adam developed testicles and Eve developed breasts. He thought that the halves of the forbidden fruit were grafted onto them, forming sex organs. In his view removal of these organs restored a person to a more pure state and relieved him or her of the burden of following Adam and Eve's sinful indulgence in sexual intercourse.

Selivanov's cult spread among all social classes and at one time may have numbered a hundred thousand. The Skoptsi practiced chastity and fasting and abstained from games, feasts, and strong alcoholic beverages. During their secret religious ceremonies they uttered prophecies and violently danced after the fashion of dervishes. They were ardent proselytizers; members who brought in twelve converts willing to undergo genital mutilation were given the rank of "apostle." They supposedly visited condemned prisoners under false pretenses and castrated them in their cells. They were said also to lend money at high rates and to forgive the debts if the borrowers agreed to enter the sect and accept mutilation. Selivanov was imprisoned when government officials sought to stop the spread of the sect among soldiers and politicians. He died in 1832.

Male members of the cult were readily identifiable because castration rendered them beardless and corpulent. The Russian government actively tried to suppress the Skoptsi, but the task proved difficult. The publicity attached to persecution attracted people to mutilate themselves to become martyrs. Some Skoptsi were shut up in monasteries, but with their ardent faith and powers of persuasion they succeeded in converting Orthodox monks to their ranks. Trials against cult members were reported as late as the 1890s when a banker and his niece were sentenced to hard labor.

Eunuchism, the large-scale practice of castration for social reasons, became quite important in the Eastern Roman Empire. The Byzantine emperors chose eunuchs for high political offices; the only position denied to eunuchs was that of emperor. Not infrequently noblemen volunteered to become eunuchs to obtain powerful governmental positions. The law recognized three types of eunuchs: those whose testicles had been cut off (*spadones*), those whose testicles had been crushed (*thlassiae*), and those whose penis and testicles had been cut off (*castrati*). Although the majority of eunuchs were *castrati* (over six thousand a year were sold as slaves and lust objects in the markets of the Eastern Roman Empire from the seventh to the ninth centuries), many of those who achieved high positions underwent less mutilative procedures.

With the rise of Islam the institution of eunuchism did not overly prosper, initially. According to Muslim tradition the prophet Muhammad forbade castration. Muhammad told a follower who asked for permission to castrate himself to avoid the temptation to fornicate, "He who castrates himself or another does not belong to my followers, for castration in Islam may consist only in fasting." The early Arabs did, however, purchase castrated slaves, who were employed as harem keepers. Beginning with the mid-thirteenth-century Mameluke period in Egypt and with the fourteenth-century Ottoman Empire in Turkey, eunuchism flourished. Eunuchs not only served in harems but also married and held the highest political positions. The Muslims did not perform the castration themselves but rather purchased eunuchs. Some monasteries in Egypt supported themselves by becoming "eunuch factories." Another center for the production of eunuchs was Khartoum, where slave raiders brought their captives to barbers, monks, and physicians to undergo castration. The trade in eunuchs was brisk and extremely profitable, fully castrated slaves being the most desirable harem employees.

In the Far East those countries that followed Buddhist precepts have little history of castration. The countries that followed Islamic precepts used eunuchs as in the Middle East, and those that followed Hindu precepts institutionalized eunuchism among some entertainers and dancers. Curran (1886) described castration of adults and children among Indian Hindus, apparently for religious reasons and financial gain. He noted that a ligature was tied very tightly around the base of the scrotum, and the penis, testes, and scrotum were cleanly cut off with a sharp barber's knife. Hot oil was spread on the wound, followed by a paste composed of boiled rice and soft clay. After an hour the paste was removed, and daily moist dressings of a cloth saturated in warm oil were applied until the wound healed.

During the sixth century B.C. in China, eunuchs were employed as servants for imperial concubines. The Chinese emperors used eunuchs to carry out household functions. Only the royal family had the right to employ eunuchs, a practice that continued through the nineteenth century. Chinese men voluntarily accepted castration to improve their social status, including many men who were married and had children. The operation was performed by royal surgeons who were themselves eunuchs. Once accepted into the royal household, the eunuchs were forbidden to leave; not a few achieved political prominence. Jamieson (1877) described castration operations performed immediately outside the palace gates. He observed that a man who volunteered for castration had his penis and scrotum bathed with a hot liquid, and he was solemnly asked if he would ever repent of his decision. If he appeared doubtful he was released; if not, his genitals were swiftly cut off by one stroke of a small, sickle-shaped knife. A pewter plug was inserted into the urethra. The wound was covered with paper soaked in cold water and firmly bandaged. For three days the volunteer received nothing to eat or drink. Healing took about one hundred days.

Monorchy

Monorchy, the ritual destruction of one testicle, certainly ranks among the strangest forms of genital mutilation. The earliest descriptions of monorchy came from European explorers among the Bushmen and Hottentots of South Africa in the 1600s. While it is tempting to dismiss these and other reports of explorers and travelers as misinterpretations or flights of fancy, one cannot dismiss references to the custom by highly regarded twentieth-century anthropologists such as Evans-Pritchard and Seligman.

Lagercrantz's review (1938) revealed differing methods and motives for monorchy. In one tribe the right testicle of each young boy was crushed between two flat stones. In another, the mother of each boy removed the right testicle with her teeth and ate it. In yet another, a tribal "surgeon" cut open the scrotum and pressed out and cut off one testicle. A ball of healing herbs was wrapped in sheep's fat and inserted into the scrotum. Then the wound was sewn closed. The primary reason given by natives for monorchy was that it made the boys swifter, more agile hunters. Other reasons stated that it prevented both sickness and the birth of twins (an evil omen) and that it was sexually attractive to women. Interpretations offered by Europeans were that it curbed the sexual appetite of young men, served as a method of birth control, and established a measure of social control; for example, a rapist would be punished by having his remaining testicle removed. As late as 1938 an anthropologist reported that "it is practised at the present day by people who are certainly not of Hottentot blood, but who must have derived their language as well as many of their customs from Hottentot conquerors in by-gone times. It stands to them in the same relation that circumcision does to many Bantu clans, that is, among them a youth cannot enter the society of men or take to himself a wife until he has become a monorch" (pp. 200–201). Extirpation of a single testicle also reportedly occurred in the Pacific Caroline Islands. There the left testicle was removed with a bamboo blade as a health measure to avoid orchitis and as a cosmetic measure to increase a youth's handsomeness.

Cutting the Penis

Mutilation of the penis is an extremely ancient practice which takes different forms, ranging from the simple slicing of the foreskin to the splitting of the penis from tip to base of the urethra. The reasons given for this practice are quite diverse and include such notions as sanitation, substitution for human sacrifice, symbolic castration, desire to be like women, elevation to the status of manhood, sexual differentiation, enhanced fertility, contraception, resolution of identity conflict, permanent incorporation into a social group, control of sexual urges, a mark of caste, a test of endurance, a covenant with God, and so on.

From studies of structurally simple societies some anthropologists hold that penis cutting results in a minimization of sexual difference between males and females; an example is Bettelheim's idea that the mutilation represents the desire of males to obtain female genitals. Others hold that the mutilation accentuates sexual differences; for example, among the Bambara of Africa the foreskin symbolically represents a vagina, the removal of which makes the subject entirely a man. Harrington (1968) rated cross-cultural socialization practices in 111 societies in order to compare differences between girls and boys in the areas of nurturance, obedience, self-reliance, responsibility, achievement, and general independence. Circumcision was linked with increased sexual differentiation but supercision (a procedure in which the prepuce is cut, but no skin is removed) was linked with low sexual differentiation. Circumcision and supercision were not isolated events. Rather, they were related to socialization processes leading toward either sexual differentiation or similarity. Reik (1975), a psychoanalyst, theorized that a man projects his unconscious hostility toward his father onto his son and therefore symbolically castrates his son through penis cutting in self-defense. In light of Reik's theory, Graber (1981) hypothesized that cultures with patrilocality (a residence pattern that brings fathers and their adult sons into continuous interaction) and enough political development to impede group fission and freedom of movement would have high rates of penis cutting. Examination of data on 250 paleos (primitive societies) supported Graber's hypothesis.

Subincision, the slitting open of the urethra, is a remarkable form of male genital mutilation performed mainly among aborigines in the northwest and central areas of Australia. It frequently is the last ordeal a young man must endure as he is initiated into manhood. Gould (1969) described these initiatory ordeals among the Yiwara. The youth first has an incisor tooth knocked out and his nasal septum pierced. Amid dancing and singing that reenact episodes of the totemic kangaroo, the boy is circumcised. He lies on his back across a living table of men, who are on their hands and knees. A relative holds the boy's penis steady, while his maternal uncle removes the foreskin with a stone knife. The foreskin is placed by a fire and, when dried, is eaten by his brothers. Months or even years later the youth must undergo a fire-walking ordeal. Finally, he undergoes subincision during which his urethra is cut open, with a sharp stone fluke, from the urethral meatus to a point about halfway to the scrotum. During these ceremonies some men who already have been subincised undergo further mutilations to enlarge their old cuts. Among the Bardi tribe, the subincision is carried out at the circumcision ceremony in which all of the skin is removed from the penis. This operation is performed several times on each youth; with each operation the subincision is enlarged until the entire urethra is laid open. The resulting artificial hypospadias sometimes heals over near the base of the scrotum, so some groups, such as the Pidjandjara, add transverse cuts in this area.

Subincision is practiced in a few other areas of the world mainly for therapeutic reasons. Rivers (1926) reported that in Fiji it was performed to evacuate blood and pathogenic bad humors. In New Guinea, Wogeo men periodically incise themselves in emulation of the purification women experience during menstruation. Some Brazilian tribes in the Amazon basin open up the urethra when it is blocked. The local rivers contain a small, transparent fish (*Cetopsis caudiru*) which may slip into a man's urethra; because of its fins it may become lodged there. Death can result from urinary retention unless the fish is surgically removed. Margetts (1960) reported a strange situation among the Kenyan Samburu, where prepubertal, uncircumcised boys perform subincisions on themselves. They do this in private without any ritual, usually during the lonely job of herding cattle.

Many investigators have tried to explain why Australian aborigines practice subincision. Basedow (1927) thought that the operation was done for contraception or for sanitation, for example, to relieve or prevent urethral inflammation caused by dirt or insects. Another theory holds that subincision is done to simulate the female genitals (Roheim 1949). Indeed, some groups use the slang word for vagina when referring to the subincised penis. This argument is enhanced by the fact that men often gash the subincised penis in order to draw blood during rituals: "Seeing that in the female the blood originated from the vulva, what is more natural than to make it come from the analogous organ in the male" (Montagu 1946–47, p. 432). Bettelheim (1955) used Australian examples to support his notion of vagina envy in men. He asserted that one purpose of male initiation rites may be to assert that men, too, can bear children and that through the operation of subincision men try to acquire sexual apparatus and functions equal to women. Another major theory is that the subincision results in a broader erection, thus enhancing the sexual act for women. Comments obtained from some aborigines — "Girls tell you straight away: you got big *burra* [subincised penis], I won't go to any other man" (Cawte 1974, p. 126) — would seem to support this theory.

A number of anthropologists favor a more general theory. They propose that circumcision, subincision, and initiation rites validate membership in a cult lodge, serve as a badge of increased ritual status and physical courage, bind the tribe together, and counteract disruptive tendencies inherent in aboriginal social and spiritual life (Elkin 1945; Gould 1969). Walbiri aborigines have explained that the practice of subincision derives from their kinship with animals, such as kangaroos and other marsupials who have a bifid penis, and from sacred myths. Thus, subincision may have evolved out of a reverence for "the marsupials as godlike ancestors whose characteristics men should imitate" (Cawte 1974). Enhanced sexual pleasure and sanitation might then be regarded as secondary gains. Cawte also proposed a *folie communiquée* theory, namely, that an innovator, possibly a psychotic person, mutilated himself or was born with a congenital penile hypospadias and persuaded others to follow: "Aware of the marsupial penis formation, this individual may have rationalized it as the raison d'etre of the procedure, and with the persuasive power of the paranoid individual in a closed community, may have succeeded in getting it generally adopted" (p. 131).

Male Circumcision

Circumcision is a very old form of mutilation, as evidenced by its practice among aborigines, by Paleolithic cave drawings of circumcised men, and by the emphasis on the use of a stone or flint knife for circumcision rites among Semitic and other groups. Joshua 5:2, for example, reads: "The Lord said to Joshua, 'make flint knives and circumcise the Israelite nation.' " The ancient Egyptians practiced the procedure as evidenced by circumcision scenes painted on the walls of tombs and by circumcised mummies. The practice has been widespread but not universal. The Mongols have never circumcised, nor is there any mention of it in the vast Sanskrit literature. Except for Athabascan tribes, circumcision was not widely practiced by North American Indians, and among South American Indians it is found in only a few tribes.

The most basic form of circumcision is a simple gash of the foreskin, a practice commonly reported among Pacific Islanders. The most brutal form, known as *salkh*, has been reported among Arab tribes in Yemen (Chabukswar 1921). In order to marry, a young man had to first undergo *salkh* without anesthesia under the careful scrutiny of friends. The ordeal consisted of flaying and removing all of the skin of the penis and the abdomen from the umbilicus to the scrotum. If the young man complained or flinched the procedure was stopped. The victim was deemed unfit for marriage and full membership in the tribe and was sold into slavery or killed. If he survived without flinching the crowd rejoiced, and he received treatment for his wounds which generally required several months to heal. Some youths died as a result of the *salkh*, while others developed urethral fistulae.

The saga of circumcision among Christians and Jews has produced an astonishing and vast literature. The Bible contains numerous references to circumcision; the first is Genesis 17 in which the Lord appeared before Abram, changed his name to Abraham, established a covenant with him and with his descendants, and promised that he would multiply exceedingly: "Circumcise the flesh of your foreskin, and that shall be the mark of the covenant between you and me." Every male child was to be circumcised at the age of eight days, and all male slaves were also to be circumcised. Anyone who failed to obey this covenant "shall be cut off from the people." Why circumcision was chosen as obligatory is puzzling since all other forms of bodily mutilation are prohibited to Jews. Further, circumcision was a widely practiced pagan custom; Jeremiah 9:25-26 lists "Egypt and Judah, Edom and the Ammonites, Moab and the desert dwellers" (Arabs) as nations that are circumcised in the flesh although not in the heart. Thus, it is difficult to understand why circumcision should be chosen as the unique mark of a special covenant.[1] If anything, circumcision would have made the Jews

1. Of all of the commentators who have tried to explain this enigma, Isaac (1967) seems to make the most sense. He notes that the Lord actually made two covenants with Abraham. In Genesis 15 Abraham is told that he will inherit Canaan. He asks for a sign and is told to split several animals in half. He then has a dream vision identifying that his descendants will indeed inherit the promised land. In the second covenant Abraham is promised offspring (even though he is 93 years old and his wife is 90) who will multiply and establish a great nation if he agrees to cut his foreskin. In each case cutting occurs, and Isaac believes that biblical circumcision may be "a special case of the ancient custom of using cutting or dismemberment rites in connection with treaty and covenant obligations" (p. 54). Although we usually associate treaties and covenants with binding, this was not always the case; for example, Alexander the Great bound Asia and Europe together when he cut the Gordian knot. Even today silk ribbons are cut to inaugurate bridges and highways, and cutting symbolizes the joining together of plans that once were separate. The ancient ritual of cutting worked *backward*, indicating that the covenant partners had been bound together in the mythical past; it also worked *forward*,

more like the Egyptians, from whom they probably learned the practice during their subjugation by the Pharaohs.

The most grisly biblical story involving penis cutting is that of David, the slayer of Goliath. King Saul, displeased with David's popularity, set a strange bride-price for the hand of his daughter, Michal. He told David to bring him the foreskin of two hundred Philistines, reckoning that David would be killed in the attempt. But, as recounted in 1 Samuel 18, "David arose and went, he and his men, and slew of the Philistines 200 men; and David brought their foreskins . . . that he might be the king's son-in-law. And Saul gave him Michal his daughter to wife." Another circumcision story is told in Genesis 34 in which Dinah was raped by Shechem, who then wanted to marry her. Her family agreed to the marriage on the condition that Shechem and all of the men of his village first be circumcised. While they were recovering from the circumcision and were still in pain, Dinah's brethren "took each man their swords, advanced against the city without any trouble, and massacred all the males."

Milah, the Jewish circumcision rite practiced for about two millennia, involved a simple cut and removal, perhaps, of only the tip of the prepuce. During the Hellenic period a number of Jews converted to paganism and tried to undo their circumcision through a surgical procedure known as *recutitio* or by using a funnel-shaped copper instrument, the *pondus Judaeum*, which covered and stretched the foreskin. The leading Jewish rabbis of that time were angered and decided to enlarge the scope of the circumcision operation. A new procedure was presented, the *periah*, in which the entire foreskin was removed, thus totally excising the glans and making a cover-up impossible.[2]

The multiple theories about the origin of circumcision have been dis-

---

indicating that the now separate partners belonged together as part of an original whole. Thus the circumcision cut re-created a mythical past "to give substance and status to an alliance directed to the future." In this context, Isaac's argument may have substance. However, no one has been able to make sense of the situation in Exodus 4 in which the Lord threatened to kill Moses but spared him after Zipporah, his wife, quickly circumcised their son and said, "You are a spouse of blood to me."

2. In the sixth century A.D., a change was made in the ritual; the circumciser moistened his lips with wine and then sucked the child's penis. This procedure, called the *metsitsah*, although widely practiced, did not become universal. In fact, in the last half of the nineteenth century many physicians and others objected to the health hazards of the *metsitsah*. The use of a glass tube was advocated instead of direct mouth-penis contact. In spite of this recommendation, illnesses such as tuberculosis undoubtedly were spread by traditionalists who transmitted the organisms through their mouths. Weiss (1962) published an investigation of Jewish circumcision throughout the world, his "attention having been called to the death of two newborn male infants shortly after their circumcision" (p. 31).

cussed previously. Early theories focused on hygiene. However, most Jewish writers have presented purely religious arguments, for example, the ritual is an act of faith. In addition, Moses Maimonides (A.D. 1135–1204) wrote in part 3, chapter 49, of his famous *The Guide of the Perplexed* that circumcision is done to weaken the penis in order to decrease sexual intercourse. "The bodily pain caused to that member is the real purpose of circumcision. . . . It is hard for a woman with whom an uncircumcised man has had sexual intercourse to separate from him; in my opinion, this is the strongest of the reasons for circumcision."

In the early Christian church there was controversy over the procedure, some factions advocating and others denying its necessity. Saint Paul had Timothy circumcised "because of the Jews of that region" (Acts 16) but eventually decided that the ritual was immaterial. "It is the same God who justifies the circumcised and the uncircumcised on the basis of faith" (Rom. 3); "Circumcision counts for nothing and its lack makes no difference either" (1 Cor. 7); "Those who are trying to force you to be circumcised are making a play for human approval—with an eye to escaping persecution for the loss of Christ" (Gal. 6); and, "Be on guard against those who mutilate. It is we who are the circumcision, who worship in the spirit of God and glory in Christ Jesus rather than putting our trust in the flesh" (Phil. 3).

As the church matured, circumcision rarely was problematic; indeed, January 1 is considered a holy day, the Feast of Jesus's Circumcision. By modern standards, however, one of the strangest chapters in the history of Christianity dealt with the status of Jesus's foreskin. At one time twelve churches in Europe claimed possession of this sacred relic, which was venerated for its ability to cure impotence and infertility and to ease labor pains (Wallerstein 1980). Among the mystical nuns who contemplated the foreskin was Saint Birgitta, who had a vision of Mary holding the foreskin in her hand, and Saint Agnes, who had visions of swallowing the foreskin. Various legends developed; one was that the foreskin was left to Saint John, Mary Magdalen, or the Apostles and was eventually possessed by Charlemagne. Another legend was that Mary was circumcised (various cults of Mary held that all the events in Jesus's life were duplicated in Mary's).

Psychoanalysts have written widely on circumcision. In *Moses and Monotheism* Freud theorized that circumcision evolved as a defense against the bisexual, orgiastic tendencies of pagan religions. The cult of Cybele, for example, required actual castration of priests and devotees. The Judaic God demanded an end to these orgies but accepted circumcision as a token of castration. In the words of the psychoanalyst Schlossman (1966), "Circumcision appears to be the last phase of a particular evolutionary process of sacrifice to the gods. The Toltecs and the Maya of Mexico sacrificed adults, the Phoenicians sacrificed children. In another phase the genitals were offered to the Mother Goddess, and finally the foreskin was offered to Jehovah as a sacrificial token" (p. 351). Glenn (1960) proposed a relationship between circumcision and anti-Semitism; the circumcised Jew is supposedly perceived as a mutilated person who seeks revenge and wants to circumcise others, giving rise to anti-Semitic prejudice.

Male Infibulation

Male infibulation is the practice of putting a clasp (fibula) or string through the foreskin. The literature on this practice is not very large, the major treatise being Dingwall's book (1925). In the first century A.D. the physician Celsus described the Roman form of infibulation in which holes were made through the foreskin with a needle and thread. When the holes became patent and healed, the thread was removed and the fibula attached. Once the fibula was in place the foreskin was unable to retract over the glans, making erection either painful or impossible.

Roman singers and actors were infibulated because it was believed that forced continence benefited their vocal ability. This notion is an old one and was first written about by Aristotle: "For in those who are wont to indulge their lust the voice changes to that of a man, which is not so in those that restrain themselves." Actors were voluntarily infibulated also because it made them sexually attractive to women who reckoned that a man denied sexual activity for prolonged periods of time would be an ardent lover when the fibula was removed. Apparently, some athletes and gladiators were infibulated as well because sexual acts were thought to weaken them for competition. This notion has persevered to the present. Only recently have professional athletes been allowed to travel with their wives. Several paintings on Greek vases depict athletes with strings through their foreskins, ostensibly to preserve their vitality.

In medical practice infibulation was prescribed to prevent illnesses thought to result from masturbation and nocturnal emissions. Karl August Weinhold, a German professor of surgery, proposed in 1827 that the human race might be bettered and the world population problems solved if the majority of men were infibulated; anyone who attempted to remove his clasp without the proper approval would be subjected to severe punishment.

Bauer, a physician in St. Louis, described the successful use of infibulation as a remedy for epilepsy and seminal losses (1879–80). His patient was a generally debilitated young man whose mind was greatly agitated and who lived in constant fear of insanity because of frequent nocturnal seminal emissions, petit mal epileptic attacks, and headaches. His condition was believed to have been caused by excessive childhood masturbation. Treatment consisted of a bland vegetarian diet, little heat in his bedroom, cold baths, a hard mattress, avoidance of lascivious reading, prompt evacuation of his bowels with cold water enemas, and, finally, infibulation with silk strings. The strings were tied at night to prevent erections and were loosened during the day. A one-year follow-up revealed that the patient was free from all symptoms.

Female Genital Mutilation

A most severe form of mutilation, introcism, was formerly practiced among Australian aborigines and was last reported in 1938. In this procedure, the vagina of a pubertal girl was slit with a knife or torn open by the fingers of the operator, the purpose being to enlarge the vaginal opening. This painful operation was immediately followed by forced intercourse with a group of young men. The spilled semen and the vaginal blood were collected and drunk as a tonic by the feeble, sick, and aged members of the tribes. The groups that practiced introcism were the same ones that practiced male subincision.

Female genital mutilation is currently a major public health problem in Africa. Most commonly midwives perform the surgery, and they may operate on thirty young girls in a day. Simple circumcision, known as Sunna circumcision in Muslim countries, consists of cutting off the clitoral prepuce and is analogous to male circumcision. Excision consists of cutting off the prepuce and the tip of the clitoris, and may include scraping away part or all of the labia minora. Infibulation, known as Pharaonic circumcision, involves removal of the clitoris, the labia minora and majora, and the mons veneris. The vagina is then sewn shut except for a small opening to permit the exit of urine and menstrual blood.

Boddy (1982) witnessed infibulation as it was performed prior to 1969, when local anesthetics became available and more sterile procedures were followed. A young girl was made to sit at the edge of a hole in the ground while her adult female relatives held her arms and legs. A midwife scraped the external genitalia with a razor. The raw tissue was pressed together, and the wound was closed by inserting thorns into the skin. The thorns were held in place by thread or bits of cloth. A piece of straw or a reed was inserted so that the vaginal scar tissue would not obliterate the opening. The girl's legs were then tied together, and she was left immobilized for a month. Boddy also witnessed the procedure in 1976 and noted the changes: a local anesthetic was injected into the genital area, and the clitoris and labia minora were cut away with scissors. The midwife then sewed the labia minora together with a surgical needle and sutures, leaving a small opening. Antiseptic lotion was liberally applied.

Knives, scissors, and razors are the most commonly used surgical instruments. If a family provides a razor, it is usually discarded after the operation. Scissors are sometimes sterilized; other times they are simply washed in water. Knives are rarely sterilized; often they are rusty and dirty. Indeed, a midwife may use the same knife for deliveries, circumcision, and housework. Although the entire procedure appears to be quite gruesome from a Western perspective, it is a cause for celebration in the African societies in which it is performed. The young girls may be dressed as brides and receive money, gold, and clothing as presents. In urban areas, printed invitation cards may be sent to guests. Singers and dancers often provide entertainment during the celebration.

Verzin (1975) listed the medical complications of these operations. Immediate or early complications include shock or death secondary to hemorrhage, infection, urinary retention, and injury to the urethra and anus. Later complications include malformation of the external genitalia that hinders or prevents medical examination, implantation dermoid cysts (some as large as a football) with subsequent abscesses, urinary tract infections, chronic pelvic sepsis, and dyspareunia. Additionally, the rigid circumcision scar often creates obstetrical problems, since the baby's head is forced backward and causes severe perineal lacerations. In addition to a posterolateral episiotomy, an anterior cut has to be made. If not done properly this may result in fistulae to the bladder and urethra.

Special problems occur for infibulated women at the time of marriage because the sewn vagina must be opened in order for consummation to take place. El Dareer (1982) noted that the customs and traditions about this matter vary widely. In one village, on the wedding night a friend of the bridegroom ties the woman to a bed. Her husband opens her vagina with a razor blade and attempts to have intercourse. Sometimes the nervous husband accidentally cuts into the rectum. Some husbands use knives or scissors. In one case a man poured acid on his bride's vulva. When he then attempted intercourse his penis was burned by the acid. The most common method, however, is for the husband simply to keep pushing into the small vaginal opening with his penis. After a few weeks complete penetration can be achieved; the vaginal tears and bleeding associated with this method are considered "normal." If this method fails, the couple may go to a midwife or a physician to have a decircumcision operation performed.

Recircumcision is also performed, usually after the birth of a child. The procedure is most commonly performed to tighten the vagina so that the husband will experience greater sexual pleasure. Widowed and divorced women may be recircumcised in order to appear as virgins when they remarry. Some women even undergo recircumcision routinely every six to twelve months to keep the vagina tight. Since those societies that practice infibulation place an enormously high value on virginity, the recircumcision operation also serves to restore the physical appearance of virginity to girls who have had premarital intercourse. As stated by El Dareer, "Thus, rather than preventing immorality, circumcision can encourage misbehavior, because girls know that they can always be stitched up again."

Although the age at which female genital operations are performed ranges from 7 days to 11 years, most are done between the ages of 6 and 10 years. How widespread are these mutilations? Hosken (1978) found that infibulation was practiced in the Sudan, Somalia, and parts of Ethiopia, Egypt, Kenya, and Nigeria. Excision is practiced in a large number of African countries, ranging from the west coast through central Africa to the east coast. Surveys taken at girls' schools in the Sudan, exclusive of Khartoum, show that practically all girls are infibulated by age 12. Surveys in Kenya show that 40–80 percent of girls are circumcised. Almost the entire female population of Somalia is said to be infibulated, while in Upper Volta 70 percent of women appearing at one hospital were found to have undergone excision. Out of a sample of 3,210 rural and urban Sudanese women, 98 percent admitted to having been operated upon. Of these, 83 percent had been infibulated, 12 percent had been excised, and 2.5 percent had been simply circumcised. The remainder were uncertain of the type of operation they had had.[3]

Gruenbaum (1982) and many others have tried to understand why these practices persist despite governmental laws prohibiting them and public health campaigns against them. The mutilative rituals serve a major purpose; they are an attempt to regulate female morality. Infibulation creates the ultimate chastity belt, one forged out of the woman's own flesh (Morgan and Steinem 1980). An infibulated woman is a guaranteed virgin most of the time and is therefore marriageable. Excision, by removing the sensitive clitoral area, is thought to attenuate sexual desires in a woman, who,

3. A recent study in Somalia found that 97 percent of nursing students had been infibulated, mainly by traditional midwives; 40 percent of the students said they would infibulate their daughters, while 55 percent would only circumcise them. While the nursing school educational program ignores the topic of infibulation, medical students are taught about the medical complications of the procedure. Interestingly, most of the male medical students stated that their families would not approve of marriage to an uncircumcised woman, noting that it would be "the equivalent of marrying a prostitute" (Gallo 1985).

freed from personal lust, can concentrate solely on pleasing her husband. In many African cultures, women whose genitals have not been modified are regarded as lustful, odd, and unworthy of being a wife and mother. The Arabic word *tahur* refers to purity, cleanliness, and circumcision; the uncircumcised woman is thought to be unclean and to have an offensive smell that emanates from her clitoris. The notion of "enclosedness" is important symbolically in many African cultures, and infibulation is one means of expressing this notion. "In that infibulation purifies, smooths, and makes clean the outer surface of the womb, the enclosure of the home of childbirth, it socializes or culturalizes a woman's fertility. Through occlusion of the vaginal orifice, her womb, both literally and figuratively, becomes a social space: enclosed, impervious, virtually impenetrable" (Boddy 1982, p. 696). The rituals are perpetuated because marriage and motherhood are the only viable social roles for women. Attempts to abolish the operations often meet with vigorous protests from the women who have endured them and from the midwives who perform them for income.

Huxley (1931) recounted that native misunderstanding of the arguments of Christian missionaries has contributed to the problem. For example, in Kenya the word *virgin*, as in the Virgin Mary, was translated *muiritu*, a Kikuyu word signifying a girl who had been circumcised and initiated but yet unmarried. As Huxley noted, "So the native Christian is confronted with a puzzle. He finds the mother of Jesus extolled and blessed in the faith he has embraced; but she is described in the Bible as a young woman who has been initiated and circumcised. And now the missionaries tell him that female circumcision is wrong" (p. 197). Efforts by Church of Scotland missionaries to forbid excision were credited by Jomo Kenyatta as being a major factor in the rise of anticolonial political activity. Kenyan men resented British interference with ancient tribal customs, especially those that threatened their domination over women. Thus, the rite of excision became an emblem of patriotism.

The government of Kenya banned female genital operations; fourteen girls reportedly have died there recently following excision. European interest was heightened in France in 1982 when a young Malian girl died as a result of a poorly done excision; the *excisuse* fled to Africa, but the girl's parents were charged with criminal negligence. Another Malian child in Paris was barely saved by French physicians. Her father had performed a clitoridectomy with a pocketknife; he brought her to a hospital after she bled sporadically for several days. French police charged the father with performing an illegal operation, but a Malian laborers' group protested. They argued that female circumcision is a customary procedure in their culture, just as male circumcision is customary in many Western cultures. Reporters in England discovered in 1982 that some wealthy African families were bringing their young girls to private surgeons in London to be circumcised. The practice has been denounced in a series of articles in English newspapers and magazines. A BBC television program on the topic was so vivid that only a curtailed version was televised. Legislation aimed at banning the "horrific operations" has been debated in Parliament, but the Royal College of Obstetrics and Gynecology opposed the bill for fear that it could prevent necessary operations. As it now stands, female circumcision is legal in England but is not a medically recommended procedure.

Debate about clitoridectomy is not new to England. In the 1860s, Sir Isaac Baker Brown, author of a widely used surgical textbook and president of the Medical Society of London, was an ardent advocate of the procedure. He believed that female masturbation gave rise to a series of diseases beginning with hysteria and eventually leading to spinal irritation, epileptoid fits, cataleptic fits, true epileptic fits, idiocy, mania, and death. Brown honestly felt that these conditions might be cured by removing the cause of peripheral nervous excitement, namely, "the clitoris and nymphae." Brown's book on the topic, *The Curability of Certain Forms of Insanity, Epilepsy, Catalepsy, and Hysteria in Females*, was published in 1866. A reviewer for the *Church Times* recommended the book highly and urged clergymen to bring their epileptic female parishioners, especially the poor ones, to medical attention in order that they might undergo the operation.

In 1867 the Obstetrical Society of London held a heated debate on Brown's procedure. It was labeled quackery, and he was portrayed as an unscrupulous profiteer. Brown was stripped of his fellowship in the Obstetrical Society and was expelled from membership.

Clinical Cases of Genital Self-mutilation in Women

The female genitalia are the object of many "assaults," such as rape, self-induced abortion, insertion of foreign bodies during masturbation, surgical procedures, and tissue damage during child birth. However, psychopathological self-mutilation of the genitalia is rarely reported. Only six publications on the topic exist in the literature (although in several other cases it is mentioned); three of these propose a specific syndrome in which the self-mutilation is found in association with an eating disorder.

The first report deals with a 24-year-old woman whose first three babies were delivered by caesarean section because of recurrent placenta previa (Gerstle, Guttmacher, and Brown 1957). Only the first child survived. During her fourth pregnancy, she confessed that she had inserted a hat pin into her vagina in an attempt to rupture the membrane and induce labor, since she was "very tired of being pregnant." By confessing to her physician, she thought she would have no incentive to indulge in further self-mutilative actions. Her pregnancy was stormy, and she admitted taking an abortifacient drug (ergotrate) without results. During the fifth month of pregnancy, she and her child "either deliberately or accidentally walked into the path of an automobile." She had several episodes of panic states and of self-induced vaginal bleeding. She was hospitalized the night before a planned caesarean section because of vaginal bleeding; a hat pin was taken from her. At the age of 18 the patient had seen her mother die: "Mother died of a complete loss of blood, which came out vaginally during her menopause. . . . she died in one hour—I was with her when she died and was terribly frightened" (p. 643). Shortly afterward the patient successfully simulated an attack of acute appendicitis. The surgeon who performed the appendectomy also performed the first three caesarean sections. The patient steadfastly denied any wish to kill her fetuses but rather said she simply wanted to terminate her pregnancies in order to see the babies born and detached from her. She related that shortly before her marriage her aunt had hexed her and prophesied that all her babies would die. When the consultant psychiatrist did not criticize her, "she made herculean efforts to convince [him] that she was evil and selfish, and accordingly deserved punishment" (p. 644).

Unexplained vaginal bleeding of two years' duration was the admitting complaint of a 19-year-old unwed mother. The bleeding began six weeks after the birth of her daughter. Over a two-year period she received three dilation and curettage operations, conization of the cervix, and multiple cauterizations. Because these procedures failed to control the bleeding and because the patient pleaded relentlessly for a hysterectomy, she was hospitalized for a thorough evaluation. When no organic pathology was found, the patient was asked about self-mutilation. She denied it but stated that she "might do something like that in my sleep, something I couldn't control" (p. 843). She agreed to have a dye (gentian violet) painted on her vaginal wall that night. The next morning she was bleeding profusely from her vagina; the dye was present on her fingernails and hands. A psychiatrist diagnosed her as having a histrionic personality disorder on the basis of her whining and childlike speech, her *belle indifference* to the bleeding, her seductive and histrionic behavior during the interview, her multiple surgeries, and a history of multiple sexual partners with little emotional involvement (Goldfield and Glick 1970).

French and Nelson (1972) reported the case of a 38-year-old married, epileptic housewife who was hospitalized for intractable overeating and self-induced vomiting. Her husband bragged about her girlish figure, but she considered herself fat. She regularly induced vomiting to keep from gaining weight, especially after episodes of binge eating. Her husband reported finding "buckets of moldy old puke hidden around the place." The woman felt isolated in her rural community and in her marriage. Although her epilepsy was well controlled, she had lost her driver's license. Her husband had once commented that in the event of a divorce he would get custody of their children because she was an epileptic. As her nervousness and vomiting increased, she was slowly extruded from family membership. Following an argument with her husband, she slashed her genital area with a razor blade; the cuts were superficial. French and Nelson noted that since her husband's interest in her was largely sexual, "she cut the only part of her he was interested in." They also noted that the dynamics underlying the patient's behavior were consistent with those of patients suffering from "dysorexia," hysteria, and anorexia-bulimia. They considered her genital self-mutilation to be a bizarre episode that could not have been predicted.

Simpson (1973) reported on a 22-year-old woman whose birth was the result of an unwanted, unplanned, and bitterly resented pregnancy. As a child she received little attention from her parents who were deeply involved in church work and who often quarreled over the wife's abhorrence of intercourse. The patient often avoided school by feigning illness. At the age of 12 she masturbated by putting pencils in her vagina, but soon stopped for fear "of doing damage." At the age of 15 she vomited after a boy put his arm around her. After leaving school she was hospitalized three times for abdominal pains, urinary problems, heavy bleeding during her periods, and intermenstrual bleeding. Fearing pregnancy after intercourse one day, she put a needle in her vagina to produce bleeding. As a result a dilation and curettage had to be performed. Shortly afterward she cut her wrists.

The next few years were marked by numerous hospitalizations for such problems as fainting, fever of unknown origin, wrist cutting, drug overdose, swallowing metal objects, smashing windows, inserting objects into her vagina and rectum, slashing her breasts, self-strangulation, cutting her vagina with a kitchen knife, severe dieting, compulsive overeating, and vomiting. She admitted that she planned her self-cutting carefully, that she enjoyed the anticipation, and that no pain accompanied the cuts. She was fascinated at the sight of her blood and felt that "something evil and tense within her [was] leaking away." A variety of treatments, including electroshock and many different types of medications, proved unsuccessful. Simpson noted that genital self-mutilation in women is a rare event, that a specific syndrome had not yet been established, and that no consistently helpful management advice could be offered. He concluded by wondering whether the female genital mutilation scene in Ingmar Bergman's film *Cries and Whispers* would inspire imitations. (The film was released in 1972–73; I have found no published or anecdotal reports implicating it in any mutilative attempts.)

Standage, Moore, and Cole (1974) reported the case of a 20-year-old woman with schizophrenia. She placed numerous objects in her vagina and ears in response to hallucinatory commands (her cervix and vaginal vault were lacerated by pieces of glass, plastic, a pin, and a pen top). She felt that people were reading her mind and that men were following her and threatening to assault her sexually. Her mutilation decreased as her psychosis abated; treatment included major tranquilizers and electroshock therapy.

In 1975 Goldney and Simpson described two women, aged 33 and 28 years, whose major symptoms were severe eating disorders and hysterical personality characteristics. Their "mutilation" consisted of repeatedly shaving off their pubic hair; this was interpreted by their psychiatrists as "a rejection of adult femininity." Another patient, a 39-year-old housewife, had three "alleged" spontaneous abortions. She carried two pregnancies to term but was hospitalized during each of them for at least five months because of vaginal bleeding. Three weeks following the delivery of her second child she was hospitalized for vaginal bleeding. Her husband caught her attempting to hide a blood-covered metal comb, but she talked him out of informing hospital staff. Following a hysterectomy the patient developed anorexia and occasional vomiting. Goldney and Simpson felt that "her difficulty in accepting the feminine role [normal sexual relations had never been established in her marriage] culminated in its rejection by genital self-mutilation and enforced hysterectomy" (p. 437). They proposed the term *Caenis syndrome* to describe the clinical triad of female genital self-mutilation, dysorexia, and hysterical personality.[4]

Clinical Cases of Genital Self-mutilation in Men

The first case of male genital self-mutilation in the medical literature dates back to 1882 (Warrington). The patient, a 29-year-old single farmer and stonemason named Isaac Brooks, claimed that several neighbors attacked

4. As described in book 12 of Ovid's *Metamorphoses*, Caenis was a beautiful girl whom many men desired although she rejected all thoughts of marriage. One day the god of the sea raped her while she was walking on a private beach. The god, Neptune, was pleased and thought she was too, so he offered to give her anything she wanted. Caenis said she wanted to become a man. Her wish was granted.

him, cut his scrotum with a knife, and pressed out his left testicle. A physician replaced the organ and the patient recovered; his assailants were sentenced to ten years of penal servitude. Two years later Brooks claimed he was attacked again by several men who severely gashed open his scrotum. With the help of his mother he partially controlled the bleeding with cobwebs, tobacco, pressure cloths, and a technique usually reserved for the treatment of castrated cattle which utilized a long needle and yarn. The physician who previously treated him was called, and the patient confessed that he had inflicted both wounds. Brooks died within a year; while on his deathbed he signed a confession that freed his neighbors from jail. Warrington noted that it was not uncommon for insane persons to mutilate their genitals. According to him, such patients often followed a similar course. They were neurotic and therefore unable to cope with sexual desires. This strain increased their nervous weakness, and their condition soon escalated to paranoia, impulsivity, and hallucinations, which directed them to do things they opposed. Their struggles led them to hypochondriasis, brooding, and irritability. Finally, in obedience to the Holy Scriptures, they cut off the offending member and then accused others of tampering with them.

Adam (1883) described the case of an 18-year-old farm servant who had been uncharacteristically dull and moody for several months. He went into the field one night with a sharp penknife and "completely and cleanly removed the whole of his penis." When asked why he did it, he responded that he had masturbated and felt it was his duty to follow the biblical injunction that "if thy right hand offend thee cut it off." He was hospitalized because of violent behavior, his belief that people were plotting against him, his refusal to eat food for fear his mother was poisoning him, and his assertion that he was Paul the Apostle. His mother attributed his self-castration to confusion resulting from his strenuous activity in putting out a farm fire the previous week. He had been unable to sleep and kept vigil at the family farm in case someone should set it on fire. He took to reading the Bible and Salvation Army publications. Initially he was uncooperative in the hospital. He became depressed and taciturn and then experienced an excited, exalted, and religiously exhilarated period. When his wound healed, his mental state returned to normal.

In 1884 two lively articles on male genital self-mutilation appeared in midwestern American medical journals. Galt reported on a small-town saloonkeeper who quarreled with his wife. She accused him of being "no good, for your penis is no account." He went on a spree, and, in a suicidal frenzy, he took a huge penknife and gashed his breast, sliced open his neck, and cut off his penis. The neck cut just missed severing the internal jugular vein and the carotid arteries. According to Galt, "The man's stump of a penis reminded one of a bloody chicken's neck after its head is wrung off. It was a clean cut; a surgeon's knife could not have performed a better amputation" (p. 226). The patient recovered rapidly. His wife filed for divorce. Galt concluded: "Bereft of his money, his wife and his penis the patient will probably for the remainder of his life spend his time either in lamenting his attempt or cursing his failure to perfect the job" (p. 228).

Whiting described the case of a 30-year-old marble cutter whose wife left him because of his excessive desire for intercourse. After she left, "his nights were spent in horrid dreams and frequent emissions and his days were one longing desire to be with some women" (p. 298). He resorted to masturbation but was so disgusted with himself that he cut open his scrotum and squeezed out his left testicle (as a child his right testicle had been surgically removed after being injured in a fall). The patient recovered and returned to his wife, but "the castration did not have the desired effect. He enjoyed the connubial felicities as of yore and was quite brutish. She only lived with him two weeks after he was out of bed—then for solace fled to parts unknown" (p. 300).

In 1901 Stroch reported the case of a 27-year-old florist with a depressive personality. He complained of chronic despondency, nervousness, poor memory, and testicular pain. He was a social recluse who never associated with women. Devoid of strong sexual feelings, he never practiced masturbation. He attributed his misery and lack of success to the condition of his sexual organs. One night, to relieve his testicular pain and free himself from the unhappy influence of his genitals, he "seized the scrotum and testicles in his left hand, and with a razor cut from above downward, with a sawing motion, severing successively all the structures. . . . The pain was not very great. . . . To the remark that he might have amputated the penis in his haste, he laughingly replied that he was careful not to do that" (p. 270). His testicles, wrapped in a handkerchief, accompanied him to the hospital. Close inspection revealed them to be free from disease.

In the first three decades of the twentieth century the theme of castration was discussed in great detail in the psychoanalytic literature. Lewis's series of articles (1927, 1928, 1931) contain most of the pertinent references. Although actual castration was not commonly encountered, the fear of castration (with the subsequent formation of a psychological "castration complex") was thought to play a vital role in both normal childhood development and later psychopathology. Castration fears were thought to lead to suicide, desire for surgical removal of body parts, fantasies that one's genitalia had been cut, delusions of being emasculated by enemies, and actual self-mutilation of the genitals to cure masturbation or to protect against perverse sexual cravings.

According to Freud and the early psychoanalysts, the male castration complex is a form of self-punishment intended to relieve guilt over incestuous oedipal desires arising in childhood. Additionally a boy supposedly desires to castrate his father because the father retains possession of the boy's mother. This desire may grow into a wish to castrate his brothers and all other males so that the boy will assume world power. Since such desires obviously can never be fulfilled, they are repressed, and they are eventually inverted so that self-castration becomes a feared punishment for these desires.

Karl Abraham, Ernest Jones, and other early analysts developed the notion that women as well as men develop a castration complex. Upon discovering that they lack a penis, little girls supposedly develop fantasies of having been "robbed" of their penis and of being left with only a gaping wound. Thus, their castration complex develops, marked by hatred toward and envy of men (because they possess a penis) and by the hope of receiving a child from the father (the child being a substitute for the penis that was taken from them). The castration complex is revived in later life by menstruation and defloration. This hatred and envy of men may be manifested by vaginismus, by dismissal of the importance of the penis (the supposed origin of the concept of an immaculate conception), and by frigidity.

In a series of somewhat rambling psychoanalytic articles, Lewis (1927, 1928, 1931) coined the term *Eshmun complex* to describe the psychodynamics of patients who mutilated themselves by actual or symbolic castration as an expression of "the incest mechanism in action."[5]

Lewis presented multiple case reports of psychotic patients who demonstrated this complex, although I must admit that in many instances the presence of an "incest mechanism" is not apparent to me. A typical case is that of a 28-year-old man who had cut out his left testicle seven years earlier for unknown reasons. Three months prior to the current hospitalization he attempted to remove his remaining testicle as a cure for chronic masturbation. His wound healed, but he lost his job. He began to have religious hallucinations, prayed incessantly, and cried a lot. In the hospital he was coquettish. He adopted feminine mannerisms, imitated the sufferings of

5. Eshmun was a handsome Phoenician nature deity. To avoid being seduced by the mother-goddess, Astronae, he castrated himself and was then transported to the heavens where he became the moon deity. Thus, Eshmun's self-castration was done to avoid incest; following the act he became associated with neutral and feminine activities (the moon with its monthly cycles).

Christ, and cut out his right testicle with a piece of glass because he wanted to be a priest. A follow-up examination nine years later revealed him to have an effeminate voice and eccentric clothing. He demonstrated frequent silly smiles, said that his castration was God's will, admitted to personal communication with God, and was convinced that he really was a priest.

Other cases of the so-called Eshmun complex include the following:

- A 32-year-old alcoholic man in a state of agitated depression slashed his arms and neck with a razor blade. While in the hospital he tried several times to cut off his penis with a piece of tin; on one occasion he tied a string around his penis to cut off its blood supply. He was preoccupied with reading the Bible and said that he was following the religious injunction "if your right arm bothers you cut it off" when he tried to cut off his penis.
- A 25-year-old man with chronic schizophrenia was destructive and uncooperative, and he sat in one spot for long periods of time repeating profane phrases. He said he was the devil, and he was usually silly and incoherent. He bit off his lower lip and gouged out both of his testicles with his fingernails for no apparent reason.
- A 59-year-old stone cutter had a history of alcoholic insanity and paranoid schizophrenia. He developed head pains and delusions of persecution, believed that people could steal his thoughts, and heard the voice of God. He obeyed God's command to cut off all of his genitalia with a razor.
- A 30-year-old schizophrenic naval officer thought that his shipmates had accused him of perverted sexual practices. He heard voices that told him to do odd things and left him bewildered and confused; while in such a state he cut off his genitals with a razor. Lewis interpreted the mutilation as a punishment for incestuous desires because the patient's father had left home when the patient was 8 years old, leaving him "wholly in possession of his mother without competition."
- A 28-year-old man who had been depressed for three years was hospitalized for serious blood loss after a self-castration attempt. He said that voices "told me they could make me take out my testicles and if I didn't do it they would make me lose my voice." He had long struggled with homosexual desires and said that he attempted castration to humiliate himself and to expiate some of his sins. During adolescence he had made a previous castration attempt following homosexual experiences: "I thought I was a terrible person. . . . it seemed that it might prevent me from indulging in sodomy" (p. 183).

Women, too, could manifest the Eshmun complex. A 39-year-old single schoolteacher developed a homosexual attachment to a nurse. While in the hospital she muttered to herself that she came from heaven and Jesus Christ was her father. She heard voices, claimed that electrical impulses passed through the walls and into her body, and destroyed property in periods of excitement. At the age of 50 she felt that her body was alive but her brain was dead. She tried to rip out her womb, pull out her teeth, tear out her umbilicus, and scratch her eyes with her fingers and a nail file.

Lewis considered the castration reaction to be "the basic theme in all life." He related it closely to suicide, noting that "one who dies, dies a temporal death, while the castrate dies externally since his germ plasm has perished" (p. 197). This proposed relationship between suicide and self-mutilation received widespread attention because of Karl Menninger's enormously popular work, *Man Against Himself* (1938), in which he theorized that "the suicidal impulse may be concentrated upon a part as a substitute for the whole" (p. 231). Menninger noted that psychotic men who feel guilty about sexual sins related to women, homosexuality, or masturbation "do the obvious thing of ridding themselves of the guilty part of their body" (p. 270). Because of conscious or unconscious homosexual impulses, castration not only accomplishes self-punishment but also converts the castrate "into a passive, penis-less individual, anatomically comparable with the female" (p. 270). Thus, while castration appears to be an act of atonement for homosexual wishes, in reality it allows a man to become closer to these wishes; it makes him incapable of the active role while predisposing him even more to the passive role.

In 1933, Bradley presented a case report to his colleagues at the St. Louis Medical Society. The patient was a 61-year-old lifelong "sexual pervert" with hyperactive sexuality. He first had sexual intercourse at the age of 9. He admitted to frequent sexual acts with cattle, sheep, and hogs and to chronic masturbation during his marriages. At the age of 40, remorseful about his hypersexuality, he went to the barn, sharpened his knife, and cut out both testicles. This did not curb his sexual appetite, however, and he married for the third time. He contracted gonorrhea, and, again feeling remorseful, cut off half of his penis with a pocketknife. Bradley was unable to present the patient to the medical group, however, noting: "Unfortunately, I am unable to show the patient tonight. He is a prisoner, charged with attempting to rape a girl 10 years old. When I asked him why he did such a thing and stated that it would have done him no good, he said he thought it might do the little girl some good" (p. 134).

A rare report on ten cases of genital self-mutilation in Southeast Asia was published by Bigot (1938). Several young Buddhist monks cut off their penises or testicles after succumbing to sexual desires; one monk castrated himself to emulate his castrated teacher. Others were driven by incestuous thoughts.

For a decade genital mutilation was not written about in the medical literature. Then, in 1948, Beilin and Gruenberg reported, primarily from a urological perspective, on five psychotic patients in state mental hospitals.

1. A 52-year-old man with hebephrenic schizophrenia and tuberculosis tied a string around his penis, causing swelling of the organ and extensive tissue destruction. He was confused, incoherent, disoriented, weak, and debilitated and was unable to recall the act or the reason for it. He died three months later.

2. A 19-year-old man with excited catatonia, the son of a Baptist minister, was guilty of committing numerous sexual acts with children. After the court recommended castration, the patient cut off his testicles with a razor blade. While in the hospital he attempted to gouge out his eyes. He died three months later.

3. A 24-year-old schizophrenic man amputated his testicle with a buckle because he was fearful of the electroshock treatments he was receiving. The patient wrapped his excised testicle in tissue paper on which he had written, "Exhibit A, one meatball."

4. A 48-year-old man with severe organic brain disease avulsed the left half of his scrotum. He was totally disoriented and unable to provide any information.

5. A 28-year-old man with hebephrenic schizophrenia developed painful and frequent urination. He was uncooperative and combative and unable to explain his dilemma. His penis was swollen and red, and pus dripped out of the urethra. The tip of a wire pin was found protruding from his penis. The patient had shoved an open safety pin into his urethra. It was removed with some difficulty.

Hemphill, in 1951, reported the case of a 66-year-old man with a past history of depression who was hospitalized for diabetes and urinary retention. He cut his wrist with a razor and then amputated his penis and one testicle. The act was followed by a feeling of enormous mental relief. At the age of 21 he had had a partial circumcision for a tight prepuce, and at the age of 30 he contracted gonorrhea and orchitis. At the age of 58 he developed a hernia, and at the age of 64 he developed diabetes and impotence. Throughout his life he was plagued by feelings of guilt about being closely bound to his mother, about an incestuous affair with a female cousin, and about his promiscuous sexual behavior. After becoming impotent he felt that his genitals "had let me down and were now no good to me—that I should get rid of the organs." He regarded them as independent sources of temptation that controlled and misled him. He did not regret his actions and claimed that they gained him moral tranquillity, since he could now live "a proper life" with his cousin. From this case and from a brief review of the literature, Hemphill concluded that several conditions appear to be necessary before genital self-mutilation can occur, namely, "an abnormal attitude toward the genitals; a tendency to regard them as being capable of exercising an independent influence over the organism as a whole and therefore inviting the possibility of rejecting the genitals in order to avoid sin or danger; . . . an abnormal integration of the concept of the body or of the body image . . . [and] a strong motive consciously understood, such as incest or fear of the destruction of the body as a whole by physical illness" (p. 294).

In 1953 Kenyon and Hyman also published several case reports. One was of a Japanese college student in New York City who became mentally disturbed because of low grades. He amputated all of his genitals with a butcher's knife. Another case was that of a 38-year-old depressed man with chronic alcoholism who "in the kitchen of his home and in the presence of his wife, also an alcoholic, placed his genitalia on the table and completely amputated them with one stroke of an ordinary bread knife" (p. 207). Bleeding profusely, he walked to a nearby police station, shook the specimen in his hand, and proclaimed "his act and his heroism" to the precinct captain. In the hospital he was diagnosed as schizophrenic. He spoke incoherently about his act, about his cowardice and courage, about his loss of sex, and his desire to become a woman.

In 1956 Cleveland reported on three men whose self-castration appeared to be "deliberate and purposeful behavior, not the random self-mutilation of a frenzied patient." The first case was that of a man who was placed in an orphanage at the age of 12. He was treated cruelly. The matrons there threatened bed wetters with castration, and girls were treated preferentially. The young man envied girls and longed to be one. At that time he injured his scrotum accidentally and felt he would be better off without such a painful appendage. When he divorced his first wife he attempted castration but stopped because the pain was too great. At the age of 25, following a second divorce, he succeeded in deeply gashing his scrotum; he was depressed over failure to gain custody of his children (a probable reenactment of his own parental desertion). At the age of 29 he felt that his problems would be resolved if he lost his disturbing sexual drive, so he carefully excised his scrotum and testicles. He was not psychotic, although he reacted to his castration with bland unconcern. The patient wrote a clear self-analysis of his mutilation and related it to his dependency, insecurity, and envy of girls.

The second case was a 44-year-old man who cut off all of his genitalia with a razor while acutely intoxicated with alcohol. He had a history of anxiety neurosis and of a renal disease that caused genital pain. Psychological testing four years prior to his castration revealed severely disorganized fantasies about bodily mutilation.

The third patient, a 31-year-old man, unsuccessfully attempted to cut off his testicles. Although he had a history of severe anxiety attacks and of one psychotic episode, he was coherent and logical at the time of his attempted self-mutilation. His mother had given him a feminine name at birth because she desired a girl. He was able to have intercourse with his wife only when angry with her; frequently he asked her to cut his genitals, and he once told her that he wanted to remove his testicles so she "could step on them and make them pop." Four years earlier he had been hospitalized with painful, swollen genitals, the result of a generalized reaction to penicillin. He was jealous of his wife's affection for their children. Cleveland concluded that self-castration in rational and coherent adult males was the culmination of a lengthy process during which the individual dissociated himself from his alien genital organ. The passive nature of such persons was noted as well as their assignment of a punitive, castrating role to women. Castration gained for the men "the primitive, parasitic stage of functioning" which they desired, according to Cleveland.

Three cases from Australia were published by Lennon in 1963. In one, a 60-year-old psychotically depressed man felt guilty over alleged sexual misdemeanors in his younger years and cut off both testicles with a razor blade. In another, a 28-year-old schizophrenic man, whose illness was characterized by inadequacy, passivity, seclusiveness, and mystical ruminations, amputated his penis for fear of becoming a homosexual. A third case, that of a 42-year-old well-educated man, provided details of self-castration performed during a manic episode. The patient had an uneventful childhood and adolescence within a stable, harmonious family, and he had a successful career. However, he had a history of five manic episodes requiring hospitalization and of a stormy marriage which he attributed to his overly demanding sexual attitude. His wife filed for a divorce. A day before the divorce became final the patient was in the midst of a severe manic episode. He saw a letter about his brother's change of address to a street with an odd sounding name. His mother wrote of the address, "This may look funny, but it isn't." The patient dwelled on the word "funny" and eventually concluded that it would be "funny" to cut off his penis. He used a rubber band for a ligature and cut off his penis with a razor. Although it was painful, he felt happy and cheerful. He drove to work after throwing his penis on the car floor. As he recovered from his mania in the hospital, he maintained a bland complacency about his amputation and jocosely stated that "I knew my divorce was coming up, and I would have no further use for it." The patient's lack of remorse and his complacency led Lennon to believe that the castration had provided a satisfactory solution to an unconscious conflict. Lennon concluded that "by amputating his penis, the symbol of his manhood, he had made himself acceptable to his wife, in so far as he could not now be accounted a man; in addition he had gotten rid of the organ he believed responsible for his marital disharmony, and had in some way contributed a peace offering towards a future reunion" (p. 81).

In 1963, Blacker and Wong published a study of four men with psychosis or borderline disorder who mutilated their genitals. In this widely quoted paper the authors identified six commonalities among the patients: (1) Their childhood experiences were severely impoverished. They came from disturbed homes in which the father was often absent and the mother was dominant. (2) Their self-castration was a culmination of a long, intense sexual confusion that resulted in a gradual disassociation of their alien genital organs from their body scheme. (3) Their relationships with women were submissive and masochistic and indicated a desire for an infantile relationship with a mother figure. Castration removed the threat of genital sexuality from such a relationship. (4) Their self-mutilation served to relieve depression and "could be considered an attenuated suicide, a compromise that averted total annihilation of the organism" (p. 175). (5) Their basic conflict revolved around confused sexual identity as manifested by strong feminine identifications. Their wishes for femininity were especially strong during periods of intoxication and psychosis. (6) They repudiated their male genitals. Unclear as to whether they were male or female, they attempted to resolve the issue in a primitive way.

Typical of the cases is a man whose childhood was characterized by poverty and deprivation. His nervous father was a religious fanatic who constantly bullied the family members. The patient's mother saw him with an erection when he was a child and said, "Shame, little boys who play with themselves have to have part of it come off." This incident made the patient reluctant to be a boy. He said that "nothing like this could happen to a girl because girls are safer." Because of malnourishment he was placed in a county home at the age of 13. He began to prick his scrotum and penis with pins and often pulled his breasts in the hope of enlarging them. He eventually married and had a responsible job. At the age of 32 he cut his

urethra in order to make himself "more like a woman." His wife later divorced him, and he married a motherly woman. After five years he began
to drink alcohol heavily, and he developed intense desires to have female
breasts, suckle children, and destroy his penis. At the age of 49 he became
sexually involved with a 65-year-old man. In a state of depression, he got
drunk and felt a savage desire to get rid of his penis. "I resented the penis
because I had been born wrong and then blamed for it." He placed his penis
on a wood block and chopped it off with a hatchet. He was disoriented and
suffered from both visual and auditory hallucinations upon hospitalization.
His condition cleared rapidly, and after two weeks he returned to work.

Kushner (1967) focused on the significance of religious delusions in the
self-castration of two paranoid schizophrenic men. The first patient was
hospitalized at the age of 26 because of auditory hallucinations, ideas of
reference, incongruity of affect, and religious preoccupations. Upon discharge he preached in public, carried a religious sign after shaving his head,
and almost died while meditating in the hills during winter. His search for
spiritual purification alternated with profound guilt following episodes of
drunkenness, aggression, masturbation, and promiscuity. At the age of 32
he cut off both testicles "as a freewill offering to God" and arrived at the
hospital carrying them in a box. Five years later, following the death of his
father, the patient drank alcohol heavily and had his first homosexual experience. He felt disgusted and turned to the Bible, where he was impressed
by Matthew 19:12: "and there be eunuchs who have made themselves eunuchs for the Kingdom of Heaven's sake." He purchased a block of wood
and a razor and waited until he felt sexual desire. He then cut off his penis,
threw it into a fire, and watched it burn. He sought help, stating, "Even if I
do get certified [as legally insane] and in the eyes of the world I am mad, it
is far better for me to have cleansed myself" (p. 295).

The second patient was a shy, withdrawn man with an excellent work
record. He was constantly afraid that people would consider him a homosexual because of his gentleness. At the age of 35 he suddenly developed
deep religious feelings. His work deteriorated as his religious preoccupation increased. He was hospitalized and received electroshock treatment.
He dwelled on the Bible and on outer space and decided that he must re-
nounce "the sex life of the world." Influenced by Matthew 19, he castrated
himself with a razor in the belief that this act of purification would qualify
him to serve as the pilot who would carry the godly to outer space.

Kushner noted that anxiety over homosexual tendencies caused patients
such as these to strive for purity and salvation; religion was the medium
they chose to obtain relief from guilt. Because society tolerates such wide

differences in religious thought, Kushner stated that it may be difficult to distinguish a religious belief from a delusion. In both patients, however, religious ideas about sin and redemption were extended into delusions that were supported by a concrete interpretation of biblical references.

Hahn and Hahn (1967) reported the case of a 20-year-old schizophrenic Korean man who amputated his penis with a razor following his first sexual experience, intercourse with a prostitute. His father, a punitive yet weak man, had died when the patient was a child. Following her oldest son's death, the patient's mother drifted from man to man. The patient, who failed in his desperate attempts to gain his mother's love, was angry and hostile toward her. He unconsciously identified the prostitute with his mother and sacrificed his penis out of guilt and depression.

In 1973 Goldfield and Glick reported the case of a 22-year-old high school graduate with a yearlong history of schizophrenia. He complained of feeling "machinelike" and thought that he was Leonardo da Vinci. He spent fifteen hours a day painting and slept only three or four hours. He laughed to himself and talked unintelligibly. Then "the voice of God" told him to castrate himself with a razor. He proceeded to remove his testicles from the scrotal sac. Although he felt an urge to cut off his penis, he did not because the voice of God became silent. In a bland and emotionless state he drove himself to a friend's house.

Anumonye (1973) was the first to report self-amputation of the penis in Africa. He presented two Nigerian patients who castrated themselves after receiving promotions (one was promoted to an important chieftaincy, the other received an accelerated promotion at work). Neither patient had manifested any premorbid psychopathology. Their elevation to a higher and more responsible social status triggered a brief psychotic episode (diagnosed by Anumonye as acute mania), which resolved rapidly. Their lack of remorse, however, suggested that the castration had resolved some unconscious conflict.

In 1974 Engelman et al. reported the case of a 26-year-old schizophrenic man who cut off the tip of his penis with a razor. His agitated, psychotic condition had been precipitated by acute drug and alcohol use. He had a history of repeated failures in traditional male roles, and his rejection of his masculinity was intermingled with strong guilt and a need for self-punishment. He regretted his actions, however, and desired to have the tip of his penis reattached surgically.

The following case from 1976 was supplied to me by Dr. Wolfgang Jilek of Vancouver, Canada. The patient, a 31-year-old man with a German-Russian ethnic background, was a practicing Mennonite. He had a clear history of chronic schizophrenia and had been in state mental hospitals many times. He was hospitalized on this occasion after he sat on a bucket of ice, took pain-killing pills, and removed both of his testicles with a razor blade. His attempts to control the bleeding failed, and he was brought to the emergency room in cardiovascular shock. He had castrated himself because he believed that people were torturing him through his testicles. He decided to end the torture. He had visual and auditory hallucinations, and a voice repeatedly told him to "squeeze them till they burst." He was fearful that male doctors and nurses would "make passes" at him, and he thought that the doctors "had changed the course of the veins" in his penis. He frequently had thoughts of blinding himself by staring at the flame of a welding torch or by sticking pencils in his eyes. Dr. Jilek believed that the patient's self-castration was a substitute for self-blinding.

In 1977 Evins, Whittle, and Rous reported the case of a 25-year-old man with paranoid schizophrenia who removed both testicles with a razor blade. He then cut the base of his penis in an abortive attempt at amputation. He was suffering from auditory hallucinations; the voice of his mother told him that he would be denied entry into the kingdom of heaven unless he cut off his penis and testicles.

In 1979 Greilsheimer and Groves described a 23-year-old unemployed Catholic man (a twin) who had been reared by a nervous and extremely religious mother; his father had left the family when the patient was an infant. Although frail as a child, he did well until high school, when he drank alcohol heavily, ceased social activities, and rebelled against his mother. At the age of 18 he decided to become a priest but was refused admission to a seminary. He became psychotic and was hospitalized with a diagnosis of paranoid schizophrenia. At the age of 23 he suffered nightmares and terrors, became withdrawn, and read the Bible incessantly. When both his dog and an injured bird that he had rescued died, he became acutely psychotic. He stated that his penis and his aunt's clitoris "were standing out at each other." On the first anniversary of his twin sister's marriage (a marriage of which the patient did not approve), he cut off his penis with a razor blade in obedience to Matthew 18:7-9. The act was sudden and painless and was followed by a sense of immediate relief.

Kalin (1979) reported an interesting case of a young man who, as an adolescent, feared that his compulsive masturbation was destroying his body and nervous system. At the age of 21 he asked a surgeon to perform a total orchiectomy in order to save him from his "hyperaggressiveness." He stated, "I'm no homosexual or transsexual. I still want a hugging and kissing relationship with a woman." After being rejected for the castration, he began medicating himself with various hormones to decrease his production of pituitary gland hormones. Additionally, he injected himself with chemicals to lower his testosterone level. He hoped this would decrease his sexual fantasies and enhance his well-being. He was hospitalized when an abscess formed, and he was diagnosed as having schizophrenia, gender identity problems, and possible temporal lobe epilepsy. He later briefly received a nonfeminizing antiandrogen hormone (medroxyprogesterone). When he was unable to find a physician willing to continue his hormone treatment, the patient performed a bilateral orchiectomy on himself. Two months later, he operated on himself again. Using mirrors and a sterile technique he tried for eight hours to denervate his adrenal glands; he had to stop because of great pain in attempting to retract his liver. After intensive research he had developed the theory that if he reduced his adrenal gland secretions his mental anguish would cease. He was unresponsive to antipsychotic medication and unable to form a working alliance with a psychotherapist.

Suk and Son (1980) reported on four schizophrenic Korean men who castrated themselves. All four were lower-social-class single men who belonged to no religious group. They had had impoverished childhoods and were depressed prior to their self-mutilation. They identified with their mothers, had confused sexual identities, and had difficulty with the male role. Three of the men revealed homosexual wishes.

Pabis, Mirla, and Tozmans (1980) reported the case of a man who had spent ten years in a class for emotionally disturbed children. A psychiatrist who saw him at the age of 17 diagnosed psychotic depression. The patient withdrew from social activities and believed that masturbation drained his brain of "nuclear material." He sought out prostitutes to perform sadomasochistic acts and served as a homosexual prostitute (although he insisted he was a heterosexual). At the age of 29 he waded into the ocean and cut off his scrotum and testicles with a kitchen knife. He brought his testicles home and handed them to his mother. He felt that his mother had "half died" at his birth; by presenting her with his testicles he intended to give back to her the life she had given him at birth. After the castration his anxiety, depression, and many of his delusions diminished. He expressed no regrets and was especially happy at the loss of some facial hair.

Clark (1981) presented the case of a middle-aged man whose early history appeared to be benign. In his thirties he was hospitalized several times for depression and was treated with electroshock. He reported periods of "overexuberance" but was never hospitalized for them. He began to drink alcohol heavily and felt guilty over his sexual interest in prepubertal girls.

Bothered by his sexual feelings, he drank, brooded, and considered suicide. After weeks of desperate deliberation on the biblical texts about plucking out one's eye and about becoming a eunuch for heaven's sake, he decided to castrate himself. He sought commitment to a mental hospital, but this was refused. He then cut off both testicles. The patient benefited from psychotherapy after his self-castration and published several books before he died of natural causes fifteen years later.

In 1981 Hall, Lawson, and Wilson reported the case of a young man whose father was a Swedish-American lumberman, and whose mother was a devout Catholic with beliefs colored by her native Mexican folklore. The family lived in a sparsely inhabited section of a rural island. As an adolescent the patient had periods of intense interest in Buddhism and reincarnation along with heavy marijuana use. Because of his "sinful" sexual thoughts he considered himself unworthy of dating. At the age of 22 he became suspicious and thought that he was disliked by his colleagues at work because of his "terrible" thoughts and dark skin color. At home when the family cat jumped into his lap, the patient became sexually stimulated and attempted sexual intercourse with the animal. He then felt guilty and hopeless and believed that God would forgive him only if he atoned for his behavior. He heard voices commanding him to amputate his hand and penis. Hungry and sleep deprived, he chopped off his right hand and the tip of his penis. He received the diagnosis of paranoid schizophrenia with a superimposed depression.

The following case history from 1981 was supplied to me by a psychiatrist in England. The patient was a 26-year-old man with paranoid schizophrenia. He had a history of childhood deprivation, numerous foster care placements, arrests for fire setting and thefts, drug abuse, an unstable work record, a fascination with blood and surgical procedures, and marked confusion about his sexual identity. He had many fantasies about "penetrating women." During an acute psychotic episode, he cut off the tip of his penis. He developed paranoid auditory hallucinations and thoughts of raping women. He attacked patients and staff because he anticipated that they would attack him. He gouged and stabbed his eyes in the belief that people were trying to kill him by looking through his eyes.

Rada and James (1982) published a thoughtful report on six men whose genital self-mutilation involved inserting objects into their urethra. All of the men were inmates in a maximum security hospital for the criminally insane. None had ever been psychotic. The number of urethral mutilations per patient varied from one to twenty-six. Most occurred during the daytime, frequently when the inmate was in seclusion.

The group was characterized by poor sexual adjustment, female identification (three were bisexual), social maladjustment and chaotic home environments during childhood, and extensive involvement with the criminal justice system. Five inmates had a history of fire setting while the sixth had "accidentally" burned his face prior to his first urethral insertion. Five had a history of self-cutting prior to their current acts; they also swallowed razor blades, open pins, or cleaning solution before or during the acts of urethral insertion. Two were adult head bangers.

None of the incidents of urethral self-mutilation was motivated by suicidal or erotic urges. Rather, the most common motive was to secure transfer to a different unit. Since the urethral insertions continued following transfer, however, Rada and James concluded that other motives were involved. They noted that the inmates experienced a buildup of tension, anger, and dysphoria prior to their self-mutilation. The acts were painless, but most inmates experienced pain later. Depersonalization was uncommon. Within minutes, news of a urethral insertion spread throughout the institution and gained a special reputation and identity for the mutilator. The contagious nature of the self-mutilative acts was clear; each mutilator had a personal relationship with at least one other mutilator, and many of the acts were temporally related.

The staff response to the acts was varied and typically focused on the patients' manipulativeness. Repulsed by the acts, many staff members stated that state money would be saved if the physician let the inmates cut off their penises. The anger of the medical staff was manifested by delays in treating the mutilators, by the withholding of analgesic medication, and by the excessive use of neuroleptic medication. The staff's need to ventilate contributed to the rapid spread of news about the acts throughout the institution. After staff agreed not to talk about the acts, new incidents of self-mutilation did not occur in other units. Three of the inmates stopped their mutilative behavior immediately after being transferred. Three other inmates, however, continued their mutilative behavior. Medications were useless. Four-point restraint was effective but resulted in struggles over control, prolonged immobility, social isolation, and regression. By being placed in chairs with hand restraints, these inmates were able to be with other people. In addition, they were told that the decision to remove the restraints was up to the physician and that the decision would be arbitrary, for example, not based on the inmates' "convincing" arguments. This approach was partially successful; two of the inmates stopped the urethral insertions and eventually were discharged from the facility.

In 1983 Thompson and Abraham reported two cases of genital mutilation occurring after paternal death. In the first case, a 24-year-old single man with no prior psychiatric history attempted to circumcise himself with a pair of scissors. He had been depressed after the death of his father one week previously, and he said that "this might lift him out of his depression." His wounds were treated surgically; he refused psychiatric help. The second case was that of a 37-year-old unemployed single man who was hospitalized for loss of blood following an attempt at self-castration; he had cut out one testicle and part of the other. He said he had led a religious movement during a previous incarnation in eighteenth-century Russia, was persecuted, and had castrated himself with a red-hot poker. He received the diagnosis of acute psychotic episode in reaction to the death of his father three days earlier. He was treated surgically and his mental state improved.

Thompson and Abraham speculated that genital self-mutilation after paternal death might indicate an unresolved oedipal complex. The general bereavement reaction might intensify previous guilt, and the son might then mutilate his genitals as a self-imposed punishment. The patient's psychiatrists apparently were unaware that his remarks about self-castration with a red-hot poker in eighteenth-century Russia were a reference to the Skoptsi sect. This appears to be the first report of a patient whose self-mutilation was influenced by knowledge of the Skoptsi.

A case on which I consulted in 1984 involved a 35-year-old man with chronic schizophrenia and mild mental retardation. He was an extremely passive individual who was deeply shaken by the death of his mother one year earlier. He had lived with a chronic schizophrenic woman for six years; she had recently been hospitalized for an exacerbation of her condition. The patient had a high sex drive and had felt very frustrated for three years because his companion had developed a "phobia" to sex and refused his sexual advances. He admitted to masturbating three to five times daily, sometimes so violently that blood came out of his penis. The patient felt very lonely during his woman friend's hospitalization, and he began to hear the voice of the devil, who told him to cut off his genitals. He got drunk one evening and the devil said, "Now you can't control yourself. Go ahead and cut it off." The patient went into a bathroom, secured his penis with a barbecue fork, and cut it off. The patient was brought to the hospital. He said he would now get along better with his woman friend because he would no longer be bothered by his penis. He had no regrets for what he had done but felt "a little embarrassed." For several days he heard the voice of the devil telling him to complete the job by cutting off his testicles, but the voice gradually diminished. The patient planned to live peacefully with his woman friend, to rejoin the Pentecostal church, and to be reborn in the Holy Spirit.

Genital Self-mutilation in the Absence of Psychosis

The literature on self-castration traditionally has emphasized the fact that the act was invariably associated with psychosis. Then, in 1954, Esman reported the case of a man whose self-castration was a nonpsychotic, isolated, impulsive act. Other cases of nonpsychotic self-castration have since appeared in the medical literature. All of these cases fall into the general diagnostic category of gender identity disorders, the most common being transsexualism. Male transsexuals have masculine genital organs but perceive themselves to be really female. For them, self-castration is often a procedure to correct a flaw of nature and to fulfill a longstanding wish to live as a female.

The patient described by Esman regarded his alcoholic, abusive father with contempt. At the age of 17 the patient started having frequent sexual experiences with prostitutes and casual pickups. He never had any homosexual contacts and regarded homosexuality as unnatural. When he was 19 years old a man suggested that he might earn a lot of money as a female impersonator. The patient bought women's clothing and tried them on but felt unattractive. Later he developed problems with alcohol and was hospitalized several times. During hospitalization at the age of 44 he said, "I want to be loved. I want to be more like a girl. I want to have my penis and scrotum cut off, have my testicles pushed up into my abdomen. . . . I want to wear my pretty dresses with lace fringes. . . . I want to be more of a child, not just a girl" (p. 80). Several months later while drunk, he cut out his testicles with a razor blade. He was neither significantly depressed nor delusional but rather told his story coherently, logically, and fluently. Esman interpreted the castration to be the isolated, impulsive act of a person with a schizoid personality structure. He concluded that the patient sought "a dependent, narcissistic oral relationship with a mother figure." Since even the possibility of genital sexuality would threaten this sort of relationship, he castrated himself.

Schneider, Harrison, and Siegel (1965) published an in-depth study of a man who experienced marked cyclic changes in sexuality although intensive examination revealed no endocrinological abnormalities. When he was an infant, bilateral inguinal hernias and bilateral cryptorchidism were diagnosed. The patient remembered always having vague feelings of uneasiness about his role as a boy. He quit high school because of the ridicule he received over the large size of his breasts. Shortly after an emergency appendectomy at the age of 23, he noticed that he was becoming increasingly feminized; his breasts grew, his voice rose, his facial hair stopped growing, and his body fat assumed a feminine distribution. This process continued for about two years when suddenly, for no apparent reason, he started to remasculinize. The eight-month period of remasculinization was trying to the patient, and he felt more comfortable when he then began to refeminize. He took to dressing and passing as a woman. He became upset when the remasculinization process started again. He then carefully and competently amputated both testicles and flushed them down the toilet. Following the castration he experienced a short cycle of feminization followed by masculinization. He was hospitalized after he attempted to amputate his penis. Six months after discharge from the hospital the patient meticulously cut off his penis.

Lowy and Kolivakis (1971) reported the case of a 35-year-old hospital attendant who came to an emergency room and announced that he had just cut off his testicles, burned them, and flushed them down the toilet. He stated that he had lost about fifty cubic centimeters of blood during the castration and that this was "the usual amount lost by a woman during menstruation." Since the age of 6 the patient had wanted to be a girl. He had been preoccupied with a desire for a sex-change operation since adolescence, when he began to cross-dress openly. He claimed that he always felt disgusted by his sexual organs, that the cross-dressing was not sexually exciting, and that he had never masturbated. He described his adoptive mother as warm, loving, and kind and his stepfather as kind but aloof and withdrawn. He said he had been a highly sensitive, lonely, and alienated child whom other boys regarded as a sissy. He was discharged from the army as medically unqualified; in the army he was regarded as a homosexual although he denied any homosexual interest. Over the years he had been arrested several times for cross-dressing. At the age of 30 he married an older woman who knew of his desire for a sex change; the marriage was never consummated. He got a job as a practical nurse. In order to prepare himself for his castration he obtained a position in the urology department, where he familiarized himself with the surgical instruments and procedure. The self-castration was not preceded by any important psychological or social stress, and he was not psychotic. He was admitted to the psychiatric ward, where he dressed bizarrely as a female, with an ill-fitting wig and false breasts. His request for a surgical penectomy and construction of a vagina was deferred, but he was placed on estrogen. Over the next four years he engaged in psychotherapy, relentlessly established his feminine identity, and even was accepted for membership in a women's church group.

Perhaps the most widely quoted study on genital self-surgery in relation to transsexualism is that by Money and DePriest (1976). One of their patients was an artist-farmer. Inspired by his study of Jungian psychology, he had developed a complicated theory about the "lost bisexual secret of the urethral orgasm," which he derived from mythical, artistic, and literary symbols. He cut an opening in his penis at the penoscrotal angle. This artificial hypospadias was designed to allow a "host penis" to reach his urethra. He thought that the intromission of a man's penis into this opening would prevent death. He likened his condition to that of Australian aborigines who practiced subincision, and he attempted to discover if they too experienced the ecstasy of urethral orgasm. At the age of 63 he was found wandering the streets in a fugue state, naked and disoriented.

Another case involved a 45-year-old paranoid man who requested that a surgeon perform an ileostomy. He had a delusional belief that while his external genitals were clearly those of a male, his internal sexual organs were female and that his vagina shared a common outlet with his rectum. He asserted that an ileostomy would keep his "vagina" cleared of feces. A year earlier he had cut off his penis with shears. To be sure that his penis would not be sutured back in place, he flushed it down the toilet. He believed so strongly in his "rectal vagina" that he attempted to become pregnant by inserting sperm into his rectum. During a ten-year follow-up it became clear that he could not cope with sex-reassignment surgery nor could he live in the female role as a transvestite. He continued to live as a male but had constant fantasies of living as a female.

A third case was that of a 51-year-old man who cut off his testicles using ice packs and a clamp marketed for the castration of farm animals. He believed that castration would allow him to feel like the girl he longed to be. Since adolescence he had a persistent compulsion to dress as a woman and to live as a female. As a form of self-therapy he had married and reared three sons. As much as he desired to be a "girl," he was deeply dependent on his wife's companionship. He removed his testicles but spared his penis, thus achieving a resolution of his conflicts.

Money and DePriest noted that all of the cases clearly contained an element of transsexualism. In the first two patients the transsexual compulsion became a paranoid proposition embedded in a delusional system, while in the third it was manifested as an idée fixe. The patients obtained no erotic pleasure from their self-surgery and, indeed, would gladly have accepted the services of a surgeon.

Although sex-reassignment surgery involving amputation of the penis and testicles, followed by construction of an artificial vagina, is currently a matter of great medical controversy, some medical centers have special gender identity clinics for the evaluation of persons (usually males) who claim to be transsexuals. The process is lengthy and often quite expensive. Some patients who are perturbed by the slowness of the evaluation may cut off their testicles to convince clinic staff of their seriousness; other patients may do so because of their inability to pay for the surgery (Haberman and Michael 1979; Krieger, McAninch, and Weimer 1982). These patients tend to remove their testicles neatly, with little tissue damage; usually they have studied the anatomy of the area in detail and have long-term goals for their self-surgery. In contrast, a psychotic person who castrates himself tends to act impulsively, to lacerate the area, and may mutilate his penis as well as his testicles.

Comments on Genital Mutilation

Deviant male genital self-mutilators tend to be psychotic at the time of the act, the most frequent diagnoses being schizophrenia and major depression; they have an average age of 32 years. Alcohol ingestion prior to the act may be a contributing factor in about 25 percent of cases. Removal of the testicles is somewhat more common than removal of the penis, which, in turn, is more common than removal of both organs. There is no correlation between a specific diagnosis and the genital organ selected for mutilation. In descending order, the reasons provided by patients for their self-mutilation are most likely to be as follows: the wish to be or delusions of being female; concerns about homosexuality; relief of physical pain or somatic illness; guilt over sexual urges such as incest; religiosity; command hallucinations; and punishment for failures in the male role.

Nonpsychotic self-mutilators are most likely to be men with character disorders who act impulsively or transsexuals who have premeditated their actions. The genital mutilations of transsexuals are usually well planned and rather neatly done. While many psychotic persons castrate themselves impulsively and with little regard to surgical technique, transsexuals typically have studied the procedure and perform it in a controlled fashion with a minimum of unnecessary trauma.

The literature on deviant female genital self-mutilation is too limited to allow for any definitive comments. The claim that a specific syndrome exists, in which female genital self-mutilation and an eating disorder are present, is only partially true. The fact is that females with an eating disorder comprise a high-risk group for *all* forms of self-mutilation.

Certainly the male genitalia are more suited for drastic mutilation than are the female genitalia. Men have a greater tendency to localize their sexual feelings to their protruding genitals, while females tend to have a more diffuse sexuality. Male genital mutilation involves a greater sacrifice than female mutilation in that successful removal of the penis, for example, eliminates the possibility of sexual functioning. Castration allows men to overcome heterosexual and homosexual urges, to gratify feminine longings, and to atone for sexual guilt. Female genital mutilation is more limited in its effects. Men can emulate women anatomically by removing their penis and testicles, but women, even if they want to, cannot emulate men by cutting tissue. For cultural and hormonal reasons men tend to be more aggressive than women, and since the phallus is an intrusive organ, one might anticipate a higher frequency of male genital mutilation. Left to their own devices, men are more apt than women to mutilate their genitals under culturally accepted conditions as well as during times of mental illness.

Culturally, male genital mutilation has been widespread, although not universal, and it has a lengthy secular and religious tradition. Culturally accepted male genital mutilation seems to cause little physical harm, although questions continue to be raised about the possible psychological harm of procedures such as infant circumcision. One current theory holds that male circumcision may play some role in the development of homosexuality. This unlikely notion stems from experiences with homosexual subgroups whose preoccupation with their lost foreskins sometimes reaches fanatical proportions. In fact, reconstruction of the prepuce through plastic surgery (a difficult procedure involving several steps over the course of a year) is now being performed in a few medical centers.

From a global and historical perspective, women, even when mentally ill, do not often voluntarily mutilate their genitals. In comparison with culturally accepted male genital mutilative practices, female practices pose clear-cut, serious physical problems to women who undergo them. Cultural explanations and rationalizations for the practices are few, and most can be linked ultimately with social control. The practices seem to stem from men's need to dominate women and to regulate what is perceived to be the rapacious female sexual appetite. In contrast, male practices have diverse explanations and rationalizations ranging from the vulgar and utilitarian to noble and profound sentiments associated with religion and amity.

DISCERNMENT AND THERAPY

III

■ ■ ■ ■ ■ ■ ■ ■ ■

Self-mutilation was described in the introduction to this book as one of the most puzzling and least understood human behaviors. Hundreds of cultural and clinical examples have been presented, setting the stage for an attempt to synthesize what is known about self-mutilation and to strip away the mysterious aura that traditionally has surrounded it.

This section classifies self-mutilative behaviors as culturally sanctioned or pathological and notes their shared purposefulness (except in cases of severe mental retardation, where cognitive capacity is minimal, and in some cases of illness with an overwhelming biological focus). In fact, such behaviors serve an identical purpose, namely, an attempt to correct or prevent a pathological, destabilizing condition that threatens the community, the individual, or both. I do not mean to imply that self-mutilative behavior is unidimensional or that the societal and personal explanations for it are invalid; nor do I wish to minimize the suffering and morbidity it causes. I contend, however, that at the deepest irreducible level self-mutilative behavior is prophylactic and salubrious for groups and for individuals threatened by death, disorganization, disease, and discomfort.

Remediation of destabilizing conditions may take many forms, including culturally sanctioned self-mutilative practices such as infibulation of females, finger chopping, and self-flagellation. These practices tend to be public events involving groups of persons. Self-mutilative practices may also represent an attempt to prevent pathological conditions from breaking out in a community. Male nose bleeding, for example, supposedly protects against illness. Practices such as penis cutting, foot binding, and scarification prevent social disorder by clearly defining statuses as well as proper comportment between the sexes and between generations. Self-mutilative and cannibalistic mortuary practices foster group solidarity and ensure the passing on of desirable traits and ritual powers. On an individual level the shaman who voluntarily endures horrible symbolic mutilation may achieve some personal gratification, but his ultimate and realizable goal is to heal the illnesses and to reverse the misfortunes of members of his community. Jesus Christ, perhaps the greatest of all cultural heroes, willingly allowed his body to be ravaged to save humankind from a life doomed by inherent, original sin and by subsequent sinful ways. The company of saints who mortified their bodies in imitation of Jesus' suffering not only achieved personal salvation but also became intercessory agents for the sick and needy.

Mentally ill persons, like communities, may feel threatened by pathological conditions and may engage in remedial self-mutilation. The most common pathological condition is tension and anxiety, often accompanied by self-anger and feelings of powerlessness. This corrodes a person's sense of stability and well-being and may create the sensation of an impending bodily explosion. Another commonly stated pathological condition is a perplexing feeling of numbness, strangeness, and unreality in regard to one's body, thoughts, and emotions as well as to persons and objects in the environment. Mentally ill persons who turn to self-mutilation usually are aware that something is wrong with them. They report feelings and thoughts about overwhelming guilt, loneliness, boredom, irresistible destructive urges, sin, persecution, helplessness (especially when confronted by hallucinatory visions and voices), demon possession, dissatisfaction with their sexual anatomy and gender identity, a desperate need for comfort and solace, and disordered social relationships. However, some mentally ill persons do not perceive their condition in pathological terms. Psychotic persons, for example, may truly believe themselves to be Jesus and may believe that their self-mutilation is in the service of humanity.

Advances over the past few years have resulted in a practical classification of pathological self-mutilation into types that have diagnostic and therapeutic relevance. This logical ordering of experience is important for clinical practice. Biological studies of self-mutilation have provided a rationale for the use of specific medications that do more than merely sedate and tranquilize. The propulsion of self-mutilation into the consciousness of both the general public and the mental health establishment has created a sense of optimism. Patients are now more willing to seek help, and they feel less ashamed of their behavior. Therapists are now more willing to provide help. These changes in attitude are remarkable in such a brief period of time.

This section also discusses various treatments, many of them new. There is no single correct therapeutic approach for all self-mutilation. For major self-mutilation, prevention is key; treatment is usually geared toward the primary illness. For stereotypic self-mutilation, behavior therapy is the primary modality, although medication often can be helpful. The use of medications that increase the activity of the neurotransmitter serotonin in the brain has proven successful for the treatment of moderate/superficial self-mutilation in many cases. This new development derives from biological research and sounds a note of optimism about dealing with clinically vexing repetitive and compulsive self-mutilators. However, medication alone works best when integrated into a comprehensive psychosocial treatment program.

9

Understanding Self-mutilation: Culturally Sanctioned Practices and Pathological Behavior

In the far distant past, primitive humans were fearful of thunder and lightning. To allay these fears, they developed theories to explain the loud heavenly noises and brilliant daggers of light that appeared in the sky. The most obvious explanation was supernatural: the events were caused by the wrath of the gods. Even though we scoff at this interpretation today because of our scientific knowledge, it was comforting back then to know that thunder and lightning were not capricious events.

Self-mutilation has been called mysterious, disgusting, incomprehensible, and a host of similar adjectives. Such negativism reflects the fear that grows out of ignorance. The predominant explanation for the behavior has been demonic possession. Jesus, for example, attributed the strange behavior of the man who repeatedly cut himself with stones to possession by the demon named Legion. With the development of science in general and of psychiatry and psychology in particular, supernatural explanations have been abandoned, and many different explanations have been offered. The multiplicity of explanations signifies that none is universally adequate and that the very concept of self-mutilation may be problematic.

In this book many examples of self-mutilation have been offered. To understand the processes and purposes of self-mutilative behaviors, I will present classifications, biological and psychosocial data, and subjective reports in this and the following chapter. Our starting point is the definition of self-mutilation as the direct, deliberate destruction or alteration of one's own body tissue without conscious suicidal intent. This definition does *not* include bona fide suicide attempts, indirect methods of self-harm (such as starvation), or swallowing objects (glass, nails) or substances (drug overdoses). Although mutilators harm themselves, this definition allows for situations in which persons willingly allow others to mutilate them.

The two major categories of self-mutilation can be portrayed thus:

Culturally sanctioned self-mutilation
Rituals
Practices

Deviant-pathological self-mutilation
Major
Stereotypic
Moderate/superficial
  Compulsive
  Episodic
  Repetitive

Culturally Sanctioned Self-mutilative Rituals and Practices

The differences between rituals and practices are often difficult to delineate. Cultural rituals imply activities that are repeated in a consistent manner over at least several generations and that reflect the traditions, symbolism, and beliefs of a society. They affect the individual participant, but since they are woven into the fabric of social life, they frequently affect the entire community. The Sun Dance of the Plains Indians is a clear example of a self-mutilative ritual. Urged on by tribal members at a yearly ceremony, spiritually and physically elite young braves gazed at the sun and struggled until the skewers that were inserted under the muscles of their chest and back broke free.

Cultural practices imply activities that may be faddish and that often hold little underlying significance. The piercing of earlobes or nose to accommodate jewelry are examples of such practices. Male circumcision is a practice when performed by Gentiles and a ritual when performed by Jews.

Because of their persistence and the "deep" meanings attributed to them by societies, self-mutilative rituals inform us about basic elements of social life. Examination of the rituals presented in this book reveals that they serve an elemental purpose, namely, the correction or prevention of a destabilizing condition that threatens the community. A few examples of destabilizing conditions are diseases; angry gods, spirits, and ancestors; failure of boys and girls to accept adult responsibilities when they mature; conflicts of all sorts, for example, male-female, intergenerational, interclass, intertribal; loosening of clear social role distinctions; loss of group identity and distinctiveness; immoral or sinful behaviors; ecological disasters.

Self-mutilative rituals (and some practices) serve to prevent the onset of these conditions and to correct or "cure" them should they occur. The rituals work by promoting healing, spirituality, and social order.

Healing

All living creatures share in the struggle for survival and the avoidance of pain. Animals are aided only by their instincts in this struggle, but human beings are able to transcend instinct and to devise strategies to deal with wounds, disease, and pain. Today we place our faith in scientific strategies, but before science existed there were other ways of dealing with threats to survival. The strategy of concern to us is that of self-mutilative rituals and practices. The origins of beliefs in the efficacy of self-mutilation to prevent and to cure diseases are obscure, but some have been present from the earliest days of human existence. Many examples of self-mutilative healing behaviors have been presented in previous chapters. For example, the Hamadsha, Muslim healers in Morocco, slash open their heads for the sake of ill persons who dip bits of bread or sugar cubes into the blood and then eat them; it is thought that a therapeutic power rests in the healers' blood. On "the island of menstruating men" in Papua New Guinea, it is believed that women are healthy because of their monthly menstrual bleeding. Men, in order to maintain their health, strength, and attractiveness, mimic the natural cycle of female self-purification by inducing periodic nasal hemorrhages. Some South African tribes used to remove one testicle to prevent sickness and used to cut off their fingertips to treat illnesses. Trephination and cutting grooves in skulls were performed originally to alleviate headaches by allowing evil spirits to exit the sick person's head. Shamans heal people through contact with the spirit world, but in order to become healers they must be cured of an initiating sickness. The curing process is horrific and involves dismemberment, scraping away of flesh, substitution of viscera, and renewal of blood during trance and dream states.

Spirituality

It is probably accurate to state that most people in all the societies that have ever existed have believed in supernatural spirits such as gods, demons, and souls. Since their power is unlimited, spirits have been implicated in every activity from crop failure to success in battle. The establishment and maintenance of the right relationship with spirits in order to avoid disaster and to promote prosperity in this world and the next has long been a major motivation for human activities. Self-mutilative ritual sacrifice and atonement are especially pleasing to spirits and, according to some mystics, are also capable of helping humans to achieve special states of ecstasy and insight. Priests devoted to the great mother goddess Cybele castrated themselves to demonstrate their mourning and identification with Attis, who had castrated himself, died, and was resurrected. The Eastern Orthodox Skoptsi sect practiced self-castration in order to avoid sinful sexual intercourse and to reclaim the pure state of Adam and Eve before the Fall. By their wounds the Old Testament Suffering Servant and the New Testament

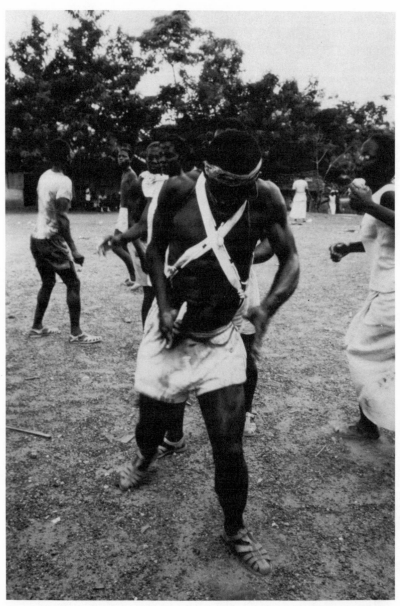

An African native from the Ivory Coast (Abidji tribe) mutilates himself while in a trance during the New Year festival. The wounds, although often severe, typically heal without problems. On the eve of the festival, tribal members meet to reconcile divisive personal and communal issues. The self-mutilation probably symbolizes the social healing that has occurred within the entire community. (Photo by Michael and Aubine Kirtley, courtesy of National Geographic Society)

In ritual subincision, the penile urethra is cut open as far as the base of the penis. Central Australian aborigines give many reasons for this procedure; most are religious myths related to the kangaroo totem. Kangaroos have a bifid penis that somewhat resembles a subincision. (See Cawte 1974; photo courtesy of Dr. John Cawte)

The breast of this elderly aboriginal woman from a Pacific island in the Gulf of Carpentaria shows scars made by her mother during a childhood illness. The procedure was intended to release a sickness-carrying rat thought to be inside the child's chest. (Photo courtesy of Dr. John Cawte)

During the Hindu festival of Thaipusum, devotees, while in a trance, put pins and rods through their tongue and cheeks painlessly and with minimal bleeding. (Photo courtesy of Dr. Ronald C. Simons)

Jesus gave salvation to humankind. Alone to the alone, the Christian desert fathers punished their bodies to achieve redemption, and for centuries the Church canonized as saints persons who zealously mortified their flesh. Some Hindus pierce their bodies to make themselves more pleasing to the god Murugan. Shiva lingam stones representing the self-castrated phallus of Shiva are among the holiest Hindu objects of veneration. Indian sadhus (holy men) engage in prodigious acts of mortification, such as sticking pins all over their bodies or stretching their penises with weights or hanging from flesh hooks, to achieve a transcendent spirituality. The Olmecs, Aztecs, and Mayans anointed sacred idols with blood from their penises as signs of devotion and penitence (Schele and Miller 1986).

Social Order

Chaos is the greatest threat to the stability of the universe. Without social order, men and women would not know how to behave properly, and many men in various cultures believe that uncontrolled female sexuality would then run riot, turning things topsy-turvy. Without order, boys and girls would not accept the responsibilities of adulthood when they came of age. People would be unable to distinguish tribal members from foes, leaders from followers, married women from unmarried ones. The alteration or destruction of body tissue helps to establish control of things and to preserve the social order. In the Sudan and other African countries, female sexuality is controlled by a surgical procedure on the genitals; in China it was done by breaking the bones in women's feet. Scarification patterns not only enhance beauty but also may indicate social status; for Tiv females in Nigeria they depict genealogical descent. A number of tribes cut off specific fingers to indicate a clan badge or sort of surname; a widow cuts off a finger upon remarriage. The Flathead Indians molded the skulls of their children to produce a clearly identifiable head shape. Circumcision of male infants has been a distinctive sign of Jewish identity for millennia. Young men of the Abidji tribe slice upon their abdomens the day after tribal members meet to reconcile divisive issues; the healing of the wounds symbolizes the social healing that has taken place within the entire community. The mutilative process is so important that the primary Indo-European cosmological myth tells about the sacrifice and mutilation of the Primordial Being from whose dismembered body parts the universe was created and the world was formed, as were the flora and the fauna and human beings, and thus everything was ordered properly.

The importance of self-mutilation is clearly demonstrated and encountered with great frequency in adolescent initiation rites. Many anthropologists (see Brown 1963; Cohen 1964; Gluckman 1962; Turner 1969; van Gennep 1909; Warner 1954; Whiting, Kluckhohn, and Anthony 1947) generally have understood the purpose of these rites to be the acquisition by adolescents of new social roles and status necessary for the orderly preservation of communal life. The mutilations that the adolescents voluntarily accept are painful and often brutal: teeth may be knocked loose, the nasal septum pierced, the penis sliced open along the length of the urethra, large areas of skin scarified. These mutilations are integral components of the initiation rites and seem to serve several important functions. They heighten the drama and significance of the ritual, focus attention on the adolescents, and allow them to demonstrate their inner strength. They also are a warning that the social group has great power and will not tolerate revolt against authority; children are transformed into adults when they overcome their fear and allow themselves to be subjected to pain and mutilation. The intense emotions of the ritual tend to foster bonding between the adolescent participants and the adults who perform the mutilation. Indeed, the painful mutilative process induces a peak emotional experience that "has the potential to mature consciousness by wasting the innocence of childhood and giving birth to the heightened self-awareness and greater consciousness of adulthood" (Morinis 1985, p. 167). In order to gain acceptance into the orderly adult world, adolescents must agree to surrender part of their autonomy as symbolized by mutilation. By voluntarily enduring pain and accepting mutilation, adolescents give visible notice of relinquishing childish ways. It is the price that must be paid in order to partake of adult communal life.

Pathological Self-mutilation

The first steps in doing something about a problem are giving it a name and a classification. Certainly clinicians were aware of self-mutilation as demonstrated by many early case reports, but there were no attempts to go beyond the general term *self-mutilation* until 1938. Karl Menninger's popular *Man Against Himself* contained a chapter in which self-mutilation was divided into four categories: neurotic, psychotic, organic, and religious. As usual, Menninger was ahead of his time. No one was ready to deal with or think about self-mutilation back then. In both popular and professional thought, self-mutilation was regarded generally as a type of suicidal behavior.

Menninger (1938) wrote about self-mutilation as an attempt at self-healing in which a suicidal impulse was focused on part of the body instead of the total body: "Local self-destruction is a form of partial suicide to avert total suicide" (p. 271). He was onto something important, but few colleagues paid attention. In his 1959 book *A Psychiatrist's World*, Menninger still was commenting that "some day" psychiatrists will talk about chronic focal self-destructive attacks that are different from acute generalized self-destruction.

The issue of the differences between suicidality and self-mutilation will be addressed later in this chapter. At this point it suffices to note that the mental health literature of the 1970s clearly recognized that not all acts of deliberate self-injury were suicidal in nature. This recognition eventually led Pattison and Kahan (1983; Kahan and Pattison 1984) to develop a differential classification of self-damaging behaviors that utilized three variables. The *direct/indirect* variable, based on the work of Farberow (1980), concerned time and awareness. Direct self-damaging behavior occurs in a brief timespan; awareness of the effects of the behavior is present, and there is a conscious intent to harm oneself. Indirect self-damaging behavior occurs over an extended time period; there is no awareness or regard of the harmful effects of the behavior, and there does not seem to be any conscious intent to self-harm. The *lethality* variable, especially as described by Litman (1980), considers the degree of possibility that the behavior will result in death. A low lethality behavior has a low possibility of death; a high lethality behavior, a high possibility. The *repetition* variable, based on a discussion by Farmer (1980), refers to single versus multiple episodes of the behavior. By using these variables, a classification can be made. A high lethality, single episode, direct self-damaging act such as a gunshot to the head is classified as suicide; an example of a similar indirect act would be termination of a vital treatment such as dialysis for kidney failure. A low lethality, multiple episode, direct behavior such as repetitive skin cutting is classified as a deliberate self-harm syndrome (more on this later), while examples of similar indirect behaviors are chronic alcoholism and heavy cigarette smoking.

The above-cited approach was a good start in the process of eliminating the linguistic and conceptual confusion that surrounded self-mutilation. Among the many terms that have been used to indicate self-mutilation are autoaggression, intentional injury, symbolic wounding, malingering, Munchausen syndrome, deliberate self-harm, self-abuse, local self-destruction, delicate self-cutting, self-injurious behavior, aggression against the self, parasuicide, attempted suicide, and focal suicide.

The classification that is widely accepted and clinically useful was reported by Favazza and Rosenthal in 1990, elaborated by them in 1993, and further modified by Favazza and Simeon in 1995. In this classification, pathological self-mutilation is divided into three observable categories based on degree of tissue destruction and the rate and pattern of behavior. The categories are major, stereotypic, and moderate/superficial. The last category has three subtypes: compulsive, episodic, and repetitive.

Major self-mutilation refers to infrequent acts — such as eye enucleation, castration, and limb amputation — that result in the destruction of significant body tissue. Stereotypic self-mutilation refers to repeated acts, such as head banging and eyeball pressing, that have a fairly fixed pattern of expression, seem to be devoid of symbolism, and are often rhythmic. Moderate/superficial self-mutilation refers to episodic or repetitive acts of low lethality and little tissue damage. This is the most common type of self-mutilation and includes behaviors such as skin cutting and burning, skin carving (words, designs, or other symbols), interference with wound healing, bone breaking, self-punching, needle sticking, hair pulling, nail biting, and skin scratching. Unlike the stereotypic type it lacks rhythmicity, usually has symbolic referents, and often requires the use of implements such as matches and a razor in a complex sequence of events.

This division of pathological self-mutilation into three categories is simplistic, as are all phenomenological classifications. It disregards etiology and is subject to change with increased knowledge, especially of biological markers and mechanisms. Its main advantage is that it is comprehensive and useful clinically. Each type of self-mutilation, for example, is usually more prevalent in certain mental disorders either as a central diagnostic feature or as an associated feature. Winchel and Stanley (1991) offered a different classification. They categorized self-mutilation by the clinical contexts in which it mainly occurs; these contexts include mental retardation, psychosis, penal institutionalization, and character disorder, primarily borderline personality disorder. Although this approach does cover much self-mutilative behavior, it does not deal with many mental and neuropsychiatric disorders where the behavior may be present.

Major Self-mutilation

Acts of major self-mutilation tend to be messy and to occur suddenly with a great deal of tissue damage and bleeding; an exception is carefully planned transsexual self-castration. These acts are not essential symptoms of any disorder but may appear as associated features. They are most commonly associated with psychosis (acute psychotic episodes, schizophrenia, mania, and depression) and acute intoxication.

An example of major self-mutilation in a psychotic person is the case of a 44-year-old man who developed apocalyptic visions of suffering people. He thought himself to be Adam, the first and the last man. He had an idea that he could control time and that he was the instrument who could give the world a new start. He then felt that he was pregnant and had to become the bride of Jesus. He took a knife and, without feeling pain, castrated himself completely. He fainted and was scared by what had happened when he recovered. Soon afterward he had a feeling of relief (Martin and Gattaz 1991).

One of the earliest reported cases of major self-mutilation exemplifies the role of intoxication. It is a brief report of a 36-year-old man who went on a four-day drinking spree. He was placed in a jail cell to dry out. That night he enucleated both his eyes (Fulton 1887).

Other cases already presented in earlier chapters demonstrate major self-mutilation in transsexualism, congenital sensory neuropathy, schizoid personality disorder, mental retardation, and acute and chronic encephalitis. It may also appear during the residual phase of schizophrenia (Talbott and Linn 1978). Acts of major self-mutilation must be distinguished on the basis of intent from similar acts of individuals who may consciously try to end their lives by deep cuts through blood vessels, self-immolation, and other gruesome acts. Even self-castration has been reported in a nonpsychotic man who wanted to bleed to death (Conacher, Villeneuve, and Kane 1991). Such bona fide suicide attempts should not be regarded as self-mutilation.

Some patients seem indifferent to their behavior and can provide no explanation for it: a teenage girl told the nurse who found her holding her right eye in her hand that it had spontaneously and painlessly fallen out of her head while she was sleeping (Goodhart and Savitsky 1933). Others offer idiosyncratic explanations that defy understanding: a 29-year-old man who castrated himself while wading in the ocean gave his severed testicles to his mother with the intention of giving back to her the life she had given him at birth (Pabis, Mirla, and Tozmans 1980). However, in many cases, explanations have a religious and/or sexual theme.

Religious themes are exemplified in numerous ways.

Influence of the Bible. Especially influential are the texts of Mark 9:47–48 and Matthew 5:28–29, which direct Christians to tear out an offending eye and to cut off an offending hand since losing part of one's body is better than being cast whole into hell. After discussing Matthew's work in a Bible study group, a young man tried to saw off his hand and to chop it off with an ax; he finally shot it off with a rifle (Goldenberg and Sata 1978). Another portentous passage is Matthew 19:12, which states, "There be eunuchs which have made themselves eunuchs for the kingdom of heaven's sake." A depressed middle-aged man brooded for weeks on that biblical passage before cutting off both testicles (Clark 1981).

Identification with Christ. A 37-year-old paranoid sailor feared that his shipmates were going to torture and kill him. Since Easter was approaching, he decided to emulate Christ, who overcame adversity by enduring the torments of his captors. He then cooked his index finger and ate half of it (Mintz 1964). A 48-year-old widow who considered herself a great sinner removed both her eyes in the belief that since Christ shed his blood, so too must hers be shed to become saintly (Bergmann 1846).

Sinfulness. Self-mutilation satisfies personal requirements for atonement, purification, and punishment for sins. A 35-year-old schizophrenic castrated himself, believing that his act of purification would qualify him to serve as pilot of a space ship that would carry pious people to outer space (Kushner 1967). In order to atone for a sinful incestuous relationship with his mother, a 50-year-old depressed man removed an eye with his fingers (Harrer 1950).

Heavenly commands. Guilt-ridden after going to a topless nightclub, a 44-year-old man shoved a pencil into his eyeball; he said that a statue of the Virgin Mary commanded him to do so (Crowder et al. 1979). A 26-year-old manic woman mutilated herself, claiming that God had ordered her to tear out her tongue, to fast, and to burn herself (Howden 1882).

Demonic influences. An adolescent enucleated his eye while experiencing an adverse reaction to LSD. He explained that the devil possessed him because his mind was weakened by the LSD. "Now I've got the devil out of my mind since I plucked my right eye out" (Rosen 1972). Believing that the Second Coming of Christ was imminent, a widow nearly severed her hand with a knife. When the surgeons found it necessary to amputate the hand, she declared that Satan had misled her (Lewis 1928).

Other religious themes. The amputation of various body parts has been explained as a mission for God (Goldenberg and Sata 1978), a freewill offering to God (Kushner 1967), and a repetition of behavior from a previous incarnation as a member of a mystical Russian sect of eunuchs (Thompson and Abraham 1983).

Persons often provide primary sexual explanations for their major self-mutilation, although a religious subtheme may be present in some cases.

Desire to be a female. A man sliced open his urethra to make himself "more like a woman"; years later he castrated himself, saying, "I resented the penis because I had been born wrong and then blamed for it" (Blacker and Wong 1963). A transsexual who had wanted to be a female ever since his childhood obtained employment as a licensed practical nurse in a urology department. After becoming familiar with surgical equipment and procedures, he neatly cut off his testicles (Lowry and Kolivakis 1971).

Fear of homosexuality. Thinking that "it might prevent me from indulging in sodomy," a man who had long struggled with homosexual desires suffered serious blood loss as a result of a self-castration attempt (Lewis 1928).

Control of hypersexuality. Afraid that he would lose his girlfriend because of his incessant sexual demands, a mentally retarded schizophrenic man drank some beer and castrated himself. He claimed that a voice told him, "Now you can't control yourself. Go ahead and cut it off."[1]

Repudiation of one's genitals. Having become impotent secondary to diabetes, an elderly man with long-standing sexual guilt castrated himself, saying that "they [his genitals] had let me down and now were no good to me" (Hemphill 1951). A 42-year-old manic man cut off his penis after his wife filed for divorce. He said, "I knew my divorce was coming up, and I would have no further use for it" (Lennon 1963).

---

1. When no reference is cited, the cases and quotations are from patients with whom I have had contact.

Obsession with amputation. Sexually excited by photographs of amputees, a 28-year-old man cut off a toe and deliberately injured a finger so that it would be removed surgically (Wakefield et al. 1977). Another man, who had constant erotic fantasies of himself as an amputee, hammered a steel pin into his tibia (a large bone in the leg). Desiring to force a surgical amputation, he repeatedly injected the wound with acne pus and with nasal and anal mucus (Money, Jobsris, and Furth 1977).

Other themes. Other reasons given by patients for their acts of major self-mutilation are to reduce testicular pain (Stroch 1901), to save the world (MacLean and Robertson 1976), to eliminate an eye perceived as bad or dangerous to others, to prevent the urge to gamble by amputating a hand, to eliminate marital anguish and to enhance general well-being (Kalin 1979), and to experience the "lost bisexual secret of the urethral orgasm" (Money and DePriest 1976).

Because of serious tissue damage, acts of major self-mutilation often are tragedies. An enucleated eye is inevitably lost; and more times than not, amputated body parts cannot be repaired or reattached surgically. The calmness that many patients exhibit after their self-mutilation suggests that the behavior may resolve unconscious conflicts. In most instances, alas, the resolution is only temporary, and the self-harm behavior may return with a vengeance. (An exception is that of some transsexuals whose self-castration may resolve certain psychological difficulties and make it more likely that professional surgical, medical, and psychological help will be made available to complete the process of changing gender.) The calmness may also reflect realistic resignation: what's done is done. When there is a clearing of consciousness in individuals whose actions were performed during a state of intoxication, the realization of their loss may be exquisitely sobering.

Stereotypic Self-mutilation

Acts of stereotypic self-mutilation are monotonously repetitive and even may have a rhythmic pattern. It is usually impossible to ascertain any symbolic meaning, thought content, or associated affect with the behaviors. The acts are more likely than those of other types of self-mutilation to occur in the presence of onlookers. Stereotypic self-mutilators seem to be driven by a primarily biological imperative to harm themselves shamelessly and without guile.

The most common behavior is head banging. It may cause self-induced seizures, vomiting, and even detachment of the retina. The highest rate was reported in an autistic, mentally retarded boy: he banged his head 5,400 times an hour (Romanczyk and Goren 1975). Among the many explanations that have been offered for stereotypic self-mutilation in general are the following: a way to obtain attention, an autoerotic response to understimulation, an expression of frustration, and a turning inward of anger and aggression. Head banging specifically has been seen as an attempt to reexperience the comfort of hearing a mother's heartbeat.

Stereotypic self-mutilation is highly prevalent in institutionalized mentally retarded persons, where it is commonly called self-injurious behavior (SIB). It is important to note, however, that not all self-mutilation in this population is stereotypic; nor are specific personality types or behaviors uniquely associated with mental retardation. As stated in the American Psychiatric Association's *Diagnostic and Statistical Manual of Mental Disorders* (4th ed., 1994), "Mental retardation has many different etiologies and may be seen as the final common pathway of various pathological processes that affect the functioning of the central nervous system." A 13.6 percent prevalence of behaviors such as head banging and hitting, orifice digging, arm hitting, throat and eye gouging, self-biting, severe scratching, and hair pulling was reported in a survey of 10,000 mentally retarded residents of state schools in Texas (Griffen et al. 1985). The prevalence of mental retardation in general is thought to be about 1,000 cases per 100,000 population; persons with severe or profound mental retardation (about 5% of cases) are at particular risk for SIB.

Self-injurious behavior may be present also as a symptom or associated feature of acute psychosis, schizophrenia, and of several disorders.

Autism. Often associated with moderate mental retardation, autism is characterized by marked and sustained impairment of social interaction and communication as well as restricted, repetitive, stereotyped behaviors, interests, and activities. Its onset occurs in early childhood. Self-injurious behavior may be present in the form of head banging as well as biting of the wrist, hand, and fingers. In some autistic persons, SIB is facilitated by excessive fearfulness and a high pain threshold. The prevalence of the disorder is probably around 35 cases per 100,000 population.

Lesch-Nyhan syndrome. This rare disorder, found only in males, is caused by an inborn error of purine metabolism, namely, defective activity of the enzyme hypoxanthine guanine phosphoribosyl transferase. Because of this enzyme defect, uric acid accumulates in the blood, and the child may develop some of the clinical findings associated with gout. Additionally, he may involuntarily develop choreoathetoid movements, mental retardation, and compulsively self-aggressive behavior. These children mutilate themselves severely by biting off their lip tissue, and it is not uncommon for them to bite off parts of their tongue or fingers. The mutilations are remarkable for their awesome rapidity; upon release from restraints, a child's hand may go instantly into his mouth, where it is bitten, accompanied by screams of pain (Christie et al. 1982). The SIB may be related to lowered dopamine activity in the area of the brain known as the striatum (Baumeister and Frye 1985) or may be related to dopamine receptor hypersensitivity (Goldstein et al. 1985). The onset of SIB is usually in the first few years of life but may be delayed until adolescence. Those affected with this syndrome "usually plead with their parents or other caretakers to keep them in restraints and they become extremely upset when the restraints are removed" (Jankovic 1988).

deLange syndrome. Children with this rare disorder are characterized by profound mental retardation, small facial bones and bushy black eyebrows that meet, and lip biting. Other behaviors include self-scratching and head and face slapping. Self-injurious behavior occurs in about half of children with this disorder (Murphy 1985; Singh and Pulman 1979).

Retts disorder. Usually associated with profound mental retardation, Retts disorder is characterized by the persistent, progressive loss of hand skills and of the ability to interact socially. Language development is seriously impaired. The disorder occurs only in females, who develop normally for the first five to thirty months of life and then demonstrate developmental regression. Repetitive hand washing movements are characteristic of the disorder. The SIB may be expressed by self-biting, head banging, and face banging (Jankovic 1988). Some social skills may develop during adolescence.

Neuroacanthosis. This disorder (really a group of disorders), possibly caused by defects in the membranes of red blood cells as well as brain cells, is associated with a wide variety of symptoms, including tics, abnormal muscle tone, muscle wasting, strange facial and mouth movements, Parkinsonism, and dementia. Perhaps its most recognizable sign is tongue and lip biting. Onset occurs mostly in adult life.

Tourette syndrome. Multiple simple and complex tics (sudden rapid, recurrent, stereotyped movements or vocal sounds) are the central feature of this disorder, whose onset is usually in childhood or early adolescence. Studies indicate that SIB occurs in at least a third of cases (Robertson, Trimbale, and Lees 1989; Shapiro et al. 1978; Van Woert, Yip, and Balis 1977; Nee et al. 1980). Self-injurious behavior includes head banging, self-hitting, tooth extraction, eyeball pressing, sticking objects in the eyeballs, joint dislocation, and biting of the lips, cheek, and tongue. The first report of the disorder in 1885 by the French physician Gilles de la Tourette described a 24-year-old man: "His mouth opens wide; when it closes again one can hear the teeth of both jaws gnashing violently. Quite often his tongue is caught between them and abruptly seizured and lacerated; moreover it is all covered with scars." (Robertson et al. 1989). Several cases of severe injury have been reported. The first patient began eye blinking at 2 years of age and then developed multiple motor and vocal tics. By age 22 his history of SIB included head banging, burning his fingers on a frying pan, self-induced bleeding by sticking his finger up his nose, and severe eye poking. Another patient bit his mouth and tongue starting at age 4. At age 18 he repeatedly punched himself in the eye, head, neck, chest, shoulder, and genitals with resultant bruising. He also shook his head so violently that on one occasion he collapsed and died due to bleeding within his skull (Robertson et al. 1989). The SIB of Tourette patients is linked both to their motor tics and to their obsessionality, compulsivity, and impulsivity. The prevalence of the disorder is about 45 cases per 100,000 population. Neither the disorder itself nor the SIB is associated with below-normal intelligence.

Moderate/Superficial Self-mutilation

Epitomized by skin cutting and burning, moderate/superficial self-mutilation is a common behavior that has been much written about recently in the lay press and professional literature. The situation is reminiscent of several decades ago when bulimia was considered a rare phenomenon. After the public and professional consciousness was awakened to the problem, bulimics came out of the closet by the droves. The same scenario fits cutting and burning, the prevalence of which is now thought to be about 1,400 cases per 100,000 population. To put this figure in perspective, the suicide rate is fairly constant at 10 to 12 per 100,000 while the attempted suicide rate ranges widely from 50 to 250 per 100,000. (These suicide statistics depend upon the definitions used, e.g., should an overdose to make a lover feel guilty be counted as a bona fide suicide attempt or is it a suicidal gesture?) In a survey of undergraduate students, Favazza, DeRosear, and Conterio (1989) found that 12 percent admitted to having deliberately harmed themselves by cutting, burning, or a similar act. There have been reports of childhood dare games that include skincutting (Lena and Bijoor 1990), and I recently met a ninth-grade student who belonged to a "cut of the month" club! That the behavior *seems* to be more common in females may be an artifact of sampling techniques. A tremendous amount of cutting and burning, for example, goes on in prison. In addition, males can easily lie about the causes of their scars (e.g., a result of a work injury, a fight, or a drunken fall).

The revelation that Princess Diana was a cutter shocked the readers of *People* magazine. The June 22, 1992, issue contained excerpts from a biography by Andrew Morton (1992). In addition to providing details of Lady Di's eating disorder, Morton wrote: "On one occasion she threw herself against a glass cabinet at Kensington Palace, while on another she slashed at her wrists with a razor blade. Another time she cut herself with the serrated edge of a lemon slicer; on yet another occasion during a heated argument with Prince Charles, she picked up a penknife lying on his dressing table and cut her chest and her thighs. Although she was bleeding, her husband scorned her. As ever, he thought she was faking her problems." In an article in *Details* magazine (May 1993), the actor and teen idol Johnny Depp displayed multiple scars on his forearm. He said that his body was like a journal and that he cut himself with a knife in order to mark special times in his life. Ironically, one of Depp's major film roles was Mr. Scissorhands.

Of the many lay articles on cutting and burning, one is especially noteworthy. Marilyn Strong's "A Bright Red Scream" appeared in the December 1993 issue of *San Francisco Focus* magazine. The reports provided by self-mutilators ring true as demonstrated in the following three anecdotes. In her high school bathroom, "Marilyn locked herself inside a stall and pressed the razor's edge into the soft skin of her wrist. It was a controlled cut, not a wild slash meant to end her life. As blood began to ooze to the surface, she felt that familiar rush of relief, like popping the lid off a pressure cooker. Sometimes she used scissors to achieve the same effect, sometimes broken bottles. The first time she punctured her skin, at age eleven, she made a pincushion of her wrist." "Melanie has cut her wrists with a razor, burned herself with cigarettes, and carved words and pictures into her arms and legs—including a happy face still visible on her left hand. Isn't it ironic, I ask her, carving a happy face into your skin? 'The whole idea of cutting yourself is ironic,' she says. 'Making yourself hurt to feel better is really a wicked and deranged thing. Yet to me, it's normal.'" Of a 17-year-old the author writes, "Upside down crosses are carved into his chest, the words 'Jenny is dead' are scratched across his stomach. Other body parts are inscribed with ominous messages: 'Die,' 'You killed me,' and 'Help.' 'It was just this primal thing,' he says. 'It started out as decoration and indifference to the world. It was like, See, this is how much pain I have, like battle scars of life.' But cutting soon became a way of calming himself, of focusing all his frustrations in one place. 'It sounds weird to say this, but it kind of kept me sane.'"

The behaviors in this category, including hair pulling and skin scratching, picking, cutting, burning, and carving, are the most commonly encountered forms of self-mutilation. They appear as symptoms or associated features of a great many disorders; a case can be made that the repetitive self-mutilation syndrome is itself a disorder of impulse control. The three types of moderate/superficial self-mutilation are the compulsive, the episodic, and the repetitive.

Compulsive Self-mutilation

The behaviors involved in compulsive self-mutilation occur many times daily and are repetitive and ritualistic. Most individuals with relatively mild symptoms do not seek professional help, while those with more severe symptoms are usually seen by dermatologists and family physicians.

Hair pulling. Hair pulling is by definition a self-mutilative behavior and is regarded as a mental disorder of impulse control. Also known as trichotillomania, this disorder involves pulling out one's hair from anywhere on the body but especially from the scalp, eyebrows, and eyelashes. The behavior may begin in early childhood, often in association with thumb sucking. These early onset cases are present equally in boys and girls, have a brief, benign course, and do not necessarily imply severe intrapsychic or familial psychopathology (Winchel 1992). Later onset cases typically begin at age 13, are ten times more likely to affect females than males, and may follow a severe, chronic course with a high evidence of co-morbid nail biting, skin scratching, and anxiety and mood disorders. In a ritualistic manner persons may select a hair that is perceived to be different (e.g., too kinky, crooked, or straight). "The hair is then plucked and examined, and the root or the entire hair sometimes eaten. Hairs may be piled before discarded. Hair-pulling sessions vary from 4 or 5 hour sessions in which several hundred hairs are pulled to brief episodes in which only a few hairs are pulled at a time, but which re-occur dozens of times each day" (Swedo and Rapaport 1991). Swallowed material can form hairballs in the stomach that may result in anemia, abdominal pain, gastric bleeding, nausea, vomiting, bowel obstruction, and perforation of the stomach or bowel (Mueller 1990).

Hair pulling usually occurs in private but sometimes occurs in the presence of family members. It increases both during periods of stress and of relaxation. Most hair pullers report mounting tension or gratification with the behavior, suggesting both compulsivity and impulsivity (Christenson et al. 1991). Hair pullers often are not consciously aware of the behavior, which may occur automatically without elaborate thought content or emotion. In this regard they are similar to patients with obsessive-compulsive disorder who have compulsions with few or no obsessions (Favazza and Simeon 1995). Although the exact prevalence is unknown, the disorder is probably fairly common and may affect 1 percent of all persons.

Psychodermatological conditions. The term *psychodermatology* was cited by Koo (1989) to describe skin disorders associated with psychological and neurological factors. Patients with delusions of parasites in their skin have been discussed in chapter 7. Since the delusion of parasitosis is usually a limited, encapsulated false belief, patients with this disorder may function well and not experience psychological deterioration. They harm themselves by injuring their skin in attempting to dig out the imaginary organisms and to destroy them with toxic substances such as lye. It should be noted that many disorders may cause persons to have tactile hallucinations. "Cocaine bugs," for example, may be reported by chronic users of that drug. Other offending drugs are "uppers," such as amphetamine and methylphenidate (Ritalin), and alcohol during withdrawal (delirium tremens). Medical disorders that may cause tactile hallucinations include multiple sclerosis, pernicious anemia, pellagra, diabetes mellitus, hyperthyroidism, and polycythemia vera. The European dermatological literature contains references to patients who experience chronic feelings of insects falling or crawling on their skin as well as biting and pricking sensations in the absence of delusions or other psychiatric findings (Conrad and Bers 1954).

Neurotic excoriations refer to skin lesions caused by perfectionistic, obsessive-compulsive persons who are compulsively driven to remove actual or imaginary skin blemishes (Koo 1989). These excoriations are present more often in females who, between the ages of 30 to 40 years, begin squeezing, scratching, and picking their skin. A subgroup is composed of younger women who compulsively pick their acne lesions. Patients with this disorder are usually unaware of their behaviors but when confronted will admit to them (Gupta et al. 1986; Doran, Roy, and Wolkowitz 1985). In contrast, other patients deliberately create skin lesions but steadfastly deny it. The methods used include cigarette and match burns and the application of phenol, acids, silver nitrate and other chemicals to their skin. This disorder, called dermatitis factitia or artefacta, was discussed in chapter 7.

Episodic Self-mutilation

The term *episodic* refers to behaviors that occur every so often. Episodic self-mutilators do not brood about this behavior, nor do they have a self-identity as a "cutter" or "burner." They deliberately harm themselves to feel better, to get rapid respite from distressing thoughts and emotions, and to regain a sense of self-control. There are many situations in which the behavior operates; among the themes most commonly articulated by patients are the following (Favazza 1989b).

Tension release. A young man who experienced mounting tension observed, "It was like looking down a tunnel into nothing. Then I saw red streaks and black fire. And then I carved my arm with a razor blade, and the pressure went away." A 39-year-old schoolteacher said, "Before every act of self-mutilation I feel emotionally overwhelmed. The sight of my blood seems to release unbearable tension. At first a bruise or scratch was effective, but later it took more blood to ease the explosive tension. Now I cut my veins to get results."

Return to reality. Patients often report that emotional deadness, the diminished ability to experience normal sensations, estrangement from the environment, and an altered perception of time result in feelings of unreality. Self-mutilation makes those patients feel real again.

Establishing control. A 22-year-old homemaker stated, "Self-harm gives me a feeling of control when I cannot find control in the environment." A 32-year-old salesman said, "When I feel hyper my mind races and I can't sleep, then I almost always harm my feet and legs. . . . Sometimes I hit myself with a hammer. . . . Then I'm calm again."

Security and uniqueness. An 18-year-old waitress said, "Cutting, burning, and poking needles into my arms is a security for me because I know that if all else fails and leaves me feeling emotionless and empty, the pain and blood will always be there for me." A 24-year-old college student admitted, "I cut myself because I need to be special. I was always taken for granted, invisible. Now, although I rarely expose my scars, I feel a smug pride. I'm not eager to give it up. Take it away from me, and I'm like everyone else."

Influencing others. A 22-year-old secretary said, "I cut my wrist [not a suicide attempt] and told my boyfriend who was very late for our date, 'This is how deeply you have hurt me.'" A 25-year-old unemployed woman stated, "Once I really needed surgery on my feet. Since then I have faked problem after problem so I could have more surgery. I am addicted to my doctor. I like the attention I get from him, and if I stopped having problems, I wouldn't feel important to anyone."

Negative perceptions. A 33-year-old homemaker explained, "My father tried to have sex with me when I was 22 years old, and I felt like a frightened child. I cut myself because I feel so much hate for myself." A 40-year-old advertising saleswoman admitted, "I feel lonely and ugly and disfigured inside. Terribly imperfect. Which leads to feeling the need to correct something outwardly, so I cut off my hair."

Pressure from multiple personalities. Patients with multiple personality disorder may attribute their self-mutilative behavior to the activities of one or more of their personalities. A 39-year-old registered nurse said, "The personalities punish one another. They sometimes use IV [intravenous] needles to get the blood running. Occasionally you wonder why for a brief moment, but the why isn't important. You just have to do it. Stick pins and needles in your skin. Hit your head with a hair brush. Scrape your vagina with a fish scaler. Sarah [a personality] cut my foot. She couldn't hurt my stepfather, so she hurt me. She just gets angry, and I get hurt. . . . She cut my wrist with a big long knife to punish me because I'm weak."

Sexuality. Some patients say that self-mutilation enhances sexual feelings, while others say the opposite. A Phi Beta Kappa college student said, "When I stick open scissors up my vagina, the cold hard steel gives me an explosive orgasm. And the blood makes it even more exciting." A 20-year-old secretary admitted, "Sometimes my mind churns up awful sexual visions, and I get rid of these bad pictures by cutting myself."

Euphoria and titillation. A 24-year-old male prisoner confessed, "When I cut myself, I get such a high feeling. It feels so good, and I feel deprived when I can't do it. I have never found a substitute for this high feeling." A 30-year-old female college instructor said, "Self-mutilation allows me to live on the edge. It is titillating to see just how far I can go and how much real pain I can endure. Too often I equivocate and am afraid to make choices. Here I can be swept away on a tidal wave of feelings."

Venting anger. A 19-year-old clerical worker said, "I get my anger out of me when I hurt myself. It would not be expressed in my family; you always had to smile. Also with my religion it is a sin to be angry. Cutting gives me a way to vent my anger." A 40-year-old disabled woman observed, "I have been set upon hard by an inoperable, intractable neck injury making me prone to violent headaches and depression that persist despite my cognitive therapy and people's platitudes. I feel I am regarded as immature by doctors or friends when I ask for help. Thus, cutting satisfies a need for justice and fairness, and I am not compelled to turn my heart against those who have failed me."

Relief from alienation. A 28-year-old librarian said, "When 'it' strikes, self-mutilation is the only thing that provides relief; 'it' being a frantic, desperate, profound sense of alienation from the rest of the world, primarily loved ones. Sometimes I think a dose of the good things—loving, hugging—would do it, but it's simpler to reach for a razor blade."

The themes that I have presented do not exhaust all the possible reasons that patients harm themselves, although the themes are fairly representative. Each person has his or her unique story to tell and reasons to give. In addition, it is important to note that all of the reasons apply to repetitive self-mutilation as well as to the episodic type.

Diagnosis of Episodic Self-mutilation

Moderate/superficial episodic self-mutilation may be present as a symptom or associated feature of many disorders.

Anxiety. Anxiety and fear are states of apprehension. Although the former theoretically refers to apprehension over unrealistic concerns and the latter to apprehension over real dangers, this distinction is difficult to make in clinical practice. The experience of anxiety ranges from the unpleasant to the horrifying. In addition to apprehension, the far-ranging manifestations of anxiety include fears (of dying, going crazy, or losing control), tension, irritability, trembling, shakiness, feelings of unreality, excessive vigilance, dizziness, hot and cold flashes, sweating, heart palpitations, chest pain, smothering sensations, difficulty with breathing and swallowing, dry mouth, cold and clammy hands, tingling in the hands and feet, nausea, diarrhea, sensation of butterflies in the stomach, panic, headaches, and disturbed sleep. For some persons, cutting and burning and similar self-mutilative acts provide relief from anxiety, especially from the symptoms of unbearable tension and fear of losing self-control.

Anxiety may be present as an associated feature of mental disorders such as schizophrenia and anorexia/bulimia nervosa (see chapter 3). It may be induced either by exposure to or withdrawal from drugs such as alcohol, stimulants (e.g., amphetamines and methylphenidate), caffeine, cannabis, cocaine, hallucinogens, inhalants (e.g., glue and paint thinners), phencyclidine, sedatives, and even anti-anxiety medication (e.g., Valium and Xanax). Anxiety may be caused by many medical disorders such as hypoglycemia, hyperthyroidism and hypothyroidism, heart arrhythmias, congestive heart failure, chronic obstructive pulmonary disease, pneumonia, hyperventilation, porphyria, and vitamin B_{12} deficiency. Ballard (1989) reported the case of a woman who cut herself to relieve the anxiety caused by benign intracranial hypertension. In another case, self-mutilation was found to be a presenting symptom in a 14-year-old girl with adrenocortical insufficiency (Addison's disease). Over a three-year period the girl repeatedly gouged pieces of skin from her limbs before falling asleep. Socially inept, often silent and withdrawn, and a poor communicator, she participated in intensive family counseling with little change in her behavior. Adrenocortical insufficiency was finally diagnosed upon hospitalization for nausea, vomiting, dizziness, and tiredness. One week following treatment with steroids, her self-mutilation stopped completely, as did her other symptoms (Rajathurai, Chazan, and Jeans 1983).

Anxiety disorders are mental illnesses in which anxiety is an essential symptom (e.g., generalized anxiety disorder and post-traumatic stress disorder [PTSD]). In PTSD, persons psychologically reexperience extremely traumatic events accompanied by anxiety. Self-mutilation has been reported in PTSD after combat (Pitman 1990). Greenspan and Samuel (1989) published case reports of self-cutting after rape. For example, six months after being violently raped several times by the same man and threatened with death if she ever told anyone, a 19-year-old woman entered therapy for severe anxiety, recurrent nightmares, a compulsion to bathe, and intermittent periods of memory loss. A few months later she started cutting her wrists, forearms, and thighs. "The secrecy that surrounded this behavior seemed to parallel the silence she felt she must maintain about the rapes. She said that cutting her arm provided a release for unbearable tension that built up as part of a rape-related flashback."

Dissociative disorders. In these disorders there is a disruption in normally integrated mental functions dealing with memory, self-identity, consciousness, and perception of the environment. In multiple personality disorder (MPD, although its official name is dissociative identity disorder), a person's behavior is controlled by two or more distinct identities or personality traits, accompanied by memory gaps for important personal information. A person with MPD usually has a primary passive identity and alternate identities with contrasting names and characteristics. In at least a third of the cases, self-mutilation may be inflicted as a punishment by one alternate personality on another (see chapter 7).

Persons experiencing depersonalization have disconcerting feelings of being detached from their bodies and mental processes. Although they observe themselves like actors in a dream or a movie, they realize the difference between reality and fantasy. Brief episodes of depersonalization are very common in persons under severe stress, especially when their lives are in danger. Some people who experience prolonged or recurrent episodes of depersonalization have an illness called depersonalization disorder. They learn that they can rapidly feel normal again by cutting themselves.

Depression. The concept and classification of depression are complicated. Everyone experiences normal feelings of dejection, disappointment, demoralization, and sadness. These feelings cross the line into the clinical illness known as dysthymia (or neurotic depression) when a person not only feels depressed but also experiences such symptoms as poor appetite or overeating, insomnia or too much sleep, low energy and self-esteem, poor concentration, and hopelessness. During a major depression, these symptoms are not only intensified but also may be accompanied by observable agitation or slowed behavior, feelings of worthlessness or excessive guilt, thoughts of death, thoughts of suicide, and attempted suicide. Depression may be present as a symptom of mental disorders (e.g., obsessive-compulsive disorder and borderline personality disorder) and of medical disorders (e.g., stroke, viral diseases, and cancer). It may be induced by a variety of drugs such as cocaine, heroin, alcohol, digitalis, steroids, major tranquilizers, and barbiturates. Depression may also follow exposure to stressful events or situations (adjustment disorder with depressed mood). Some depressed persons find that cutting and burning may effect a temporary respite from their misery. Self-mutilation may, for example, alleviate guilt through self-punishment.

Personality disorders. Personality refers to the more or less enduring psychological and emotional characteristics of a person. Personality develops slowly, starting with infancy. It is not something that a person has, but rather is a major essence of a person. Our personality comprises numerous, different qualities that describe our general pattern of thinking, feeling, perceiving, acting, and relating to the world across time and across most social situations. A person might be described as being devoted or dramatic or adventuresome or meticulous. Although these are positive characteristics, when they become intense and hypertrophied, they may be transformed into dependency, histrionics, criminality, and obsessive-compulsive behavior. When personality characteristics cause some functional impairment or subjective distress, they are known as pathological personality traits; when the impairment or distress is severe, they are classified as personality disorders. Moderate/superficial self-mutilation is commonly encountered in antisocial, borderline, and mixed personality disorders.

Antisocial personality disorder. Sometimes known as sociopathy or psychopathy, this disorder is manifested by persons who persistently disregard and violate the rights of others. They are frequently deceitful, impulsive, aggressive, reckless, irresponsible, manipulative, and lacking in remorse about their mistreatment of others. Typical psychopathic behaviors include using aliases, spouse and child abuse, committing crimes, defaulting on debts, getting into physical fights, speeding and driving while intoxicated, and not showing up for work. People often describe psychopaths as callous, self-centered, arrogant, superficially charming when things are going their way, hedonistic and sexually exploitative, easily bored, and prone to malingering, depression, tension, drug abuse, and getting multiple tattoos. In a general population, it is thought that 3 percent of males and 1 percent of females are psychopaths. Among prisoners the prevalence of the disorder is 75 percent.

Prisons and detention centers are hotbeds of cutting and burning (see chap. 7). In these settings self-mutilation may be "normal" to a subculture that values unorthodox methods of outwitting rules. Thus, prisoners may self-mutilate in order to force authorities to transfer them to a preferred cell block or work assignment. The behavior also may stem from psychopathology, or the need to control the mounting tension and to assuage the depression that psychopaths are apt to experience when they are unable to roam free and practice their regular impulsive and deceitful life-style. Self-mutilation provides psychopaths with stimulation to combat dreaded boredom; some even claim it provides a feeling of euphoria. The behavior may be a genuine, desperate cry for attention as well as a maneuver to instill guilt in others, for example, in a relationship that is threatening to end. Outside of prison, psychopaths who deliberately harm themselves usually explain away scars and burn marks by saying that they are the result of a fight.

Borderline personality disorder (BPD). To many clinicians, BPD is synonymous with moderate/superficial self-mutilation. Diagnosed more often in females, the disorder is thought to be present in about 2 percent of the general population (and in about 20% of hospitalized psychiatric patients). The already large literature on BPD continues to grow rapidly, and much of what is known about the mental state of self-mutilators comes from the study of borderlines. As a diagnosis, BPD has existed for only a few decades. Previously, persons with borderline characteristics were diagnosed as having an inadequate or emotionally unstable personality disorder or even schizophrenia. Especially well known is the case of Deborah Blau, the central character in the popular autobiographical novel _I Never Promised You a Rose Garden_ (Greenberg 1981). At age 5, Deborah developed urinary incontinence, which her governesses tried to cure through the use of shame, threats, and whippings. A urethral tumor was diagnosed and operated upon. Deborah vividly recalled the "searing stroke of the instrument" and the use of probes and needles "as if the entire reality of her body were concentrated in the secret evil inside that forbidden place." She felt that the tumor was never fully removed and that she carried "Deborah rot" within her. As she grew up she became aware of her father's incestuous feelings toward her, became a compulsive eater, developed insomnia, and endured the anti-Semitic remarks directed at her by children at camp. While at camp she mentally constructed a fanciful world with strange gods who sent her omens and made demands on her. Shortly before her sixteenth birthday, she was hospitalized for cutting her wrists. During her hospitalization she painlessly cut and burned herself, beat her head on tiled floors, and hurled her body against walls. Through the slow process of intensive psychotherapy (with occasional medications and icy wet packs to control her behavior), she became well. In real life, the author was treated by the well-known psychoanalyst, Frieda Fromm-Reichmann, who diagnosed her as schizophrenic. Although in a modern review of the case Murray (1993) states that "perhaps" the correct diagnosis should have been post-traumatic stress disorder and dissociative disorder, most psychiatrists would add borderline personality disorder.

In addition to self-mutilation, persons with BPD are characterized by fears of abandonment; short-lived episodes of dissociation, depersonalization, psychotic-like symptoms, anxiety, irritability, and depression; intense and rocky relationships; a vacillating self-image and sense of self; rapidly fluctuating emotions; chronic feelings of emptiness; intense and inappropriate anger; suicidal behaviors; and impulsive acts such as binge eating, abusing drugs, and going on spending sprees. Their lives are often tumultuous and filled with real and imaginary crises that result in such discontinuities as failed marriages, lost jobs, and incomplete educational experiences. Many, but not all, borderlines are reared in unpleasant circumstances (family conflicts, sexual and physical abuse, neglect, and early parental loss or separation). Episodic self-mutilation is present more in BPD than in any other disorder. It is so prevalent because it works: it ends the depersonalization and mounting anxiety ("Cutting myself is like popping a balloon"), provides solace, stabilizes emotional swings, and so forth. The popular film _Fatal Attraction_, in which the heroine (or villain, depending upon one's perspective) cuts herself, is a fairly accurate portrayal of a borderline.

Mixed personality disorder (_or personality disorder not otherwise specified_). Many persons have personality problems that do not coincide with recognized diagnostic disorders. Thus, a person may have _some_ borderline characteristics intermingled with other problematic characteristics, such as histrionic traits that include excessive emotionality, a flair for dramatic attention-seeking behavior, and flirtatiousness (in previous classifications "suicidal gestures," some of which would today be regarded as self-mutilation, were considered a feature of histrionic personality disorder). The combination of borderline and/or histrionics and/or antisocial traits is favorable for the emergence of self-mutilative behavior, as are other personality traits such as narcissism, dependency, perfectionism, paranoia, and eccentricity.

Repetitive Self-mutilation

Episodic self-mutilation becomes repetitive when the behavior becomes an overwhelming preoccupation in those persons who may adopt an identity as a "cutter" or "burner" and who describe themselves as addicted to their self-harm. The self-mutilative behavior seems to assume an autonomous course. There is not a set number of self-mutilative episodes that marks the switch from episodic to repetitive. In some persons the switch may occur between the fifth and tenth episode; in others between the tenth and twentieth. Unlike episodic self-mutilation, which is best considered a symptom or associated feature of a mental disorder (such as BPD or generalized anxiety disorder), the repetitive type is best considered a separate disorder of impulse control known as the repetitive self-mutilation syndrome. This syndrome usually begins in early adolescence and persists for decades, during which the self-harm periodically heats up and cools down and may coexist with other impulsive behaviors, such as eating disorders, alcohol and substance abuse, and kleptomania (stealing unnecessary objects) (Favazza and Rosenthal 1990, 1993).

The historical development of this syndrome began many decades ago when a wrist-cutting syndrome was described. According to Graff and Mallin (1967), the typical wrist slasher was "an attractive, intelligent, unmarried young woman, who is either promiscuous or overtly afraid of sex, easily addicted and unable to relate to others. . . . She slashes her wrists indiscriminately and repeatedly at the slightest provocation, but she does not commit suicide. She feels relief with the commission of her act." Eighty percent of women with this proposed wrist-cutting syndrome had cut themselves more than five times and many more than forty times.

Rosenthal et al. (1972) provided more data on the wrist-cutting syndrome in a study of female inpatients, half of whom were "habitual cutters" (defined as more than five cutting episodes). In comparison with a study group of females with a history of suicidality but no self-mutilation, Rosenthal's patients had histories of eating disorders, childhood physical trauma or surgery, chronic feelings of emptiness, and depreciation of their femininity. Self-cutting with consequent reintegration was the culmination of a process in which separation or rejection resulted in feelings of anger, self-hatred, or fear that led to numbness and depersonalization. In retrospect, my colleague Richard Rosenthal now realizes that he was describing something more than a wrist-cutting syndrome since most of his patients cut other parts of their bodies, traumatized fresh fractures, scratched and gouged their faces, and rubbed glass fragments into their skin. Several years earlier, Pao (1969) had given a different name to this type of self-mutilation. He called it the syndrome of "delicate self-cutting" and described young women who were so extremely sensitive to feelings of abandonment that they repeatedly hurt themselves in a superficial manner.

Interest in self-mutilative syndromes was affected dramatically in the

1970s when two flawed epidemiological studies were published. The first used data from police reports on "a large and relatively unselected population of persons who attempted suicide" (Clendenin and Murphy 1971). The study found that 40 percent of subjects who attempted suicide by wrist cutting were males, compared with only 28 percent of those who used other methods. Wrist cutters were no more likely than those who used other methods to make repeated suicide attempts or to confine themselves to a single method. The authors concluded that different kinds of studies were needed to determine the existence of a specific wrist-cutting syndrome. A second study essentially replicated these findings, concluding that "the stereotype of persons who cut their wrists as distinct from other suicide attempters did not hold" (Weissman 1975). Both studies unfortunately regarded cutting solely as a suicide attempt, and they examined only isolated cutting episodes severe enough to require a police report or hospital treatment. They did not distinguish repetitive from single-episode cutters, yet they included references that emphasized both this distinction and the fact that cutting rarely represents a conscious suicide attempt. The first study excluded persons who cut parts of their bodies other than wrists, while the second excluded cases of "compulsive minor self-mutilation."

In England, Morgan (1979) first used the term "non-fatal, deliberate self-harm" to describe behavior in which suicide was clearly not intended. Morgan included suicide gestures and drug overdoses as well as self-mutilation in his concept. In Denmark, Bille-Brahe (1982) studied and identified two groups of suicide attempters: one group engaged in single, acute attempts, while the other engaged in lower lethality repetitive attempts. These ideas stimulated Pattison and Kahan (1983; Kahan and Pattison 1984) to develop the concept of a deliberate self-harm syndrome, a concept that marks the beginning of modern interest in self-mutilation. A "prototype" model of the syndrome, derived from analysis of fifty-six published reports, was characterized by multiple episodes and types of self-harm, low levels of lethality, onset in late adolescence, and duration of many years. Anxiety, despair, anger, and cognitive restriction were the prominent pathological symptoms associated with the syndrome. Predisposing factors included lack of social support, male homosexuality, drug and alcohol abuse, and suicidal ideation in women. Overdoses were excluded since they tended to be mainly single events with clinical ambiguity about intent (bona fide suicide attempts were excluded from the syndrome). Noting that Ross and McKay (1979) found no clear association between self-mutilation behaviors and specific personality disorders, Pattison and Kahan (1983) contended that the syndrome occurred more frequently but not necessarily or exclusively in borderline and histrionic persons. They concluded by classifying the deliberate self-harm syndrome as a disorder of impulse control.

This prototype model has been refined and renamed over the past decade. Data collected on 240 female, habitual self-mutilators, for example, described a typical subject as "a 28-year-old Caucasian who first deliberately harmed herself at age 14. Skin cutting is her usual practice, but she has used other methods such as skin burning and self-hitting, and she has injured herself on at least 50 occasions. Her decision to self-mutilate is impulsive and results in temporary relief from symptoms such as racing thoughts, depersonalization, and marked anxiety. She now has or has had an eating disorder, and may be concerned about her drinking. She has been a heavy utilizer of medical and mental health services, although treatment generally has been unsatisfactory. In desperation over her inability to control her self-mutilative behavior this typical subject has attempted suicide by drug overdose" (Favazza and Conterio 1989).

Diagnosis of the Repetitive Self-mutilation Syndrome

The repetitive self-mutilation (RSM) syndrome as developed by myself and my colleague Dr. Richard Rosenthal is presented utilizing the format of the American Psychiatric Association's *Diagnostic and Statistical Manual*.

Repetitive self-mutilation should be listed on Axis I among the "impulse control disorders not elsewhere classified." Other disorders in this class include intermittent explosive disorder, kleptomania, pyromania, pathological gambling, and trichotillomania.

The essential feature of RSM is recurrent failure to resist impulses to harm one's own body physically without conscious suicidal intent. The most common act of self-harm is skin cutting; other behaviors include skin burning, self-hitting (e.g., punching oneself in the face), pin sticking, interfering with wound healing, severe skin scratching, head banging, bone breaking, insertion of foreign objects into the urethra, and vaginal laceration. People with the disorder usually use multiple methods to harm themselves and report that their acts often provide rapid, albeit short-lived, relief from a variety of unpleasant symptoms, such as heightened anxiety and tension, intense anger and rage, racing thoughts, depersonalization, depression, and feelings of loneliness. The diagnosis is not made when the self-harm behavior is associated with an organic condition — such as serious mental retardation; the Lesch-Nyhan, deLange, and Tourette syndromes; a preexisting inflammation of the skin — or when the behavior is in response to a delusion, hallucination, or transsexual fixed idea.

Although self-harm results from a failure to resist an impulse, people with the disorder may brood about harming themselves for hours and even days and may go through a ritualistic sequence of behaviors, such as tracing areas of their skin and compulsively putting their self-harm paraphernalia in a special order. Self-harm acts are usually performed in private. Even seemingly bizarre behaviors as drinking one's blood or saving it in small vials are not associated with psychosis. People with this disorder often describe it as an "addiction" and may avidly seek professional help. As the disorder progresses, the acts of self-harm may escalate in frequency and intensity. Bona fide suicide attempts may result from demoralization over an inability to control the behavior.

Associated features. RSM is often associated with concurrent disorders, especially borderline, histrionic, and antisocial personality disorders, multiple personality disorder, and post-traumatic stress disorder. Some persons demonstrate traits found in the personality disorders during the course of RSM, but then these traits may subside or disappear when the syndrome remits. People with the syndrome frequently have problems with eating and may develop or have a history of anorexia and/or bulimia nervosa. Some people may have a history of, or may develop, episodic alcohol abuse and/or kleptomania. When an eating disorder or alcohol abuse develops, self-mutilative behavior often diminishes but sometimes returns as the eating disorder or alcohol abuse abates. In some persons these compulsive behaviors occur simultaneously.

People with RSM recognize and may try to exploit the particularly unsettling effect that self-mutilation has on others. Thus, the behavior may be used in an attempt to engender a caring response in a significant other and to instill guilt in others for a perceived wrong. Institutional inmates may use their disorder to gain a transfer to a more desirable location. For some, the self-mutilative act and its consequent scar impart a sense of security and uniqueness that is difficult to give up.

Age at onset and course. RSM usually begins in late childhood or early adolescence. It waxes and wanes and may become chronic. In many patients the disorder lasts ten to fifteen years, although isolated episodes of self-mutilative behavior may persist.

Impairment and complications. Physical disfigurement from scars or wound infections may result in social rejection and isolation. Some people may feel so embarrassed by their appearance that they rarely appear in public. Others will avoid wearing short-sleeved shirts, revealing clothes, or bathing suits. Eating disorders, kleptomania, and problems with alcohol and substance abuse may complicate the course. Bona fide suicide attempts, often made in desperation over an inability to control the disorder, are common; however, they will typically occur by means other than self-mutilation, such as a drug overdose.

Predisposing factors. Although RSM is regarded as "multidetermined," its onset has been linked to stressful situations. Significant predisposing factors appear to be physical and/or sexual abuse in childhood, an early history of surgical procedures or illness, parental alcoholism or depression, and residence in a total-care institution. Other possibly significant factors include a proneness to accidents, perfectionistic tendencies, dissatisfaction with body shape or sexual organs, and an inability to tolerate and express feelings. The most common precipitants are real or perceived rejection and situations that produce feelings of helplessness, anger, or guilt.

Prevalence. Although occasional self-mutilating acts appear to be common, especially in adolescence, the prevalence of the disorder is unknown (combined episodic and repetitive self-mutilation may affect 1,400 persons per 100,000 population per year). It is more common in people with borderline, histrionic, and antisocial personality disorders, multiple personality disorder, post-traumatic stress disorder, and a history of an eating disorder.

Familiar pattern. No information.

Sex ratio. The disorder is apparently more common in females.

Differential diagnosis. In schizophrenia, major depression, bipolar disorder, transsexualism, and psychoactive substance-induced organic mental disorders, self-mutilative acts such as eye enucleation and amputation of a body part are singular, potentially lethal events in response to a delusion, hallucination, or fixed idea. In obsessive-compulsive disorder, repetitive behaviors are designed to prevent or produce some future event or situation. In trichotillomania, primarily scalp and facial hairs are pulled out. In factitious disorder with physical symptoms, the person simulates illness to get medical attention and to assume a "patient" role. In stereotypy/habit disorder, especially in its more severe forms, acts of self-harm are frequently associated with mental retardation, become stereotyped and often rhythmic, and the person usually does not seem distressed by the behavior. In borderline, histrionic, and antisocial personality disorders, transient self-mutilative acts may occur. When these acts become established as repetitive responses to disturbing psychological symptoms or environmental events, the Axis I diagnosis of RSM should be recorded. In sexual masochism, acts of self-harm are associated with intense sexual urges and fantasies of being humiliated, beaten, bound, and otherwise made to suffer.

The diagnostic criteria for RSM are:

1. preoccupation with harming oneself physically;

2. recurrent failure to resist impulses to harm oneself physically, resulting in the destruction or alteration of body tissue;

3. increasing sense of tension immediately before the act of self-harm;

4. gratification or a sense of relief when committing the act of self-harm; and

5. the act of self-harm is not associated with conscious suicidal intent and is not in response to a delusion, hallucination, transsexual fixed idea, or serious mental retardation.

Notably, the proposed diagnosis of RSM contains all the essential features of an impulse disorder: failure to resist an impulse, drive, or temptation to perform a harmful act; an increasing sense of tension or arousal prior to the act; and an experience of either pleasure, gratification, or release at the time of the act. Immediately after the act, there may or may not be genuine regret, self-reproach, or guilt. Siomopoulos (1974) was the first to regard repetitive skin cutting as an impulse neurosis.

Impulsivity

Impulsivity is a problematic behavior in psychiatric diagnosis. It may be present in many disorders, such as bulimia, mental retardation, paraphilias, substance use disorders, personality disorders, multiple personality disorder, and psychotic disorders. According to the current diagnostic manual, impulsivity also is a key feature of five specific disorders in which the behavior must occur "recurrently" (kleptomania, trichotillomania), "frequently" (pathological gambling), "on more than one occasion" (pyromania), or as "several discrete episodes" (intermittent explosive disorder). Repetitive self-mutilation falls within this very broad range of impulsive behaviors.

A significant number of repetitive self-mutilators demonstrate problems with other forms of impulsivity. Lacey and Evans (1986) reviewed the literature on impulsivity and found within each clinical population of patients with "uni-impulsive" disorders a significant number of patients that displayed more than one such problem. Some patients identified as self-mutilators, for example, may also have problems with bulimia, kleptomania, and alcohol abuse. The authors suggest that if such a patient's alcohol abuse is addressed, the patient may stop drinking but may begin impulsive behaviors involving food or cutting.

Evans and Lacey (1992) studied fifty women attending an alcohol treatment unit. These women demonstrated other impulsive behavior: one-quarter cut themselves deliberately, 16 percent had an eating disorder, half described impulsive physical violence, and half acknowledged a period of promiscuity. Fichter et al. (1994) reported on thirty-two "multi-impulsive bulimics." Among their impulsive behaviors were self-mutilation (75%), shoplifting (78%), alcohol dependence (34%), drug abuse (22%), and sexual promiscuity (53%).

These findings are consistent with those of Favazza and Conterio (1989) that about half of repetitive self-mutilators develop or have a history of anorexia, bulimia, or both and that about 20 percent develop or have a history of episodic alcohol abuse. There is no fixed sequence, and one of the three self-harm behaviors usually predominates at any time. Patients claim that alcohol abuse is the easiest behavior to overcome and that self-mutilation is the hardest.

An objection to the identification of RSM syndrome is that impulsivity and self-mutilation are key elements in already existing personality disorder diagnoses, especially BPD. In a comparison of self-mutilating and non-self-mutilating personality disordered individuals, Simeon et al. (1992) found that all the subjects had higher than normal impulsivity; the self-mutilators also had greater aggression, "which when combined with poor impulse control takes the form of self-mutilation rather than less aggressive impulsive behaviors assessed by the Schedule for Interviewing Borderlines such as gambling, promiscuity, over-eating, and oversleeping." Two interpretations of the data were offered: self-mutilation may be a marker for more severe borderline pathology or self-mutilation might best be viewed as a distinct Axis I impulse control disorder. Both interpretations may be correct. Self-mutilation is one of eight diagnostic criteria for BPD but by itself is neither necessary nor sufficient to establish a diagnosis. Its presence may indicate a more severe form of the disorder. When the behavior becomes repetitive, it may develop into the RSM syndrome.

Many Axis I disorders coexist with BPD; Gunderson and Zanarini (1987) listed panic disorder, substance abuse, gender identity disorders, factitious disorders, disorders of impulse control, attention deficit disorder, and eating disorders. Concurrent depression is also frequently cited. Because the criteria for BPD include symptoms of all the disorders listed above, the existence of a concurrent disorder often depends on the quantity of the symptoms in question. Occasional binge eating or shoplifting episodes, for example, are consonant with the construct of BPD, but a pattern of frequent, uncontrolled, repetitive episodes warrants the additional diagnoses of bulimia nervosa and kleptomania.

An identical argument can be made for moderate/superficial self-mutilation. Patients with the RSM syndrome demonstrate a pattern of uncontrolled and repetitive self-harm in response to disturbing psychological symptoms or environmental events, are captive to their preoccupation with acts of self-harm, experience cravings to self-mutilate and withdrawal symptoms when prevented from indulging their cravings (just as pathological gamblers do if unable to gamble), and may assume an identity as a cutter. These patients should not to be confused with those who sporadically cut their wrists. In addition, some patients' RSM syndrome remits, and they no longer demonstrate a full-fledged personality disorder, although they may possess pathological personality traits. The situation is analogous to that of an alcoholic whose "personality disorder" disappears after prolonged sobriety.

In England, Tantam and Whitaker (1992) reviewed these issues and favored the concept of a separate "diagnostic category of repeated, deliberate self-harm, sui generis, which could also include other compulsive and self-destructive behaviors." A special advantage of this concept is that it would then be possible to study the effect of repeated self-mutilation on relationships and emotions: "whether, in other words personality abnormality may be consequent on, rather than antecedent to, repeated self-harm."

Case History: Repetitive Self-mutilation

The patient, an articulate 31-year-old farm worker, sought me out after reading about my interest in self-mutilation because he wanted to discuss his experiences and to learn about his prognosis.

He was born and reared in a large East Coast city where his father was an engineer. He described his mother as understanding but distant, and his father as a nice but noncommunicative and "closed-in" person. The patient has two younger brothers, both of whom are successful and doing well.

The patient remembers that as a child he preferred to stay at home rather than to seek out playmates. He had excellent grades until he contracted mononucleosis during his sophomore year in high school. His grades dropped, and he felt he was not learning as well as he could. Despite this, he achieved a high score on the national college entrance examination and was accepted by a local college, one of the most prestigious in the nation.

He decided to attend a state college, however, because he wanted to get away from home and assert his independence. During two years in college, he majored in ancient history and had a B average, but he was discontent with his tendency to avoid intimate relationships. After a long hike in the woods during a snowstorm, he made a major decision to break down the defensive shell he had erected around himself.

He took a summer job in a large city and took night college courses. Although he made a few friends, he still felt isolated, and he was especially sensitive about not wanting to "use" people by asking favors. He was disappointed with his life and felt that he was not doing as well as he had expected. He then experienced an episode of mounting tension: "It was like looking down a tunnel into nothing. Then I saw red streaks and black fire. And then I carved my arm with a razor blade and the pressure went away."

Always an avid reader, he started to read anthropological books about shamanism and hallucinogens as a way to gain insight and healing. He took LSD a few times and gained some insights about himself, but as a result of one "trip," he began to dwell on his childhood faults. Once again he felt a mounting tension, and he relieved it by cutting the skin on his chest and stomach. He sought professional help, but he claims that a psychiatrist thought that he was attempting suicide. He could not convince the psychiatrist that he had no suicidal intent.

He then became involved with the drug subculture and used phencyclidine (PCP, or "angel dust") and intravenous heroin for four months. He lost his job and cut himself on the chest several more times "to relieve the pressure." He again sought psychiatric help and was diagnosed as a suicide-prone schizophrenic. He was sure that he was not prone to suicide and, after reading intensively, concluded that he was not schizophrenic either. He developed a close relationship with a street girl who supported herself by part-time prostitution.

After voluntarily participating in a drug rehabilitation program, he moved in with his parents, stopped cutting his skin and using drugs, and took a civil service job, which he held for eight years. He then moved into an apartment and cut his chest again — twelves times over a two-year period. He concealed these cutting episodes from everyone. Each episode was similar: he would introspect about his life, become angry with himself for his past mistakes and for his inability to do better, experience intense pressure, and then cut himself for relief. During this period he reentered the drug subculture and used heroin, LSD, and amphetamines.

Then, the patient stated, "All of a sudden I came into focus, without being able to explain such a change." He stopped taking drugs and cutting himself. He dated, developed self-confidence, and began to meet new people and establish friendships. He took college courses again and got married. His wife had a large financial debt, and he worked two jobs to pay it off. To help him stay awake at work he used amphetamines, but he did not cut himself. His wife filed for divorce and ran off with a rock musician. The patient's last cutting episode occurred on the day he signed the divorce papers. He experienced depersonalization and enormous pressure. Relief came after he slashed his chest, stomach, and arm. He contemplated suicide but decided against it.

Although deeply hurt by his wife's departure, the patient continued working two jobs until he paid off her debt. During this time he developed numerous friends, "dabbled" in occasional drug use and drank alcohol ("more than I should have"). A close friend invited the patient to work on his farm in the Midwest, and he accepted. At the time of the interview, the patient had been working on the farm for over a year. He explained that he was content, experienced no stress, drank beer for relaxation, and had no desire to take drugs or cut himself. He recognized that he had a bad attitude toward women but hoped that he could "work on the problem." He planned to buy some farmland of his own.

■

Why is it important to identify repetitive self-mutilation as a separate syndrome? First, it is not uncommon for mental health professionals to automatically associate self-cutting, burning, and similar acts with BPD. The construct of BPD is so broad that it presents tremendous problems in treatment. Where does the therapist begin? What should therapy focus on? In fact, none of the major advances in psychiatric treatment has involved personality disorders. Especially in light of data indicating that repetitive self-mutilation does have a distinct course, treatment for the behavior would have a clear focus and the therapist would have a more optimistic attitude. Second, recognition and acceptance of RSM syndrome may make patients more willing to seek help for their often secret behavior. Once bulimia became accepted as a syndrome, for example, a large number of persons who indulged in this behavior were willing to ask for help. Third, acceptance of the syndrome will lead to research into its causes, prognosis, and treatment. Early identification and treatment might result in a cure or in a shortening of the natural course of the syndrome (typically, five to ten years). Additionally, some persons with this syndrome who might eventually have committed suicide may be prevented from doing so.

10

Biological and Psychosocial Findings

—— —— —— —— —— —— —— ——

In the previous chapter I attempted to clarify self-mutilation by classifying the different categories and types and by focusing on issues of diagnosis. This chapter examines the biological, psychological, and social dynamics of self-mutilation. I begin with an account of biological studies, many of which are very complex and difficult to interpret. They often involve broad concepts such as "impulsivity" and "aggression," small samples of patients, and inferences about what actually is going on in a person's brain. Childhood experiences of self-mutilators are then examined, especially the controversial issue of sexual and physical abuse, followed by a discussion of the relationship between suicide and self-mutilation. The lengthiest section in this chapter deals with the numerous psychological theories and mechanisms that are operative in self-mutilation. In any single case, any number of psychological forces may come into play; no one grand theory or mechanism can explain a behavior as complex as deliberate self-harm. The focus then shifts to the role of social mechanisms. The discussion concludes with my personal comments and a brief list of summary statements.

Neurochemistry

By far the greatest amount of research deals with episodic and repetitive self-harm. Since the late 1970s, the neurotransmitter serotonin has been implicated in "impulsive aggression." As a neurotransmitter, serotonin facilitates the passage of impulses between the connections of a few nerves (probably less than 1 percent) in the brain. The highest concentration of serotonin is found in a part of the brain known as the raphe nuclei. Nerves from this area connect to all areas of the brain but mostly to a region called the hypothalamus, a structure that plays a role in regulating impulsivity and aggression as well as appetite, mood, and the sleep-wake cycle. The dietary amino acid tryptophan is chemically transformed into serotonin, which is then metabolized with a chemical called 5-HIAA (5-hydroxyindoleacetic acid).

The first clinical study of interest to the discussion here found low levels of 5-HIAA in the cerebrospinal fluid (fluid in the brain and spinal cord) of depressed persons who attempted suicide (Asberg, Traskman, and Thoren 1976). Other studies have found reduced levels in male borderlines (Brown et al. 1982). These studies inferred that the low 5-HIAA levels probably reflected low serotonin activity in the brains of persons who engaged in impulsive aggression.

Utilizing a better measurement of probable serotonin activity in the brain (technically called a fenfluramine challenge test), Coccaro et al. (1989) found that low serotonin in persons with a personality disorder was correlated with suicide attempts and with ratings of assaultiveness, instability, aggression, and impulsiveness. "In other words, a reduction of central serotonergic system function was associated with an increased risk of impulsive aggression against both self and others, probably depending on the circumstances leading up to the act" (Markowitz and Coccaro 1995). Simeon et al. (1992) used yet another measure of serotonin activity (a blood platelet binding test) in a landmark controlled study of self-mutilating and non-self-mutilating persons with personality disorders. The self-mutilators had significantly more personality pathology, greater lifetime aggression, more antisocial behavior, and lower levels of serotonin activity. The authors concluded that low serotonin may facilitate self-mutilation. Indirect evidence for this finding is the efficacy of medications that increase brain serotonin levels and decrease self-mutilative behaviors such as cutting, burning, and hair pulling (this will be discussed in chap. 11).

A group of neurotransmitters called enkephalins may also play a role in self-mutilation. The enkephalins are opium-like substances produced by the brain and various glands; among their actions are the suppression of pain and the regulation of emotions. One theory is that since enkephalins have a generally pleasurable effect (similar to what is experienced by taking opium or heroin), self-mutilators harm themselves to induce their production. "As in opiate addiction, tolerance develops, requiring repetitive self-injurious behavior to prevent 'withdrawal'" (Russ 1992). In this autoaddictive model the pain associated with self-mutilation results in the release of pain-reducing and pleasurable enkephalins. Persons learn to associate self-mutilation with positive feelings, and whenever they feel dysphoric they cut or burn themselves in order to feel better (Konicki and Schultz 1989). A controlled study found markedly increased blood plasma enkephalin levels in ten habitual self-cutters diagnosed as having BPD; in addition, five had an eating disorder, while four had a psychosexual disorder of gender identity or dysmorphophobia. They all stated that their acts of self-cutting were painless and provided temporary relief from dysphoria, tension, or depersonalization. The highest enkephalin levels correlated with the most severe and recent of the self-mutilative acts. The levels returned to normal as the patients' condition improved. It is not known, unfortunately, whether plasma levels of enkephalin accurately reflect brain levels or whether enkephalin is a healing response to self-mutilation rather than a causal, or precipitating factor (Coid, Allolio, and Rees 1983). In applying the autoaddictive theory, it should be noted that a major problem is the claim of self-mutilators not to experience pain when they cut or burn themselves. In the Favazza and Conterio (1989) study of 240 patients, 64 percent experienced little or no pain, and only 10 percent felt great pain.

Some self-mutilators may produce high levels of endogenous analgesic chemicals, and some may have neuroanatomical flaws that diminish their perception of pain. Under the right circumstances these forms of pathology may facilitate self-mutilation. From a different perspective one might speculate that some patients who seem to actively seek surgical operations and painful medical diagnostic tests have a low sensitivity to pain. Such patients are not uncommon; they truly seem to relish being operated upon and may go from hospital to hospital with fantastic and often convincing symptoms. This condition, sometimes called mania operativa, is a polysurgical addiction that may be associated with alcoholism, drug dependency, self-mutilation, hypochondriasis, and psychopathic personality. A study (Hunter and Kennard 1982) presented eight cases in which patients with mania operativa underwent unnecessary limb amputation as a result of their masterful display of symptoms. Less dramatic but probably more common are patients who sporadically trick dentists and physicians into performing minor surgical procedures.

Another theory relates to stereotypic self-mutilation. It holds that an abnormality in the enkephalin system may result in an elevation of a person's pain threshold and a reduction in response to sensory stimuli. Thus, persons may repeatedly harm themselves (e.g., bang their heads) in order to stimulate themselves. An interesting application of the enkephalin theory will be discussed later in this chapter in the section on childhood experiences of self-mutilation.

Norepinephrine and dopamine (collectively known as catecholamines) are important neurotransmitters even though they facilitate the passage of impulses at less than 2 percent of the brain's nerve terminals. Abnormalities of the dopamine system have been implicated in the stereotypic self-mutilation found in Lesch-Nyhan and Tourette syndromes (see Winchel and Stanley 1991). Drug-induced stereotypic behavior such as skin picking secondary to amphetamine use may be mediated by dopamine dysfunction (Van Putten and Shaffer 1990). In moderate/superficial self-mutilation there is a good probability of interactions between the catecholamine and serotonin systems; the former may account for arousal and irritability that then triggers serotonin-mediated acts of self-harm (Siever, Trestman, and Silverman 1992).

A final neurotransmitter we shall consider is GABA (gamma-aminobutyric acid). It inhibits the transmission of nerve impulses in about one-third of all the brain's nerve terminals and mediates anxiety, pain, and behavioral activity. Although medications such as Valium and Xanax produce tranquilization by affecting GABA, sometimes unexpected and paradoxical rage may occur (Eichelman 1987). One study found that seven of twelve persons with BPD who received Xanax demonstrated an increased incidence of self-mutilation (Gardner and Cowdry 1985).

Other Biological Factors

Except for neurochemical studies, the biology of human self-mutilation remains relatively unexplored. Differences in pain perception have been reported. Using a standard painful stimulus test (placing a hand in cold water), borderlines who said they experienced pain during acts of self-mutilation were compared with those who said they did not experience pain. The pain ratings in response to the test were consistent with reports of pain during self-mutilation. Additionally, those who reported no pain during self-mutilation reported an improvement in mood following the cold water test. The no pain group "seemed" to have an earlier onset of self-injurious behavior and, perhaps, a more chronic course, with more lifetime episodes (Russ et al. 1992). The authors concluded that subtypes of self-mutilating borderline patients might be differentiated according to their perception of pain, mood improvement after self-harm, age of onset, and severity of childhood abuse.

Another approach has been to examine brain wave recordings (electro-encephalograms, or EEGs). Although some studies indicate EEG abnormalities in borderlines, "no finding has reached a level of reliability that would make it clinically useful" (New, Trestman, and Siever 1995). Epilepsy refers to a group of disorders characterized by paroxysmal disturbances of brain function that often can be identified by EEGs. Based on the similarity of symptoms seen in some types of epilepsy and in patients who mutilate themselves (depersonalization, mood swings, distortions in perception), Gardner and Cowdry (1986) have theorized that some self-mutilation may be epileptic in origin. While it is true that *occasionally* some self-mutilators improve when treated with an antiepileptic medication (Tegretol, or carbamazepine, which is also used in the treatment of manic-depressive disorder), the linkage between epilepsy and self-mutilation lacks EEG confirmation and is, at best, very tenuous.

As pointed out by Russ (1992), family and adoption studies have not addressed any possible genetic contribution to self-mutilation. In an interesting report from Singapore, six of nine children in a family became self-cutters; the effect of genetics versus child-rearing and other family factors was impossible to determine in this case. However, one child, who was adopted out at birth and who had no contact with its biological family, also was a self-cutter (Lim and Seng 1985).

In a psychophysiological study, male self-mutilators and control groups used guided imagery of a self-mutilative act while measurements of arousal and tension reduction were recorded. The subjects were presented with scripts that described the setting at the onset of the act, then events that led up to the act, then the self-mutilative act itself, and, finally, reactions to the act. While the subjects were imagining this sequence of events, their heart and respiratory rates, skin resistance level, and finger blood volume and pulse amplitude were measured. Results supported the often reported clinical observation that self-mutilation successfully reduces tension and, thus, reinforces and maintains itself as a coping behavior. A significant finding is that "participants reported continued negative feelings despite reduced psychophysiological arousal." This result suggests that it is the alteration of psychophysiological arousal that may operate to reinforce and maintain the behavior, not the psychological response (Haines et al. 1995). This lag interval between the physiological and psychological response to an act of self-mutilation could possibly be a target for a therapeutic medication and cognitive-behavioral intervention.

The last biological finding to be discussed here pertains to rare situations in which there is physical damage to nerves that process sensations from the periphery of the body. Damage might occur, for example, to infants during a difficult delivery or to adults in an auto accident. The results are unpleasant body experiences such as numbness, pins and needles, tingling, itching, burning, crushing, and the sensation of insects crawling. Over the past few years there have been several case reports of persons biting off their fingertips in response to these unpleasant sensations (Procacci and Maresca 1990; Rossitch et al. 1992).

Childhood Experiences of Self-mutilators

Most studies that provide information about childhood experiences of self-mutilators are of females. Fifty-four percent of female, habitual self-mutilators in a major study selected the adjective "miserable" to describe their childhood, 8 percent selected "happy," and the rest selected "average" (Favazza and Conterio 1989).

Childhood abuse was noted by 62 percent of the subjects. Of these, 29 percent reported both sexual and physical abuse; 17 percent reported only sexual abuse; and 16 percent reported only physical abuse. The average age of onset of sexual abuse was 7 years, and the average duration was twenty-four months. The sexually abusive people most commonly listed were a family friend (43%), brother (25%), father (23%), uncle (13%), mother and stepfather (6% each), and grandfather (4%). The average age of onset of physical abuse was 6 years and the average duration was five years. The physically abusive people most commonly listed were mother (50%), father (45%), brother (16%), other (16%), stepfather (4%), and sister and uncle (3%).

A study of sixteen abused and neglected children, ages 2.5 to 5 years, reported self-mutilation and suicidal behavior (Rosenthal and Rosenthal 1984), while another study reported skin cutting and burning as well as head banging and self-biting in 41 percent of physically and sexually abused children (Green 1978). Simpson and Porter (1981) found a history of sexual abuse in nine of twenty hospitalized self-mutilators. The most comprehensive study followed seventy-four persons with either a personality disorder or recurrent major depression with hypomanic episodes for an average of four years and monitored them for "self-destructive behavior," such as suicide attempts, self-mutilation, and eating disorder (van der Kolk, Perry, and Herman 1991). At the beginning of the study, 56 percent of the subjects had made at least one suicide attempt, 25 percent reported at least five episodes of self-mutilation, 11 percent had cut themselves once or twice, and about half had histories of binge eating and/or anorexia. During the follow-up period, 7 percent made one or two suicide attempts, another 7 percent made more than three suicide attempts, and 8 percent engaged in at least five cutting episodes. A history of major disruptions in parental care was found in 89 percent of the self-mutilators; 79 percent reported significant childhood trauma (sexual abuse, physical abuse, witnessing domestic violence). Sexual abuse was the type of trauma most strongly related to all forms of self-destructive behavior; the earlier the age when abuse was experienced, the more likely there was cutting behavior. Childhood separation from parents, environmental chaos, and physical and emotional neglect were significantly associated with self-cutting but not with suicide attempt. High total neglect scores predicted continued cutting and suicide attempts, as did prolonged separation from caregivers. Dissociative experiences correlated highly with histories of trauma, neglect, and cutting;

ongoing dissociation was associated with cutting. The authors noted the similarity between the pattern of self-destructive behaviors (minor stress causes intense physiological disorganization, which then results in either impulsive and aggressive actions or to dissociation, psychic numbing, and physical analgesia) and the pattern of behaviors experienced by survivors of severe trauma (minor emotional stressors result in extremes of under-arousal and overarousal that do not extinguish over time). Since stress hormones play a role in the symptomatology of adults with post-traumatic stress disorder, the authors theorized, "It is likely that the *immaturity* of the central nervous system of children makes them more vulnerable than adults to developing lasting biological changes in response to trauma and neglect. . . . Dissociation, self-destructiveness, and impulsive behavior may all prove to be hormonally mediated responses that are triggered by reminders of earlier trauma and neglect."

In 1987 Kirmayer and Carroll proposed a neurobiological model for chronic self-mutilation. They noted that persons who experience repeated shock or injury become physiologically less sensitive to pain; the effect may be mediated by enkephalins. Abused children may develop consistently high enkephalin levels, which provide them with partial analgesia. Their diminished response to pain could provoke greater abuse by the angry, punitive parent, further stimulating enkephalin production. Chronically abused children with persistently high enkephalin levels might become habituated and relatively insensitive to their enkephalin production. In times of calm or isolation, enkephalin levels would drop, "creating a relative withdrawal state with an increase in tension and dysphoria." Self-mutilation might then be a method of increasing enkephalin production to alleviate tension and dysphoria.

Childhood physical and, especially, sexual abuse have been proposed as significant events in the pathogenesis not only of self-mutilation but also of other pathological behaviors. Certainly many cases are horrific, as exemplified by the following summary from an article by Shapiro (1987).

Elaine is 24 years old. She remembers her mother as frequently going into delusional states during which her mother would manifest dramatic personality changes that included sadistic and controlling behaviors such as inflicting knife cuts around Elaine's breasts and vagina. Elaine was used as a sexual object by her mother, father, brother, and friends of her father. She said that, in addition to the cumulative sexual abuse, her father would beat her and force her to take part in painful sexual acts in which he would insert an object, such as a tool or a gun barrel, into her anus or vagina and then force her to walk around the room with the foreign body still retained. Elaine's parents also participated in a sex ring that included the use of themselves and their children for purposes of pornography. The duration of Elaine's sexual abuse was approximately sixteen years. Her leaving home at 18 was the event that facilitated the cessation of incest. Elaine first attempted suicide at age 7, when she took an overdose of drugs and was brought to the emergency room (where she stayed overnight). She became more involved with mutilating herself from ages 11 through 23.

We must always keep in mind that not all self-mutilators are the victims of childhood abuse. For example, in Favazza and Conterio's study (1989), 38 percent of female habitual self-mutilators did not admit to childhood abuse. I have encountered patients who were told by therapists that sexual abuse, usually by the patient's father, *must* have occurred and that the "dirty secret" *must* be brought into the open. Distraught patients, eager to find an answer for the cause of their uncontrolled cutting, often accept their therapist's formulation. In most of the cases with which I am familiar, the patient's accusations usually resulted in the fragmentation of a family already under duress in dealing with the patient's self-mutilation. Fathers who often were very supportive of their daughters were newly perceived as enemies. Several recent, highly publicized cases in which the father successfully sued the daughter's therapist may cause a decline in the well-intentioned but disastrously wrong practice of routinely inferring abuse.

Perhaps the most commonly mentioned mechanism in the linkage between sexual child abuse and self-mutilation involves the dissociative process of depersonalization; the child deals with the tension of the abuse by depersonalizing and, thus, by becoming numb and distant from the abuse. Years later, whenever the depersonalization process recurs, self-mutilation serves to end the depersonalization and allows the person to feel real again. Many clinical cases attest to the accuracy of this formulation. However, a recent study of female self-mutilating and non-self-mutilating borderline patients failed to find any relationship between either sexual or physical abuse and dissociation. Although both the frequency of child abuse and the score on a dissociative experiences scale were greater among self-mutilating than non-self-mutilating borderlines, a statistical multivariate analysis did not uncover any discriminating risk factors. "In other words, the difference between self-mutilating and nonself-mutilating BPD patients was not mediated by abuse variables and their parameters or by levels of dissociation. In summary, this study does not provide support for the theory that dissociation with a history of abuse explains why BPD patients self-mutilate" (Zweig-Frank, Paris, and Grizder 1994a). The same findings pertained to an identical study of male borderlines (Zweig-Frank, Paris, and Grizder 1994b).

In addition to physical and sexual abuse, many self-mutilators report hypercritical or absent fathers, excessively protective and dominant mothers, loss of a parent through divorce or death, stormy parental relations, and mental illness (especially alcoholism) in family members. As children, self-mutilators often experience a sense of abandonment, of loneliness, and of unlovability, and they may carry these feelings into adolescence and adult life. They may believe that they are responsible for causing family problems and, therefore, are in need of some form of punishment.

A recurrent finding among male self-mutilators is long-standing confusion about their sexual identity, as manifested by envy of females, desire to be a female, repudiation of their penises, bisexuality, cross-dressing, and concerns about homosexuality. They may report having been treated as a girl by their parents and having been threatened with castration for bedwetting or masturbation. Their erotic fantasies may center on amputation, for example, making love to a stump or utilizing pictures of amputees as masturbation aids. Many female self-mutilators report disgust over menarche, menstruation, and intercourse, sometimes accompanied by fantasies of prostitution and sexual humiliation. In the study of Rosenthal et al. (1972), more than 60 percent of the self-cutting by women took place at the time of their menses. (This finding has not been reported in other studies, however.) Both male and female self-mutilators typically experience sexual guilt. They often have difficulty dealing with sexual relationships and assuming an appropriate masculine or feminine role. Some have patterns of childhood and adolescent hypersexuality and promiscuity.

The backgrounds of a fair number of deviant self-mutilators include special medical contacts such as employment in medical or rehabilitation agencies. Rosenthal et al. (1972) found that sixteen of twenty-four female self-cutters had experienced surgery, hospitalization for serious illness, or lacerations requiring multiple sutures before the age of 12. None of the twenty-four women in a control group of noncutting suicide attempters had such a history. Patients sometimes mutilated organs that were unintentionally injured or diseased during childhood (e.g., castration of a testicle previously affected by mumps orchitis or amputation of a limb in which a bone had been broken). In other instances, the mutilated organs had been deliberately injured during childhood.

Suicide and Self-mutilation

The ideas of Sigmund Freud have greatly influenced psychiatric thought. His early work emphasized the concept of a life instinct (eros) as a general biological principle that supported behavior conducive to the creation and maintenance of life. Possibly because of the experiences of World War I, in 1920 Freud postulated a death instinct (thanatos) that gave rise to aggressive instincts. Suicide and self-mutilation were regarded as manifestations of an instinctive push toward death and were qualitatively identical for Freud.

Although the notions of a life — and, especially, of a death — instinct have been discarded by psychiatrists, the belief that self-mutilation is a suicidal behavior lingers. Karl Menninger (1938) was the first major psychiatrist to modify Freud's belief. He regarded self-mutilation as a form of self-healing in that a person might avert total self-destruction by substituting the destruction of a body part such as an eye, genital, organ, or limb. "In this sense it represents a victory, even though sometimes a costly one, of the life instinct over the death instinct" (p. 285). Menninger's substitution theory is reminiscent of the biblical exhortation to pluck out an offending eye or cut off an offending limb because it is better to reach heaven with only part of a body than to be cast into hell with a whole body. Today we know that in *rare* cases suicide can be averted by the sacrifice of a significant body part. In most cases, however, self-mutilation has little to do with suicidality.

For all practical purposes, self-mutilation has not been as much of a concern to psychiatry as has suicide. The origin of the modern concept of self-mutilation started in 1964 when Stengel wrote about the differences between suicide and attempted suicide, which included any type of self-harm that threatened life. In 1977 Kreitman described overdoses and self-mutilation as parasuicidal acts because they were like attempted suicide. It was during this time that attention was given to wrist-cutting "syndromes," and the typical wrist cutter was noted by Graff and Mallin (1967) to feel relief after the cutting but "does not commit suicide." Pao (1969) called attention to "delicate self-cutting" as distinct from attempted suicide. Simpson (1976) boldly declared self-mutilation to be "an act of antisuicide, for the cutting is used as a direct reliable and rapidly effective way of coming back to life from the dead unreal preceding state." In 1979 Ross and McKay wrote that self-mutilation was counterintentional to suicide and that self-mutilation cannot be understood in terms of explanations of suicide. In 1979 Morgan's book *Death Wishes*? used the phrase "non-fatal, deliberate self-harm." Although Morgan's term included "failed suicides" as well as behavior in which actual self-destruction was not intended, the concept of deliberate self-harm influenced Pattison and Kahan (1983), who presented a deliberate self-harm syndrome that excluded suicide attempts. Among the ways that deliberate self-harm behavior differed from suicidal behavior were its prevalence in young people, low lethality, chronic pattern, sense of relief after the behavior, and different methods used by the same person. The publication of *Bodies under Siege* in 1987 and Walsh and Rosen's *Self-Mutilation* in 1988 solidified the understanding that self-mutilation is distinct from suicide. Recent major reviews have upheld this distinction (Winchel and Stanley 1991; Tantam and Whitaker 1992), which is now recognized as valid by mental health professionals, although many physicians and others in the helping professions still are not aware of the distinction.

It may seem odd that the concept of self-mutilation does not include drug overdoses (self-poisoning). The best explanation for this is offered by Walsh and Rosen (1988): "In the case of ingesting pills or poison, the harm caused is uncertain, ambiguous, unpredictable, and basically invisible. In the case of self-laceration, the degree of self-harm is clear, unambiguous, predictable as to course, and highly visible. In addition, the self-laceration often results in sustained or permanent visible disfigurements to the body, which is not the case with overdose. In these various ways, therefore, these two forms of self-harm are quite different; the danger in combining them in a single category is that these important differences (including their clinical implications) are overlooked" (p. 32).

Having clarified the differences between self-mutilation and suicide, it is now important to note that self-mutilators are at increased risk for suicide. In Favazza and Conterio's study (1989), 59 percent of female habitual self-mutilators had overdosed on drugs; half of these had overdosed four or more times. A third of the total sample expected to be dead in five years. Repetitive self-mutilators often become demoralized or depressed over an inability to control their acts of self-harm. They feel helpless in the face of what they perceive to be an overwhelming "addiction." Additionally, their visible scars and burn marks cause them to endure social isolation. In such a situation, suicide attempts are understandable. In persons with borderline, histrionic, or antisocial personality disorders as well as other disorders in which episodic self-mutilation occurs, suicide attempts are inherent in the basic disorder and might be anticipated even in the absence of self-mutilation (although the presence of self-mutilation might indicate an increased seriousness of psychopathology). Although persons who commit or attempt suicide and persons who self-mutilate may share some common characteristics, behaviors, and neurochemical abnormalities (Stanley et al. 1992), the act of suicide and the act of self-mutilation are dissimilar. Suicide is an exit into death, but self-mutilation is a reentrance into a state of normality. Suicide is an act of escape, but self-mutilation is a morbid act of regeneration. A person who attempts suicide seeks to end all feelings, but a person who self-mutilates seeks to feel better. A fifteen-year follow-up study of severely ill psychiatric inpatients revealed that most with serious suicidal intent who did *not* go on to kill themselves had histories of impulsivity, manipulative suicide attempts, or self-mutilation (Dingman and McGlashan 1988). Accidental deaths during self-mutilation may occur, such as cutting through an artery, but I have never encountered such a case personally.

Psychological Theories and Mechanisms of Self-mutilation

Examination of the case examples in this book reveals self-mutilation by mentally ill persons to be a private, solitary act that often temporarily alleviates pathological symptoms. This remedial effect is extremely rapid. Persons suffering from intolerable tension and anxiety or from an episode of numbing unreality may obtain relief, sometimes instantaneously, by slicing their skin. Likewise, a psychotic person suffering from paranoid persecution or sexual guilt may experience a swift diminution or removal of these symptoms upon, for example, castrating himself. There are many problems associated with this form of symptom-reducing self-therapy, but let us try to understand why it works from psychological points of view. The large number of psychological theories and mechanisms that have been proposed indicate that none can be applied universally.

In everyday life it is possible to obtain some respite from moderately heightened levels of tension and anxiety through such methods as increased physical activity, orgasm, meditation, and muscle relaxation exercises. But when tension and anxiety reach truly pathological levels, none of these methods has much effect. An act of self-mutilation, however, may be quite efficacious in reducing the tension and anxiety. One explanation for this effect relates to the problematic theory of "psychic energy." Briefly stated, this theory holds that the mind-brain system operates best within a certain range of tension levels. If the level gets too high, the mind-brain system will operate automatically to divest itself of "quantities of excitation." When tense patients cut themselves, they in fact often describe the results in words such as "It's like lancing a boil," or "It's like popping a balloon." The implied metaphor is clear: in cutting their skin they provide an opening through which the tension and badness in their bodies can rapidly escape. What does leave the body as the result of skin cutting is blood, a precious substance that throughout human history has been associated with the cure of illness, preservation of health, salvation and resolution of social conflict. Many cutters like to watch the blood drip from their wounds; it is a scene sometimes reminiscent of paintings of Jesus on the cross with his blood spurting out. It seems likely that the outward flow of tension following self-mutilation is linked with the flow of blood, with all its symbolic connotations. We use the term *bad blood*, for example, to indicate inimical relationships, especially among close friends and family members. Self-cutters may feel relief because they have eliminated some "bad blood," thus symbolically decreasing the tension arising from impaired relationships. Some self-mutilators burn rather than cut their skin. This does not draw blood but, as several patients have told me, the procedure is efficacious because badness and tension slowly leak out of their bodies in the serous fluid caused by the burn. In fact, a fluid-filled blister serves as a safety valve that can be "popped" when needed.

Another mechanism through which self-mutilation may exert therapeutic effects is the cathartic release of anger. As stated by one patient, "Often I can feel the pressure build up internally until self-mutilation can create a cathartic reaction. It is as if I need to purge myself in some medieval ritual." Many self-cutters are angry with themselves for not living up to their expectations, for causing misery for others, or for being "no good." They may be angry with their parents and other important people in their lives or with institutions such as mental hospitals, schools, or prisons that have failed them. Often they are angry with their fate and with the unjust universe. By wounding their bodies, such persons provide an outlet for their anger. Certainly self-mutilation is a safer outlet than the direct expression of anger toward parents and important people who might retaliate. As an expression of anger against institutions, private self-mutilation is not as effective as writing letters to newspapers, picketing, public fasting, or immolation by fire on a busy thoroughfare, but it is some sort of action and is preferable at a personal level to passivity and resignation.

Kernberg (1987) feels that self-mutilators develop "feelings of resentment, rage, and impotence in an effort to control an important person (including the therapist), and that the experience of self-mutilation is the relieving enactment of revenge." The expression of anger is important in another formulation: abused children may mutilate themselves to punish the original perpetrators of the abuse in effigy, using their own skins as a symbol for the offending persons (Stone 1987). Rarely, the intense anger will be directed outward as well as inward, but social forces "conduce women to inhibit the direct expression of violent feelings against the offending parties, whereas men who feel violated tend more readily to become aggressive" (Stone 1987). Girls at a repressive correctional institution carved their skin as a demonstration of autonomy; the authorities at the institution tightly controlled the girls' lives but were relatively helpless in stopping the carving (Ross and McKay 1979).

Self-mutilation in some cases, however, may be "the product of introjects which are excessively cathected with primitive aggression. . . . The primitive self carries out the functions and activities that have been modeled and acted out in reality by a very disturbed parental figure" (Figueroa 1988). Aggression is a plastic drive that seeks expression when a person is frustrated. Early childhood self-attack, for example, results when aggression is forced inward because its expression outward is blocked. Blockage may be caused by a child's physical disability, external restrictions on physical expression, physical distance from the object of aggression, or fears of loss of love, fears of punishment, and fears of destroying the love object (Cain 1961). Anna Freud (1946, p. 56) referred to turning against the self as an early defense mechanism that was "as old as the instincts themselves, or at least as old as the conflict between instinctual impulses and any hindrance which they may encounter on their way to gratification." In a regressive slide from object to self, an object of hate may be incorporated or introjected so that the internalized representation becomes the target of aggression. Studies of adult self-mutilation report lifetime histories of greater aggression than in non-self-mutilating personality-disordered controls, as well as a correlation between the frequency of self-mutilation and chronic anger (Simeon et al. 1992).

The pathological condition, mentioned previously, in which a person experiences an alteration in the perception or experience of the self and of reality is known in psychiatry as a depersonalization disorder. Mild depersonalization episodes appear to be common in young adults but are not associated with significant impairment or self-mutilation. Severe episodes of depersonalization, however, are very frightening. Depersonalized individuals may feel that their bodies are unreal, that time and the environment have mysteriously changed, and that they are becoming insane. As noted by Nemiah (1985), "It is a curious paradox that, even though the patient complains of being emotionally dead and estranged, he is capable of being emotionally upset by that very sense of loss. Indeed, all the manifestations of depersonalization are acutely unpleasant and not only motivate the patient to seek medical help but often drive him to vigorous activity or to inducing intense sensations in himself in order to break through the prison walls of his sense of unreality" (p. 955). Self-mutilation, especially skin cutting, is usually very effective in ending an episode of depersonalization.

Waltzer (1968) thought that depersonalization facilitated the expression of unconscious, self-destructive impulses. However, it is now apparent that the self-mutilative acts associated with depersonalization are not suicide attempts but rather are therapeutic attempts to end the unpleasant feelings of the disorder. As stated by a patient, "I'd rather die than face being unreal. You go through life doing things automatically, like a machine. And then at the end of the day you try to match events with an emotion and try to experience them as a whole being. It's all right to hurt yourself because it proves you are real." Sometimes it is the pain, but more often it is the sight of blood that seems to be effective in restoring a sense of reality to the self-mutilator. Asch (1971) described a sequence of events leading to wrist scratching in a group of adolescent girls. When threatened by rejection, they experienced depersonalization, which was relieved by wrist scratching. In the words of one girl: "There was too much white, white nurses, white doctors, white sheets, white walls. It was such a relief to cut and see the red blood flow" (p. 632). The sensation of pain and the presence of blood not only interrupt the monotony of depersonalization but also indicate that the cutter is, indeed, alive and that the body's border of skin is intact and in place.

The relationship of the psyche to the functions of the skin is significant to understanding the self-mutilative process, according to some psychoanalysts (Hibbard 1994). The skin encloses and maintains the body, and the "skin ego" maintains and encloses the psyche. Infants first internalize their mothers through skin contact. Before the mind develops, the infant's skin is the earliest site of sensations. The skin "is one of the most primitive channels for preverbal communication, where nonverbalized affects may be somatically experienced and observed. Through her handling of the child the mother's skin may convey the full range of emotions from tenderness and warmth and love to disgust and hate" (Gaddini 1982, p. 315). There is supposedly an initial merging of the mother and the infant. Eventually infants establish their own sense of self, but a maternal core remains within them (the internalized mother). If an infant's skin ego is impaired because of diffuse instinctual anxiety, as an adult "he wraps himself in suffering" (Anzieu 1989, p. 102) and may use the physical pain of self-mutilation to repair his outer shell. If the skin ego is impaired because of unsatisfactory early nurturing, the adult may attack the internalized mother by self-mutilation. Self-cutters demonstrate unresolved issues dealing "with the very first assault on their bodies, the site of which is the skin" (Hibbard 1994).

Self-mutilation sometimes serves as a remedy for depression. The word *depression* has a variety of connotations, including feeling blue, sad, demoralized, guilt ridden, nihilistic, and deserving of punishment and even death. Persons suffering from clinical depression think poorly of themselves and truly believe their symptoms to be the just deserts of bad thoughts or deeds. They cannot escape harsh self-judgment but can hope for some relief by paying for their "crimes," just as criminals may be reconciled with society by suffering in a penitentiary. If depressed persons imagine them-

selves to have committed truly heinous crimes, they may sentence themselves to death by suicide. Of course, for less serious "crimes" the sentence
may be lighter and the punishment less great; for example, self-cutting or
sticking needles into one's skin may suffice to bring the relief that follows
paying for one's transgressions. As one patient said, "I feel that I have to be
punished and after harming myself I feel relief. I never wanted to die. I just
want my emotions to die." In psychoanalytic terms, self-mutilation in these
cases represents the workings of a harsh superego that functions as police-
man, judge, jury, and jailer to enforce punishment on a criminal.

Feelings of badness and hostility may find relief in acts of self-mutilation
through the mechanism of localization. Rather than consider themselves
totally bad, persons may localize the bad part to a specific organ, such as
the eye; removal of the organ provides a method for removing the badness
or demon as well.

For some persons self-mutilation serves to remedy perceived internal or
external flaws. One patient stated, "I feel lonely and ugly and disfigured
inside. Terribly imperfect. Which leads to feeling the need to correct something outwardly so I cut off my hair. I think about death a lot." According
to another patient, "I feel hopeless and helpless. As I must wash and fix my
hair each morning and can't stop cutting it, I dread even getting out of bed.
I feel deformed—like I have to fix or change myself all the time. In reality
I am an attractive woman but I feel ugly. I don't want to die but think of
death as the only answer to ending this malady. I'm afraid of me." More
drastic is the use of self-castration among men whose psychopathology
centers on problems with gender identity, functioning in the male role,
and sexual conflicts. Men who perceive themselves to be women may regard self-castration as a surgical remedy to correct a flaw in their anatomy.
Other men may castrate themselves in order to fulfill a desire to be "like"
a woman, to enhance or to establish a relationship with a woman (such as
mother) by removing the threat of sexuality, and to resolve conflicts over
homosexual desires.

Although suicide attempts have been called "a cry for help," there is a
great difference between a true suicide attempt and a "gesture." Persons
who make suicide "gestures" have no intention of killing themselves; thus,
use of the word *suicide* is imprecise. One intent of these persons is to demonstrate their desperation; their hope is that someone will respond and
make things better. Self-cutting of an exposed area of the body can be
a most effective demonstration of desperation. "My self-harm began my
senior year in high school. I watched a movie where a guy killed himself
and was—strangely—moved by it. One of the girls in my class had tried to

kill herself that night. She had taken pills to die but her favorite method was the blade. I began scraping myself with a key and by cutting the words 'HELL ME' on my arm. I was scared to death the next morning and told my teacher. She saw the words as 'HELP ME.' I purposely did *not* write that because it is too conventional. She helped me start seeing a psychologist." A possible explanation of this behavior has been proposed by Benjamin (1987): abused children learn that acknowledging inflicted pain often ends the perpetrator's attacks and may then result in nurturance. A pattern is established so that later in life persons faced with seemingly terrible problems inflict suffering on themselves through self-mutilation in the expectation that the problems will end and nurturance will follow: "The internal phenomenology of the self-mutilator is a replay of family history."

Sometimes self-mutilation can be a manipulative ploy to gain attention and to coerce others into providing a caring, mothering response (Kwawer 1980). As emotional blackmail, self-mutilation often works. It is difficult enough to see strangers, much less family members or loved ones, cut and burn themselves without intervening. Especially as self-mutilators escalate the frequency and intensity of their acts, observers become overwhelmed by guilt and acquiesce to their demands.

Self-mutilation can be an attention getter in a negative way. It is an unappealing behavior; indiscriminate scars and burn marks are ugly and even frightening at times. The legend of Saint Lucy tells how she drove away an unwanted suitor by enucleating her eyes and sending them to him. Figueroa (1988) notes, "Especially when sexual abuse has occurred, the mutilation may be an attempt to turn away future sexual contact/abuse by ensuring that one is physically unattractive and, thus, undesirable."

In his book on symbolic wounds, Bettelheim (1955) addresses female adolescent self-mutilation. His theory is that girls in their transition to adult status may demonstrate an identification with their mother by symbolically creating a vagina (the cut skin) and menstruation (the bloody wound). Bettelheim was aware of tribal rites of passage; his theory is not as far fetched as it would seem at first glance. Identification with the mother also is the major theme in a different formulation of self-mutilation: "The induced bleeding in the cutting is an attempt to undo the current separation by identifying with the bleeding woman (mother) symbolic of this mother-infant unit in the past" (Asch 1971).

The perturbations of sexual drives commingled with aggressive drives serve as the basis of several psychoanalytic theories. Menninger (1935) referred to self-mutilation as "a rash expression of the aggressive, destructive tendency by erotization." He also regarded self-castration as the prototype of all self-mutilation and regarded the substituted organ (skin, eyes, etc.) as the unconscious representative of the genitals. This formulation has been repeated over the years. Friedman et al. (1972), for example, state that the unconscious fantasy in self-mutation is destruction of the genitals through displacement: "Whatever part of the body is attacked then represents the genitals." Psychoanalysts also write about the pleasure of self-mutilation. Biven (1977) writes about the excitable, elated, sexualized orgasmlike feelings associated with the behavior; and Daldin (1990) notes that "cutting the skin also represents a self-stimulating masturbatory (autoerotic) activity involving both the attempted expression of masturbatory sexual gratification as well as a punishment for the impulse to stimulate the self." Siomopoulos (1974) describes cuts as producing little female genitalia, which may then be touched and manipulated uninhibitedly.

In a psychoanalytic case history, Daldin (1990) describes an adolescent who stuck a pin "through the skin of her left forearm and then through the skin between the thumb and first finger. She said, 'See, I can stick it in . . . and pull it out . . . and I don't feel a thing' . . . She (said) sarcastically, 'I'm sure I'm getting great sexual pleasure from doing this! I told my mother I cut my arm because I like it. . . . I get off on it but I don't get any orgasms' . . . She imagined cutting herself open from the navel to the genitals. . . . She explored how her menses had been both terrifying and fascinating. . . . She then went back to talk of her father as being a 'pin dick,' and using her by 'sticking me with all the chores.'" The author's formulation considers the patient both a feminine, receptive object and a masculine, phallic, penetrating object. "Remaining in the feminine, receptive position, with a penis, resulted in her feeling hopeless, worthless, vulnerable and angry. The site of her arm created a stage for the creation of a mutilated, castrated, bleeding vagina as well as symbolizing a cutting (castration) of the phallic-like arm."

A great deal of attention recently has focused on self-mutilation as a method to relieve emotional dysphoria, which is usually precipitated by issues of separation, loss, and failure (Liebenluft, Gardner, and Cowdry 1987). The psychological mechanisms for this relief include reduction in guilt through self-punishment; the redirection of pain away from disturbing thoughts and feelings; cutting as a counterstimulus; arousal and amplification of distantly and nebulously perceived conflicts so that they are clearer, more easily understood, and less frightening; and the amplification of pleasurable emotions (e.g., masochistic sexual practices) (Figueroa 1988).

One of the most common reasons given for self-mutilation is that it helps reestablish control over racing thoughts, rapidly fluctuating emotions, and an unstable environment. "I didn't 'decide' on self-abuse. I just did it because it calmed me down. I would be so hurt and angry I'd feel like I was exploding. Better cut me than someone else. The pain gave me a focal point, then I'd put whatever was bothering me out of my mind." "Self-harm gives me a feeling of control when I cannot find control in the environment. It also makes me feel real. I enjoy it. It makes me feel better. Release from emotional pain. A form of security." Persons who feel a loss of control in other areas find that self-mutilation is a behavior over which they have total control. Only they can start it, and only they can stop it. Women who experience dyscontrol of their blood during their periods may cut themselves not only to prove that they can at least control something but also to attempt to divert the blood away from the vaginal area.

Self-mutilation may be symptom reducing by providing stimulation to certain persons. Institutionalized children living in a sterile environment, for example, are prone to head banging and face slapping as a means of satisfying their need for stimulation. Persons with an antisocial personality disorder appear to have an inordinate need for excitement and stimulation. When such persons are locked in a prison cell or placed in a restrictive environment, they experience mounting tension because of stimulation hunger. Self-mutilation provides the stimulation they crave and effectively lowers their level of tension.

In earlier chapters, I presented many cases of psychotic persons whose drastic acts of self-mutilation (e.g., castration, eye enucleation, and limb amputation) occurred within a religious context. Chronic, low-lethality self-mutilation, however, also may have religious underpinnings: "I have carved a cross on my chest so many times that there is a raised red scar and have made cuts on my sides. I keep thinking of something said when they baptize babies in our church: 'Receive the sign of the cross on the forehead and chest that you have been redeemed by Christ the crucified.' I also think of the 'stripes' Christ received when I cut my side. I understand that Christ died for everyone but, somehow in my mind, not for me."

Self-mutilation may occur in response to hallucinations or intensely intrusive thoughts. Voices may command psychotic persons to mutilate themselves, or visions may be interpreted to indicate that self-mutilation is necessary. When the hallucinations indicate that self-mutilation would be the fulfillment of a higher destiny, such as God's will, mentally ill persons may feel exalted because they have been so chosen and may feel compelled to act out the role assigned to them. In Christian culture, persons may find reinforcement for their acquiescence to the demands of a higher destiny in biblical paragraphs that sanction the self-mutilation of the eyes, hands, and genitals. When the voices are persecutory, the act of self-mutilation may be a gesture of appeasement; for example, "I have hurt myself, therefore you no longer need to persecute me." Hallucinations may range from continuous, pesky noises to extremely frightening visions (especially when drug induced); self-mutilation may represent a desperate attempt to distract attention away from the hallucinations or to end a frightening episode.

Among female habitual self-mutilators, multiple scars are located on their arms (74%), legs (44%), abdomens (25%), head (23%), chest (18%), and genitals (8%) (Favazza and Conterio 1989). Self-mutilation may also be therapeutic because of the symbolism associated with the formation of scar tissue; scar tissue indicates that healing has occurred. Thus, with a few strokes of a razor the self-cutter may unleash a symbolic process in which the sickness within is removed and the stage is set for healing as evidenced by a scar. The cutter, in effect, performs a primitive sort of self-surgery, complete with tangible evidence of healing. Scarring serves an additional purpose in that it can "mark" a hurtful occasion. Just as a significant event symbolically can be burned in one's memory, so too it literally can be burned into one's skin.

In order to put all the cited theories and mechanisms into some perspective, it is instructive to note the most common reasons for self-mutilation given by female habitual self-mutilators: to control their mind when it is racing (72%), feel relaxed (65%), feel less depressed (58%), feel real again (55%), feel less lonely (47%), atone for sins (40%), respond to "voices" (20%), and respond to evil spirits (12%) (Favazza and Conterio 1989).

Most of the psychological explanations and mechanisms for stereotypic self-mutilation, called SIB (self-injurious behavior) in the mental retardation literature, are phrased in behavioral terms. Stereotypic self-mutilation such as head banging, gouging, and scratching, is most commonly described as a learned operant. The concept of reinforced attention seeking holds that the behavior is shaped and maintained by positive social attention. The concept of escape holds that the behavior may be shaped and maintained by negative reinforcement. For example, "an institutionalized girl would bang her head against the bars of her crib when put to bed against her wishes. She did so presumably to escape from the crib" (Carr 1977). The self-stimulation hypothesis holds that some persons who do not experience sufficient stimulation will engage in SIB to gratify their "stimulation hunger" (Collins 1965). In other psychological terms, SIB is associated with death wishes and with an attempt to differentiate the self from the object world. Rhythmical SIB supposedly represents attempts to reexperience the comforting heartbeats of mother (Fitzherbert 1950).

Social Explanations of Self-mutilation

Social setting may greatly influence the onset, course, and spread of self-mutilative behavior. Podvoll (1969) notes that self-mutilators who assume an identity as a cutter or a slasher develop a distinctive, functional role on a hospital ward. Their acts evoke intense feelings among the members of the ward community. One the one hand, staff and other patients perceive the behavior as a pathological symptom that must be controlled; on the other hand, they may also perceive it "as something seemingly more honest, pure, or disciplined" than other behaviors and therefore the object of respect, envy, and collusion. Thus, the continuance or cessation of a self-mutilator's behavior may depend in great part on the ward community's reaction to that behavior.

Self-mutilation has been known to occur as an epidemic. Hundreds of cases of self-inflicted eye injuries have been reported among soldiers who wished to avoid unpleasant duty (Somerville-Large 1947). Examination of epidemics of self-mutilation that have occurred on psychiatric inpatient units (Matthews 1968; Crabtree and Grossman 1974) supports the finding of a relationship among four variables: the self-mutilative behavior, the rituals and ceremonies of a hospital unit, the meaning and coherence of the unit's social organization, and the unit's therapeutic effectiveness (Kroll 1978). Walsh and Rosen (1988) state that self-mutilation within groups is a primitive method of communicating needs, is used to manipulate the behavior of members, and may be a requisite of group membership or high status. I have encountered cutter "groupies"; these all have been females who are attracted to cutters and who then cut themselves to become closer to them.

Endemic self-mutilation often exists in repressive settings such as correctional institutions. Self-mutilation in such settings has generally been interpreted as a coping mechanism that offers a means to express defiance, gain a transfer to a different unit, or attract sympathetic medical help.

It is of interest that the most commonly encountered type of pathological self-mutilation is skin cutting by adolescents. Although the cutting is most directly related to relief of psychological distress, it is symbolically associated with healing and salvation. It also has a symbolic association with the mutilative rites of adolescent initiation. At an intuitive level, the self-mutilative acts of mentally disturbed adolescents represent attempts to escape feelings of loneliness and abandonment and to attain the heightened self-awareness that often leads to change and maturity. They are desperate, primitive attempts to achieve social acceptance and integration into the adult world. They are pacts, unconscious and sealed with blood, indicating the adolescent's desire to be reconciled with society.

Comments on Self-mutilation

Self-mutilation is a multidetermined behavior and can be understood only by attention to interactions among psychological and biological functioning, the environment and social setting, and the overarching web of culture. Depending upon the circumstances, differing factors may assume primary importance. Biology, for example, is the driving force behind the Lesch-Nyhan syndrome, while the social setting may drive self-harm in prisoners. Psychodynamic approaches may best "explain" cutting and burning, while behavioral considerations seem to apply best to many types of stereotypic acts of self-harm.

Many of the constructs used to understand self-mutilation are subject to criticism. Levels of chemicals in the blood or urine, for example, may not correspond accurately with levels in the brain. Impulsivity is a problematic concept in psychiatry; among the "impulse control disorders not elsewhere classified" in *DSM-IV*, for example, a criterion for the diagnosis of pyromania is deliberate, purposeful fire setting on *more than one occasion*. A frequency of two acts could establish a diagnosis but hardly jibes with most notions of impulsivity. Psychiatric diagnosis may be reliable (raters may agree among themselves), but validity is another matter. A German study (Herperz 1995), for example, diagnosed 19 percent of female moderate/superficial self-mutilators as schizophrenic, but it is doubtful that American psychiatrists would make that diagnosis. Many clinicians and researchers, I among them, regard the syndrome of repetitive self-mutilation as valid, but there are others who consider it a "borderline" phenomenon. Psychodynamic psychology is often derided as unscientific, while behavioral psychology, based on the measurement of observable acts, is seen as valid. However, there are many problems associated with a behavioral approach to self-mutilation. For example, deCatanzaro (1978) points out difficulties: (1) Developmental variables may be involved; the continued occurrence of SIB may be more dependent on early experience than on maintained contingencies of reinforcement; (2) the SIB may occur relatively spontaneously in frustrating situations, where a previously learned response is not rewarded, or singly as a result of change in routine; (3) most attempts to extinguish SIB by removing all extrinsic reinforcement have failed to eliminate this behavior; the ability of punishment to suppress SIB does not prove that SIB is learned behavior; (4) it is difficult to envisage how patterns of social reinforcement could support rhythmicity, rates sufficiently high to exclude all other forms of operant behavior, and multiple forms of SIB in the same individual; and (5) the relationship between SIB and IQ cannot be explained by the learning model.

On the cultural scene, body piercing first became faddish, especially in the homosexual, lesbian, and rock music subcultures, but has spread into mainstream culture. *Modern Primitives* (Vale and Juno 1989), a comprehensive book complete with many startling photographs, describes piercing of such body parts as the penis, scrotum, nipples, labia, and nasal septum. The Gauntlet Stores in Los Angeles, San Francisco, and New York, as well as many other piercing parlors, supply hypoallergenic rings and pins that are inserted after the piercing is completed. *Piercing Fans International Quarterly* and *Body Play and Modern Primitives Quarterly* are journals for aficionados. A descriptive study of nipple piercing in 292 men and 70 women, the majority of whom were solicited from among readers of a piercing magazine, reported a median age for women at the time of piercing of 34 years, with a range of 22 to 60 years; median age for men was 43 years, with a range of 24 to 76 years. Over 60 percent of the men and half of the women had at least a college education; the same percent of each group described themselves as homosexuals. For most, the nipples became more of an erotic focus after the piercing (e.g., nipple stimulation during masturbation). At least half the sample reported an increased awareness of being sexually "turned on" throughout the day. Almost all the women and 80 percent of the men had other piercings in the ear lobe, nose, genital organs, and navel (Moser et al. 1993).

The most common piercing fad today, other than earrings, consists of navel rings. When I was asked during an interview why so many teenagers were getting piercings, I replied, "It makes them feel good in a coming-of-age experimental sense; it looks sexy; and its upsets their parents." There are other answers to the question. It is a way to establish some individuality, but if a specific piercing becomes relatively commonplace, then more complex piercings may be sought as well as other types of body modification such as scarification and branding (the "kiss of fire"). By the way, a proficient brander is able to create an "artistic" mark that lasts for differing lengths of time. Inexperienced branders, such as those in some college fraternities, usually produce crude marks that last a lifetime.

Although most body piercing is purely decorative, some of its advocates √ speak of a deeper meaning. A Californian known as Fakir Musafar coined the term *modern primitivism* and is its foremost spokesperson. He has mastered body modification by contortion, constriction, deprivation, encumberment, fire, penetration, and suspension. Examples of these categories include penis stretching, corsets, encasement of body parts in plaster, wearing heavy iron manacles, branding, flagellation, body piercing, and suspension by body hooks. Musafar claims that these ordeals can result in psychological and spiritual awakenings through an alteration of consciousness. Some professional body piercers claim that "the art of being cut and surviving is a very strengthening and powerful experience for people. Especially for people who've been either in abusive situations or have gone through a lot of 'stuff' in their lives. To ask to be cut (not in a violent situation, but in a loving, supportive, trusting situation) and then bleed and then end up with something beautiful . . . and then it heals and you have it and you're proud of it—that can be very empowering. It can be a reclaiming for a lot of people" (Vale and Juno 1989, p. 105).

Body modification takes the center stage in "performance art," during which artists pierce, brand, and execute the acts of body modification on willing performers before an audience. One artist of my acquaintance sews various body parts of dead animals (e.g., a pig's tail) onto men (sometimes the parts are only pasted on). Another artist concluded a philosophical discussion of deconstructionism when he decorated a human Christmas tree by stapling ornaments into the skin of a woman. A well-known performance artist, Ron Athey, ritually cuts performers and rubs paper on bleeding wounds to produce unique pieces of art. Athey, who was reared by his evangelical aunts to become a preacher, utilizes martyr symbols and the stigmata in his performances. He says that his art is about "redemption from self-destruction and suicide" (Breslauer 1994).

In addition to performance artists, there are just plain performers (not illusionists or tricksters) who are capable of amazing physical acts. A European named Mirin Dajo (Esperanto for "something miraculous") is hypnotized by a colleague. Then a third member of the team sticks a sword all the way through Dajo's back until it exits through the chest on the other side of his body. The sword has a blunted tip so as not to cut internal organs. Obviously the placement of the sword is crucial. X-rays taken at the City Hospital of Basel, Switzerland, show that the sword does, indeed, go through Dajo's body.

The most spectacular group performers are Sufi (a branch of Islam) male dervishes who belong to an order known as Tariqa Casnazaniyyah (the first word is Arabic for "way," while the second word is Kurdish for "that is known by no one"). Among the feats they perform are inserting skewers and spikes into the body (face, neck, arms, breast, abdomen), hammering knives into bones (skull and clavicle), swallowing glass shards and razor blades, holding red-hot iron plates in their bare hands as well as their teeth, and eating poisonous snakes and scorpions after being bitten by them! They consider these acts to be miracles (since no pain is felt, no blood is shed, and the wounds heal immediately) that are demonstrated to win converts. Upon request they will deliberately contaminate the spikes that they drive into their bodies. Since 1982 a group of physicists and physicians in Jordan (Paramann Programme Laboratories) has been studying the group (Hussein et al. 1993; Al-Dargazelli 1993–94) in order to find a way for all human beings to access the ability to control pain and heal wounds. They report that the feats can be performed not only in a religious context but also in the most sterile environment; no preparation is needed and tired subjects performed even after only one to two hours of sleep. Measurements of brain wave (EEG) activity, electrical skin resistance, skin temperature, blood pressure, heart and respiratory rates, and unspecified chemical tests of the subjects' blood, urine, and feces failed to show any systematic changes either during or after the demonstrations. The finding of no EEG changes is most interesting since both American and German researchers found changes (onset of alpha waves and increased theta waves) in two subjects who allowed spikes and needles to be inserted into their bodies (Green and Green 1977; Larbig 1982). Since these changes are associated with meditative and trance states, the absence of EEG changes in the Tariqa group suggests that the dervishes do not perform during an altered state of consciousness. The Paramann Programme group's scientific credibility, unfortunately, becomes suspect when they state their belief that the dervishes' abilities were spontaneously transmitted to them during an initiation ceremony when ritualistically shaking the hand of a Califa (an especially distinguished dervish) and reciting a brief religious vow. The dervishes' abilities are thought to derive from the Master of the Tariqa, whose authority and spiritual powers are in turn derived from the prophet Muhammad.

A modern American named Tim Cridland, whose stage name is "The Torture King," is able to perform spectacular feats without recourse to supernatural explanations or mystical mumbo-jumbo. He is a connoisseur of oddities concerning the human body. He studies films and videos very closely and is impressed that fakirs and dervishes know exactly where to pierce for maximum penetration with minimal damage. He was intrigued by a specific piercing after he saw a photograph of a boy who had slipped while trying to climb a fence. A sharp post on top of the fence penetrated under his chin and out his mouth, leaving him hanging by the jaw. He was stuck like this for some time. Rescuers freed him and took him to the hospital with the fence still sticking from his mouth. Surprisingly the boy sustained little damage. As Cridland wondered about piercing himself in the mouth and out near the throat, he saw photographs of the Sufi group where this piercing (as well as many others) was done. He concluded that it was safe and went to Santa Cruz, California, where a master piercer named Eric Dakota worked with him. He learned how to pass a skewer through his biceps and then perfected a procedure for placing a skewer in his mouth and out near his neck. It is now part of his act. He has told me that he "never takes a blind stab in the dark." He studies each piercing in great detail and notes that "I have no intention of putting myself in an emergency room." He dislikes pain and bleeding; he is able to control both through self-hypnosis. He is acutely aware of what he is doing during a piercing: "I don't want to hit an artery or harm myself." He denies any masochistic pleasure from his performances. He has mastered the ability to change the experience of pain into "just another type of sensation as though someone were touching me." He can achieve this state of self-hypnosis rapidly and with little effort. In addition to using skewers, his act includes placing hundreds of pins in his flesh and muscle tissue, walking barefoot up and down a ladder of sharp blades, eating glass, and putting white-hot metal in his mouth. As a counterpoint, he also is able to walk on eggs without breaking them. He is currently attempting to learn more about a fakir piercing in which a small sword is inserted through the neck from side to side, going behind the windpipe and in front of the spine. He has high admiration for the Sufi piercers and speculates that their knowledge was gained "at the expense of a number of lives."

Summing Things Up

The following statements summarize our current state of understanding of self-mutilation:

- Self-mutilation is best regarded as a morbid form of self-help.
- Self-mutilation is antithetical to suicide, although mentally ill self-mutilators are at increased risk for suicide.
- Culturally sanctioned mutilative rituals are linked to physical healing, spiritual salvation, and social orderliness.
- Pathological self-mutilation not only reduces troublesome and painful symptoms temporarily but also serves the deeper purposes of healing, salvation, and order.
- Classification of pathological self-mutilation into three basic types (major, stereotypic, moderate/superficial), although subject to change with new discoveries, is useful clinically.

- Major self-mutilation is most often, but not exclusively, associated with psychosis and intoxications.
- Stereotypic self-mutilation is most often, but not exclusively, associated with severe mental retardation.
- Moderate/superficial self-mutilation is most often, but not exclusively, associated with borderline, histrionic, and antisocial personality disorders.
- The syndrome of repetitive self-mutilation is a distinct disorder of impulse dyscontrol, the biological underpinning of which may be lowered functioning of serotonin, a neurotransmitter in the brain.
- A psychiatric diagnosis *cannot* be presumed in persons who engage in body piercing, branding, tattoos, and so forth, although as a group such persons probably have increased levels of psychopathology.

11

Treatment

▬ ▬ ▬ ▬ ▬ ▬ ▬ ▬ ▬

Despite the antiquity, ubiquity, and relatively high prevalence of deviant self-mutilation, psychiatric attention has seldom been focused upon it because of the perception—shared by the general public and many mental health professionals—that it is a senseless, repugnant, frightening, mysterious behavior.

Even though self-mutilation may provide temporary relief from a host of ills, it is not a joyous activity. Self-mutilators, deep down, feel miserable about their behavior, and one goal of my work is to give public voice to their laments. The behavior is also tough on those who naturally care for the self-mutilator (parents, siblings, friends, spouses, children) and those who attempt to provide professional care. Alcoholics, drugs abusers, and self-mutilators are all exasperating persons to deal with. Their promises are usually worthless and their crises never ending. No matter how many times we remind ourselves that they are "sick" and that part of their sickness is the abrogation of personal responsibility, we cannot help but be upset when we are called in the middle of the night to tend to an alcoholic on yet another bender or a cutter intent on feeling bloody better.

Self-mutilators have a difficult life. There is significant physical morbidity when an irreplaceable body part such as an eye, hand, or penis is destroyed. Chronic self-mutilators often require medical attention for their cuts and burns. Hair pullers and others who interfere with wound healing may endure repeated infections. Many will make bona fide suicide attempts in desperation over their inability to control their behavior. Social morbidity also may be great. In addition to disfiguring scars, most chronic self-mutilators usually feel empty inside, misunderstood by all, a burden to others, and scared when close to anyone.

Put simply, no one loves self-mutilators. Their very presence seems to threaten the sense of mental and physical integrity of those around them. Even surgical personnel who are used to amputating limbs and treating mangled accident victims may display uncharacteristic poor judgment when confronted with these patients; for example, only a half-hearted (or no) attempt may be made to reattach a severed genital. Not a few chronic cutters have recounted that, because of the brutish treatment they have sometimes received in emergency rooms, they will falsely admit to a suicide attempt in order to facilitate a warmer reception. Even experienced psychotherapists are hard-pressed to maintain equanimity with chronic self-mutilators. Publications about psychotherapy with these patients universally contain lengthy discussions of countertransference. Frances (1987) neatly summed up the situation:"Of all disturbing patient behaviors, self-mutilation is the most difficult to understand and treat. . . . The typical clinician (myself included) treating a patient who self-mutilates is often left feeling a combination of helpless, horrified, guilty, furious, betrayed, disgusted, and sad."

Frances's remarkable litany of adjectives reflects the extraordinary power of the self-mutilative act. Although suicide is shocking, the grief of mourners may be assuaged by a host of convenient rationalizations, such as, "It is all part of God's great plan"; and at least the victim is dead. But self-mutilation is horrific in its seeming senselessness, and the victim is very much alive and able to haunt us in the flesh.

The power of self-mutilation to mystify and horrify even seasoned therapists seems to derive from more than what are generally considered to be the sources of countertransference. In addition to the standard reasons, I believe that self-mutilation challenges our equanimity because its bloody tendrils reach out to touch the Sacred. In the scenario of the travelers to the Holy Temple (chapter 2) I tried to portray a sense of the Sacred. It is a scary place, so scary that all the trappings of organized religion may be defenses against the true religious experience of the Sacred. Through the mechanism of transubstantiation, the Sacred becomes palatable; a wafer of grain is digested more easily than the liver of a Man-God, and a sip of red wine is less likely to stick in one's throat than His blood. Although it is unfashionable in these days of molecular biology to speak of energy, early anthropologists such as Tyler and Frazer and Smith noted the powerful energy that is released at the moment of religious sacrifice. The release of symbolic sacrificial energy during the act of self-mutilation contributes to its unsettling potential. Another disturbing factor of self-mutilation is its symbolic connection to ritual timelessness as described by Turner (1968). In sum, even though deviant self-mutilators are not liminal beings, even though their acts have no real transcendency, even though their use of religious symbolism is based on private rather than public delusions, they open a window onto the turbulent, bloody space of the Sacred. It is a space that truly great shamans can visit briefly, although the voyage is dangerous and fearful. So can adepts of Tantric Buddhism who have achieved the great liberation through hearing in the bardo meditations (Rinpoche 1975). For most of us, however, it is a space in the cosmos and in ourselves that remains hidden. When self-mutilators draw us to this space, we resist and feel "helpless, horrified, guilty, furious, betrayed, disgusted, and sad."

Our feelings are hurt when self-mutilators reject our care and clever interpretations, feelings that may even turn to "hate" (Winnicott 1949). Our negative feelings may be reflected in justifying "either harsh or indifferent treatment . . . apparently therapeutic maneuvers such as ECT, high-dose medication, or even the transfer of care may on occasions be a means of getting rid of a frustrating patient or even punishing her for her refractoriness" (Tantam and Whittaker 1992).

The reason for this lengthy discourse is that the treatment of self-mutilation demands more equanimity on the part of the therapist than in dealing with other patients. The general clinical wisdom is that two cutters and burners are the maximum that most therapists should deal with intensively at any one time. I have, more or less, come to grips with my feelings and will describe in this chapter the therapeutic strategies that I employ to help my patients and maintain my sanity. I am at a loss to explain my composure when dealing with self-mutilators (however, I find it almost impossible to deal with severely burned patients or young quadriplegics without feeling emotionally overwhelmed). Perhaps it is a result of my long reading on the topic followed by emotionally "safe" research. By the time I first provided serious clinical care, I was well prepared. A major factor certainly was my good fortune in having several patients who served as my teachers. I still continue to learn from patients but try to avoid generalizing "insights" from one patient to others.

Biological Treatment

The most promising discovery of recent years is the ability of medications that enhance serotonin to decrease and even eliminate moderate/superficial self-mutilation. These medications are classified as SSRIs (selective serotonin reuptake inhibitors), and they are marketed as antidepressants even though they are used to treat panic disorder, obsessive-compulsive disorder, and eating disorders, as well as depression and self-mutilation. Their side effect profile is generally favorable in that they produce little sedation or blood pressure changes, a very low level of anticholinergic symptoms (blurred vision, dry mouth, urinary retention), few cardiac effects, and are relatively safe when taken as overdoses in suicide attempts. The most common side effects are headache, nausea, and anxiety; up to a third of patients may experience some sexual dysfunction. Fluoxetine (Prozac) was the first

SSRI to become available and was soon followed by sertraline (Zoloft), paroxetine (Paxil), and fluvoxamine (Luvox). There are some differences among them, such as the length of time they last in the blood system and the degree to which they bind to proteins in blood plasma, but they all theoretically use the same mechanism to affect serotonin. Despite this similarity, some patients may tolerate or respond to one medication better than another.

Although published studies of the efficacy of SSRIs in the treatment of self-mutilation are few and involve small numbers of patients, they are the first consistently positive reports. Twelve subjects with borderline or schizotypal personality disorder who were chronic self-mutilators were treated with fluoxetine for twelve weeks; their cutting episodes were reduced by 97 percent (Markovitz et al. 1991). The dose given was 80 milligrams a day (the usual dose for depression is 20 to 40 milligrams). At the end of twelve weeks only two patients were still cutting themselves, and in these patients the rate was greatly reduced. Since fluoxetine is marketed as an antidepressant, it is important to note that the presence or absence of clinical depression did not affect the outcome. I have treated repetitive self-mutilators with high doses of fluoxetine (up to 120 milligrams; at this dose very careful monitoring is necessary) with no side effects; one patient who demonstrated every symptom of the repetitive self-mutilation syndrome simultaneously (cutting, eating disorder, kleptomania, and alcohol and substance abuse) stopped all these behaviors. After several months, however, the cutting returned, albeit at a lower rate. The patient said that the medication seemed to lose its effectiveness. A number of clinicians have told me that they have had the same experience. My patient also reported that she "missed" the cutting very much and welcomed its return.

It is clear that SSRIs do not selectively treat self-mutilation but rather affect impulsivity. They also affect compulsivity, and there are positive reports of their effectiveness in treating nail biting, skin picking, scratching, and hair pulling (Gupta et al. 1986; Jan Stout 1990; Leonard et al. 1991; Stein et al. 1993; Swedo et al. 1989; Winchel et al. 1992). It should be noted that other medications also may increase serotonin, although not as selectively as SSRIs. Clomipramine, especially useful for hair pulling, also helped an obsessive-compulsive patient who injured himself by repeatedly pushing in his eyeballs; he still thought about blinding himself but no longer acted on this thought (Primeau and Fontaine 1987). Another patient, a typical cutter and burner, responded to trazodone (Patel 1988).

Many medications have been used to treat moderate/superficial self-mutilation. With the exception of lithium for hair pulling (Christenson et al. 1991), none has proven terribly helpful. Neuroleptics (major tranquil-izers, antipsychotics) are not at all helpful, except for the treatment of delu-sional parasitosis, where pimozide, a drug marketed primarily for the treat-ment of tics associated with Tourette syndrome, may be effective. Lithium and propranolol, a medication marketed primarily for hypertension and heart arrhythmias, occasionally help with outward-directed aggression but rarely with self-mutilation (Wickham and Reed 1987). Minor tranquiliz-ers such as the benzodiazepines (Valium and Xanax) are not very helpful either; seven of twelve borderline patients increased their self-mutilation after receiving a minor tranquilizer (Gardner and Cowdry 1985). A case has been made for using monoamine oxidase inhibitors such as Nardil and Par-nate (marketed as antidepressants) in the belief that they reduce "rejection-induced dysphoria" (Liebowitz 1987), but they are rarely prescribed.

In one study, the "suggestions" of neurological dysfunction that were found in four female self-mutilators prompted speculation about a cortical deficiency in experiencing stimulation (Lycacki, Josef, and Munetz 1979). The four patients were treated with methylphenidate (Ritalin), a stimulant drug thought to affect the reticular activating system; two responded favor-ably. With occasional success, clinicians sometimes prescribe stimulants, such as amphetamines, for chronic self-mutilators. The enkephalin theory repeatedly stimulates calls for treatment with opiate antagonists (such as naloxone and naltrexone); unfortunately, they do not work with cutters and burners (although the recent approval of these drugs for the treatment of alcoholism may revive interest in studies with self-mutilators). Many clinicians are prescribing carbamazapine (Tegretol) and valproate (valproic acid), medications developed as anticonvulsants but used in psychiatry as mood stabilizers. Anecdotal reports indicate a modest rate of success, and they are worth a trial (Gardner and Cowdry 1986).

The best form of treatment for major self-mutilation is prevention. Therapeutic efforts can prevent self-mutilation in high-risk situations, for example, in psychotic patients with command hallucinations, persecutory delusions, and preoccupations with sexual or religious thoughts, especially when the patients are confined against their will. A potentially ominous sign is intensive reading of the Bible by a psychotic person. Time and time again, psychotic persons find a final justification for their self-mutilation from the portentous biblical passage about removing an offensive eye or hand. Although it is not feasible to deny these patients access to a Bible, one might consider removing or crossing out the troublesome paragraphs. A history of previous self-mutilation is another danger signal. I recently was asked to see a psychotically depressed prisoner who enucleated his left eye after being placed in a restrictive cell for punching a guard; two years previously, the patient had enucleated his right eye under the same circumstances. An easily observable harbinger of impending major self-mutilation in psychotic persons is a self-imposed change in appearance, such as head shaving or severe hair plucking (Sweeney and Zamecnik 1981). Prevention of major self-mutilation, usually single events such as eye enucleation or castration, entails close observation and active treatment, for example, the rapid administration of high doses of neuroleptics (major tranquilizers) such as haloperidol (Haldol) or fluphenazine (Prolixin).

The use of medication for stereotypic self-mutilation is common, confusing, and often ineffective. Many medications, especially neuroleptics and beta blockers, have been tried, and every so often a patient will respond favorably (Arnold and Aman 1991). One report favors buspirone (Ratey et al. 1991). As Winchel and Stanley (1991) pointed out, most studies about the use of drugs in treating self-mutilation involve the mentally retarded and are very problematic. Often self-mutilation is equated with aggression in general, thus compromising results."Nonspecific sedating effects (as with neuroleptics and benzodiazepines) or the presence of nondiagnosed mood disorders (which may respond to lithium and carbamezapine) complicate the interpretations of beneficial results" (Winchel and Stanley, 1991). Moreover, carbamezapine's occasional efficacy may be a result of its anticonvulsant effect; the mentally retarded have high rates of seizure disorders and EEG abnormalities. Evidence for the efficacy of opiate antagonists is mixed. A recent report cites extremely good results in three mentally retarded adults (Buzan et al. 1995). One patient with a ten-year history of hitting herself intensely on the nose decreased this behavior to one episode a day after receiving naltrexone. Another patient had a long history of 140 self-injurious episodes an hour (hitting her face with both hands and kicking her head) and required padded arm splints twenty-three hours a day. Within a month of receiving naltrexone (50 milligram dose) the episodes were reduced to 10 per hour when out of splints and to none when wearing splints. However, an increase in the dose to 100 milligrams resulted in an increase of self-harm episodes to 120 per hour.

Patients whose self-mutilation is a consequence of a medical disorder obviously need to receive specific treatment, such as replacement hormones for Addison's disease, although they may also need adjunctive tranquilizers. Exciting work in genetic engineering points to the possibility of curing disorders such as the Lesch-Nyhan syndrome by replacing the patient's defective genes with normal ones.

Finally, a very small literature exists on the use of neurosurgical operations for the control of self-mutilation. While the early history of psycho-surgery reveals rather crude procedures, modern psychosurgery is quite precise and can be directed at minute areas of the brain such as specific nuclei. Vaernet and Madsen (1970) reported on the effect of destruction of the amygdala (small areas of brain tissue in the limbic system that are thought to be the substrate of emotions) in twelve institutionalized patients with violently aggressive behavior and a "tendency" toward self-mutilation. In almost all of the patients, the psychosurgical procedure resulted in a marked improvement in or disappearance of episodes of aggression, hostility, and destructiveness. Although some of the patients had several psychosurgical operations, the amygdalotomy appears to have been the crucial one. The general public and mental health professionals look upon psychosurgery with a great deal of distrust, and, favorable as the one study was, it is unlikely that in the foreseeable future psychosurgery will be utilized for the treatment of self-mutilation.

Psychological and Social Treatments

Since the first edition of this book in 1987, several instructive articles have been published that outline general principles of treatment. After presenting these, I will look at psychodynamic, cognitive, and behavioral approaches, as well as my personal system.

Tantam and Whittaker (1992) review the treatment literature and then list treatment principles for repetitive self-mutilators:

1. Making and maintaining a relationship: understanding, staying calm, reframing self-mutilation as an expression of feeling, avoiding threats or promises, sticking to limits, leaving the responsibility with the patient, sticking with the patient;

2. Breaking the habit: coping with withdrawal symptoms, increasing determination to change;

3. Maintaining change: rewards for new behavior, minimizing medicalization, resolving emotional conflicts, tackling coercion, training in intimacy.

The authors note that self-mutilation should be understood in the context of persistently disordered relationships "but do not consider that terming these a 'personality disorder' is particularly illuminating." They also warn against trying to save patients from themselves or from their families. As for extraordinary services such as involuntary commitment or home visits or emergency therapy sessions, if a special need has been met, patients will recognize it; but "if the decision is wrong, patients will either feel rejected because their real need has been unrecognized or cheated because the caregiver has been unable to trust them to sort out the situation for themselves."

Hawton (1990) also considers principles of management:

1. Analyze the precipitating events, such as arguments or rejection. Identify thoughts ("I hate myself," "I am a failure," etc.), emotions (anger, low mood, tension), associated behaviors (seeking isolation and a cutting implement), factors that increase the likelihood of cutting (such as alcohol or isolation), and factors that delay or prevent cutting (such as contacting a friend or exercising). Note where the act of self-mutilation occurs, implement used, extent and number of wounds, emotional state, and presence or absence of pain. Consider the goals of the act (e.g., to reduce tension or manipulate others) the benefits (e.g., tension reduction and a sense of well-being), and the negative consequences (e.g., disgust, guilt, scars, need to conceal cuts).

2. Gain control over cutting. Can precipitating events or aggravating factors (e.g., alcohol) be avoided? Emphasize factors that decrease the likelihood of self-mutilation. Initially focus on controlling the cutting through a change in thinking, ventilation of emotions, relaxation techniques (although they work better later in the treatment), physical exercise, physical contact with another person, and medications.

3. Once the cutting is controlled, examine the underlying problems. Focus on improving the patient's self-esteem and mood disturbances. Cognitive therapy is especially useful. The patient's communication problems may be helped by individual therapy, including role-playing and role reversal, group therapy, and assertiveness training. For this phase of treatment, at least six months may be required.

4. Inpatient treatment should be brief. A written contract with the patient and a clear policy about the treatment approach and restrictions should be known by all ward staff. Excessive restrictions are unhelpful "because the patient will often find a means of cutting in spite of them and they can become a major focus of dispute." If cutting occurs, it should be tended to with minimal fuss. If the cutting behavior spreads to other patients, discuss this at a ward community meeting; sometimes a patient (or two) central to the epidemic may need to be transferred to another unit.

Self-mutilating patients on inpatient units have most of their contacts with nursing staff. Pawlicki and Gaumer (1993) discuss nursing interventions. The nurse coordinator should collaborate with the patient in developing a plan of care, and the patient should be assigned a different "shift associate" for each work shift. Nursing staff should help patients to use self-soothing techniques "such as listening to a relaxation tape, taking a warm bath, holding a teddy bear." Staff can also teach anger management skills such as writing in a journal, exercising, asking for medication, talking, using a safe place on the ward, or asking to be put in restraints. Patients should collaborate with nursing staff in identifying high-risk times for self-mutilation, early warning signs, and precipitating events. A plan is then developed, written down, and posted by patients in their rooms. The plan lists methods for helping patients to feel in control and to avoid self-harm and includes increasing involvement with others, physical activity such as vigorous walking, self-soothing activities, and the processing of feelings by talking or by writing in a journal. *Short-term* contracts should be developed (e.g., the patient agrees not to self-mutilate while taking a shower)."Longer term contracts are usually unrealistic for the patient and reflect wishful thinking by the staff." Patients should be taught how to care for their own wounds. Nursing staff should also constantly monitor patients' suicide potential. Providing "an atmosphere for appropriate ventilation of staff feelings is essential because it allows for validation and explanation of nurse-patient dynamics."

Marsha Linehan (1987) is developing a treatment known as dialectical behavioral therapy (DBT) that appears to be very successful. It focuses on all forms of self-harm (self-mutilation as well as suicide attempts) and views these acts as faulty problem-solving behaviors in persons with low distress tolerance, inadequate coping skills, and expectancies of self-harm. The treatment involves individual and group treatment; the latter is educational and stresses the acquisition of interpersonal effectiveness, emotional regulation, distress tolerance, and self-management abilities. Individual treatment targets the replacement of self-harm behavior with more adaptive solutions by using problem-solving strategies. Also dealt with are behaviors that interfere with therapy (missing sessions, interruptive crises, lying, etc.);"escape" behaviors such as drug abuse and antisocial acts; increasing and integrating into daily life the skills taught in the group; and specific patient goals such as developing intimate relationships, getting off welfare, clarifying career directions, remediating troublesome relationships, and dealing with past traumas. (A person who successfully stopped cutting as a result of participating in a DBT program provided me with her perspective:"It just wasn't worth cutting myself because then I had to spend hour after hour discussing it. All these discussions were like torture. It was easier not to cut. Eventually I learned that I could survive without harming myself.") A DBT manual explains the various strategies used (e.g., problem solving, capability enhancement, relationship, contingency). I believe that we can expect a slow but steady increase in the practice of this therapy.

Psychodynamic Therapy

Individual psychodynamic psychotherapy is probably the most used long-term treatment for moderate/superficial self-mutilation, although the number of therapists trained in this approach is decreasing. Expressive (insight-oriented) therapy is the form most written about. O. H. Kernberg (1987), a psychoanalyst who has written extensively on this subject, sees patients several times a week over many months and even for up to seven years. He stresses interpretation of transference and primitive defensive operations. Using clarification and confrontation, he deals initially with the "here and now"; interpretations dealing with the childhood genesis of the behavior come later in the treatment process. Setting limits helps to control severe acting out, and auxiliary therapists or structured social settings provide environmental support. "The expectation is that self-mutilating behavior will gradually be transformed into more direct, verbally communicated behavior patterns in the transference, and will be resolved by the means of transference interpretation."

To illustrate what may transpire during the course of intensive psychotherapy with habitual self-mutilators and which issues may need to be dealt with and interpreted, several cases will be presented.

The first published psychoanalytic study of a self-mutilator dealt with a 23-year-old woman (Emerson 1933). As a child she was frightened of her father, a cruel man who beat his sons. At age 8 the patient was seen trampling her father's garden by her uncle. He threatened to report her unless she agreed to his sexual advances, and for five years she allowed him to masturbate her. At age 13 her periods began but were irregular, and she thought this to be the cause of severe headaches.

Her headaches persisted. At age 20, while she was suffering a severe headache, a cousin sexually assaulted her. In the scuffle she accidentally cut herself with a knife and noticed that her headache vanished. She said, "After I had let blood my headache went away, and I thought that the cutting of my wrist, and letting the blood flow had cured it" (p. 44). From that time on she cut herself in order to relieve her headaches.

She wanted to have a baby but, because of her shameful childhood experiences, she thought marriage an impossibility. In a moment of agony over this conflict she cut her breast with a razor, thinking that her breasts were useless if she could not have a baby. "My head began to ache. I could not stand it. I thought a moment, then I cut over the left breast as deeply as the razor would go in, and I laughed" (p. 47). She decided to have a child out of wedlock but was unable to become pregnant. Later a suitor wished to marry her. She felt it necessary to reveal her past to him. He rejected her angrily and called her a whore, whereupon she carved the letter *W* on her leg with a razor. Eight months later she gashed her vagina with a knife, feeling that if she would only menstruate she would be all right. She continued to cut herself at various times. "The feeling I always had whether I had a headache or not was: What does it matter? Nobody cares enough to stop you. Of course there were people who did help me" (p. 48).

Emerson interpreted the cutting and its pain as a symbolic substitute for masturbation. When her uncle first masturbated her she experienced pain, and then the pain and sexual stimulation became intimately related. The pain also was a form of self-punishment for her acquiescence in her misdeeds. Her cutting, too, symbolized menstruation and her desire to be like other little girls. Emerson thought that since cutting is a masculine, aggressive act, "her sadistic impulses, probably strongly inherited from her father, got satisfaction while she satisfied her masochistic inclinations, inherited from her mother" (p. 52).

In treatment, "she analyzed her own complexes and thereby gained much self-control. And most important of all, opportunity for sublimation was obtained for the patient and she was given a chance" (p. 53). When the article was written, the patient had not mutilated herself for fourteen months.

Crabtree (1967) provided an account of his successful therapy with a 16-year-old habitual self-mutilator named Jane. Her mother was a cold, logical woman who, according to Crabtree, had "tremendous underlying destructive urges toward Jane." While changing Jane's diaper, for example, she once dropped a stone into Jane's mouth as a pacifier, and the child almost choked to death. She displayed affection only when Jane was ill or terrified because of recurrent nightmares and fears of death. Jane's father, a successful scientist, was dominated by his wife.

At age 13, soon after menarche, Jane became infatuated with a male schoolteacher and began to scratch her arms, neck, and face with pins. She confessed her behavior to him. "At first he seemed very understanding but then became angry and I did it all the more. I don't know why but this scratching had something to do with my feelings about him" (p. 93). Because of this behavior she was hospitalized for over a year. Intensive individual psychotherapy, group therapy, and medications failed to control her mutilation. Her facial scratching gave way to deep cuts on her arms. She broke windows, attacked other patients, eloped from the hospital, took an overdose of aspirin, and swallowed a needle. Her symptoms were worse during menstruation. She was placed in a school for the mentally disturbed for six months. Nothing seemed to help, however, so she was rehospitalized. She began twenty months of psychotherapy.

Crabtree noticed that focusing on feelings and fantasies served to stimulate her and to aggravate her inclination to cut herself. "Jane was no longer cutting herself simply in response to an array of external events. She was now cutting herself in relation to me, a fact both disquieting and exasperating" (p. 95).

Although Jane's unabated self-mutilation gained her close physical contact with staff, Crabtree maintained his distance. He told her that she was responsible for her behavior and for its consequences. He urged her to experiment with alternative solutions, for example, to take warm milk instead of medications. Gradually the therapist encouraged the staff to follow his lead by becoming "more spontaneously and directly expressive of the actual feelings aroused by her — especially angry ones." He insisted that Jane handle her feelings in some other way. She then stopped her cutting, as she realized that while it once forced people to react to her with feeling, it now caused people pain and pushed them away. For Crabtree the turning point in therapy was his communication to Jane of his genuine experience of their relationship and of his feelings of being torn apart by her self-mutilation. As caveats for the treatment of self-mutilators, he warned against an initial introspective approach with a focus on fantasy and feelings because this fostered regression and might lead to increased self-mutilation. He also warned against becoming too nurturant or "maternal" since this might also increase the patient's need for self-punishment.

In a published symposium several psychotherapists discussed their experiences with habitual self-mutilators. Kafka (1969) stressed the need for the therapist to overcome any countertransference and to "experience" the self-mutilating patient as a living person. He believed that self-cutters experienced their skin as something foreign and that the analysis of transference and countertransference contributed to the reformation among patients of a "more bodily-ego-syntonic membrane." Once self-cutters truly experience their skin as an integral part of themselves, then, according to Kafka, their self-mutilation will cease. Pao (1969) regarded patients' self-cutting episodes as indexes of underlying conflicts over abandonment and separation, with a consequent fear of hurting or being hurt by the therapist. Podvoll (1969) focused on the hospital setting where the self-mutilator's behavior engages the ward community in a struggle to resolve a basic conflict over caring versus punishment. He thought that such patients tend to polarize the world around them, and "it becomes of crucial importance to the management of these patients that surrounding splits and conflicts be continually and agonizingly confronted and resolved and that this take place through the effort of the patient and staff community" (p. 216). He noted that patients, after making revelations to the therapist of sexual fantasies, seem to cease their self-mutilative behavior and to become more involved in their treatment. Podvoll asserted, however, that changes in the patients often are preceded by successful exposure and resolution of on-going splits within the ward community. Thus, one of the major tasks of the hospital treatment process is to invade patients' privacy, to make patients aware of their share in a larger part of humanity, and to let them know they are "not so uniquely alone but rather a teeming center of participation." In his comments summarizing the symposium, Burnham (1969) noted the powerful effects that self-mutilators had on hospital staff, and he recalled some chronic cutters and swallowers at a large hospital who became campus celebrities. One patient provoked the staff into performing a prefrontal lobotomy; this procedure ended her self-cutting and "she afterwards busied herself cutting out paper dolls."

Novotny (1972) regarded self-cutting as a manifestation of a phallic conflict in which the cuts symbolized "the wished for and feared penetration by the father." He felt that self-mutilators had a disturbed mother-child relationship during infancy and that the more bizarre the self-mutilation, the greater the degree of ego impairment. Novotny considered self-mutilation to be an act that served to reinforce bodily ego boundaries and to emotionally "blackmail" others into paying attention and expressing concern. He advocated flexible treatment that utilized different approaches, depending upon the most significant factors in the patient's intrapsychic life at the time of the mutilation. In order to discourage emotional blackmail, for example, self-mutilation should be handled matter-of-factly. With some patients, interpretation of dependency needs and wishes may be helpful, while with others interpretations of anger and hostility should be made. With still others, substitute stimulations of the skin may be efficacious.

A more recent report of successful intensive psychotherapy with a habitual self-mutilator was the case of a 23-year-old woman named Gloria (Kwawer 1980). She was seen four times weekly in a residential hospital, and during an eighteen-month period she mutilated herself with broken glass, razor blades, pins, and knives. Previously she had been in psychotherapy with several therapists for five years, and also had had three short-term hospitalizations because of self-mutilation. Her diagnosis was borderline personality disorder.

Several patterns and themes emerged during therapy. Her cutting often occurred when she feared being abandoned, for example, when her therapist was on vacation. She became preoccupied with her blood and even saved it, "allowing it to drip into a small receptacle which was kept hidden in her closet and treasured especially during stressful times when it had a calming effect" (p. 211). She regarded her menstruation as particularly loathsome and disgusting. Her feelings of powerlessness were intense, and she had frequent fantasies of tying strings on her therapist and pulling on them like a puppet. She attempted to "blackmail" the staff and therapist, threatening that her blood would be shed on their behalf. She tried to polarize the staff by sharing "secrets" with certain people and then pledging them to secrecy.

In therapy, despite her protests, self-mutilation was constantly presented to her as a symptom of underlying problems. Great efforts were made to help staff deal with Gloria's attempt to polarize them and to force them into a caring, mothering response. When Gloria complained of night terrors and begged for drugs to dull her senses, she was offered people instead. She was encouraged to use the nursing staff to assist her during difficult times and to use psychotherapy "to continue self-exploration." Boundaries were reinforced to provide her with consistent and predictable reality experiences. "This approach entailed maintaining firm limits in the face of angry demands, which were responded to with an appreciation of their sadistic and controlling intent, while remaining attentive to and curious about the underlying neediness in her behavior" (p. 215). Her conflicts over her relationship with her psychotic mother, her fears of separation and individuation, and her faulty perception of sexuality and of womanhood were explored and resolved. Therapy consisted of factual sex education in addition to exploration of her fantasies about homosexuality, prostitution, and masturbation. As Gloria improved she became more actively involved in the ward community, learned to drive, secured a part-time job, and planned to live outside of the hospital.

Michael Stone (1987) is another psychoanalyst who has done much work with borderline patients. He notes that when self-mutilation is mostly related to traumatic loss, such as a death of a parent, therapy "should consist of partial compensation of the loss through the human relationship with the therapist." This is a long-term process with several sessions weekly and "will diminish the need for symbolic replay of the trauma and fantasied revival of the dead" through self-mutilation. A different situation occurs when the patient has been abused by a sadistic parent or sibling. The capacity for trust is demolished, and supposedly helpful persons (including the therapist) are seen as malicious and dangerous. It may take years for the therapist "to establish his or her basic innocence, let alone helpfulness." The next step is "to enable the patient to believe in the possibility of tenderness" in a love partner. The final task is "helping the patient develop new habits of sexual excitement (ones less chaotic and violent; more able to fit in with the patterns of more ordinary and less harmful partners)."

Nelson and Grunebaum's (1971) follow-up study of ten patients found that improvement was associated with increased verbal capacity to express angry, sad, or anxious feelings. This was accomplished initially through a long-term relationship with an accepting therapist. A case example is that of a highly impulsive woman who was promiscuous, drank alcohol heavily, and slashed her wrists in periods of emotional upheaval. She learned to talk about her feelings with her therapist over a two-year period and stopped her slashing and destructive behavior. Soon after terminating therapy, she married a man who gratified her sexually and who, like her therapist, gave her permission to verbalize her feelings. Improvement also occurred when patients learned to use constructive behavior, for example, by identifying with healthy persons (therapists and others) who behaved in socially acceptable ways. An obsessive patient, for example, identified with "the adaptive, organized, and planned behavior of the therapist" and ceased his mutilative behavior by learning to deal with his angry feelings in a structured way. He established specific times during which he formulated plans to

---

The drawings on the following pages were made by a 21-year-old female patient during six months of intensive psychotherapy. When treatment began, she was cutting or burning her arms, chest, abdomen, and legs several times a week. Previous therapists had diagnosed her as having a variety of mental disorders, including manic-depressive psychosis and borderline personality disorder. In reality, her illness was hysterical in nature and was dominated by unresolved oedipal conflicts. (a) The true histrionic (hysterical) nature of her illness is evident in her colorful and crowded drawings during this period. Depicted in this drawing are her cutting paraphernalia (razor, salt solution, gauze, trash can with Mickey Mouse on it for collecting her blood) and frightening figures, present in her mind since childhood, who urged her to harm herself. (b) After three months, the patient depicted herself as a wooden figure held together by stitches. She is tortured, trapped, and devoured by monsters representing her family members. (c) A week later, she vented her anger graphically by chopping up the monsters while Mickey Mouse laughed at them. (d) Shortly afterward, she portrayed herself as an innocent, sexless child surrounded by confusion. She is trying to see herself as a real person, different from the monsters and hopeful about the future. (e) After six months of therapy, she drew her "mixed-up" family (the Scrabble tiles). She is a pawn and a frightened cat in a game dominated by her parents. She is the Joker, caught between her father, the King of Hearts, and her mother, the Queen of Clubs.

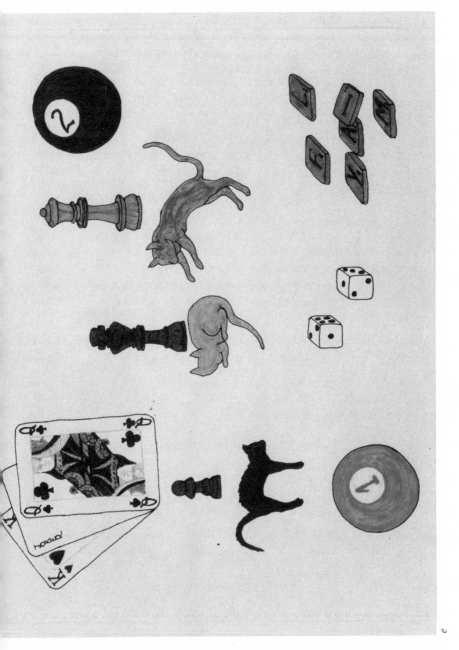

express his anger constructively. The third factor Nelson and Grunebaum associated with improvement was control of psychotic symptoms, such as delusions and hallucinations, through the use of medications and supportive psychotherapy. A significant negative finding was that "insight into the genesis of slashing behavior was not helpful."

Psychodynamically oriented supportive therapy does not emphasize insightful interpretations of transference or of unconscious conflicts. Although not written about very much, it is more widely used than the expressive (insight-oriented) type of therapy. Rockland (1987) notes the supportive techniques used in treating self-mutilators. General support includes maintaining a positive rapport and therapeutic alliance with the patient; providing education, reassurance, an attitude of hopefulness, encouragement, and praise; giving suggestions and advice; clarifying and, when appropriate, confronting; setting limits and prohibitions; emphasizing the patient's strengths and talents; intervening in the patient's environment; encouraging sublimations; using medications and somatic treatments liberally; helping patients develop a more objective view of their life situation. In this approach the therapist is "real" (rather than a neutral blank screen), offers advice while encouraging patients to make their own decisions, and accentuates the positive.

Cognitive Therapy

Cognitive therapy aims to change maladaptive thoughts (cognitions). A good discussion of this approach can be found in *Self-Mutilation* (Walsh and Rosen 1988) where four categories of thoughts that lead to self-mutilation are identified.

1. *Self-mutilation is acceptable.* Thoughts of this nature are always present either consciously or unconsciously and form a value that regulates the self-mutilator's behavior.

2. *One's body and self are disgusting and deserving of punishment.* Thoughts about the repulsiveness of one's body are used to justify self-mutilation. Low self-esteem is present.

3. *Action is needed to reduce unpleasant feelings.* Thoughts that some action must be taken are coupled with thoughts that self-mutilation will provide relief.

4. *Overt action is necessary to communicate feelings to others.* The thought here is that only through self-mutilation will other people comprehend the terrible suffering that a person is experiencing.

Cognitive therapy demonstrates to patients the connection between their
thoughts and their self-mutilative behavior; this can be facilitated by redirecting patients' attention away from environmental conflicts and toward
their own thoughts. According to Walsh and Rosen, the next step is to challenge these thoughts: "The eventual elimination of the acts of self-harm
rests on the perception that self-mutilation is unacceptable, since it represents disrespect for oneself" (p. 160). Patients are instructed to replace
thoughts that lower self-esteem with thoughts about their positive qualities. Intense feelings may be dissipated by labeling them, by thinking of the
necessity to maintain self-control, and by then pushing the feelings out of
conscious thought. "In effect, the feelings are turned on or off by switching
thoughts on or off" (p. 162). Patients are then taught to speak about rather
than use actions to communicate their feelings and to think about the ad-
vantages of a lifestyle without mutilation (e.g., "I really want to be stable. I
want to have relationships that don't revolve around hurting myself. I will
like myself and my life much better once I stop mutilating" [p. 164]).

One type of symptomatic and pragmatic measure that is useful in the
hands of a skilled therapist has been described by Taylor (1969). Conducted within the context of a positive relationship that includes concern
and caring for a suffering patient, the measure consists of a challenging interpretation of self-mutilative symptoms, "given with the express intention
of arousing such an emotional response as will counteract the symptom.
This can be achieved by an interpretation that attaches unacceptable ideas
and emotions to the target symptom" (p. 410). Sexual challenging interpretations are especially effective (e.g., "I am afraid that your skin cutting
is a perverted form of masturbation"). When the patient angrily attacks
the interpretation as untrue, the therapist does not argue but rather comments, "The interpretation must be valid because otherwise you would not
be so angry about it." Another challenging measure is the admission of
therapeutic failure to patients who are pessimistic about their inability to
improve: "I am afraid you have not responded to any of my treatment."
Such a statement sometimes changes the patient into an optimist who will
then present evidence of improvement in order to console the therapist. A
more provocative challenge is the announcement that therapy may have to
end since it has not been successful. When a strong, positive relationship
is present, the fear of ending therapy may mobilize a patient to resist self-
mutilative urges. It must be emphasized that challenging statements are
palliative, that is, they are meant to reduce a target symptom and not to
get at underlying conflicts (although they sometimes do so). They should

be used sparingly and should be *avoided* with severely depressed patients who may be sent into even deeper despair. When successful, challenging measures will temporarily halt self-mutilative behavior and will encourage patients to proceed with psychotherapy.

Behavioral Therapy

The literature on behavioral therapy for self-mutilation is large and complicated. Most articles deal with mentally retarded patients and view self-mutilation as a learned behavior maintained by positive social reinforcement. Therapy, therefore, focuses on the removal of positive reinforcement by such techniques as withholding attention following an act of self-mutilation, isolating the person to exclude any form of reinforcement ("time out"), or "shaping" the self-injurious behavior into a benign act. In cases where negative reinforcement appears to maintain the behavior, approaches such as counterconditioning and desensitization have been utilized. An adolescent girl, for example, banged her head against the bed when she was awakened by nightmares. Successful therapy consisted of desensitizing her to her nightmares (Ross, Meichenbaum, and Humphrey 1971). Readers interested in behavioral approaches to self-mutilation are referred to the following representative articles: shaping (Schaefer 1970), positive reinforcement (Ragain and Anson 1976), reinforcement of other behaviors (Repp and Deitz 1974), counterconditioning (Ernst 1973), punishment and aversive conditioning (Myers and Deibert 1971; Ball et al. 1975), and comparisons of behavioral approaches (Corte, Wolff, and Locke 1971; Lucero et al. 1976).

The use of multiple behavioral approaches is well described in an article about a 20-year-old schizophrenic man with a sixteen-month history of severe eye poking and a six-month history of lip and tongue biting (Cautela and Baron 1973). He had received inpatient psychiatric treatment, electroshock, multiple medications, and psychotherapy with no improvement. At one point his eyes were sewn shut to prevent further damage, and he was kept in restraints almost constantly. By the time he entered into a behavioral treatment program he was completely blind, and his mouth opening was reduced in size because of the buildup of scar tissue from constant biting.

In the first phase of treatment both the patient and the hospital staff were told that his self-mutilative behavior was a learned habit that he needed to unlearn. Since this behavior was preceded by restlessness and by an urgent thought or feeling that he must mutilate himself, the patient was taught how to relax whenever he felt tense or had an urge to mutilate. He also was instructed in "thought-stopping," that is, he consciously forced himself to resist the thought of self-mutilation. He was instructed also to imagine a sequence of events leading to lip biting; when he clearly imagined having an "urge" to bite, he then imagined feeling sick to his stomach. Covert reinforcement was used to promote periods of feeling calm and relaxed. The patient made a therapeutic contract to practice these techniques. If he did them as assigned and did not injure himself for two months, then he would be evaluated for surgical repair of his lips. Since the patient was afraid of social contacts with new people, systematic desensitization was used to eliminate this fear. Ward staff learned techniques for dealing with his disruptive behavior. For example, when he yelled for help to keep from biting, he was quietly escorted to his room and encouraged to use self-control techniques. This phase of treatment lasted two and a half months, during which both threatened and actual self-mutilative behavior continued at a high rate.

The second phase of treatment, lasting five months, emphasized more practice in self-control techniques, especially in regard to "convulsive-like" behaviors that preceded and accompanied his self-mutilation. The patient underwent behavioral rehearsals to handle social problems better and reinforcement sampling to strengthen behaviors incompatible with self-mutilation. Staff paid extra attention to him when his behavior was appropriate and when he carried out his ward jobs. In this phase no new injuries to his eyes or mouth occurred, the number of convulsivelike episodes decreased, and the patient experienced only occasional "urges" to harm himself.

During phase three, lasting three months, all destructive or disruptive behavior ceased. Treatment consisted of elimination of maladaptive thoughts, continued reinforcement sampling, and corrective plastic surgery. The patient was discharged from the hospital, completed a vocational rehabilitation program, entered college, and married. He seemed happy and enthusiastic about the future and no longer mutilated himself during a two-and-a-half-year follow-up period.

Romanczyk and Goren (1975) reported their attempts to treat a 6-year-old mentally retarded, autistic child. In various social contexts and in response to any stimulus, the child would scratch himself, slap his face, or bang his head at a rate of 5,400 times an hour. The major treatment approach was punishment with an apparatus that delivered an electric shock. However, other techniques such as time out, shaping, and reinforcement were needed to modify the child's problematic screaming, fear of loud noises, and inability to feed himself. While his self-mutilative behaviors were suppressed briefly in the controlled hospital environment, they could not be controlled in any other setting. After more than one thousand therapy hours over a ten-month period, the child was placed permanently in an institution. He had improved somewhat, however, and at last count indulged in self-injurious behavior "only" five to fifteen times per hour.

Strikingly absent from the behavioral literature, with the exception of DBT, are reports on attempts to modify the habitual self-mutilative acts, such as skin cutting and burning, of persons demonstrating the repetitive self-mutilation syndrome. These patients are aware of mounting levels of tension and have learned that an act of self-mutilation will provide instantaneous relief. It may be possible to change the usual sequence of events in these patients by behavioral techniques. One could, for example, provide the patient with a painful stimulus such as an electric jolt at the moment of cutting in the hope of associating the act of self-mutilation with a negative consequence instead of a pleasant one. Possibly a more efficacious technique would be to utilize thought-stopping; for example, the patient who experiences intrusive thoughts and feelings as a prelude to self-mutilation would be encouraged to delay the cutting by saying "Stop!" and by visualizing a large stop sign. In addition, covert sensitization could be tried. A patient might be instructed to think of the pleasant feelings that come immediately after cutting. One would then encourage negative imagery, for example, that people were watching and were laughing at the patient, or that queasy feelings existed in his or her stomach. One could even ask a patient to visualize the cutting but, just as the imaginary cut was being made, suggest that the patient visualize the cut being made on a beloved pet or on another person. To my knowledge, there are no reports in the literature of systematic attempts to utilize these behavioral techniques in habitual self-cutters. It may be that the complex symbolism and multiple intrapsychic conflicts encountered in such patients vitiates the efficacy of behavioral approaches.

As with any therapeutic endeavor, the best results are obtained with highly motivated patients. Many habitual self-cutters are motivated to get "well" but are reluctant to give up their self-cutting totally. This is not an unexpected finding when one considers the complex symbolism surrounding blood and the relationship of self-mutilation to ancient notions of healing, religion, and the creation of order from chaos.

In the management of cutters and burners, behavioral techniques are often used in combination with other types of therapy. Sometimes the behavioral components are acknowledged, as in DBT, and sometimes they are not. When nursing staff treat self-inflicted wounds in a matter-of-fact manner and teach self-mutilators to care for their own wounds, the effect is to minimize positive reinforcement. The psychoanalyst who calmly tells a patient,"It is unfortunate that you have harmed yourself. Perhaps you should have the wound tended to," is also minimizing positive reinforcement.

Self-mutilators may gain reinforcement when their acts of self-harm successfully stop unwanted situations from continuing (e.g., arguments or the threatened termination of a relationship). Walsh and Rosen (1988) discuss several behavioral methods to alter these situations. Desensitization entails learning to cope with unpleasant feelings in incremental steps. As an example,"if a mutilator finds criticism extremely aversive and immediately attempts to avoid or escape from the situation, the desensitization progresses by having the client tolerate slightly more of the stimulus before he or she escapes or avoids it. The client is always in control and can regulate his or her degree of exposure to the aversive experience" (p. 170). Helping patients to listen a little longer each time they are criticized may produce a delay between the criticism and the onset of self-mutilation. The goal is to produce longer and longer delays until the patient is able finally to respond to real or perceived hurt by listening. The next step is to help the self-mutilator develop new social skills to replace the self-mutilation:"Mutilators need to feel powerful and competent in the face of aversive experiences without having to resort to self-mutilation as a weapon" (p. 172). The therapist can facilitate the process by praising and approving each success of a patient, such as ever-lengthening delays before cutting or superficial cuts as opposed to previous deep ones. Another tactic is to work with the patient and family members to develop behavioral contracts (e.g.,"If I do not cut, burn, or hurt myself in any way, I will receive $5 a day over the next two weeks"). Rewards other than money, such as favorite foods or going to a movie, may be used. Contracts should be time limited and constantly renegotiated.

Administrative Therapy

Several studies report a reduction in self-mutilation following changes in institutional policies. Offer and Barglow (1960) reported eighty-one incidents of self-mutilation among twelve patients, ages 14 to 22, in a general psychiatric hospital. These incidents were ushered in by a three-day "epidemic" of self-mutilation. The initial response of hospital personnel was fragmented and diffuse, with widespread confusion, guilt, heated arguments, and breakdowns in communication, resulting in an untherapeutic environment. Hospital policy had been to withhold extra attention from self-mutilators, but this policy was challenged one evening by a resident physician who convinced the hospital administrator to allow the transfer of such patients to a more controlled unit. Anger and criticism of this change in policy ensued. A special hospital committee was established to study the problem. Staff, therapists, and patients were interviewed to learn their impressions about the causes of the increased self-mutilation. A wide variety of responses were elicited, for example, "When you hurt yourself, people really care"; "More discipline is needed"; "The personnel must realize that self-mutilation is part of the patient's illness."

Five recommendations were made and established as hospital policy. The first was that every unit should establish its own policy for dealing with self-mutilators. The second was that adolescent patients should be "screened" for acting-out tendencies, and those at high risk for self-mutilation should not be admitted to the hospital. Third, more occupational therapy should be made available to young patients during evenings and weekends along with an additional group worker. Fourth, a "young adult group" was formed to meet weekly with the staff to plan group events. Fifth, patients who continued to self-mutilate despite attempts to control this behavior were to be transferred to another hospital. The number of self-mutilative episodes was reduced to their "usual" prevalence after these policies were put into practice.

One of the most successful administrative changes reported was that on an adolescent psychiatric unit (Crabtree and Grossman 1974). This locked unit had a high incidence of self-mutilation, patient elopement from the hospital, and other disruptive behaviors. Crabtree and Grossman associated the locked doors with "the breeding of institutional mistrust, the development of staff mistrust and rigidity, and the promotion of regressive behaviors" (p. 350), although they provided some measure of containment, safety, and security in dealing with acutely psychotic, suicidal, and impulsive patients. After numerous preparatory meetings among staff and patients, the unit's doors were unlocked. The results were astounding. In the first month there was a 94 percent decrease in self-mutilation, as well as a 73 percent decrease in elopements and a 69 percent decrease in disruptive incidents. Over the course of a year the decrease in self-mutilative episodes was 67 percent. Additionally, these episodes were fairly well separated and there were far fewer "epidemics" of self-mutilation. For the majority of patients and staff, the open setting was accompanied by an increased sense of security and safety.

Perhaps the most detailed report dealing with administrative therapy is a "carving study" at a Canadian correctional facility for girls. Eighty-six percent of the 136 girls in the institution had carved their bodies. The administration, unable to cope with the situation with traditional remedies such as solitary confinement, medications, lectures, threats, counseling, and increased recreational activities, brought in Ross and McKay (1979). Ross and McKay tried intensive psychotherapy but noted that this approach increased carving among the girls tenfold. Then they tried various behavior modification programs. In a token economy program, the girls earned poker chips for good behavior and could purchase goods and privileges with the chips. In addition, staff refrained from responding to the carving with counseling, reprimands, or discussions. Instead, they imposed the programmatically determined consequences in a matter-of-fact way. This approach failed, so a new factor was added: "Girls in the token economy were provided with specific training in reinforcement therapy principles and encouraged to utilize these principles in attempting to modify the behavior of their peers" (p. 130). This new program reduced the total number of carving incidents somewhat but certainly did not solve the problem. Sixty-six percent of the girls in the program still carved themselves.

What finally worked was a strategy of co-opting based on an understanding of the carving by the girls as "the epitome of personal freedom by which they could reassure themselves that they had some mastery over their fate" (p. 135). Co-opting involved persuading the girls that their carving played into the hands of institutional personnel whose control they opposed; for example, the carving made life exciting and interesting for the staff. Ross and McKay successfully convinced the girls "that they could better proclaim their autonomy by refusing to carve." The girls were converted from research subjects to research assistants; the most influential girls became paraprofessional therapists and, finally, program directors for a cadre of girls. Immediately after girls were proclaimed "therapists," their adjustment to the institution improved markedly. The use of this approach on one troubled and troublesome girl is instructive. Her pathology was relabeled by referring to "her manipulativeness as social skill, her unreliability as flexibility, her domineering as leadership, her histrionics as creativity, her callousness as pragmatism, her suspiciousness as insight" (p. 143). Once she became a "therapist," she manipulated her friends into working for her and selected several as assistants. She trained them in simple behavioral techniques for use not only with girls whose behavior caused withdrawal of privileges for the group but also with staff whose behavior was thought to be in need of modification. Throughout the co-opting program not one incident of carving occurred among the girls who acted as therapists.

After five months, however, the co-opting program was stopped. Ross and McKay attributed this to disgruntled staff and noted that "perhaps acceptance of our recommendations meant rejecting traditional roles, accepting reduced authority and responsibility, and living with lessened status. Implied by our comments was the conclusion that clinicians were not needed" (p. 154). The old programs of individual and group psychotherapy and behavior modification were reinstituted along with some new programs. According to Ross and McKay, however, "there also followed a resurgence of carving. We should have co-opted our colleagues."

Personal Reflections on Treatment

In treating stereotypic self-mutilation, behavioral programs form the core of therapy, but I have used adjunctive medication with some success. I usually end up practicing polypharmacy because single medications rarely prove effective. The medications I use most commonly are a major tranquilizer such as thioridazine (Mellaril) or fluephenazine (Prolixin), followed by an antiepileptic mood stabilizer such as carbamazapine (Tegretol) or valproate, followed by an SSRI such as fluoxetine (Prozac), sertraline (Zoloft), or Paxil (paroxetine). If there is no response to one medication, I stop it and try another. If there is a partial response, I keep using it and add a second medication. If the response improves, then I may add a third medication. The more medications that are used, the more difficult it is to know exactly what the effect is of each drug. Polypharmacy also presents problems with decisions about which drug to decrease eventually. The goal should always be to use the lowest effective dose of a medication for the shortest period of time. Some types of stereotypic self-mutilation seem unrelenting and will require year after year of drug use. Especially when dealing with patients whose IQs permit effective communication, it is often possible to adjust medication doses down over time.

Most acts of major self-mutilation occur during psychotic episodes of schizophrenia, manic-depressive illness, and depression. I treat the psychosis aggressively with major tranquilizers, deal with correcting the mania or depression, and place the patient on one-to-one nursing (to prevent further acts of major self-harm) until I am convinced that the underlying illness is under control. Patients are at risk for a second act of major self-mutilation as long as the psychosis, mania, or serious depression is operative. Physical restraints may be necessary until chemical restraints take effect. Surgical consultation should be gotten rapidly if there is any chance to reattach organs. The best prognosis occurs when patients deeply regret their action.

Undoubtedly the most troublesome of all self-mutilating patients are those who have spent most of their life in various mental institutions. These are career patients whose psychiatric problems often started in childhood. Despite efforts to move them to less restrictive environments, they always seem to end up back in secure mental hospitals. A patient that I remember well was a husky woman whose body was a mass of scars from self-cutting and burning. A victim of childhood abuse, she frequently directed her aggression outward as well as inward and had beaten staff and broken their arms. Although she was never psychotic, her behavior often resulted in her receiving large doses of tranquilizing medication as well as being placed in restraints. I recommended that legal charges be filed against her when she savagely attacked a nursing aide. My hope was that she would be placed in a prison where some "tough" prisoners would deal with her harshly when she became violent. Indeed, she was sent to prison, but her self-mutilation escalated to such a degree that she was transferred back to the maximum security state mental hospital. She was wise to the ways of institutional life and resisted all attempts to allow her to live outside of the hospital. Another patient I was asked about was a penis cutter. After years of institutional life he did not harm himself any more while in the hospital and seemed to enjoy living in a community group home. However, after a few weeks he invariably started cutting his penis and would be transferred back to the hospital. This scenario was repeated time and time again. He steadfastly said that he would not castrate himself, but no group home could tolerate his cutting. A case in which I had some success was that of a long-term prisoner who swallowed light bulbs, nails, bottle tops, and whatever else he could get his hands on. He had had over twenty surgical procedures to remove the objects. Upon talking with him I discovered that when he no longer could stomach prison life he swallowed things so he could go to a hospital "for a vacation." My solution was a practical one to which he agreed: whenever he felt a need to get away from the prison (usually once or twice a year), he was to alert the warden, who would then arrange his transfer to a state hospital for a week or two of "rest and relaxation." This certainly was less expensive and less traumatic than undergoing surgery.

The most vexing patients to treat effectively are repetitive cutters and burners. If they are actively harming themselves several times a week, they may require hospitalization. Before the advent of SSRIs, I utilized a month-long, addiction-model hospital stay with intensive nursing care. Visitors were kept to a minimum because they sometimes brought razor blades onto the unit (it is very easy to tape one under a chair seat). Nowadays I prefer a brief (seven- to ten-day) hospital stay during which an SSRI is prescribed. It often takes high doses (e.g., 80 to 120 milligrams of Prozac) to quell the impulses for self-harm. Sleeping pills may be used the first few nights.

Patients must be instructed to inform ward staff whenever they feel the urge to cut. They may experience "withdrawal" symptoms such as restlessness, irritability, and sweating that may require a lot of reassurance, nursing attention, and even a day or two of minor tranquilizers. As an external aid, bulky gloves may be tied or taped on patients' hands during periods of extreme tension to interfere with skin gouging and attempts to mutilate with can tops, eating utensils, and other items. I have found it useful for patients to have portable radios or cassette players with plugs for each ear. Listening to loud music sometimes alleviates dissociative experiences (SSRIs help with dissociation also).

Once the acute crisis has passed, the arduous work of outpatient therapy must begin. Intensive DBT seems like an excellent approach. Unfortunately, very few persons have been trained in this approach, and it will be many years before it becomes generally available (assuming that it produces good results).

Since the course of treatment is apt to last several years, I am convinced that no therapist can do the job alone, especially since the patient's symptoms may switch to substance abuse or an eating disorder. I can stay the course with a patient provided that I do not have to deal with day-to-day crises and roller-coaster rides of emotions. I see myself as a constant figure in the patient's therapy, the person who provides overall direction and who is always available in a special way. I help patients to find therapists willing to work with them; patients usually go through several therapists in the course of treatment. I may prescribe medications and meet with a patient once a month (or at even longer intervals) for hourlong sessions. Obviously, I do more than simply prescribe drugs. I hold out hope for recovery, am always supportive, help patients develop a vision of what they might achieve in the future, and ask patients to help me understand their illness. If they harm themselves, I freely express displeasure (but never rejection). I encourage them to work with their therapist but may intervene if I perceive therapy to be going sour. I urged a patient to change her therapist, for example, when I discovered that the therapist was trying to convince her that she had MPD and was trying to "bring out" the supposedly submerged other personalities. (There are rare patients with the disorder, but not in this case.) On another occasion a therapist, totally exasperated, wanted the patient to consult a faith healer in order to exorcise "demons" that oppressed her. Much trickier was the time when the therapist jumped on the child abuse bandwagon and tried to convince a patient that she "must" have been sexually abused, despite a total lack of evidence, because "all self-mutilators have been abused." That statement is false. Perhaps 60 percent have been abused, but it was certainly not the case with the patient in question. Had I not intervened, the patient would have unnecessarily alienated her parents, with whom she had a good relationship and who provided her with a great deal of support.

I usually try to refer patients for vocational rehabilitation. Getting off the disability roll and holding a job are extremely important. If a patient develops a substance abuse problem or an eating disorder, I work with the therapist in finding appropriate treatment. I encourage socialization with as many "normal" persons as possible. Living in a group home with other troubled persons can be a disaster or a blessing, depending upon who lives there.

I always discuss scars with patients. A favorable prognostic sign is a patient's desire to have plastic surgery on scars. They rarely do have surgery; it is enough that they desire it. It often indicates that the self-mutilative process is winding down.

I do not respond to crises personally but rather try to ensure that the patient is cared for. By maintaining some "distance," I find that I actually can get closer to a patient. Patients may disappoint their therapists, but not me. Similarly, patients may feel rejected by their therapists, but rarely by me. Regarding medication, I have not been impressed with the ability of SSRIs to maintain their effect over a long period of time. Once a patient's active cutting is under control so that it occurs only sporadically, I may switch to carbamazepine and/or valproate. One of the dangers of these medications is their lethality in case of overdose. Repetitive self-mutilators often become demoralized over the slow progress and frequent setbacks that they suffer during treatment; this places them at high risk of a suicide attempt. If they become clinically depressed or if their self-harm behavior escalates, I then return to high doses of an SSRI. The SSRIs appear to be more effective, at least with self-mutilators, when used intermittently.

Final Words

In the mid-1980s, when I was preparing the first edition of *Bodies under Siege*, there were few colleagues with whom I could share ideas. Mansell Pattison, the dynamic chair of the Department of Psychiatry at the Medical College of Georgia, was such a person. The way in which our thoughts and interests coincided was almost eerie. His untimely death in a senseless automobile accident was a great loss to me, but it made me determined to carry on. Karen Conterio, a therapist in Chicago, who had the grit and foresight to establish the first inpatient program for self-mutilators (at Hartgrove Hospital), was another source of inspiration. She has done a tremendous job in revealing the plight of self-mutilators to the general public. We have collaborated on several papers and have maintained an easy friendship.

There are now a number of psychiatrists and psychologists who are knowledgeable about self-mutilation and who are conducting important research both in the United States and in Europe. Interest is especially high in the biological processes involved in self-mutilative behavior, in prison populations who are at high risk for deliberate self-harm, and in the development of effective treatment strategies. The media, particularly magazines that cater to women, are awakening to the large numbers of people whose lives are troubled by self-mutilation.

Through it all, I have been kept amazed constantly by self-mutilating patients who have reciprocated my interest in them by pouring out their hearts to me. Whatever understanding I possess has come directly from self-mutilators themselves, not from any preconceived theories about behavior. They have been willing teachers, with a marvelous capacity to jolt me out of complacency.

Just as I was about to throw away my psychoanalytic texts, along came a patient reared in the cornfields of Iowa who would have been at home in turn-of-the-century Vienna. Janet was a severe repetitive cutter and burner caught up in a clear-cut oedipal drama. Her father was a man with characterological as well as depressive problems. He and Janet had formed a strong alliance against the rest of the family. The special attention he devoted to her during childhood continued to the present; for example, during a hospital visit he carved their initials in a wooden bench and kissed her. He convinced her that they had special magical powers and that their lives were mysteriously entwined. Her greatest fantasy was to run off with her father, care for him, and protect him against the cruel world.

The sexualized aspect of her love for father, however, created enormous conflicts for Janet that were central to her self-mutilation. She cut herself as a punishment for her incestuous guilt and for her hateful feelings toward her mother and sister. The hatred she had for the female aspects of her body resulted from the recognition that had she been a boy, she would not have to endure so many tribulations. In fact, she regarded her vagina as a "disgusting wound" and believed that she really possessed a penis; supposedly, it was once external but was pushed inside of her when she had an accident while riding her brother's bicycle. During a session in which we were trying to understand why she seemed to enjoy rubbing the scar tissue of her cuts, she blushed and said, "It's because it is hard and gets red like a penis." She detested her menstrual periods, and sometimes she cut herself in the hope of diverting blood away from her vagina. To my surprise, she exclaimed that the cuts on her skin were like little vaginas and that she liked to have her cuts sewn closed just as she would like to have her vagina sewn closed. She felt particularly "proud" of her stitches and lavished great care over them. Her tender descriptions of how she kept the wound area clean, used powder, and applied fresh bandages sounded very much like the words of a mother changing a baby's diaper. If my interpretation is correct, then the cuts, representing a vagina, were "impregnated" by the sutures, representing her father's sperm, resulting in scar tissue, which represented a baby. Thus, her cuts had multiple symbolic meanings related to sexuality.

Just as I renewed my interest in psychodynamics, along came a patient whose impulsive behaviors were so prodigious that no professional caregiver could deal with her for more than a month at a time. She was a human cutting machine. When a therapist told her to go for long drives in her car to avoid cutting, she gladly complied stating, "Great! Now I can use the cigarette lighter to burn myself in the peace and quiet of my car!" She also devoured entire boxes of doughnuts as well as Ex-Lax in quantities so gigantic as to defy belief. Discontent with laxatives, she developed a novel scheme to lose weight—eating tapeworms gathered from repugnant sources. She also drank vodka instead of water and took 1,000 milligrams of Benadryl (an antihistamine whose usual dose is 25 milligrams) to help her sleep. To top it off, she was arrested several times for shoplifting items she did not need. Psychology be damned, nothing short of a straitjacket could stop her impulsive actions. Then along came Prozac. A lot of it, and even more. The result: all the impulsive behaviors ceased. Just like that.

Just as my interest in the biology of self-harm blossomed, along came the "modern primitives," with their passion for piercing, branding, tattoos, and body modification. A lot of it was for fun, for rebelliousness, for a sexual turn-on, but some of it was serious enough. In large cities, especially San Francisco, a support system has developed for persons with urges to put holes in their bodies. It is difficult not to be impressed by Fakir Musafar, the philosopher of modern primitives who has experimented with ritual behaviors ranging from hanging by flesh hooks inserted into his chest muscles (the Native American O-Kee-Pa ceremony) to corseting (Ibitoe waist training). According to him, "to not have encumberments, to not have holes in your body, to not have tattoos may be debilitating—this is something people have to consider. They may not be getting the most out of life because they don't do these things—that's the point. People may be missing beautiful, rich experiences because of cultural bias and conceit" (Vale and Juno 1989, p. 15).

Self-mutilation is a complicated act the meanings of which cannot be inferred by simple observation of the behavior itself. The presence of sanctioned self-mutilative practices across latitudes, longitudes, and centuries reflects the dynamic process of social life. With each marriage, birth, and death, with each change of season, with the ascendancy of each pathogen, with each covetous glance, are sown the seeds of social disruption. Mutilative rituals acknowledge disruptions within the social body and provide a mechanism for the reestablishment of harmony and equilibrium. Through the spilling of blood and the removal of limbs, the garden of relationships among humans, god, and nature is watered, pruned, and cultivated. Through the myths and personal dramas of dismemberment and reassembly, of wounding and healing, are played out the eternal struggles between men and women, parents and children, friends and enemies, humankind and the environment, the world of the flesh and the world of the spirit.

The individual human body mirrors the collective social body, and each continually creates and sustains the other. Misperceptions of reality, feelings of guilt, negative self-images, antisocial acts, and all the other symptoms we associate with personal mental illness defy understanding without reference to the psychological, social, cultural, and physical integrity of the communal "body."

So I have come full circle. Self-mutilation cannot be understood and dealt with without recourse to psychology, biology, and culture. When dealing with patients, I recognize self-mutilation not only as a pathological behavior but also as an expression of a struggle to reenter a "normal" life. A cut in the skin may let out "bad blood" but also provides an opening to the interior. Everyday life is primarily a surface phenomenon, but the examined life—getting to the heart of things—involves the painful process of dissection. For most of us, dissection is a metaphor for intellectual examination, but for others it is a physical act. Intellectually can we not at least entertain the notion that extirpation of a "bad seed" might be accomplished as well by cutting its roots as by poisoning it with drugs or chanting psychomantras and interpretive insights? It is easy to forget that dripping blood may accompany birth as well as death. The scars of the process are more than the artless artifacts of a twisted mind. They signify an ongoing battle and that all is not lost. As befits one of nature's greatest triumphs, scar tissue is a magical substance, a physiological and psychological mortar that holds flesh and spirit together when a difficult world threatens to tear both apart. Self-mutilators seek what we all seek: an ordered life, spiritual peace—and maybe even salvation—and a healthy mind in a healthy body. Their desperate methods are upsetting to those of us who try to achieve these goals in a more tranquil manner, but the methods rest firmly on the dimly perceived bedrock of the human experience.

EPILOGUE

Body Play: State of Grace or Sickness?

Fakir Musafar

▬ ▬ ▬ ▬ ▬ ▬ ▬ ▬

As Dr. Armando Favazza suggests in this book, the phenomenon of "self-mutilation" is "not purely a biological, or psychological, or socially determined act but rather involves a combination of these factors as they operate within the web of culture." If we can take a broad, multicultural view of this "whole web," the phenomenon may very well snap into focus. But to truly understand may also require an adjustment in our mindset — perhaps a calculated and deliberate attempt to rise above the cultural biases by which we have been observing and describing this behavior.

In my personal experimentation and work with self-mutilators over the past fifty years, I have been brought very close to the subject. So close, in fact, that I have sometimes been called the "father of the modern primitive movement." I was bitten by the urge to modify my own body at a very early age; I found nondestructive ways to satisfy that urge and practiced them in secret for thirty years. Unfortunately, I was driven into deep isolation and shame, as are so many others, for lack of any social sanction. I was a bright boy. I knew that if I let it be known what I felt and what I was doing, I would probably have been institutionalized.

For years I haunted libraries, searched archives, and listened to tales of Native American elders in South Dakota, where I grew up. I was looking for any trace of sanction for what I felt and practiced in secret. In other cultures I did find acceptance, reasons, and traditions honoring this urge to "self-mutilate." In fact, the mental and emotional states associated with the act (ecstasy, trance, disconnection, and disassociation) were frequently considered "states of grace" instead of sickness.

I ended my isolation when a wise and understanding mentor encouraged me to "go public" with what I had been doing in secret. He arranged a showing at the only place where I might find a receptive audience — the first International Tattoo Convention, held in Reno, Nevada, in 1978. There I did it all: body piercings, contortions, display of my blackwork body tattoos, disconnection from body sensation while on beds of sharp blades and spikes. The highly tattooed and pierced audience ate it up. They understood and honored in me what had also moved them to mark and pierce their own bodies. We made our own new culture of social sanctions. After this warm welcome, I openly searched for others who viewed "life in a body" very differently from most around them. I found them by the hundreds, and eventually thousands. We had all heard the sound of a "different drummer" and responded to the beat. But the beat we heard was *not* the beat of Western Judeo-Christian culture.

Whether we were Native Americans returning to traditional ways or urban aboriginals responding to some inner universal archetype, one thing was clear: we had all rejected the Western cultural biases about ownership and use of the body. We believed that our body belonged to us. We had rejected the strong Judeo-Christian body programming and emotional conditioning to which we had all been subjected. Our bodies did *not* belong to some distant god sitting on a throne; or to that god's priest or spokesperson; or to a father, mother, or spouse; or to the state or its monarch, ruler, or dictator; or to social institutions of the military, educational, correctional, or medical establishment. And the kind of language used to describe our behavior ("self-mutilation"), was in itself a negative and prejudicial form of control.

At first, these newer views about the body and what it could be used for were expressed or practiced only in the budding subcultures of the 1960s and 1970s — in hippie, punk, radical sex, gay, sadomasochistic, tattooing, and body-piercing circles. My own connections with the subcultures began as far back as 1955, when I started to do body piercing and other body rites with individuals and various cultural subgroups. I needed a meaningful name to call our now socialized (versus isolated) practices. To me it had always been "play," so I coined the term *body play*.

In the 1970s, an eccentric millionaire in Los Angeles brought a number of "body players" together. We used to meet monthly in the back of Los Angeles restaurants for what we then called "T&P (tattoo and piercing) Parties." The numbers were small, never more than ten to fourteen persons (which was all we could gather in those days). We shared experiences, did "show and tell," and arranged to help each other with our next body modifications. At one meeting, in 1975, I recall that we tried to list everyone we knew of in the subcultures of Western society who had pierced nipples. There were only seven people — all males except for one woman who had been pierced in 1965. None of us in that group could conceive that some of us would, within a few years, pierce hundreds of nipples. And many in that group of hundreds would also pierce hundreds of nipples. So by the late 1980s the sight of pierced nipples, thousands of them, was commonplace at all large subculture gatherings.

Our Los Angeles T&P group was a major core of what eventually became the modern body-piercing movement, with body-piercing studios that were located in most large American and European cities and that offered an ever-expanding range of piercings from eyebrows, tongues, labrets, and nose bridges to several dozen sexual enhancement piercings for both male and female genitals. By the early 1990s, the practice of body piercing was rapidly seeping out of the subcultures and into the mainstream. I heard business executives on commuter trains, for example, in serious debate about whether they should allow their teenage daughters to have a navel piercing. There were thousands of others, all ages, who didn't get anybody's permission; they felt the urge and just did it.

By the late 1980s, other forms of body modification and socialized body ritual were also emerging from the shadows of American subculture: cutting and scarification, branding and body sculpting, for example. And I now know that I was responsible for encouraging some of it. In a quiet way in 1983, I had proposed production of a book on body modification and body rites to ReSearch Publications of San Francisco. They began the project by taping twenty-seven hours of interviews with me. Along with this edited text, I provided about seventy photographs of myself that I had taken during my thirty years of secret experimentation with body play. To round out the book, the publishers added other individuals who were also pioneers in modern body liberation.

I suggested the title *Modern Primitives*, a term that I coined in 1978 to describe myself and a handful of other "atavists" I knew. The result was a book of unprecedented popularity and influence in the subcultures. Since its release in 1985, *Modern Primitives* has been reprinted six times, with more than 60,000 copies now in circulation. As a result of this one book, thousands of people, mostly young, were prompted to question established notions of what they could do with their bodies—what was ritual, *not* sickness, what was physical enhancement, *not* mutilation. The role models and archetypes that they found in *Modern Primitives* encouraged a whole new generation of people to use their bodies for self-expression—to search and experiment with the previously forbidden "body side" of life. The Modern Primitive movement had been born.

During the 1980s, since I had "gone public," I also found new opportunities for personal exploration. Instead of isolation, there were now kindred spirits—others to give me sanction and encouragement—to help me try a whole other round of body play. I asked sympathetic friends to put me into the Kavadi frame, akin to that of the Savite Hindus. I was pierced by ninety 4-foot-long steel rods in my upper chest and back. I danced for hours with this 50-pound load while I went into a state of ecstasy and drifted out of my body. It was sweet. It was bliss. I got to know what the Tamil Hindus had experienced probably 2,000 years ago. I repeated "taking Kavadi" many times after that one and was eventually asked by other modern primitives of several subculture groups to put them in it too. I did it and also acted as a shaman who guided them on trips to unseen spaces.

In another body-oriented adventure, I invited trusted friends to pierce my chest with two large hooks and suspend me by these two piercings in the style of the Native American Oglalas Sioux Sun Dance and Mandan O-Kee-Pa ceremony. That experience proved to be truly transformative. I lifted out of my body, drifted up to a white light that radiated incredible love and understanding. The light said, "Hello, I'm you!" I was never the same after that remarkable trip. Years later, I discovered many others had had a similar transformative experience during what is now called the "near-death experience." I repeated the hanging many times after the first one; each had its own lesson and special place to visit. My fifth hanging was beautifully filmed for a documentary by Mark and Dan Jury. This movie, released in 1985, is titled *Dances Sacred and Profane*.

By 1990, the Modern Primitive movement, with its intricate web of body expression and exploration, had come to bloom. Body piercing, for example, was now a main-street business in large cities, mostly as a result of the diligence of a handful of people in the original 1970s T&P group. In 1990 and 1991, I worked as a commercial piercer in one of the largest of these studios in San Francisco. Since I also did, and had done for some years, private ritualized piercing, I couldn't help but introduce this element into what appeared to be a rather normal-looking personal service business. I was curious. Why did these hundreds of people, mostly young, get pierced? I knew from years of research many of the reasons that people in other cultures did it. But what about these contemporary modern primitives?

In the so-called primitive tribal societies that I had studied, about a dozen reasons kept appearing for the practice of body-piercing, marking, and modification rites:

1. rites of passage
2. creation of lifelong peer bonding
3. sign of respect or honor for elders and ancestors
4. symbol of status, belonging, bravery, or courage
5. initiation into greater mysteries or unseen worlds
6. protection from evil spirits/energies

7. opening for beneficial spirits/energies
8. rebalancing of body and/or spirit energies
9. healing of diseased body, self, and others
10. healing of wounded psyche, self, and others
11. healing of tribal disorder and creation of tribal bonding
12. tribal/community connection to greater forces, especially in times of chaos or disaster

Since I was now doing ten to twenty piercings a day, I had plenty of opportunity to ask reasons of contemporaries. In the privacy of the piercing booths that we used in the commercial studio, I would encourage ritual and would ask, "You don't have to answer me if you don't want to, but if you don't mind, could you tell me why you are getting your nipples (or whatever) pierced today?" or, "Have you been thinking about doing this for very long? Does it have any special meaning for you?" To my surprise, most piercing clients gave me answers. The reasons were not very different, in many cases, from those I had found in other cultures where body piercing was sanctioned and a part of the cultural tradition. But some of the reasons were radically skewed from those of other cultures, reasons never or seldom heard in tribal cultures.

For example, one that came up often, especially among women who had been raped, is a sad commentary on the abusiveness and disregard for others' sacred space in our society: "I'm getting pierced to reclaim my body. I've been used and abused. My body was taken by another without my consent. Now, by this ritual of piercing, I claim my body back as my own. I heal my wounds." Some reasons were more obvious: for example, the identification and status marking of certain subgroups, like bikers or the Club Fuck girls of Los Angeles, who all wore small colored rings in their nasal septums. The most common reason given for a body piercing usually dealt with a rite of passage or memorial.

In 1990, I met Dr. Favazza when we both appeared on a television talk show in San Francisco. The program was on self-mutilation, primarily that of young women who locked themselves in a private space and slashed themselves with razor blades. In addition to Dr. Favazza and myself, the program also featured Raelyn Gallina, who is renowned for and openly does cutting on others (primarily women) in socialized ritual, as well as a young woman "cutter" from Los Angeles who had a long history of isolated cutting and psychiatric treatment. I felt sorry for Dr. Favazza. He did not get much of a chance to present his side of the story on the program. Raelyn and I had filled the audience with highly modified people, all of whom were pierced, tattooed, or cut with intricate patterns — *and* were very vocal and positive about their experiences.

After the program, the young woman cutter from Los Angeles connected with other women in the audience whose urge to express feelings by body acts had been more social and sanctioned than hers. In listening to their conversation, I had the feeling that if this woman had been in the San Francisco area and had connected sooner with a supportive peer group like this one, her shame and negative experiences as an isolated cutter might have taken a different turn. Who knows? I also gave Dr. Favazza a fast tour of the widespread display and acceptance of body modification in San Francisco. I hoped that this tour would add new dimensions to his work.

By 1991, the Modern Primitive movement was receiving widespread public notice, which in itself was a type of sanction. Rock stars and models began to appear in mass media with body piercings and tattoos. Maverick clothing and hairstyles became fashionable. I gave countless interviews and wrote extensively for the alternative press. Hundreds of young persons responded to the message. They wanted more — more information, more opportunity and guidance in body arts and ritual practices, more instruction in safe and social ways to express themselves through the body. To provide a reliable channel of information, I started a magazine called *Body Play & Modern Primitives Quarterly*. It has not only lasted three years but has even become a commercial success, distributed through such mainstream outlets as Tower Records. For those who wanted personal exploration, I started a series of workshops on ecstatic shamanism; these workshops have been given in major cities such as Los Angeles, Dallas, and San Francisco. And close to my heart, I started the Fakir Professional Body-Piercing Intensives to teach the art, science, safe medical practice, and magic of body piercing. To date, this educational effort has produced the majority of body piercers who operate studios in Western culture. In 1993, I started similar instruction on branding.

All of these activities brought me hundreds of young people eager to modify their own and other's bodies. Some were sincere and stable, open to advice and counsel. Others were so overwhelmed with passion and the urge that they were prone to ignore caution, physical safety, and tradition. From the onset, I adopted a practice of stalling any rash or risky actions. I advised those persons to study the tradition of the practice and consider the risks and possible dangers — physical, mental, spiritual, and psychic. If, for example, a young man wanted to do the Sun Dance, I would encourage him to learn all he could about the Native American tradition from which

Modern Primitive Sid Ziarra is highly pierced, tattooed, and cut. Here she displays her lip and tongue piercings for *Body Play* magazine. (Photo courtesy of Fakir Musafar)

Socialized, ritual cutting/scarification by Raelyn Gallina. An intricate Celtic knot pattern is cut with a scalpel and filled with ashes while the female subject goes into a light trance. (Photo courtesy of Fakir Musafar)

Modern Primitive Mercedes
shows the results of her
thirty-six-strike brand some
months after it was made in
a socialized ritual in Santa
Cruz, California. Mercedes
loves body ritual and has
many piercings, cuttings,
and tattoos as well. Her genetic makeup allowed her
branding to keloid and thus
produce a raised, three-
dimensional pattern that
is both visual and tactile.
(Photo courtesy of Fakir
Musafar)

it came. I would advise him to find a trustworthy medicine man or shaman
who was experienced in the ritual and to do the ritual only if that mentor
felt he was properly prepared and ready.

Since the late 1980s, I have had a number of people ask me to help them
take the Spear Kavadi of the Hindus. One woman, a Christian, asked me
dozens of times. I made her wait two years until I felt her motives were
clear and she was appreciative of the Hindu tradition from which it came.
Then I asked her to prepare herself so that finally, on a sunny summer day
in California, I could put her into the Kavadi frame for half a day. She had a
marvelous transformative experience during the rite. Others who facilitate
modern-day body modification have adopted a similar practice; Raelyn
Gallina, for example, was recently asked by a protegé body piercer trained in
my courses to make a series of slashes across his face. The requested modi-

fication was radical; the decision to do it was somewhat impulsive. When he went to Raelyn to get this cutting, she asked him if he had given it much thought and seriously considered the consequences. She made three lines with a permanent red marker where he wanted the slashes on his face. She told him to wear the marks for seven days. If he still wanted the cutting at the end of the waiting period, she would do it. This is the type of approach that serious, responsible body modifiers are taking. But not everyone involved in the modern trend to practice old body rituals is this conscientious. Some see the trend as a way to commercialize and exploit this "urge" that runs so deep.

Why have peoples through all ages and most cultures sought expression of life through the body, through its sensations and modification? I've felt the "urge" myself and have come to terms with it. I've investigated this phenomena for almost fifty years, and I've found it to be a significant part of human development. The more I look, the more convinced I am that the phenomenon wells up from some deep inner source—perhaps a behavioral archetype that may be encoded in our genes. This past year, I had the opportunity to explore the phenomenon's universality. As a young man, I was emotionally moved by the body worship of the Savite Tamil Hindus in such cultural rites as the Thaipusam Festival. As a teenager, I had seen photographs of these Hindus in old *National Geographic* magazines— on the streets in Southern India with hundreds of limes or other objects suspended from their bodies by hooks pierced through the skin, in huge arched frameworks supported by long iron spears embedded in the chest and back, with long spikes pierced through their tongues and cheeks. The glazed look in the eyes, their seeming indifference to pain, said something.

I vowed to witness this event some day, to soak in and understand firsthand what was happening inside these people whom I had only observed externally in pictures. So after waiting nearly fifty years, I finally had my chance to attend the Thaipusam in Penang, Malaysia. I was not disappointed. Over 200,000 people had gathered in Penang, 500,000 in Kuala Lumpur, and another 250,000 in Singapore. These were not tourists but devotees with their priests, family, and friends assembled for openly sanctioned public worship through the body. In Penang, the procession streets were purified by smashing over two million coconuts; the milk was believed to clear the way for the passing of the image of Lord Muruga (also known to the Tamils as Murugan, Subramanya, Velan, Kumara, and many other names, each indicating an aspect of an unseen deity).

The atmosphere on the morning of the body-piercing and procession ritual was intoxicating. As I watched group after group of Tamil Hindus get pierced to cries of "vel, vel" and let themselves enter deep trance states, I began to feel the utter reality of the deities whom they were invoking. Murugan was there. Lord Siva was there. Goddess Kali was there. All welling up from somewhere deep inside the devotees. I had felt this before in my own rituals and in the ones I had conducted for others in California. But never of this magnitude. What I felt in Penang was not sickness, but rather a state of grace.

References

Abraham K. 1942. Restrictions and transformations of scopophilia in psychoneurotics. In *Selected Papers of Karl Abraham*. London: Hogarth Press.

Adam J. 1883. Cases of self-mutilation of the insane. *J Ment Science* 29:213–19.

Albert DM, Burns WP, Scheie HG. 1965. Severe orbitocranial foreign-body injury. *Am J Ophthalmology* 60:1109–11.

Al-Dargazelli S. 1993–94. New findings in healing research. *Doctor-Healer Network Newsletter* (England) (Winter):12–17.

Alexander HB. 1967. *The World's Rim: Great Mysteries of the North American Indians*. Lincoln: University of Nebraska Press.

Allyn G, Demye A, Begue I. 1976. Self-fighting syndrome in macaques: A representative case study. *Primates* 17:1–22.

Amin P, Yeragani VK. 1987. Control of aggressive and self-mutilative behavior in a mentally retarded patient with lithium. *Can J Psychiatry* 32:162–63.

Anaclerio AM, Wicker HS. 1970. Self-induced solar retinopathy by patients in a psychiatric hospital. *Am J Ophthalmology* 69:731–36.

Ananth J, Kaplan HS, Lin K-M. 1984. Self-enucleation of the eye. *Can J Psychiatry* 29:145–46.

Anderson JR, Chamove AS. 1980. Self-aggression and social aggression in laboratory-reared macaques. *J Abnorm Psychology* 89:539–50.

———. 1981. Self-aggressive behavior in monkeys. *Curr Psychological Rev* 1:139–58.

Anumonye A. 1973. Self-inflicted amputation of the penis in two Nigerian males. *Nigerian Med J* 3:51–52.

Arens W. 1979. *The Man-Eating Myth*. New York: Oxford University Press.

Arnold LE, Aman MG. 1991. Beta blockers in mental retardation and developmental disorders. *J Child Adolescent Psychopharmacology* 1:361–73.

Arons BS. 1981. Self-mutilation: Clinical examples and reflections. *Am J Psychotherapy* 25:550–58.

Asberg M, Traskman L, Thoren P. 1976. 5-HIAA in the cerebrospinal fluid: A biological suicide predictor. *Arch Gen Psychiatry* 33:1193–97.

Asch SS. 1971. Wrist scratching as a symptom of anhedonia. *Psychoanalytic Quar* 40:630–37.

Assaad MB. 1980. Female circumcision in Egypt. *Studies in Family Planning* 11:3–16.

Axenfeld T. 1899. Über Luxation, Zerstörung und Herausreissung des Augapfels als Selbstuerstummelung bei Geisteskranken. *Z für Augenheilkunde* 1:128–51.

Bach-Y-Rita G. 1974. Habitual violence and self-mutilation. *Am J Psychiatry* 131:1018–20.

Backman JA. 1972. Self-injurious behavior. *J Abnorm Psychology* 80:211–24.

Balduzzi E. 1961. Contributo alla psicopatologia degli stati ossessivi. *Riv Sper Freniat* 85:314–31.

Ball TS, Sebback L, Jones R, Steele B, Frazier L. 1975. An accelerometer-activated device to control assaultive and self-destructive behaviors in retardants. *J Behav Therapy Exp Psychiatry* 6:223–28.

Ballard CG. 1989. Benign intracranial hypertension and repeated self-mutilation. *Br J Psychiatry* 155:570–71.

Ballinger BR. 1971. Minor self-injury. *Br J Psychiatry* 118:535–38.

Baroff GS, Tate BG. 1968. The use of aversive stimulation in the treatment of chronic self-injurious behavior. *J Am Acad Child Psychiatry* 7:454–70.

Barr MW. 1920. Some notes on asexualization. *J Nerv Ment Disease* 51:231–41.

Basedow H. 1927. Subincision and kindred rites of the Australian aboriginal. *J Roy Anthropol Institute* 57:123–56.

Bates WJ, Smeltzer DJ. 1982. Electroconvulsive treatment of psychotic self-injurious behavior in a patient with severe mental retardation. *Am J Psychiatry* 139: 1355–56.

Battey R. 1873. Practice of Scoptzi in Roumania. *Atlanta Med Surg J* 11:483–86.

Battle RJV, Pollitt JD. 1964. Self-inflicted injuries. *Br J Plastic Surg* 17:400–412.

Bauer L. 1879–80. Infibulation as a remedy for epilepsy and seminal losses. *St. Louis Clinical Record* 6:163–65.

Baumeister AA, Frye GD. 1985. The biochemical basis of the behavioral disorder in the Lesch-Nyhan syndrome. *Neurosci Biobehav Review* 9:169–78.

Beattie JHM. 1980. On understanding sacrifice. In *Sacrifice*, edited by Bourdillon MFC, Fortes M. New York: Academic Press.

Beilin LM, Gruenberg J. 1948. Genital self-mutilation by mental patients. *J Urology* 59:635–41.

Benezech M, Bourgeois M, Boukhabza D, Yesavage. 1981. Cannibalism and vampirism in paranoid schizophrenia. *J Clin Psychiatry* 42:290.

Benjamin LS. 1987. An interpersonal approach. *J Personality Disorders* 1:334–39.

Beresford TP. 1980. The dynamics of aggression in an amputee. *Gen Hosp Psychiatry* 3:219–25.

Bergmann GH. 1846. Ein Fall von religioser Monomanie. *Allgemeine Z für Psychiatrie* 3:365–80.

Berndt R. 1962. *Excess and Restraint.* Chicago: University of Chicago Press.

Best JW, Angelo LL, Milligan B. 1962. Complete traumatic amputation of the penis. *J Urology* 87:134–38.

Bettelheim B. 1955. *Symbolic Wounds.* London: Thames and Hudson.

Betts WC. 1964. Autocannibalism. *Am J Psychiatry* 121:402–3.

Bhattacharya SK, Jaiswal AK, Mukhopadhyay M, Datla KP. 1988. Clonidine-induced automutilation in mice as a laboratory model for clinical self-injurious behavior. *J Psychiatric Research* 22:43–50.

Bigot A. 1938. Recherches sur le penis des Tonkinois, suivies d'une note sur les automutilations genitales. *Rev Med France d'Extreme-Orient* 16:717–23.

Bille-Brahe V. 1982. Persons attempting suicide in the Danish welfare system. *Social Psychiatry* 17:181–88.

Bisset RDN. 1949. Self-castration. *Br Med J* 2:59.

Biven B. 1977. A violent solution: The role of skin in severe adolescent regression. *Psychoanal Stud Child* 32:327–52.

Blacker KH, Wong N. 1963. Four cases of autocastration. *Arch Gen Psychiatry* 8: 169–76.

Bliss EL. 1980. Multiple personalities. *Arch Gen Psychiatry* 37:1388–97.

Bloch M. 1992. *Prey into Hunter: The Politics of Religious Experience*. New York: Cambridge University Press.

Blondel C. 1906. Les automutilateurs. Medical Thesis, Paris.

Boddy J. 1982. Womb as oasis: The symbolic context of Pharaonic circumcision in rural Northern Sudan. *Am Ethnol* 9:682–98.

Boehm C. 1984. *Blood Revenge: The Anthropology of Feuding in Montenegro and Other Tribal Societies*. Lawrence: University Press of Kansas.

Bohannon P. 1956. Beauty and scarification among the Tiv. *Man* 51:117–21.

Bonnard A. 1960. The primal significance of the tongue. *Intl J Psychoanalysis* 41: 301–7.

Bourdillon MFC, Fortes M (eds). 1980. *Sacrifice*. New York: Academic Press.

Bowen DI. 1971. Self-inflicted orbitocranial injury with a plastic ballpoint pen. *Br J Ophthalmology* 33:427–30.

Bowker J. 1970. *Problems of Suffering in Religions of the World*. Cambridge: Cambridge University Press.

Bowman KM, Engle B. 1957. Medicolegal aspects of transvestism. *Am J Psychiatry* 113:583–88.

Bradford DT. 1990. Early Christian martyrdom and the psychology of depression, suicide and bodily mutilation. *Psychotherapy* 27:30–41.

Bradley JM. 1933. A case of a self-made eunuch. *Weekly Bulletin St. Louis Med Soc* 28:133–54.

Brain R. 1979. *The Decorated Body*. New York: Harper and Row.

Breslauer J. 1994. The body politics. *Los Angeles Times*, 2 July, pt. F, p. 1, col. 4.

Breytenbach B. 1985. *The True Confessions of an Albino Terrorist*. New York: Farrar, Straus and Giroux.

Brody S. 1960. Self-rocking in infancy. *J Am Psychoanalytic Assn* 8:464–91.

Bromberg W, Schilder P. 1933. Psychologic considerations in alcoholic hallucinosis-castration and dismembering motives. *Intl J Psychoanalysis* 14:206–24.

Brothwell D, Sandison AT (eds). 1967. *Diseases in Antiquity*. Springfield, IL: Charles C. Thomas.

Brown BZ. 1970. Self-inflicted injuries of the eye. *Trans Pacific Coast Oto-ophthalmol Soc* 51:267–76.

Brown GL, Ebert MH, Goyer PF. 1982. Aggression, suicide, and serotonin. *Am J Psychiatry* 139:741–46.

Brown J. 1963. A cross-cultural study of female initiation rites. *Am Anthropol* 65: 837–53.

Brown K. 1993. Blood-letting in bulimia nervosa. *Br J Psychiatry* 163:129.

Brown P, Tuzin D. 1983. *The Ethnography of Cannibalism.* Washington, DC: Society for Psychological Anthropology Special Publication.

Bryan D. 1921. Blindness and castration. *Intl J Psychoanalysis* 2:71.

———. 1922. Note on tongue. *Intl J Psychoanalysis* 3:481–82.

Bryson Y, Sakati N, Nyhan WL, Fish CH. 1971. Self-mutilative behavior in the Cornelia deLange syndrome. *Am J Ment Deficiency* 76:319–24.

Burkert W. 1983. *Homo Necans.* Berkeley: University of California Press (originally published in German in 1972).

Burnham RC. 1969. Symposium on impulsive self-mutilation. *Br J Med Psychology* 42:223–27.

Burns ME. 1980. Droperidol in the management of hyperactivity, self-mutilation and aggression in mentally handicapped patients. *J Internal Med Rsch* 8:31–33.

Burton RV, Whiting JWM. 1961. The absent father and cross-sex identity. *Merrill-Palmer Quar Behav Dev* 7:85–95.

Burton-Bradley BG. 1976. Cannibalism for cargo. *J Nervous Ment Disease* 163:428–31.

Buzan RI, Dubovsky SL, Treadway JT, Thomas MI. 1995. Opiate antagonists for recurrent self-injurious behavior in three mentally retarded adults. *Psychiatric Services* 46:511–12.

Byman S. 1974. Suicide and alienation: Martyrdom in Tudor England. *Psychoanalytic Rev* 61:355–73.

———. 1978. Ritualistic acts and compulsive behavior: The pattern of Tudor martyrdom. *Am Historical Rev* 83:625–43.

Byrnes VA. 1949. A case of self-mutilation involving both eyes. *Am J Ophthalmology* 32:268–69.

Cain AC. 1961. Presuperego turning-inward of aggression. *Psychoanalytic Quar* 30:171–208.

Caine ED. 1985. Gilles de la Tourette's syndrome. *Archives Neurology* 42:393–397.

Cameron N. 1963. *Personality Development and Psychopathology.* Boston: Houghton Mifflin.

Campbell J. 1962. *The Masks of God: Oriental Mythology.* New York: Viking Press.

Cansever G. 1965. Psychological effects of circumcision. *Br J Med Psychology* 38:321–31.

Carr EG. 1977. The motivation of self-injurious behavior. *Psychological Bull* 84:800–816.

Carroll J, Schaffer C, Spensley J, Abramowitz SI. 1980. Family experience of self-mutilating patients. *Am J Psychiatry* 137:852–53.

Carroll MP. 1982. The rolling head. *J Psychoanalytic Anthropol* 5:29–56.

Carson DI, Lewis JM. Ocular auto-enucleation while under the influence of drugs: A case report. 1971. *Adolescence* 6:397–403.

Cautela JR, Baron MG. 1973. Multifaceted behavior therapy of self-injurious behavior. *J Behav Therapy Exp Psychiatry* 4:125–31.

Cawte J. 1974. *Medicine Is the Law.* Honolulu: University Press of Hawaii.

Cawte J, Djagamara N, Barrett MG. 1966. The meaning of subincision of the urethra to aboriginal Australians. *Br J Med Psychology* 39:245–53.

Chabukswar YV. 1921. A barbaric method of circumcision among some of the Arab tribes of Yemen. *Indian Med Gaz* 56:48–49.

Chalupecky H. 1895. Luxatio bulbi. *Wiener klin Rundschaw.*

Chamove AS, Anderson JR. 1981. Self-aggressive, stereotypy, and self-injurious behavior in man and monkeys. *Curr Psychological Rev* 1:245–56.

Chamove AS, Anderson JR, Nash V. 1984. Social and environmental influences on self-aggression in monkeys. *Primates* 25:319–25.

Chamove AS, Bayart F, Nash V, Anderson JR. 1985. Dominance, physiology, and self-aggression in monkeys. *Aggressive Behav* 11:17–26.

Chamove AS, Harlow, HS. 1970. Exaggeration of self-aggression following alcohol ingestion in rhesus monkeys. *J Abnorm Psychology* 75:207–9.

Channing W. 1877–78. Case of Helen Miller. *Am J Insanity* 34:368–78.

Chevigny H, Braverman S. 1950. *The Adjustment of the Blind.* New Haven: Yale University Press.

Chowance GD, Josephson AM, Coleman C, David H. 1991. Self-harming behaviors in incarcerated male delinquent adolescents. *Am Acad Child Adolescent Psychiatry* 30:202–7.

Christenson GA, Popkin MK, Mackenzie TB, Realmuto GM. 1991. Lithium treatment for chronic hair pulling. *J Clinical Psychiatry* 52:116–20.

Christie R, Bay C, Kaufman IA, Babey B, Borden M, Nyhan WL. 1982. Lesch-Nyhan disease. *Dev Med Child Neurology* 24:293–306.

Clark RA. 1981. Self-mutilation accompanying religious delusions: A case report and review. *J Clin Psychiatry* 42:243–45.

Cleckley H. 1964. *The Mask of Sanity.* St. Louis: Mosby.

Clendenin WW, Murphy GE. 1971. Wrist cutting: New epidemiological findings. *Arch Gen Psychiatry* 25:465–69.

Cleveland SE. 1956. Three cases of self-castration. *J Nerv Ment Disease* 123:386–91.

Coccaro EF, Astill JL, Szeeley PJ, Malkowica DE. 1990. Serotonin in personality disorders. *Psychiatric Annals* 20:587–92.

Coccaro EF, Siever LJ, Klar HM. 1989. Serotonergic studies in patients with affective and personality disorders: Correlates with suicidal and impulsive aggressive behavior. *Arch Gen Psychiatry* 46:587–99.

Cohen E. 1969. Self-assault in psychiatric evaluation. *Arch Gen Psychiatry* 21:64–67.

Cohen J, Hawkins R. 1983. Medicine or mutilation? *World Medicine* 22 Jan, 24–25.

Cohen Y. 1964. *The Transition from Childhood to Adolescence.* Chicago: Aldine.

Cohn N. 1958. *The Pursuit of the Millennium.* New York: Essential Books.

Coid J, Allolio B, Rees CH. 1983. Raised plasma metenkephalin in patients who habitually mutilate themselves. *Lancet*, 3 Sept, 545–46.

Coid J, Wilkins J, Coid B, Everitt B. 1992. Self-mutilation in female remanded prisoners II: A cluster analytic approach towards identification of a behavioral syndrome. *Criminal Behavior Mental Health* 2:1–14.

Collins DT. 1965. Head banging: Its meaning and management in the severely retarded adult. *Bull Menninger Clin* 29:205–11.

Conacher GN, Westwood GH. 1987. Autocastration in Ontario federal penitentiary inmates. *Br J Psychiatry* 150:565–66.

Conacher N, Villeneuve D, Kane G. 1991. Penile self-mutilation presenting as rational attempted suicide. *Can J Psychiatry* 36:683–85.

Conklin BA. 1995. Mortuary cannibalism in an Amazonian society. *Am Ethnologist* 22:75–101.

Conn JH. 1932. A case of marked self-mutilation presenting a dorsal root syndrome. *J Nerv Ment Disease* 75:251–62.

Connor L. 1979. Corpse abuse and trance in Bali: The cultural mediation of aggression. *Mankind* 12:104–18.

Conrad K, Bers N. 1954. Die Chronischer taktile halluzinose. *Fortschrift Neurol* 22: 254–70.

Coons PM, Ascher-Svanum H, Bellis K. 1986. Self-amputation of the female breasts. *Psychosomatics* 27:667–68.

Coons PM, Milstein V. 1990. Self-mutilation associated with dissociative disorders. *Dissociation* 3:81–87.

Cooper AF, Fowlie HC. 1973. Control of gross self-mutilation with lithium carbonate. *Br J Psychiatry* 122:370–71.

Cooper SN. 1968. Self-inflicted ocular injuries. *J All India Ophthal Soc* 16:213–16.

Cooper WW. 1859. *On Wounds and Injuries of the Eye.* London: John Churchill.

Copenhaver RM. 1960. A report of an unusual self-inflicted eye injury. *Arch Ophthalmology* 63:266–72.

Corte HE, Wolff MM, Locke BJ. 1971. Comparison of procedures for eliminating self-injurious behavior of retarded adolescents. *J Applied Behav Anal* 4:201–7.

Coxon A. 1962. The Kisii art of trephining. *Guy's Hospital Gaz* 76:263–66.

Crabtree LH. 1967. A psychotherapeutic encounter with a self-mutilating patient. *Psychiatry* 30:91–100.

Crabtree LH, Grossman WK. 1974. Administrative clarity and redefinition for an open adolescent unit. *Psychiatry* 37:350–59.

Crapanzano V. 1973. *The Hamadsha.* Berkeley: University of California Press.

Cross HA, Harlow HF. 1965. Prolonged and progressive effects of partial isolation on the behavior of macaque monkeys. *J Exp Res Personality* 1:39–49.

Cross L. 1993. Body and self in feminine development: Implications for eating disorders and delicate self-mutilation. *Bull Menninger Clinic* 57:41–68.

Crouigneau. 1887. Arrachement traumatique du muscle droit inférieur de l'oeil dans une observation d'automutilations répetées chez une mélancholique. *J Med Paris* 22:671–80.

Crowder JE, Gross CA, Heiser JF, Crowder AM. 1979. Self-mutilation of the eye. *J Clin Psychiatry* 24:420–23.

Cullen RB, Nater T. 1982. A secular rite on trial. *Newsweek*, 1 Nov, 55.

Culliford L. 1987. Autocastration and biblical delusions in schizophrenia. *Br J Psychiatry* 150:407.

Curran W. 1886. The making of eunuchs. *Provincial Med J*, 1 Apr, 149–51.

Daldin H. 1988. A contribution to the understanding of self-mutilating behavior in adolescence. *J Child Psychotherapy* 14:61–66.

———. 1990. Self-mutilating behavior in adolescence with comments on suicidal risk. *Bull Anna Freud Centre* 13:279–93.

Daniel A, Shekim WO, Koresko RL, Dekirmenjian H. 1980. Congenital sensory neuropathy with anhydrosis. *Dev Behav Pediatrics* 1:49–53.

Darche MA. 1990. Psychological factors differentiating self-mutilating and nonself-mutilating adolescent inpatient females. *Psychiat Hospital* 21:31–35.

Darnton R. 1984. *The Great Cat Massacre.* New York: Basic Books.

Dearborn GVN. 1932. A case of congenital pure analgesia. *J Nerv Ment Disease* 75: 612–15.

deCatanzaro DA. 1978. Self-injurious behavior. *Motivation and Emotion* 2:45–65.

Dehn. 1894. Ein Beitran zur kenntoris der Luxatio bulbi. *Arch für Ophth* 40:2.

deLissovoy V. Head-banging in early childhood. 1961. *J Pediatrics* 58:803–5.

DeMuth GW, Strain JJ, Lombardo-Maher A. 1983. Self-amputation and restitution. *Gen Hosp Psychiatry* 5:25–30.

Dennis SG, Melzack R. 1979. Self-mutilation after dorsal rhizotomy in rats. *Exp Neurol* 65:412–21.

Desoff J. 1943. The eye and related functional disturbances. *Med Ann District Columbia* 12:97–101.

Despagnet M. 1893. Arrachement de l'oeil. *Ann d'Oculistique* 53:109–10.

Devereux G. 1966. The cannibalistic impulses of parents. *Psychoanalytic Forum* 1: 114–24, 129–30.

Dingman CW, McGlashan TH. 1988. Characteristics of patients with serious suicidal intentions who ultimately commit suicide. *Hospital Community Psychiatry* 39:295–99.

Dingwall EJ. 1925. *Male Infibulation.* London: John Bale, Sons and Danielson.

———. N.d. *Very Peculiar People.* London: Rider (year of publication not listed in book, probably 1930s).

———. 1931. *Artificial Cranial Deformation.* London: John Bale, Sons and Danielson.

Dollard J, Doob L, Miller N, Mowrer OH, Sears RR. 1939. *Frustration and Aggression.* New Haven: Yale University Press.

Dollfus M-A, Michaux L. 1957. Un cas d'oedipisme suivi d'un double décollement de retine. *Bull Soc Ophthal France* 3:161–63.

Doran AR, Roy A, Wolkowitz OM. 1985. Self-destructive dermatoses. *Psychiatric Clinics North America* 8:291–98.

Dubovsky SL. 1978. "Experimental" self-mutilation. *Am J Psychiatry* 135:1240–41.

Dubovsky SL, Groban S. 1975. Congenital absence of sensation. *Psychoanalytic Study Child* 30:49–73.

Duke-Elder WS. 1949. *Textbook of Ophthalmology.* St. Louis: Mosby.

Dupeyrat A. 1954. *Savage Papua.* New York: Dutton.

Durham ME. 1928. *Some Tribal Origins, Laws and Customs of the Balkans.* London: Allen and Unwin.

Earls JH. 1967. Tatooed sailors. *Military Med* 132:48–53.

Eastwell HD. 1982. Australian aborigines. *Transcultural Psychiatric Rsch Rev* 19:221–47.

Eibl-Eibelsfeldt I. 1972. *On Love and Hate.* New York: Holt Rinehart Winston.

Eichelman B. 1987. Neurochemical and psychopharmacologic aspects of aggressive behavior. In *Psychopharmacology: The Third Generation of Progress*, edited by Meltzer HY. New York: Raven.

Eigner EH. 1966. Self-induced solar retinitis. *Am J Ophthalmology* 61:1546–47.

Eisenhauer GL, Woody RC. 1987. Self-mutilation and Tourette's disorder. *J Child Neurology* 2:265–67.

El Dareer A. 1982. *Women, Why Do You Weep?* London: Zed Press.

Eliade M. 1960. *Myths, Dreams and Mysteries*. New York: Harper and Row.

———. 1974. *Shamanism*. Princeton: Princeton University Press.

———. 1975. *Rites and Symbols of Initiation*. New York: Harper and Row.

Elkin AP. 1945. *Aboriginal Men of High Degree*. Sydney: Angus and Robertson.

Elwin V. 1943. Vagina dentata legend. *Br J Med Psychology* 19:439–53.

Emerson LE. 1933. The case of Miss A: A preliminary report of a psychoanalytic study and treatment of a case of self-mutilation. *Psychoanalytic Rev* 1:41–54.

Emma M. 1932. Cottributo allo studio della patogenesi della auto-mutilazioni: Enucleazione di un occhio in un sogetto postencephalitico. *Arch di Antropologia Criminale* 52:203.

Engelman ER, Polito G, Perley J, et al. 1974. Traumatic amputation of the penis. *J Urology* 112:774–78.

Engle BS. 1936. Attis: A study of castration. *Psychoanalytic Rev* 23:363–72.

Ernst FA. 1973. Self-recording and counterconditioning of a self-mutilative compulsion. *Behav Therapy* 4:144–46.

Esman AH. 1954. A case of self-castration. *J Nerv Ment Disease* 120:79–82.

Evans C, Lacey JH. 1992. Multiple self-damaging behavior among alcoholic women. *Br J Psychiatry* 161:643–47.

Evans-Pritchard EE. 1956. *Nuer Religion*. Oxford: Clarendon Press.

Evins SC, Whittle T, Rous SN. 1977. Self-emasculation. *J Urology* 118:775–76.

Farberow N. 1980. *The Many Faces of Suicide: Indirect Self-Destructive Behavior*. New York: McGraw-Hill.

Farmer R. 1980. The differences between those who repent and those who do not. In *The Suicide Syndrome*, edited by Farmer R, Hirsch S. London: Croon Helm.

Favazza A. 1979. The eyes have it. *MD* 23:17–19.

———. 1989a. Normal and deviant self-mutilation. *Transcultural Psychiatric Research Review* 26:113–27.

———. 1989b. Why patients mutilate themselves. *Hosp Community Psychiatry* 40:137–45.

———. 1991. Masturbation or mutilation? *Medical Aspects Human Sexuality* (May):45–46.

———. 1992. Repetitive self-mutilation. *Psychiatric Annals* 22:60–63.

Favazza A, Conterio K. 1988. The plight of chronic self-mutilators. *Community Mental Health J* 24:22–30.

———. 1989. Female habitual self-mutilators. *Acta Psychiatrica Scandinavica* 79:283–89.

Favazza A, DeRosear L, Conterio K. 1989. Self-mutilation and eating disorders. *Suicide Life-Threatening Behavior* 19:352–61.

Favazza A, Dos Santos E. 1985. Depersonalization episodes in self-mutilation. *Am J Psychiatry* 142:1390.

Favazza A, Rosenthal R. 1990. Varieties of pathological self-mutilation. *Behavioral Neurology* 3:77–85.

———. 1993. Diagnostic issues in self-mutilation. *Hosp Community Psychiatry* 44: 134–40.

Favazza A, Simeon D. 1995. Self-mutilation. In *Impulsivity and Aggression*, edited by Hollander E, Stein D. New York: Wiley.

Federn P. 1952. *Ego Psychology and the Psychoses*. New York: Basic Books.

Female circumcision. 1983. *Lancet*, 12 Mar, 569.

Fenichel O. 1953. The scopophilic instinct and identification. In *The Collected Papers of Otto Fenichel*, edited by Fenichel H. and Rapoport D. New York: W. W. Norton.

Ferenczi S. 1959. On eye symbolism. In *Sex in Psychoanalysis*. New York: Basic Books.

Ferguson G. 1954. *Signs and Symbols in Christian Art*. New York: Oxford University Press.

Ferguson-Rayport SM, Griffith RM, Straus EW. 1955. The psychiatric significance of tatoos. *Psychiatric Quar* 29:112–31.

Fichter MM, Quadflieg N, Rief W. 1994. Course of multi-impulsive bulimia. *Psychological Medicine* 24:592–604.

Figueroa MD. 1988. A dynamic taxonomy of self-destructive behavior. *Psychotherapy* 25:280–87.

Fisch RZ. 1987. Genital self-mutilation in males: Psychodynamic anatomy of a psychosis. *Am J Psychotherapy* 41:453–58.

Fitzherbert J. 1950. The origin of head banging. *J Ment Sci* 96:793–95.

Fleischer K. 1980. Uvula-excision in Afrika. *Curare* 3:19–22.

Fleishel MF. 1960. A man's fantasy of a crippled girl. *Am J Psychotherapy* 14:741–48.

Fleming JB. 1960. Clitoridectomy: The disastrous downfall of Isaac Baker Brown. *J Ob Gyn Br Empire* 67:1017–34.

Flugel JC. 1925. A note on the phallic significance of the tongue and of speech. *Intl J Psychoanalysis* 6:209–15.

Foulks E, Freeman D, Kaslow F, Madow L. 1977. The Italian evil eye. *J Operational Psychiatry* 8:28–34.

Frances A. 1987. Introduction [to the section on self-mutilation]. *J Personality Disorders* 1:316.

Frances A, Munro A. 1989. Treating a woman who believes she has bugs under her skin. *Hospital Community Psychiatry* 40:1113–14.

Francheschetti A. 1923. Beitrag zur Kenntis der Evulsio nervi optici. Medical Thesis, Zurich.

Frankel F, Simmons III JQ. 1976. Self-injurious behavior in schizophrenic and retarded children. *Am J Ment Deficiency* 80:512–22.

Frazer JG. 1904. The origin of circumcision. *Independent Rev* 4:204–18.

———. 1958. *The Golden Bough*. New York: Macmillan (originally published in 1922).

Freeman L. 1918. Primitive surgery of the Western Hemisphere. *JAMA* 70:443–48.

French AP, Nelson HL. 1972. Genital self-mutilation in women. *Arch Gen Psychiatry* 27:618–20.

Freud A. 1946. *The Ego and the Mechanisms of Defense*. New York: International Universities Press.

Freud A, Burlingham DT. 1944. *Infants without Families*. New York: International University Press.

Freud S. 1930. *Civilization and Its Discontents*. London: Hogarth Press.

———. 1950. *Totem and Taboo*. New York: W. W. Norton (original work published in 1913).

Friedman M, Glasser M, Laufer E, Laufer M, Wohl M. 1972. Attempted suicide and self-mutilation in adolescence. *Intl J Psychoanalysis* 53:179–83.

Fromm E. 1973. *The Anatomy of Human Destructiveness*. New York: Holt Rinehart Winston.

Fruensgaard K, Flindt-Hansen H. 1989. Disease patterns seen in self-mutilating patients. *Nordisk Psychiatrisk Tidaskrift* 42:281–89.

Fulton JF. 1887. A case of almost complete self-enucleation of both eyeballs. *Am J Ophthalmology* 4:179–80.

Furst R. 1928. Ein Fall von schwerer Selbstverletzung des Auges. *Psychiatrisch-Neurologische Wochenschrift* 30:548–49.

Gaddini E. 1982. Early defensive fantasies and the psychoanalytic process. *Int J Psychoanalysis* 63:379–88.

Gajdusek DC. 1977. Unconventional viruses and the origin and disappearance of kuru. *Science* 197:943–60.

Gall PG. 1985. Views of future health workers in Somalia on female circumcision. *Med Anthropol Quar* 17:71–73.

Galleher EP, Kiser WS. 1953. Injuries of the corpus cavernosum. *J Urology* 70:648–55.

Galt J. 1884. Suicidal amputation of the penis. *Med Herald* 6:225–28.

Gandy DT. 1936. Feigned or self-induced eruptions. *Texas Med* 31:712–15.

Gardiner M. 1971. *The Wolf-Man*. New York: Basic Books.

Gardner AR, Gardner AJ. 1975. Self-mutilation, obsessionality, and narcissism. *Br J Psychiatry* 127:127–32.

Gardner DL, Cowdry RW. 1985. Alprazolam-induced dyscontrol in borderline personality disorder. *Am J Psychiatry* 142:98–100.

———. 1986. Positive effects of carbamazepine on behavioral dyscontrol in borderline personality disorder. *Am J Psychiatry* 143:519–22.

Gardner R, Heider KG. 1968. *Gardens of War*. New York: Random House.

Garfinkel PE, Moldosky H, Garner DM. 1980. The heterogeneity of anorexia nervosa. *Arch General Psychiatry* 37:1036–40.

Garn SM, Block WD. 1970. The limited nutritional value of cannibalism. *Am Anthropologist* 72:72–106.

Genovese E, Napoli PA, Bolego-Zonta N. 1969. Self-aggressiveness: A new type of behavioral change induced by pemoline. *Life Sci* 8:513–14.

Gerhard M. 1968. A propos des automutilations oculaires. *Bull Soc Ophthal France* 68:622–26.

Gerlich F. 1929. *Die stigmatisiete Therese Neumann von Konnersreuth.* Munich: Kosel and Pustet.

Gerstle ML, Guttmacher AF, Brown F. 1957. Recurrent malingered placenta previa. *J Mt Sinai Hospital* 24:641–46.

Gifford ES. 1955. Psychogenic ocular symptoms. *Arch Ophthalmology* 53:318–29.

Gillette PJ. 1966. *The Complete Marquis de Sade.* Los Angeles: Holloway House.

Gillman MA, Sandyk R. 1985. Opiatergic and dopaminergic functions and Lesch-Nyhan syndrome. *Am J Psychiatry* 142:1226.

Giradot NJ. 1983. *Myth and Meaning in Early Taoism.* Berkeley: University of California Press.

Girard R. 1977. *Violence and the Sacred.* Baltimore: Johns Hopkins University Press (originally published in French as *La Violence et Le Sacre,* 1972).

Gittleson NL, Wallen GPD, Dawson-Butterworth K. 1969. The tatooed psychiatric patient. *Br J Psychiatry* 115:1249–53.

Glenn J. 1960. Circumcision and anti-Semitism. *Psychoanalytic Quar* 29:395–99.

Gluckman M. 1962. *Essays on the Ritual of Social Relations.* Manchester, England: Manchester University Press.

Goffin. 1887. Ein Fall von schwerer Selbstverummelung. *Bull Med Mentale de Belgique* 3:8.

Goldberg BZ. 1930. *The Sacred Fire (Skoptsi).* New York: Horace Liveright.

Golden S, Chosack A. 1964. Oral manifestations of a psychological problem. *J Periodontology* 35:349–50.

Goldenberg E, Sata LS. 1978. Religious delusions and self-mutilation. *Curr Concepts in Psychiatry* (Sept/Oct):2–5.

Goldfield MD, Glick IA. 1970. Self-mutilation of the female genitalia. *Dis Nerv System* 31:843–45.

———. 1973. Self-mutilation of the genitalia. *Med Aspects Human Sexuality* 7:219–32.

Goldney RD, Simpson IG. 1975. Female genital self-mutilation, dysorexia and the hysterical personality: The Caenis syndrome. *Can Psychiatric Assn J* 20:435–41.

Goldsmith W. 1973. Self-enucleation: Further views. *Am J Psychiatry* 130:329.

Goldstein IC, Dragan AI. 1967. Self-inflicted oral mutilation in a psychotic adolescent. *J Am Dental Assn* 74:750–51.

Goldstein M, Anderson LT, Reuben R. 1985. Self-mutilation in Lesch-Nyhan syndrome is caused by dopamine denervation. *Lancet* 1:338–39.

Goldstein N. 1979. Psychological implications of tatoos. *J Dermatol Surg Oncology* 5:883–88.

Goldstein N, Sewell M. 1979. Tatoos in different cultures. *J Dermatol Surg Oncology* 5:857–64.

Goodhart S, Savitsky N. 1933. Self-mutilation in chronic encephalitis. *Am J Med Science* 185:674–84.

Goosen C. 1981. Abnormal behavior patterns in rhesus monkeys: Symptoms of mental illness? *Biological Psychiatry* 16:679–716.

Gordon BL. 1937. Oculus fascinus (fascination, evil eye). *Arch Ophthalmology* 17:290–319.

Gorin M. 1964. Self-inflicted bilateral enucleation. *Arch Ophthalmology* 72:225–26.

Gould GM, Pyle WL. 1956. *Anomalies and Curiosities of Medicine.* New York: Julian Press (originally published in 1896).

Gould RA. 1969. *Yiwara: Foragers of the Australian Desert.* New York: Scribner's.

Graber RB. 1981. A psychocultural theory of male genital mutilation. *J Psychoanalytic Anthropol* 4:413–34.

Grabman JM. 1975. The Witch of Mallegem; print by Bruegel the Elder. *J Hist Med Allied Sciences* 30:385.

Graff H, Mallin R. 1967. The syndrome of the wrist cutter. *Am J Psychiatry* 124:36–42.

Graillot H. 1912. *Le Culte de Cybele.* Paris.

Graver D. 1995. Violent theatricality. *Theatre Journal* 47:43–64.

Green AH. 1967. Self-mutilation in schizophrenic children. *Arch Gen Psychiatry* 17:232–44.

———. 1978. Self-destructive behavior in battered children. *Am J Psychiatry* 135:579–82.

Green E, Green A. 1977. *Beyond Biofeedback.* New York: Melroyd Lawrence.

Greenacre P. 1926. The eye motif in delusion and fantasy. *Am J Psychiatry* 82:553–79.

Greenberg J. 1981. *I Never Promised You a Rose Garden.* New York: Holt Rinehart Winston.

Greenspan GC, Samuel SE. 1989. Self-cutting after rape. *Am J Psychiatry* 146:789–90.

Greilsheimer H, Groves JE. 1979. Male genital self-mutilation. *Arch Gen Psychiatry* 36:441–46.

Griffin JA. 1971. Is a cannibal a criminal? *Melanesian Law Journal* 1:79–81.

Griffin JC, Williams DE, Stark MT. 1985. Self-injurious behavior: A statewide prevalence survey. *Applied Research Mental Retardation* 7:105–16.

Griffin N, Webb MGT, Parker RR. 1982. A case of self-inflicted eye injuries. *J Nerv Ment Diseases* 170:53–56.

Gruenbaum E. 1982. The movement against clitoridectomy and infibulation in Sudan: Public health policy and the women's movement. *Med Anthropol Newsletter* 13:4–12.

Grunebaum HV, Klerman GL. 1967. Wrist slashing. *Am J Psychiatry* 124:527–34.

Gualtieri CT. 1989. The differential diagnosis of self-injurious behavior in mentally retarded people. *Psychopharmacology Bulletin* 25:358–63.

Guiard E. 1930. *La trepanation cranienne chez les neolithiques et chez les primitifs modernes.* Paris: Masson.

Gunderson JG, Zanarini MC. 1987. Current overview of the borderline diagnosis. *J Clin Psychiatry* 48 (Suppl.):5–11.

Guntert H. 1923. *Der Arische Weltkonig und Heiland.* Halle: Niemeyer.

Gupta MA, Gupta AK, Haberman HR. 1986. Neurotic excoriations. *Comprehensive Psychiatry* 27:381–86.

Haberman MA, Michael RP. 1979. Autocastration in transsexualism. *Am J Psychiatry* 136:347–48.

Hahn DS, Hahn DS. 1967. A case of penis amputation. *Korean Med J* 12:113–16.

Haines J, Williams CL, Brain KL, Wilson GV. 1995. The psychophysiology of self-mutilation. *J Abnormal Psychology* 104:471–89.

Hall DC, Lawson BZ, Wilson LG. 1981. Command hallucinations and self-amputation of the penis and hand during a first psychotic break. *J Clin Psychiatry* 42:322–24.

Hall JR, McGill JC. 1986. Hypnobehavioral treatment of self-destructive behavior: Trichotillomania and bulimia in the same patient. *Am J Clinical Hypnosis* 29:39–46.

Halprin KM. 1966, 1967. The art of self-mutilation. *JAMA* 198:777, 1207; 199:119.

Hamburger E, Lacovara DJ. 1963. A study of tatoos in inmates. *Military Med* 128: 1205–11.

Hand E. History of circumcision. 1950. *J Michigan State Med Soc* 49:573–78.

Hare RD. 1970. *Psychopathy Theory and Research*. New York: Wiley.

Harner M. 1977. The ecological basis for Aztec sacrifice. *Am Ethnologist* 4:117–135.

Harrer VG, Urban HJ. 1950. Zur Selbstblendung und Selbstverstummelung. *Wiener Medizinische Wochenschrift* 100:37–40.

Harrington C. 1968. Sexual differentiation in socialization and some male genital mutilations. *Am Anthropol* 70:951–56.

Harris M. 1977. *Cannibals and Kings*. New York: Random House.

Hart HH. 1949. Eye in symbol and symptom. *Psychoanalytic Rev* 36:256–75.

Hartman DE, Powander SM. 1987. Identification with a brain-damaged parent: Theoretical considerations on a case of self-mutilation. *Psychoanalytic Psychology* 4:171–78.

Hartmann H. 1926. Self-mutilation. *Arch Neurol Psychiatry* 15:384–86.

Hawton K. 1990. Self-cutting. In *Dilemmas and Difficulties in the Management of Psychiatric Patients*, edited by Hawton K, Cowen P. Oxford: Oxford University Press.

Hay T. 1971. The windigo psychosis: Psychodynamic, cultural, and social factors in aberrant behavior. *Am Anthropologist* 73:1–9.

Hays HR. 1964. *The Dangerous Sex*. New York: Putnam.

Hays TE, Hays PH. 1982. Opposition and complementarity of the sexes in Ndumba initiation. In *Rituals of Manhood*, edited by Herdt GH. Berkeley: University of California Press.

Helmuth H. 1968. Cannibalism in paleoanthropology and ethnology. In *Man and Aggression*, edited by Montagu A. New York: Oxford University Press.

Hemphill RE. 1951. A case of genital self-mutilation. *Br J Med Psychology* 24:291–95.

Hemphill RE, Zabow T. 1983. Clinical vampirism. *South African Med J* 63:278–81.

Herdt GH. 1982. Sambia nosebleeding rites and male proximity to women. *Ethos* 10:189–231.

Herpertz S. 1995. Self-injurious behavior. *Acta Psychiatrica Scandinavica* 91:57–68.

Hibbard SK. 1994. The mechanisms and meanings of self-cutting. *Modern Psychoanalysis* 19:45–54.

Hillbrand M, Krystal JH, Sharpe KS, Foster HG. 1994. Clinical predictors of self-mutilation in hospitalized forensic patients. *J Nerv Mental Disease* 182:9–13.

Hoffman E, McCoy J. 1981. *Concrete Mama: Prison Profiles from Walla Walla.* Columbia: University of Missouri Press.

Hoffman HA, Baer PN. 1968. Gingival mutilation in children. *Psychiatry* 31:380–86.

Hogbin HI. 1970. *The Island of Menstruating Men.* Scranton, PA: Chandler.

Hollender MC, Abram HS. 1973. Dermatitis factitia. *Southern Med J* 66:1279–85.

Holloway TB. 1911. Case report by Dr. Mary Buchanan on avulsion of the eyeball. *Ann Ophthalmology* 20:433.

Hong CC, Ediger RD. 1978. Self-mutilation of the penis in C57BL/6N mice. *Laboratory Animals* 12:55–57.

Horton PC. 1981. *Solace.* Chicago: University of Chicago Press.

Hosken FP. 1978. The epidemiology of female genital mutilations. *Tropical Doctor* 8:150–56.

Howden JC. 1882. Mania followed by hyperaesthesia and osteomalacia: Singular family tendency to excessive constipation and self-mutilation. *J Ment Sci* 28:49–53.

Hrdlicka A. 1939. Trepanation among prehistoric people. *CIBA Symposia* 1:170–77.

Hubert H, Mauss M. 1899. Essai sur la nature et la fonction du sacrifice. *L'Année sociologique* 2 (published in English as *Sacrifice: Its Nature and Function.* London: Cohen and West, 1964).

Hunter A, Kennard AB. 1982. Mania operativa: An uncommon, unrecognized cause of limb amputation. *Can J Surgery* 85:96–98.

Hussein JN, Fatooki LJ, Al-Dargazelli S, Almuchtar N. 1993. The deliberately caused bodily damage phenomena: Mind, body, energy, or what? Paramann Programme Laboratories, Amman, Jordan.

Huxley J. 1931. *Africa View.* London: Chatto and Windus.

Hyneck RW. 1932. *Konnersreuth: A Medical and Psychological Study of the Case of Therese Neumann.* New York: Macmillan.

Ideler. 1871. Fall von Selbstverstummelung bei einer Geisteskranken. *Allgemeine Z für Psychiatrie* 27:717–21.

Inman WS. 1939. The symbolic significance of glass and its relation to diseases of the eye. *Br J Med Psychology* 18:122–40.

Isaac E. 1967. The enigma of circumcision. *Commentary* 43:51–56.

Jacobi W. 1923. *Die Stigmatisiertia: Bertrage für Psychologie der Mystik.* Munich: Bergmann.

Jacobs BW, Isaacs S. 1986. Pre-pubertal anorexia nervosa. *J Child Psychology Psychiatry* 27:237–50.

Jacobs S. 1943. Ritual circumcision. *Urologic Cutaneous Rev* 47:679–81.

James EO. 1962. *Sacrifice and Sacrament.* London: Thames and Hudson.

Jamieson RA. 1877. Chinese eunuchs. *Lancet,* 28 July, 123–24.

———. 1882. Self-mutilation in China. *Br Med J* 1:397–98.

Jan Stout R. 1990. Fluoxetine for facial picking. *Am J Psychiatry* 147:370.

Jankovic J. 1988. Orofacial and other self-mutilations. In *Advances in Neurology,* vol. 49, *Facial Dyskinesias,* edited by Jarkovic J, Tolsa E. New York: Rowen Press, pp. 365–81.

Janssens PA. 1957. Medical views on prehistoric representations of human hands. *Med History* 1:318–22.

Jilek WG, Jilek-Aall L. 1978. Initiation in Papua–New Guinea. *Papua–New Guinea Med J* 21:252–63.

Johnson EH, Britt B. 1967. *Self-mutilation in Prison: Interaction of Stress and Social Structure.* Carbondale: Southern Illinois University Center for the Study of Crime, Delinquency, and Corrections.

Johnson F, Frankel B, Ferrence R, Jarvis G, Whitehead P. 1975. Self-injury in London, Canada. *Can J Public Health* 66:207–316.

Johnson R. 1978. Youth in crisis: Dimensions of self-destructive conduct among adolescent prisoners. *Adolescence* 13:461–82.

Jonaitis A. 1988. Women, marriage, mouths and feasting: The symbolism of Tlingit labrets. In *Marks of Civilization*, edited by Rubin A. Los Angeles: Museum of Cultural History, UCLA.

Jones A. 1986. Self-mutilation in prison. *Criminal Justice and Behavior* 13:286–96.

Jones IH. 1969. Subincision among Australian Western desert aborigines. *Br J Med Psychology* 42:259–63.

———. 1982. Self-injury: Toward a biological basis. *Perspec Biol Med* 26:137–50.

Jones IH, Barraclough BM. 1978. Auto-mutilation in animals and its relevance to self-injury in man. *Acta Psychiatrica Scandinavica* 58:40–47.

Jones IH, Congiv L, Stevenson J, Frei B. 1979. A biological approach to two forms of human self-injury. *J Nerv Ment Disease* 167:74–78.

Jones R. 1961. Flagellants. In *Hasting's Encyclopedia of Religion and Ethics*, vol. 6, edited by Hasting J. New York: Scribner's.

Kafka JS. 1969. The body as a transitional object: A psychoanalytic study of a self-mutilating patient. *Br J Med Psychology* 42:207–12.

Kahan J, Pattison EM. 1984. Proposal for a distinctive diagnosis: The Deliberate Self-Harm Syndrome. *Suicide and Life Threatening Behavior* 14:17–35.

Kalin NH. 1979. Genital and abdominal self-surgery. *JAMA* 241:2188–89.

Kaminer Y, Shaher A. 1987. The stress inoculation training management of self-mutilating behavior. *J Behavior Therapy Experimental Psychiatry* 18:289–92.

Kanner L. 1928. The tooth as a folkloristic symbol. *Psychoanalytic Rev* 15:37–52.

Kayser B. 1918. Evulsion des Bulbus und Nervus Opticus mit Chiasmatrennung. *Kleinische Monatsblatter Augenheilkunde* 61:657–60.

Kehoe AB. 1979. The Sacred Heart: A case for stimulus diffusion. *Am Ethnol* 6:763–71.

Keleman P. 1967. *Baroque and Rococco in Latin America.* New York: Dover.

Kennedy JG. 1973. Cultural psychiatry. In *Handbook of Social and Cultural Anthropology*, edited by Honigmann JJ. Chicago: Rand McNally.

Kenyon HR, Hyman RM. 1953. Total autoemasculation. *JAMA* 151:207–10.

Kernberg O. 1987. A psychodynamic approach. *J Personality Disorders* 1:344–46.

Khandelwal SK, Varma UK, Gupta R. 1981. Auto-castration review with a case report. *Indian J Psychological Med* 4:119–21.

King RA, Riddle MA, Chappell PB, Hardin MT, Anderson GM, Lombroso P, Schaill

L. 1991. Emergence of self-destructive phenomena in children and adolescents during fluoxetine treatment. *J Am Acad Child Adolescent Psychiatry* 30:179-86.

Kirmayer LJ, Carroll J. 1987. A neurobiological hypothesis on the nature of chronic self-mutilation. *Integrative Psychiatry* 5:212-13.

Kirtley M, Kirtley A. 1982. The Ivory Coast. *Nat Geographic* 162:94-124.

Klauder JV. 1938. Stigmatization. *Arch Dermatology Syphilology* 37:650-59.

Knapp PH. 1953. The ear, listening and hearing. *J Am Psychoanalytic Assn* 1:672-89.

Koch F. 1945. Patron saints of the eyes. *Am J Ophthalmology* 28:160-72.

Konicki E, Schulz C. 1989. Rationale for clinical trials of opiate antagonistic in treating patients with personality disorder and self-injurious behavior. *Psychopharmacology Bulletin* 25:556-63.

Koo JYM. 1989. *Current Concepts: Psychodermatology.* Kalamazoo: Upjohn Company.

Koorten JJ, VenDorp A. 1975. Self-mutilation in a case of 49, XXXXY chromosomal constitution. *J Ment Deficiency Rsch* 19:63-71.

Krahn DD, Nairn K, Gosnell BA, Drewnowski A. 1991. Stealing in eating disordered patient. *J Clinical Psychiatry* 52:112-15.

Kramrisch S. 1981. *Manifestations of Shiva.* Philadelphia: Philadelphia Museum of Art.

Kravitz H, Rosenthal V, Teplitz A, Murphy JB, Lesser CE. 1960. A study of head-banging in infants and children. *Disease Nerv System* 21:203-8.

Kreitman N. 1977. *Parasuicide.* Chichester, England: Wiley.

Krickeberg W. 1968. *Pre-Columbian American Religions.* London: Weidenfeld and Nicolson.

Krieger MJ, McAninch JW, Weimer SR. 1982. Self-performed bilateral orchiectomy in transsexuals. *J Clin Psychiatry* 43:292-93.

Kroll JL. 1978. Self-destructive behavior on an inpatient ward. *J Nerv Ment Disease* 166:429-34.

Krupp NE. 1976-77. Self-caused skin ulcers. *Psychosomatics* 17-18:15-19.

Kushner AW. 1967. Two cases of auto-castration due to religious delusions. *Br J Med Psychology* 40:293-98.

Kwawer JS. 1980. Some interpersonal aspects of self-mutilation in a borderline patient. *J Am Acad Psychoanalysis* 8:203-16.

Lacey JH. 1982. Anorexia nervosa and a bearded female saint. *Br Med J* 285:1816-17.

Lacey JH, Evans CDH. 1986. The impulsivist. *Br J Addictions* 81:641-49.

Lafon C. 1907. Les auto-mutilations oculaires. *Rec d'ophthalmologie* 29:561-73.

Lagercrantz S. 1935. Fingerverstummelungen und ihre Ausbreitung in Afrika. *Z für Ethnologie* 67:129-55.

———. 1938. Zur Verbreitung der Monorchie. *Z für Ethnologie* 70:199-208.

Landwirth J. 1964. Sensory radicular neuropathy and retinitis pigmentosa. *Pediatrics* 34:519-24.

Larbig W. 1982. *Schmerz und Schmerzbehandlung.* Stuttgart: Kohlhammer.

Lastres JB, Cabieses F. 1960. La trepanacion del craneo en el Antiguo Peru. Lima: Universidad Nacional Mayor de San Marcos.

Lauerma H. 1994. Ear stuffing and psychosis. *J Nervous Mental Disease* 182:412-13.

Lawton K, Fagg J, Marsak P, Wells P. 1982. Deliberate self-poisoning and self-injury in the Oxford area, 1972–1980. *Social Psychiatry* 17:175–80.

Lea HC. 1973. *The Ordeal*. Philadelphia: University of Pennsylvania Press (originally published in 1866).

———. 1973. *Torture*. Philadelphia: University of Pennsylvania Press (originally published in 1866).

Leach ER. 1976. *Culture and Communication*. Cambridge: Cambridge University Press.

Leash AM, Beyer RD, Wilber RG. 1973. Self-mutilation following Innovaret injection in the guinea pig. *Lab Animal Science* 23:720–21.

Lechler A. 1933. *Das Rätsel von Konnersreuth in Lichte eines neuer Falles von Stigmatisation*. Munich: Elberfeld.

Leigh I. 1954. *In the Shadow of the Mau Mau*. London: Allen.

Lena SM, Bijoor S. 1990. Wrist cutting: A dare game among adolescents. *Can Med Assn J* 142:131–32.

Lennon S. 1963. Genital self-mutilation in acute mania. *Med J Australia* 50:79–81.

Leonard HL, Lenane MC, Swedo SE, Rattew DC, Rappaport JL. 1991. A double-blind comparison of clomipramine and desipramine treatment of severe onychophagia. *Arch Gen Psychiatry* 48:821–27.

Letts RM, Hobson DA. 1975. Special devices as aids in the management of child self-mutilation in the Lesch-Nyhan syndrome. *Pediatrics* 55:853–55.

Levine MD, Gordon TP, Peterson RH, Rose RH. 1971. Urinary 17-OHCS response of high- and low-aggressive rhesus monkeys to shock avoidance. *Physiolog Behav* 5:919–24.

Levison CA. 1970. Development of head banging in a young rhesus monkey. *Am J Ment Deficiency* 75:323–28.

Levy HS. 1968. *Chinese Footbinding*. New York: Bell.

Levy J, Sewell M, Goldstein N. 1979. A short history of tatooing. *J Dermatol Surg Oncology* 5:851–56.

Lewis NDC. 1927, 1928. The psychobiology of the castration reaction. *Psychoanalytic Rev* 14:420–46; 15:53–94, 174–209, 304–23.

———. 1931. Additional observation on the castration reaction in males. *Psychoanalytic Rev* 18:146–65.

Lidz RW, Lidz T. 1977. Male menstruation. *Intl J Psychoanalysis* 58:17–31.

Liebenluft E, Gardner DL, Cowdry RW. 1987. The inner experience of the borderline self-mutilator. *J Personality Disorders* 1:317–24.

Liebowitz MR. 1987. A medication approach. *J Personality Disorders* 1:325–27.

Lim YC, Seng BK. 1985. Self-mutilation in a family. *Singapore Med J* 26:482–84.

Lincoln B. 1975. The Indo-European myth of creation. *History Religion* 15:121–45.

———. 1981. *Emerging from the Chrysalis*. Cambridge: Harvard University Press.

Linehan MM. 1987. Dialectical behavioral therapy: A cognitive behavioral approach to parasuicide. *J Personality Disorders* 1:328–33.

Linnoila M, Virkunnen M, Scheinin M, Nuutila A, Rimon R, Goodwin FK. 1983. Low cerebrospinal fluid 5-HIAA concentration differentiates impulsive from non-impulsive violent behavior. *Life Sciences* 33:2609–14.

Lion JR. 1975. Conceptual issues in the use of drugs for the treatment of aggression in man. *J Nerv Ment Disease* 160:76–82.

Lion JR, Conn LM. 1982. Self-mutilation: Pathology and treatment. *Psychiatric Ann* 12:782–87.

Lipinski JF. 1991. Clomipramine in the treatment of self-mutilating behaviors. *New Eng J Med* 324:1441.

Litman R. 1980. Psychodynamics of indirect self-destructive behavior. In *The Many Faces of Suicide*, edited by Farberow N. New York: McGraw-Hill.

Lloyd HGE, Stone TW. 1981. Chronic methylxanthine treatment in rats. *Pharmacol Biochem Behav* 14:827–30.

Lloyd KG, Hornykiewicz O, Davidson L, Shannak K, Farley J, Goldstein M. 1981. Biochemical evidence of dysfunction of brain neurotransmitters in the Lesch-Nyhan syndrome. *New England J Med* 305:1106–11.

Loeb EM. 1923. The blood sacrifice complex. *Am Anthropological Assn Memoirs*, no. 30:3–40.

Long CH. 1963. *Alpha: The Myths of Creation.* New York: Braziller.

Lopez-Ibor JJ, Saiz-Ruiz J, de los Cobos JCP. 1985. Biological correlations of suicide and aggressivity in major depressions. *Neuropsychobiology* 14:67–74.

Lorenz K. 1954. *Man Meets Dog.* Cambridge, MA: Riverside Press.

———. 1966. *On Aggression.* New York: Harcourt Brace World.

Lowie R. 1920. *Primitive Society.* New York: Boni and Liveright.

Lowry FH, Kolivakis TL. 1971. Autocastration by a male transsexual. *Can Psychiatric Assn J* 16:399–405.

Lubin AJ. 1961. Vincent Van Gogh's ear. *Psychoanalytic Quar* 30:351–84.

Lucero WJ, Fireman J, Spoering K, Fehrenbacher J. 1976. Comparison of three procedures in reducing self-injurious behavior. *Am J Ment Deficiency* 180:548–54.

Lycacki H, Josef NC, Munetz M. 1979. Stimulation and arousal in self-mutilators. *Am J Psychiatry* 136:1223–24.

McCallum D. 1988. Historical and cultural dimensions of the tattoo in Japan. In *Marks of Civilization*, edited by Rubin A. Los Angeles: Museum of Cultural History, UCLA.

McEvedy CP. 1963. Self-inflicted injuries. Academic D.P.M. diss., University of London.

McHenry LC. 1985. Neurological disorders of Dr. Samuel Johnson. *J Royal Soc Medicine* 78:485–91.

McKerracher DW, Strect DRK, Segal LJ. 1966. A comparison of the behavior problems presented by male and female subnormal offenders. *Br J Psychiatry* 112:891–97.

MacKinlay JG. 1887. Complete self-enucleation of eyeball. *Trans Ophthalmological Soc U.K.* 7:298–300.

McKinney WT. 1974. Primate social isolation: Psychiatric implications. *Arch Gen Psychiatry* 31:422–26.

McKinney WT, Bunney WE. 1968. Animal model of depression. *Arch Gen Psychiatry* 21:240–48.

MacLean G, Robertson BM. 1976. Self-enucleation and psychosis: Report of two cases and discussion. *Arch Gen Psychiatry* 33:242–49.

Majno G. 1975. *The Healing Hand*. Cambridge: Harvard University Press.

Malavitis A, Arapis D, Stamatinis C. 1967. A case of auto-enucleation. *Bull Soc Hellenique Ophtalmologie* 23:200–201.

Malcolm LWG. 1934. Prehistoric and primitive surgery. *Nature*, 10 Feb, 200–201.

Malcove L. 1933. Bodily mutilation and learning to eat. *Psychoanalytic Quar* 2:557–61.

Maple T, Erwin J, Mitchell G. 1974. Sexually aroused self-aggression in a socialized, adult male monkey. *Arch Sex Behav* 3:471–75.

Marano L. 1982. Windigo psychosis. *Current Anthropology* 23:385–412.

Margetts EL. 1960. Subincision of the urethra in the Samburu of Kenya. *East African Med J* 37:105–8.

———. 1967. Trepanation by medicine men: Present day East African practice. In *Diseases in Antiquity*, edited by Brothwell D, Sandison AT. Springfield, IL: Charles C. Thomas.

Margo GM, Newman JS. 1989. Venesection as a rare form of self-mutilation. *Am J Psychotherapy* 43:427–32.

Markovitz PJ, Calabrese JR, Schulz SC, Meltzer HY. 1991. Fluoxetine in the treatment of borderline and schizotypal disorders. *Am J Psychiatry* 148:1064–67.

Markowitz PI, Coccaro EF. 1995. Biological studies of impulsivity, aggression, and suicidal behavior. In *Impulsivity and Aggression*, edited by Hollander E, Stein DJ. New York: John Wiley & Sons.

Martin T, Gattaz WF. 1991. Psychiatric aspects of male genital self-mutilation. *Psychopathology* 24:170–78.

Martinenq L, Cortyl E. 1884. Automutilations répetés chez une mélancholique. *Ann Med Psychol* 12:425–36.

Marx P, Brocheriou J. 1961. Automutilation oculaire chez un malade atteint de schizophrénie. *Bull Soc Ophthal France* 2:98–101.

Marziali EA, Munroe-Blume H. 1987. A group approach. *J Personality Disorders* 1:340–43.

Matthews PC. 1968. Epidemic self-injury in an adolescent unit. *Intl J Social Psychiatry* 14:125–33.

Mellon CD, Barlow C, Cook J, Clark LD. 1989. Autocastration and autopenectomy in a patient with transsexualism and schizophrenia. *J Sex Research* 26:125–30.

Mendez R, Kiely WF, Morrow JW. 1972. Self-emasculation. *J Urology* 107:981–85.

Menninger K. 1935. A psychoanalytic study of the significance of self-mutilation. *Psychoanalytic Quar* 4:408–66.

———. 1938. *Man against Himself*. New York: Harcourt Brace World.

———. 1959. *A Psychiatrist's World*. New York: Viking Press.

Meyer-Holzapfel M. 1968. Abnormal behavior in zoo animals. In *Abnormal Behavior in Animals*, edited by Fox FW. Philadelphia: Saunders.

Michael KD, Beck R. 1973. Self-amputation of the tongue. *Intl J Psychoanalytic Psychotherapy* 2:93–99.

Miller F, Baskhin E. 1974. Depersonalization and self-mutilation. *Psychoanalytic Quar* 43:638–49.

Mintz IL. 1964. Autocannibalism: A case study. *Am J Psychiatry* 120:1017.

Mishara BL, Robertson B, Kastenbaum R. 1973. Self-injurious behavior in the elderly. *Gerontologist* 13:311–14.

Mitchell J. 1984. *Eccentric Lives and Peculiar Notions*. London: Thames and Hudson.

Mitchell JE, Boutacoff CI, Hatsukami D, Pyle RL, Ekert ED. 1986. Laxative abuse as a variant of bulimia. *J Nerv Ment Disease* 174:174–76.

Mitchell WM. 1968. Self-insertion of urethral foreign bodies. *Psychiatric Quar* 42: 479–86.

Mizuno T, Yasumi Y. 1974. Self-mutilation in Lesch-Nyhan syndrome. *Lancet* 1:761.

Money J. 1988. The Skoptic syndrome. *J Psychology Human Sexuality* 1:113–29.

Money J, DePriest M. 1976. Three cases of genital self-surgery and their relationship to transsexualism. *J Sex Rsch* 12:283–94.

Money J, Jobsris R, Furth G. 1977. Apotemnophilia: Two cases of a self-demand amputation as a paraphilia. *J Sex Rsch* 13:115–25.

Money-Kryle R. 1930. *The Meaning of Sacrifice*. London: Hogarth Press.

Monroe RR. 1970. *Episodic Behavioral Disorders*. Cambridge: Harvard University Press.

Montagu A. 1937. *Coming into Being among the Australian Tribes*. London: Routledge and Kegan Paul.

———. 1946–47. Ritual mutilation among primitive people. *CIBA Symposia* 8:421–36.

———. 1973. *Man and Aggression*, 2d ed. London: Oxford University Press.

Moodie RL. 1920. The amputation of fingers among ancient and modern primitive peoples and other voluntary mutilations indicating some knowledge of surgery. *Surgical Clinic Chicago* 4:1299–1306.

Moran EC, McKinney WT. 1975. Effect of chlorpromazine on the vertical chamber syndrome in rhesus monkeys. *Arch Gen Psychiatry* 32:1409–13.

Morgan HG. 1979. *Death Wishes?: The Understanding and Management of Deliberate Self-Harm*. New York: Wiley.

Morgan HG, Burns-Cox CJ, Pocock H, Pottle S. 1975. Deliberate self-harm. *Br J Psychiatry* 127:564–74.

Morgan HG, Pocock H, Pottle S. 1975. The urban distribution of non-fatal deliberate self-harm. *Br J Psychiatry* 126:319–28.

Morgan OG. 1944. Discussion: Ocular psychoneuroses. *Trans Ophthalmological Soc U.K.* 64:57.

Morgan R, Steinem G. 1980. The international crime of genital mutilation. MS.

Morinis A. 1985. The ritual experience. *Ethos* 13:150–74.

Morris D. 1967. *The Naked Ape*. New York: McGraw-Hill.

Morton A. 1993. *Diana: Her True Story*. New York: Simon and Schuster.

Moser C, Lee J, Christensen P. 1993. Nipple piercing: An exploratory-descriptive study. *J Psychology Human Sexuality* 62:51–61.

Moskovitz RA, Byrd T. 1983. Rescuing the angel within: PCP-related self-enucleation. *Psychosomatics* 24:402–6.

Mueller K, Hsiao S. 1980. Pemoline-induced self-biting in rats and self-mutilation in the deLange syndrome. *Pharmacol Biochem Behav* 13:627–31.

Mueller K, Nyhan WL. 1983. Clonidine potentiates drug induced self-injurious behavior in rats. *Pharmacol Biochem Behav* 18:891–94.

Mueller K, Saboda S, Palmour R, Nyhan WL. 1982. Self-injurious behavior produced in rats by daily caffeine and continuous amphetamine. *Pharmacol Biochem Behav* 17:613–17.

Mueller SA. 1990. Trichotillomania: A histopathologic study in sixty-six patients. *J Am Acad Dermatology* 23:56–62.

Muluka EA. 1986. Severe self-mutilation among Kenyan psychotics. *Br J Psychiatry* 149:778–80.

Murphy GH. 1985. Self-injurious behavior in the mentally handicapped. *Newsletter Assn Child Psychology Psychiatry* 7:2–11.

Murray BJ. 1993. I never promised you a rose garden: Compulsive self-mutilation. In *Rediscovering Childhood Trauma*, edited by Goodwin JM. Washington, DC: American Psychiatric Press.

Murray TJ. 1979. Dr. Johnson's movement disorder. *Br Med Journal* i:1610–14.

Myers JJ, Deibert A. 1971. Reduction of self-abusive behavior in a blind child by using a feeding response. *J Behav Therapy Exp Psychiatry* 2:141–44.

Nadeau G. 1941. Indian scalping. *Bull Hist Med* 10:178–94.

Nagera H. 1967. *Vincent Van Gogh: A Psychological Study.* London: Allen and Unwin.

Nee LE, Caine ED, Polinsky RJ, Eldrige R, Ebert MH. 1980. Gilles de la Tourette syndrome. *Annals Neurology* 7:41–49.

Neil JF. 1958. Self-mutilation of the tongue. *J Laryngology Otology* 72:947–50.

Nelson SH, Grunebaum H. 1971. A follow-up study of wrist slashers. *Am J Psychiatry* 127:1345–49.

Nemiah J. 1985. Dissociative disorders. In *Comprehensive Textbook of Psychiatry*, 4th ed., edited by Kaplan HI, Sadock B. Baltimore: Williams and Wilkins.

Nettleship E. 1886. Meningitis after excision of eyeball. *Trans Ophthalmological Soc U.K.* 6:476–80.

New A, Trestman RL, Siever LJ. 1995. Borderline personality disorder. In *Impulsivity and Aggression*, edited by Hollander D, Stein DJ. New York: Wiley.

Newman G. 1982. The implications of tatooing in prisoners. *J Clin Psychiatry* 43:231–34.

Newman PL. 1965. *Knowing the Gururumba.* New York: Holt Rinehart Winston.

Newman PL, Boyd DJ. 1982. The making of men: Ritual and meaning in Awa male initiation. In *Rituals of Manhood*, edited by Herdt GH. Berkeley: University of California Press.

Novotny P. 1972. Self-cutting. *Bull Menninger Clin* 36:505–14.

Nunberg H. 1949. *Problems of Bisexuality as Reflected in Circumcision.* London: Imago.

Nyhan WL. 1972. Behavioral phenotypes in organic genetic disease. *Pediatric Rsch* 6:1–9.

———. 1976. Behavior in the Lesch-Nyhan syndrome. *J Autism Childhood Schizophrenia* 6:235–52.

Offer D, Barglow P. 1960. Adolescent and young adult self-mutilation incidents in a general psychiatric hospital. *Arch Gen Psychiatry* 3:194–204.

Ortner DJ, Putschar WGJ. 1981. *Identification of Pathological Conditions in Human Skeletal Remains.* Washington, DC: Smithsonian Institution Press.

Pabis R, Mirla MA, Tozmans S. 1980. A case study of autocastration. *Am J Psychiatry* 137:626–27.

————. 1981. Autocastration as a counterphobic focal suicide. *Suicide and Life Threatening Behav* 11:3–9.

Pao P-N. 1969. The syndrome of delicate self-cutting. *Br J Med Psychology* 42:195–206.

Parker S. 1960. The wiitiko psychosis in the context of Ojibwa personality and culture. *Am Anthropologist* 62:603–23.

Parkin JR, Eagles JM. 1993. Bloodletting in bulimia nervosa. *Br J Psychiatry* 162:246–48.

Parry A. 1934. Tatooing among prostitutes and perverts. *Psychoanalytic Quar* 3:476–82.

Parry-Jones B, Parry-Jones WL. 1993. Self-mutilation in four historical cases of bulimia. *Br J Psychiatry* 163:394–402.

Patel H, Bruza D, Yeragani VK. 1988. Treatment of self-abusive behavior with trazodone. *Can J Psychiatry* 33:332–33.

Pattison EM, Kahan J. 1983. The deliberate self-harm syndrome. *Am J Psychiatry* 140:867–72.

Pawlicki CM, Gaumer C. 1993. Nursing care of the self-mutilating patient. *Bull Menninger Clinic* 57:380–89.

Peffer-Smith PG, Smith EO, Byrd LD. 1983. Effects of d-amphetamine on self-aggression and posturing in stumptail macaques. *J Exp Anal Behav* 40:313–20.

Peters JM. 1967. Caffeine induced hemorrhagic automutilation. *Arch Intl Pharmacodynamics* 169:139–46.

Peto A. 1960. The development of ethical monotheism. In *The Psychoanalytic Study of Society.* New York: International Universities Press.

Philips RH, Akan M. 1961. Recurrent self-mutilation. *Psychiatric Quar* 35:424–31.

Pierloot RA, Wellens W, Houben ME. 1975. Elements of resistance to a combined medical and psychotherapeutic program in anorexia nervosa. *Psychotherapy Psychosomatics* 26:101–17.

Pitman RK. 1990. Self-mutilation in combat related post-traumatic stress disorder. *Am J Psychiatry* 147:123–24.

Podvoll EM. 1969. Self-mutilation within a hospital setting. *Br J Med Psychology* 42:213–21.

The Poems of Catullus. 1969. Translated by Michie J. New York: Random House.

Pond C, Rush HG. 1983. Self-aggression in macaques: Five case studies. *Primates* 24:127–34.

Poole FP. 1983. Cannibals, tricksters, and witches: Anthropophagic images among Bimin-Kuskumin. In *The Ethnography of Cannibalism,* edited by Brown P, Tuzin D. Washington, DC: Soc Psychological Anthropology.

Preston RJ. 1980. The Witiko. In *Manlike Monsters on Trial*, edited by Halprin MH, Ames MH. Vancouver: University of British Columbia Press.

Price BJ. 1978. Demystification, enriddlement, and Aztec cannibalism. *Am Ethnologist* 5:98–115.

Primeau F, Fontaine R. 1987. Obsessive disorder with self-mutilation. *Can J Psychiatry* 32:699–701.

Prince R. 1960. Curse, invocation, and mental health among the Yoruba. *Can Psychiatric Assn J* 5:65–79.

Procacci P, Maresca M. 1990. Autotomy. *Pain* 43:394.

Provence S, Lipton R. 1962. *Infants in Institutions*. New York: International Universities Press.

Putnam FW, Guroff JJ, Silberman EK, Barban L, Post RM. 1986. The clinical phenomenology of multiple personality disorder: Review of 100 recent cases. *J Clin Psychiatry* 47:285–93.

Putnam N, Stein M. 1985. Self-inflicted injuries in childhood. *Clin Pediatrics* 24: 514–18.

Rada RT, James W. 1982. Urethral insertion of foreign bodies: A report of contagious self-mutilation in a maximum-security hospital. *Arch Gen Psychiatry* 39:423–29.

Rado S. 1933. Fear of castration in women. *Psychoanalytic Quar* 2:425–75.

Ragain RD, Anson JE. 1976. The control of self-mutilating behavior with positive reinforcement. *Ment Retardation* 14:22–25.

Rajathurai A, Chazan BI, Jeans JE. 1983. Self-mutilation as a feature of Addison's disease. *Br Med J* 287:1027.

Rasmussen KLR, Reite M. 1982. Loss-induced depression in an adult macaque monkey. *Am J Psychiatry* 139:679–81.

Ratey J, Sovner R, Parks A, Rogentine K. 1991. Buspirone treatment of aggression and anxiety in mentally retarded patients. *J Clin Psychiatry* 52:159–62.

Razzak A, Fujiwara M, Oishi R, Ueki S. 1977. Possible involvement of a central noradrenergic system in automutilation induced by clonidine in mice. *Japan J Pharmacology* 27:145–52.

Razzak A, Fujiwara M, Ueki S. 1975. Automutilation induced by clonidine in mice. *European J Pharmacology* 30:356–59.

Read KE. 1965. *The High Valley*. New York: Scribner's.

Read PP. 1974. *Alive: The Story of the Andes Survivors*. Philadelphia: J. B. Lippincott.

Reik T. 1975. *Ritual*. Westport, CT: Greenwood Press.

Remondino PC. 1891. *History of Circumcision*. Philadelphia: F. A. Davis.

Repp AC, Deitz SM. 1974. Reducing aggressive and self-injurious behavior of institutionalized retarded children through reinforcement of other behavior. *J Appl Behav Analysis* 7:313–25.

Richardson JS, Holmlund JA, Gutkin A. On the role of endogenous opioids in the maintenance of self-mutilation. *Intl J Neuroscience* (in press).

Richardson JS, Zaleski WA. 1983. Naloxone and self-mutilation. *Biol Psychiatry* 18: 99–101.

———. 1986. Endogenous opiates and self-mutilation. *Am J Psychiatry* 143:938–39.

Rinpoche G. 1975. *The Tibetan Book of the Dead*. Berkeley: Shambala.

Rivers WHR. 1926. *Psychology and Ethnology*. London: Kegan Paul, French and Trubner.

Robertson MM, Trimbale MR, Lees AJ. 1989. Self-injurious behavior and the Giles de la Tourette syndrome. *Psychological Medicine* 19:611-25.

Rockland LH. 1987. A supportive approach: Psychodynamically oriented supportive therapy–treatment of borderline patients who self-mutilate. *J Personality Disorders* 1:350-55.

Rogers T, Pullen I. 1987. Self-inflicted eye injuries. *Br J Psychiatry* 151:691-93.

Roheim G. 1932. Psychoanalysis of primitive cultural types. *Intl J Psychoanalysis* 13: 1-224.

————. 1949. The symbolism of subincision. *Am Imago* 6:321-29.

Romanczyk RG, Goren ER. 1975. Severe self-injurious behavior. *J Consulting Clin Psychology* 43:730, 739.

Roper-Hall MJ. 1950. Self-inflicted conjunctivitis. *Br J Ophthalmology* 34:119-20.

Rosen DH. 1972. Focal suicide. *Am J Psychiatry* 128:1009-11.

Rosen PM, Walsh BW, Rode SA. 1990. Interpersonal loss and self-mutilation. *Suicide Life-Threatening Behavior* 20:177-84.

Rosenthal PA, Rosenthal S. 1984. Suicidal behavior by preschool children. *Am J Psychiatry* 141:520-25.

Rosenthal RJ, Rinzler C, Walsh R, Klausner E. 1972. Wrist-cutting syndrome: The meaning of a gesture. *Am J Psychiatry* 128:1363-68.

Ross RR, McKay HB. 1979. *Self-Mutilation*. Lexington, MA: Lexington Books.

Ross RR, Meichenbaum DH, Humphrey C. 1971. Treatment of nocturnal head-banging by behavior modification techniques. *Behav Rsch Therapy* 9:151-54.

Rossitch E, Oakes WJ, Ovelman-Levitt J, Nashold BS. 1992. Self-mutilation following brachial plexus injury sustained at birth. *Pain* 45:209-11.

Roy A. 1978. Self-mutilation. *Br J Med Psychology* 51:201-3.

Rudofsky B. 1971. *The Unfashionable Human Body*. New York: Doubleday.

Russ MJ. 1992. Self-injurious behavior in patients with borderline personality disorder: Biological perspectives. *J Personality Disorders* 6:64-81.

Russ MS, Roth SD, Lerman A, Kakuma T, Harrison K, Shindledecker RD, Hull J, Mattis S. 1992. Pain perception in self-injurious patients with borderline personality disorder. *Biol Psychiatry* 32:501-11.

Russel (Lord of Liverpool). 1954. *The Scourge of the Swastika*. London: Cassell.

Sackett GP. 1968. Abnormal behavior in laboratory-reared rhesus monkeys. In *Abnormal Behavior in Animals*, edited by Fox MW. Philadelphia: Saunders.

Sagan E. 1974. *Cannibalism*. New York: Harper and Row.

Saint Margaret Mary. 1931. *Gems of Thought from Saint Margaret Mary*. New York: Benziger.

Sanday PR. 1986. *Divine Hunger: Cannibalism as a Cultural System*. New York: Cambridge University Press.

Schaefer HH. 1970. Self-injurious behavior. *J Appl Behav Anal* 3:111-16.

Schaffer CB, Carroll J, Abramowitz SI. 1982. Self-mutilation and the borderline personality. *J Nerv Ment Disease* 170:468-73.

Schecter DC. 1962. Breast mutilation in the Amazons. *Surgery* 51:554–60.

Schele L, Miller ME. 1986. *The Blood of Kings*. Fort Worth, TX: Kimbell Art Museum.

Schilder P. 1950. *The Image and Appearance of the Human Body*. New York: International Universities Press.

Schiller G. 1972. *Iconography of Christian Art*, vol. 2: *The Passion of Jesus Christ*. Greenwich, CT: New York Graphic Society.

Schlossman HH. 1966. Circumcision as a defense: A study in psychoanalysis and religion. *Psychoanalytic Quar* 35:340–56.

Schneider SF, Harrison SI, Siegel BL. 1965. Self-castration by a man with cyclic changes in sexuality. *Psychosomatic Med* 27:53–70.

Schnier J. 1950. The blazing sun: A psychoanalytic approach to Van Gogh. *Am Imago* 7:143–62.

Schwartz RH, Cohen P, Hoffman NG, Meeks JE. 1989. Self-harm behaviors (carving) in female adolescent drug abusers. *Clinical Pediatrics* 28:340–46.

Schweitzer I. 1990. Genital self-amputation and the Klingsor syndrome. *Austral New Zealand J Psychiatry* 24:566–69.

Scullica L. 1962. Ceratocono acuto post-traumatico da autolesioni in paziente affetto da psicoastenia ossessiva. *Bull Oculisto* 41:270–77.

Segal P, Mrzyglod S, Alichniewicz-Czaplicka H, Dunin-Horkawicz W, Zwyrzykowski E. 1963. Self-inflicted eye injuries. *Am J Ophthalmology* 349–62.

Shapiro AK, Shapiro E, Bruun RD, Sweet RD. 1978. *Giles de la Tourette Syndrome*. New York: Raven Press.

Shapiro AK, Shapiro E, Eisenkraft GH. 1983. Treatment of Giles de la Tourette's syndrome with pimozide. *Am J Psychiatry* 140:1183–86.

Shapiro S. 1987. Self-mutilation and self-blame in incest victims. *Am J Psychotherapy* 41:46–54.

Shea S. 1993. Personality characteristics of self-mutilating male prisoners. *J Clinical Psychology* 49:576–85.

Shear CS, Nyhan WL, Kirman BH, Stern J. 1971. Self-mutilative behavior as a feature of the deLange syndrome. *J Pediatrics* 78:506–9.

Shelley WB. 1962. Abstract of discussion on congenital absence of pain. *Arch Dermatol* 85:338–39.

Shodell MJ, Reiter HH. 1968. Self-mutilative behavior in verbal and non-verbal schizophrenic children. *Arch Gen Psychiatry* 19:453–55.

Shore D. 1979. Self-mutilation and schizophrenia. *Comp Psychiatry* 20:384–87.

Shore D, Anderson DJ, Cutler NR. 1978. Prediction of self-mutilation in hospitalized schizophrenics. *Am J Psychiatry* 135:1406–7.

Siever LJ, Trestman RL, Silverman JM. 1992. Validation of personality disorder assessment of biologic and family studies. *J Personality Disorder* 6:301–12.

Silva JA, Leong GB, Weinstock R. 1989. A case of skin and ear self-mutilation. *Psychosomatics* 30:228–30.

Simeon D, Stanley B, Frances A, et al. 1992. Self-mutilation in personality disorders. *Am J Psychiatry* 149:221–26.

Simpson CA, Porter GL. 1981. Self-mutilation in children and adolescents. *Bull Menninger Clin* 45:428-38.

Simpson MA. 1973. Female genital self-mutilation. *Arch Gen Psychiatry* 29:808-10.

———. 1975. Symposium-self injury: The phenomenology of self-mutilation in a general hospital setting. *Can Psychiatric Assn J* 20:429-34.

———. 1976. Self-mutilation and suicide. In *Suicidology: Contemporary Developments*, edited by Schneidman ES. New York: Grune and Stratton.

Sinclair E. 1886-87. Case of persistent self-mutilation. *J Ment Science* 32:44-46.

Singh NN, Pulman RM. 1979. Self-injury in the deLange syndrome. *J Ment Deficiency Research* 23:79-81.

Siomopoulos V. 1974. Repeated self-cutting: An impulse neurosis. *Am J Psychotherapy* 28:85-94.

Slawson PF, Davidson PW. 1964. Hysterical self-mutilation of the tongue. *Arch Gen Psychiatry* 11:581-88.

Smith GE, Dawson WR. 1924. *Egyptian Mummies*. London: Allen and Unwin.

Smith HW. 1952. *Man and His Gods*. Boston: Little, Brown.

Soderstrom J. 1938. Die Rituellen Fingerverstummelungen in der Sudsee und in Australien. *Z für Ethnologie* 70:24-47.

Soebo J. 1948. Automutilation bulborum. *Acta Ophthalmologica* 26:451-53.

Somerset IJ. 1945. Self-inflicted conjunctivitis. *Br J Ophthalmology* 29:186-204.

Somerville-Large LB. 1947. Self-inflicted eye injuries. *Trans Ophthalmological Soc U.K.* 67:185-201.

Spencer RF. 1946-47. The cultural aspects of eunuchism. *CIBA Symposia* 8:406-20.

Stabinsky H, Stabinsky S, Wiener A. 1984. Post psychotic depression in a patient who castrated himself. *Jefferson J Psychiatry* 2:35-37.

Standage KF, Moore JA, Cole MG. 1974. Self-mutilation of the genitalia by a female schizophrenic. *Can Psychiatric Assn J* 19:17-20.

Stanley B, Winchel R, Molcho A, Simeon D, Stanley M. 1992. Suicide and the self-harm continuum: Phenomenological and biochemical evidence. *Int Rev Psychiatry* 4:149-55.

Stannard K, Leonard T, Holder G, Shilling J. 1984. Oedipism reviewed: A case of bilateral ocular self-mutilation. *Br J Ophthalmology* 68:276-80.

Stein DJ, Hutt C, Spitz J, Hollander E. 1993. Compulsive picking and obsessive-compulsive disorder. *Psychosomatics* 34:177-81.

Stellwag von Carion C. 1858. Extirpation des Bulbus. In *Die Ophthalmologie*. Verlag von Ferdinand Enke.

Stengel E. 1964. *Suicide and Attempted Suicide*. Baltimore: Penguin Books.

Steward TD. 1958. Stone age skull surgery. Annual Report of the Board of Regents of the Smithsonian Institution, 1957. Publication no. 4314. Washington, DC: U.S. Government Printing Office.

Stewart GR. 1960. *Ordeal by Hunger: The Story of the Donner Party* (new ed.). Cambridge: Riverside Press.

Stinnett JL, Hollender MH. 1970. Compulsive self-mutilation. *J Nerv Ment Disease* 150:371-75.

Stoller RJ, Herdt GH. 1982. The development of general identity: A cross-cultural contribution. *J Am Psychoanalytic Assn* 30:29–59.

Stone M. 1987. A psychodynamic approach. *J Personality Disorders* 1:347–49.

Storr A. 1968. *Human Aggression.* New York: Atheneum.

Story WH. 1887. *Castle St. Angelo: The Evil Eye.* London: Chapman and Hall.

Strack HL. 1909. *The Jew and Human Sacrifice,* 8th ed. London: Cope and Fenwick.

Stroch D. 1901. Self-castration. *JAMA* 36:270.

Strong M. 1993. A bright red scream. *San Francisco Focus,* Dec, 58–144.

Suh-ho. 1915. In praise of footbinding. *New Republic,* 18 Dec, 170–72.

Suk JH. 1974. Wrist-cutting syndrome. *Neuropsychiatry* (Seoul, Korea) 13:100–104.

Suk JH, Son BK. 1980. A study on male genital self-mutilation. *Neuropsychiatry* (Seoul, Korea) 19:97–104.

Swedo SE, Leonard HL, Rapoport JL, Lenane MC, Goldberger EL, Cheslow DL. 1983. A double-blind comparison of clomipramine and desipramine in the treatment of trichotillomania. *N Eng J Med* 321:497–501.

Swedo SE, Rapoport JL. 1991. Annotation: Trichotillomania. *J Child Psychology Psychiatry* 32:401–9.

Sweeny S, Zamecnik K. 1981. Predictors of self-mutilation in patients with schizophrenia. *Am J Psychiatry* 138:1086–89.

Talbott JA, Linn L. 1978. Reactions of schizophrenics to life-threatening disease. *Psychiatric Quar* 60:218–27.

Tantam D, Whittaker J. 1992. Personality disorder and self-wounding. *Br J Psychiatry* 161:451–64.

Tapper CM, Bland RC, Danyluk L. 1979. Self-inflicted eye injuries and self-inflicted blindness. *J Nerv Ment Disease* 167:311–14.

Taylor FK. 1969. Prokaletic measures derived from psychoanalytic technique. *Br J Psychiatry* 115:407–19.

Terson A. 1911. L'auto-enucleation des deux yeax dans la mélancolie avec délire religieux. *Ann d'Oculistique* 145–46:81–87.

Thomas EWP. 1937. Dermatitis artefacta: A note on an unusual case. *Br Med J* 1: 804–6.

Thompson CC, Park RI, Prescott GH. 1980. Oral manifestation of the congenital insensitivity-to-pain syndrome. *Oral Surg* 50:220–25.

Thompson JN, Abraham TK. 1983. Male genital mutilation after paternal death. *Br Med J* 287:727–28.

Thurston H. 1952. *The Physical Phenomena of Mysticism.* London: Burns and Oates.

Tinklepaugh DL. 1928. The self-mutilation of the male macacus rhesus monkey. *J Mammol* 9:293–300.

Toch H. 1975. *Men in Crisis.* Chicago: Aldine.

Tolentino I. 1957. Transvestism and transsexualism: A case of auto-castration in a transsexual subject. *Riv Sper Freniat* 81:909–40.

Trad PV. 1989. Self-mutilation in a new mother. *Am J Psychotherapy* 43:414–26.

Tsunenari S, Idaka T, Kanda M, Koga Y. 1981. Self-mutilation: Plastic spherules in penile skin in yakuza, Japan's racketeers. *Am J Forensic Med Pathology* 2:203–7.

Turner TH, Toffler DS. 1986. Indications of psychiatric disorders among women admitted to prison. *Br Med J* 292:651–53.

Turner V. 1968. *Drums of Affliction*. Oxford: Clarendon Press.

———. 1969. *The Ritual Process*. Ithaca: Cornell University Press.

———. 1977. Sacrifice as quintessential process. *History Religions* 16:189–215.

Urechia M. 1931. Autophagie des doits chez un paralytique en rapport avec une pachymeningite cervicale. *Revue Neurologique* 55:350–52.

Vaernet K, Madsen A. 1970. Stereotoxic amygdalotomy and basofrontal tractotomy in psychotics with aggressive behavior. *J Neurology Neurosurgery Psychiatry* 33:856–63.

Vale V, Juno A. 1989. *Modern Primitives*. San Francisco: Research Publications.

van der Kolk BA, Perry C, Herman JL. 1991. Childhood origins of self-destructive behavior. *Am J Psychiatry* 148:1165–73.

van Gennep A. 1909. *The Rites of Passage*. London: Routledge Kegan Paul.

Van Moffaert M. 1989. Management of self-mutilation. *Psychotherapy Psychosomatics* 51:180–86.

Van Putten T, Shaffer I. 1990. Delirium associated with buproprion. *J Clin Psychopharmacology* 10:234.

VanWoert MH, Yip LC, Balis ME. 1977. Purine phosphoribosyltransferase in Giles de la Tourette syndrome. *New England J Med* 296:210–12.

Vermasseren MJ. 1977. *Cybele and Attis: The Myth and the Cult*. London: Thames and Hudson.

Verzin JA. 1975. Sequelae of female circumcision. *Tropical Doctor* 5:163–69.

Virkkunen M. 1976. Self-mutilation in antisocial personality (disorder). *Acta Psychiatrica Scandinavica* 54:347–52.

Voget FV. 1964. Welfare and the integration of Crow culture. In *Explorations in Cultural Anthropology*, edited by Goodenough WG. New York: McGraw-Hill.

Wackenheim A, Becker Y, Nevers J. 1956. L'automutilation oculaire. *Cahiers de Psychiatrie* 11:108–18.

Waddell H. 1957. *The Desert Fathers*. Ann Arbor: University of Michigan Press.

Wakefield EG, Dellinger SC. 1939. Possible reasons for trephining the skull in the past. *CIBA Symposia* 1:166–69.

Wakefield PL, Frank A, Meyers RW. 1977. The hobbyist: A euphemism for self-mutilation and fetishism. *Bull Menninger Clin* 41:539–52.

Waldenberg SSA. 1972. Wrist cutting: A psychiatric inquiry. M. Phil. diss., University of London.

Walsh BW, Rosen P. 1985. Self-mutilation and contagion. *Am J Psychiatry* 142:119–20.

———. 1988. *Self-mutilation: Theory, Research, and Treatment*. New York: Guilford.

Walter G, Streimer J. 1990. Genital self-mutilation: Attempted foreskin reconstruction. *Br J Psychiatry* 156:125–27.

Waltzer H. 1968. Depersonalization and self-destruction. *Am J Psychiatry* 125:399–401.

Warlomont E. 1875. *Louise Lateau: Rapport médical sur la stigmatisée de Bois-d'Haine, fait à l'Académie royale de médecine de Belgique*. Paris: Ballière.

Warner L. 1954. *The Living and the Dead*. New Haven: Yale University Press.

Warrington. 1882–83. The case of Isaac Brooks. *J Ment Science* 33:69–74.

Wehrli GA. 1939. Trepanation in former centuries. *CIBA Symposia* 1:178–86.

Weinstock R. 1988. Self-amputation of the ear. *Can J Psychiatry* 33:242–43.

Weiser M, Levy A, Neuman M. 1993. Ear stuffing. *J Nervous Mental Disease* 181:587–88.

Weiss C. 1962. A worldwide survey of the current practice of milah (ritual circumcision). *Conference on Jewish Social Studies*, 30–48.

Weissman MM. 1975. Wrist cutting: Relationship between clinical observations and epidemiological findings. *Arch Gen Psychiatry* 32:1166–71.

Westermeyer J, Serposs A. 1972. A third case of self-enucleation. *Am J Psychiatry* 129:484.

Whitehead PC, Johnson FG, Ferrence R. 1973. Measuring the incidence of self-injury. *Am J Orthopsychiatry* 43:142–48.

Whiting JWM. 1964. Effects of climate on certain cultural practices. In *Explorations in Cultural Anthropology*. New York: McGraw-Hill.

Whiting JWM, Kluckhohn R, Anthony A. 1947. The functions of male initiation ceremonies at puberty. In *Readings in Social Psychology*, edited by Macoby E, Newcomb T, and Hartley E. New York: Holt Rinehart Winston.

Whiting M. 1884. Self-castration. *Peoria Med Monthly* 5:297–300.

Whitlock FA, Hynes JV. 1978. Religious stigmatization. *Psychological Medicine* 8: 185–202.

Wickham ER, Reed JV. 1987. Lithium for the control of aggressive and self-mutilating behavior. *Intl Clinical Psychopharmacology* 2:181–90.

Wilkins J, Coid J. 1991. Self-mutilation in female remanded prisoners I: An indicator of severe psychopathology. *Criminal Behavior Mental Health* 1:247–67.

Wilson J. 1992. *The Bleeding Mind*. London: Weidenfeld and Nicolson.

Wilson WA. 1955. Oedipism. *Am J Ophthalmology* 40:563–67.

Winchel R. 1992. Trichotillomania: Presentation and treatment. *Psychiatric Annals* 22:84–89.

Winchel RM, Jones JS, Stanley B, Molicho A, Stanley M. 1992. Clinical characteristics of trichotillomania and its response to fluoxetine. *J Clin Psychiatry* 53:304–8.

Winchel RM, Stanley M. 1991. Self-injurious behavior: A review of the behavior and biology of self-mutilation. *Am J Psychiatry* 148:306–17.

Winnicott DW. 1949. Hate in the counter-transference. *Intl J Psychoanalysis* 30:69–74.

———. 1958. Transitional objects and transactional phenomena. In *Collected Papers*. New York: Basic Books.

Wise TN, Dietrich AM, Segall E. 1989. Female genital self-mutilation. *J Sex Marital Therapy* 15:269–74.

Woods J. 1988. Layers of meaning in self-cutting. *J Child Psychotherapy* 14:51–60.

Wurfler P. 1956. Selbstblendung eines cocainsuchtigen Betrugers. *Nervenartz* 27: 325–26.

Yamamoto J, Seeman W, Lester BK. 1963. The tatooed man. *J Nerv Ment Disease* 136:365–67.

Yang HK, Brown GC, Magargal LE. 1981. Self-inflicted ocular mutilation. *Am J Oph-thalmology* 91:658–63.

Yaroshevsky F. 1975. Self-mutilation in Soviet prisons. *Can Psychiatric Assn J* 20: 443–46.

Yaryura-Tobias JA, Neziroglu F. 1978. Compulsions, aggression, and self-mutilation: A hypothalamic disorder? *Orthomolecular Psychiatry* 7:114–17.

Yellowlees AJ. 1985. Anorexia and bulimia in anorexia nervosa. *Br J Psychiatry* 146: 648–52.

Young FW. 1962. The function of male initiation ceremonies. *Am J Sociology* 67: 379–96.

———. 1965. *Initiation Ceremonies*. Indianapolis: Bobbs-Merrill.

Young LD, Feinsilver DL. 1986. Male genital self-mutilation: Combined surgical and psychiatric care. *Psychosomatics* 27:513–17.

Yudofsky S, Williams D, Gorman J. 1981. Propanolol in the treatment of rage and violent behavior in patients with chronic brain syndromes. *Am J Psychiatry* 138: 218–20.

Zaidens SH. 1951. Self-inflicted dermatoses and their psychodynamics. *J Nerv Ment Disease* 113:395–404.

Zambrowsky P. 1930. Avulsio bulbi. *Russki Optalmologicheskii Z* 1:103–6.

Zillboorg G. 1939. The discovery of the Oedipus complex: Episodes from Marcel Proust. *Psychoanalytic Quar* 8:279–302.

Zweig-Frank H, Paris J, Grizder J. 1994a. Psychological risk factors for dissocia-tion and self-mutilation in female patients with borderline personality disorder. *Can J Psychiatry* 39:259–64.

———. 1994b. Psychological risk factors and self-mutilation in male patients with BPD. *Can J Psychiatry* 39:266–68.

Index